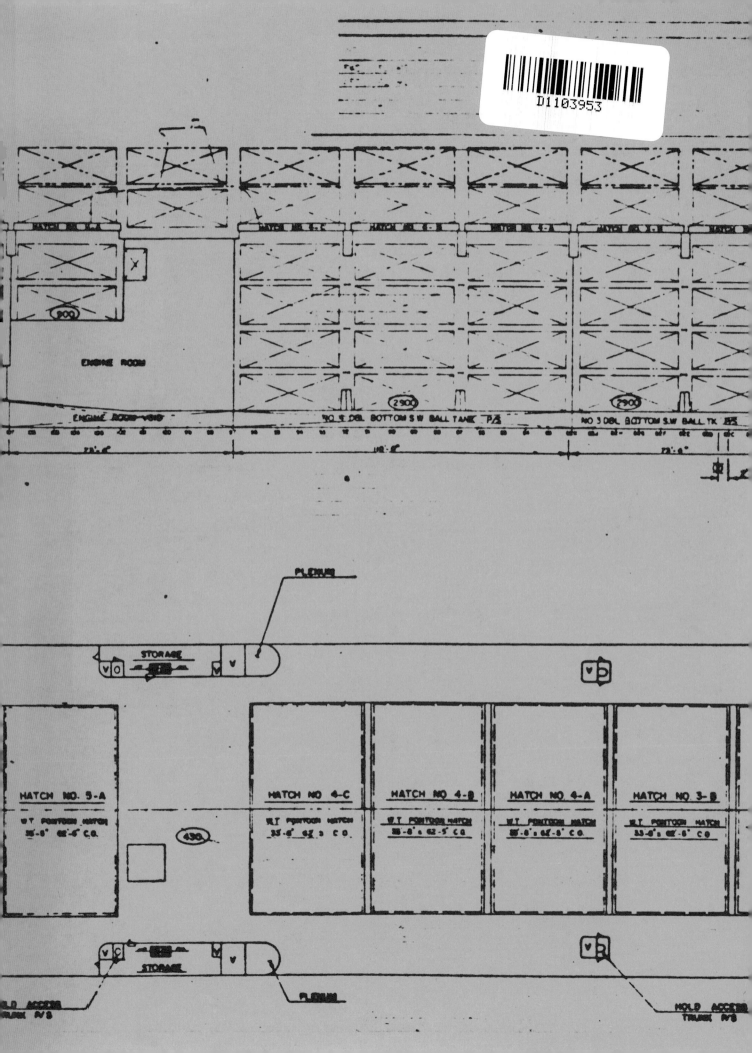

Not For Widows And Orphans

The Chronology of International Shipholding
Corporation from 1947 to 2007

"...Thou must consider the duty thou owest to the
other owners of this ship – widows and orphans..."

Herman Melville, *Moby Dick*

Not For Widows And Orphans

*The Chronology of International Shipholding Corporation
from 1947 to 2007*

By Niels W. Johnsen
Edited by Margaret Stocker

6/27/07

Dear Marshall

*Hope you enjoy reading
about some of our experiences over
the last 60 years. Regards
Niels*

INTERNATIONAL SHIPHOLDING CORPORATION

ISBN 978-0-9796235-0-9

International Shipholding Corporation

RSA Battle House Tower Office Building
11 North Water Street
Suite 18290
Mobile, Alabama 36602

One Whitehall Street
20th Floor
New York, NY 10004

www.intship.com

Design by Bruce Campbell
Type set by Aardvark Type
Printed by Worzalla Printing. Manufactured in the United States

Dedicated to the memory of

Julia Anita Winchester Johnsen

A N D

Niels Frithjof Johnsen

Contents

The bark *Baron Holberg* was built in 1877 at Söderhamn, Sweden, 613 gross tons, 560 net tons, home port, Larvik, Norway.

Prologue

Nils Olsen was born in Ula, Norway, on September 8, 1844, and later lived in the town of Larvik, on the southwest coast of the Oslo Fjord. On December 3, 1871, he married Jeannette Oibye in the Larvik Church and lived in a house called "Minde."

Nils Olsen went to sea as a deck boy in 1860 and rose through the ranks to become master and, by 1883, owner of a bark named *Baron Holberg,* built in Skien, Norway, in 1857. He was fondly known as "Baron Olsen." His ship, the *Baron Holberg,* was named in honor of Ludwig Holberg (1684-1754), who left his native Bergen, Norway, at age 20 to travel by ship and on foot throughout Britain, the Netherlands, France and Italy in search of knowledge. His poetry, plays and histories brought the Age of Enlightenment to Scandinavia. Ludwig Holberg was ennobled "Baron of Holberg" by Frederik V, King of Denmark and Norway in 1747.

In 1896, while Captain Olsen was at home in Larvik, the *Baron Holberg* was wrecked during a storm off Folke-stone, England. The ship was lost but the entire crew was saved. In 1898, after a few years ashore, Captain Olsen and a group of Larvik men including his son-in-law Johannes Johnsen purchased the *Blenda,* a three-masted bark built in the late 1870s in Söderhamn, Sweden. They naturally renamed her *Baron Holberg.* About 1906, the *Baron Holberg* sustained major heavy weather damage on one of her voyages. Captain Olsen sent the ship to a shipyard for repairs and, at the same time decided to have her re-rigged as a schooner. The *Baron Holberg* left the yard as the largest schooner-rigged ship under Norwegian flag and the pride of Captain Olsen's fleet, which also included the barks *Strathearn* and *Sterling.* "Baron Olsen" continued as Master of the *Baron Holberg* until he retired from the sea in 1914. A year later the *Baron Holberg* was sold. Those were the glory days of sailing ships before the advent of steam and motor vessels.

The last days of the *Baron Holberg* are captured in a newspaper article that appeared in the Norges Handels-og

Jeannette Oibye Olsen and Captain Nils Olsen, circa 1900.

A scale model of the *Baron Holberg,* sails furled, in Erik F. Johnsen's office.

"Leif Eriksson Discovering America," a tapestry after a painting in the collection of the Oslo Ship Museum, Bygdoy, which Niels F. Johnsen gave to the Company.

Sjofartstidende dated March 29, 1952, written by reporter Michael West:

> During a visit to Stavanger some time ago I noticed an old wreck lying partly submerged in Bangarvagen just north of the town. It was easy to see that it was the remainder of what had once been a sailing vessel, but none of the people I asked in the surrounding farms knew what ship she had been.
>
> On my return to Stavanger I met Harbourmaster Lura and asked him. Yes, said Lura, what you saw is all that is left of a sailing ship, which in her time was well known, bearing the proud name of *Baron Holberg*. Her homeport was in Southeast Norway and many years ago she was rigged down and used as a barge. Just after the Second World War she was used for salvage work here, but since then the hulk has been lying at Bangarvagen and is of course steadily deteriorating. It is also an obstacle to the traffic there, and the harbour authority will now order it to be removed . . .
>
> Enroute from Sunderland to Kristiania in November 1919 the ship sprang a leak and having sustained also other damage, she was abandoned by the crew. The people on board were saved, and some days later the ship was towed to England and condemned. She was however taken back to Norway, converted into a barge and was then used until just a few years ago. Soon, the last remains will have disappeared. Captain Olsen, who through his long life as

a sailor, was linked to the two Barons, which he commanded and to an extent also owned, became a very old man. He died in 1933 in his 90th year.

One of Nils and Jeannette Olsen's six children, Klara, married Johannes Johnsen in 1894 and raised their family in a house called "Villa Nora" in Larvik. Their first son (grandson of Nils Olsen) was born on April 29, 1895, and named Niels Frithjof Johnsen. Frithjof, as he was known in his youth, began his employment in 1911 in the Larvik office of Christian Nielsen & Company A/S (Whale Fishery, Ship Owners, Steam & Sailing-Ship Brokers, Chartering & Commission Agents). In 1914, at the age of 19, Frithjof left Norway to continue work in that company's offices in Perth and Fremantle, Western Australia. A letter dated "Fremantle, Western Australia, November 11, 1918" signed by the Norwegian consul, Mr. Aug. Stang, states

> Mr. F. Johnsen (meaning Niels F. Johnsen) has been in my employ as Accountant and Book keeper during the last 3½ years. During this period he has performed his duties to my entire satisfaction. He is an energetic, sober and willing worker with an excellent knowledge of shipping and accountancy, and it is with regret that I am losing his services.

Niels Frithjof Johnsen must have carried this letter of recommendation when he immigrated to the United States in 1919. He settled in New Orleans, Louisiana, and became a United States citizen in 1921. First he worked with Kerr Steamship Company, Inc., which had been established five years earlier. In a letter dated June 22, 1921, Kerr's Southern manager writes to Mr. F. Johnsen:

> On the eve of your departure for Norway, I want to express to you my appreciation of the valuable assistance you have been to me during the last two years you have had charge of the Freight Department in this office. It is with sincere regret that I see you leave our employ, and I hope that circumstances may later permit our resuming the very pleasant and satisfactory business relations existing heretofore. With best wishes for a good voyage, believe me. Charles Harrington.

Apparently this trip to Norway in 1921 was a short visit, because he married Julia Anita Winchester, daughter of Louise Olivier and Peter Sydney Winchester of New Orleans, in June 1921. By 1924 he had joined the

New Orleans office of Norton Lilly & Company, which started as Norton & Co. in New York in 1841 and became Norton Lilly & Company in 1907. Frithjof worked directly with Mr. Furman B. Pearce, who was in charge of handling operations in Norton Lilly's New Orleans office, primarily for cotton exports from the Southern United States. Norton Lilly & Company represented U.S.-flag and foreign-flag companies, including the Isthmian Line, a subsidiary of the U.S. Steel Corporation, mainly in its round-the-world service.

In 1935, after approximately 12 years in the employ of Norton Lilly & Company in New Orleans, Niels F. Johnsen joined States Marine Corporation, a growing American firm established by Henry Mercer in 1930 as agents for Reardon Smith Line, one of the old line British shipping companies. States Marine gradually developed scheduled liner services by managing and then owning ships.

After forming Central Gulf Steamship Corporation together with his sons Niels W. Johnsen and Erik F. Johnsen in 1947, Niels F. Johnsen continued with States Marine until 1956, when he decided to avoid conflict of interest between Central Gulf, an unsubsidized line, and States Marine. States Marine had become active in the ownership and operation of U.S.-flag ships and at one point contemplated an operating subsidy. States Marine Corporation purchased the 24 U.S.-flag C-3 fleet owned by Isthmian Line, Inc. from U.S. Steel in 1956. Ironically, Niels F. Johnsen had handled Isthmian Line ships that called at New Orleans when he was with Norton Lilly & Company.

As Central Gulf and its associated companies developed and thrived, Niels F. Johnsen was recognized as an industry leader and innovator. Three foreign governments honored Niels F. Johnsen. In 1966 King Olav V of Norway decorated him for "distinguished services to Norway and humanity" as Knight First Class of the Order of St. Olav. In 1967 the Republic of India named him First Honorary Consul for the State of Louisiana. Then the Japanese government in 1968 decorated him for his "contributions to U.S./Japanese industrial and trade relations" awarding him the Order of the Rising Sun. In 1969 the World Trade Club of New Orleans cited Niels F. Johnsen for his "fifty years of service to world trade" and gave him an honorary lifetime membership in that organization. He was a member of the American Bureau of Shipping, the Navy League of the United States, the National Defense Transportation Association, the American Scandinavian Foundation and the Japan Society of America. He was also a member of France-Amerique de la Louisiane, International House and a number of other New Orleans business and civic organizations.

Niels F. Johnsen was a prolific letter writer ever since he left Norway in 1914. Envelopes for the correspondence he mailed from Australia to the United States indicate his meticulous planning to expedite delivery. Before there was a regular transatlantic airmail service, he would send letters by domestic airmail from New Orleans to New York timed to arrive for the scheduled sailing of certain ships, and then specify air mail from their port of arrival in Europe to Norway. One of his letters was carried on the first transatlantic crossing of the German dirigible (rigid airship) Hindenburg in 1936.

He enjoyed writing these letters either in his florid longhand or pecked out on a typewriter himself. Many

Airmail envelope containing a letter written by Niels F. Johnsen on May 9, 1936, to his mother and sent via dirigible Hindenburg, approximately one year before the dirigible exploded and burned at Lakehurst, N.J.

Clipping from the Oslo newspaper *Aftenposten,* February 26, 1943, sent to Niels F. Johnsen in New Orleans by his brother J. Anker Johnsen, during the period in World War II that Norway was occupied by Nazi Germany. Article contains (in Norwegian) an edict issued by Quisling with new work rules for the citizens of Norway.

passed through the censors during the two world wars. Norway in World War I was neutral but letters from Australia were subject to censors of the Allied forces. In World War II the German Nazis occupied Norway from 1940 to 1945 and censored mail as it entered Norway. Niels F. Johnsen also received mail in the United States from Norway during the German occupation, including a clipping that contained an edict by Quisling that was published on the front page of the daily Oslo newspaper *Aftenposten* on February 26, 1943.

With the end of World War II in 1945 and the passage of the Merchant Ship Sales Act of 1946 by the U.S. Congress, Niels F. Johnsen was on the verge of achieving his ambition of becoming a shipowner, following in the footsteps of his ancestors.

Introduction

World War II had ended with the surrender of Japan on September 2, 1945. Of the almost 6,000 merchant ships built in United States shipyards under Maritime Commission and War Shipping Administration contracts between 1939 and 1945, approximately 1,768 had been either sunk, damaged, captured or detained due to war activity. When hostilities ceased, the United States government owned a fleet of more than 4,000 war-built merchant vessels: Liberty ships, Victory ships, C-1's, C-2's, C-3's, and C-4's (in addition to about 500 T-2 tankers) which were now surplus.

To reestablish the privately owned U.S. Merchant Marine and replace merchant vessels lost by Allied nations, Congress passed and President Harry S. Truman signed the Merchant Ship Sales Act of 1946. The disposal of the U.S. government-owned fleet began. American and foreign buyers converged on Washington: The rush was on!

The U.S. government decided as a matter of policy to offer the surplus ships to U.S. citizen shipowners first. The government gave first options on the preferred C-2, C-3 and C-4 ships to (1) U.S.-flag dry-cargo operators who had received Operating Differential Subsidy contracts pre-war under the Merchant Marine Act of 1936, and (2) certain shipowners who held Interstate Commerce Commission certificates for services in the U.S. domestic coastwise, interstate via the Panama Canal and (3) between the U.S. mainland and U.S. noncontiguous territories. The government then offered Liberty and Victory ships to all other U.S. citizen operators. After satisfying the requests of U.S. citizen operators, the U.S. government then offered Victory and Liberty ships to qualified operators of former Allied nations for foreign-flag registry.

After September 1945 the United States shifted from being the "arsenal of democracy" to the leader of the free world in restoring financial and political stability to the wartime victors and, for that matter, even the economies of the defeated powers. War-torn areas of the globe had to be rebuilt. Populations worldwide had to be fed. America was the major post-war source of the materiel, foodstuff, and other commodities needed for reconstruction. The Congress passed and President Truman signed legislation authorizing the Marshall Plan, to help Europe rebuild after World War II.

America was also the only country in the world capable of providing the ships required for the ocean transportation needed to implement the Marshall Plan.

DRY-CARGO SHIPS OFFERED FOR SALE
UNDER THE MERCHANT SHIP SALES ACT OF 1946

Type	LOA Feet	Beam Feet	DWT Tons	Gross Tons	Disp. Tons	Max. HP	Capacity (Bale)	Speed (Knots)
Liberty (EC-2)	441	56	10,844	7,180	14,270	2,500 (1)	475,000	11
Victory (AP-2)	455	62	10,800	7,600	15,200	6,600	495,000	15.5
C-1 B	417	60	9,510	6,750	13,270	4,400	451,620	14
C-2	468	63	11,330	8,230	15,500	6,600	540,000	15.5
C-3	492	69	12,348	7,995	18,210	9,350	677,000	17
C-4	520	72	15,348	10,780	19,850	9,900	744,000	16

Timeline

1936   Congress passes Merchant Marine Act of 1936.

1939   September 1: World War II begins.

1941   December 7: Japan attacks Pearl Harbor. U.S. enters WWII. U.S. economy shifts to production of armaments including ocean-going vessels.

1945   April 12: President Franklin D. Roosevelt dies in office; Vice President Harry S. Truman becomes president of the U.S.

May 8: VE Day.

August 6, 9: First atomic bomb dropped on Hiroshima, Japan, and second on Nagasaki, Japan.

August 14: Japan surrenders. WWII ends.

1946   Merchant Ship Sales Act enacted: 847 war-built ships sold to U.S. investors; 1,113 ships sold to foreign shipowners.

1947   April 19: Central Gulf Steamship Corporation (CG) is founded by Niels F. Johnsen and sons Niels W. and Erik F. Johnsen.

June 8: CG purchases first vessel, the war-built Liberty ship SS *Horatio Allen,* renamed SS *Green Wave.*

November 30: Company's Total Assets: $820,739. Net Worth: $311,494.

1948   November: Truman wins U.S. presidential election.

June 24: Berlin Airlift begins.

1949   June: CG purchases second ship, war-built AP-2 Victory SS *Ouachita Victory,* renamed SS *Green Valley.*

1950   January: Gen. L. Kemper Williams is elected to CG board of directors.

June 25: Korean conflict begins.

August 9: *Green Valley* is first CG ship chartered to Military Sea Transportation Service.

October: SS *Green Wave* is sold for $512,500 for delivery in December 1950.

1951   January 15: CG purchases third ship, the war-built AP-2 Victory SS *Cooper Union Victory,* renamed SS *Green Harbour.*

September 30: Total Assets: $2,270,120, Net Worth: $741,495.

October: Erik F. Johnsen receives honorable discharge as U.S. Navy lieutenant after service in WWII and Korean War, and is elected to CG Board of Directors and named vice president.

1952   November: Gen. Dwight D. Eisenhower is elected U.S. president.

1953   July 27: Korean conflict ends.

1954   October: Two CG affiliates, Overzeese Scheepvaart Maatschappij, N.V., the Netherlands, and Compania Maritima Unidas, S.A., Liberia, are established.

1956   April 26: Container ship era begins when Pan-Atlantic Steamship Corporation (later renamed Sea-Land) sails converted tanker *Ideal X* from Port Newark, N.J., to Houston, Texas, with 58 loaded containers on deck.

July 26: Egypt nationalizes the Suez Canal. War breaks out between Israel and Egypt. Closure of Suez Canal causes ship freight rates to soar.

August: In strong freight market, CG books a total of 57 such cargoes by mid-1957.

October: Central Gulf opens independent offices in New Orleans and New York. N.W. Johnsen and Co., Inc. opens in New York as ship/cargo brokers.

November: Eisenhower is re-elected U.S. president.

1957   April: Suez Canal reopens. Freight market crashes.

October: CG begins a liner berth service between U.S. Gulf and East Coast ports and ports in the Red Sea, India and Pakistan.

December 31: Consolidated Total Assets: $2,671,509. Consolidated Net Worth: $100,694. (Reduced net worth reflects the depressed market conditions before coal contracts booked in 1956-57 shipping boom.)

1958   February 25: CG applies to U.S. Maritime Subsidy Board for Operating Differential. Subsidy for 16 to 24 voyages annually on Trade Routes 18 and 17.

July 18: G.E. Gillis, Jr., founding board member, dies. Mrs. G.E. Gillis and George Denegre fill vacancies.

August: Robert S. Labry resigns from board and as secretary-treasurer.

1959   Central Gulf increases unsubsidized liner service between U.S. Gulf/U.S. East Coast and Red Sea, India and Pakistan to 36 sailings annually.

1960   June 24: SS *Green Bay* (ex-SS *Noordzee*) sinks Ambrose Light Ship while departing New York Harbor in dense fog.

July 5: Central Gulf establishes Mid-Gulf Stevedores, Inc.

September 23: Maritime Subsidy Board offers ODS to Central Gulf for 24 sailings annually on Trade Routes 18 and 17, which Central Gulf declines.

November: John F. Kennedy is elected U.S. president.

December 31: Consolidated Total Assets: $7,155,732. Consolidated Net Worth: $602,849.

1961   May 5: Alan B. Shepard Jr. becomes first U.S. astronaut in space.

August 13: East Germany begins erecting Berlin Wall.

1962   September: New York office moves to One Whitehall Street from 19 Rector Street.

October: Cuban missile crisis.

1963   Central Gulf Lines Agency Ltd. opens office in Bombay, India.

March: Joseph Merrick Jones, founding director and general counsel, and his wife, Eugenie Elizabeth Penick, perish in fire at home.

November 22: President Kennedy is assassinated, Vice President Lyndon B. Johnson becomes president.

December 29: CG contracts with Uraga Heavy Industries Ltd., Japan, for construction of first newbuilding ship, Hull #858, a 48,000-DWT bulk carrier christened MV *Baron Holberg*.

December 31: Consolidated Total Assets: $11,816,329. Consolidated Net Worth: $2,394,061.

1964 March 2: Nicholas Johnson is appointed U.S. maritime administrator.

July 8: CG contracts with Uraga Heavy Industries Ltd., for construction of second newbuilding, Hull #868, a 57,897-DWT tanker christened MT *Sterling*.

November: Lyndon B. Johnson wins U.S. presidential election.

1965 U.S. deploys ground troops in Vietnam.

India and Pakistan engage in border conflicts.

June 21: CG contracts with Uraga Heavy Industries Ltd., for construction of third newbuilding, Hull #878, a 52,000-DWT bulk carrier christened MV *Strathearn*.

August 18: MV *Baron Holberg* (Hull #858) is delivered by Uraga Heavy Industries Ltd.

September 9: Hurricane Betsy hits New Orleans.

1967 June 5: Suez Canal is closed after Six-Day War, as Israel occupies Sinai Peninsula. Canal remains closed until 1975.

October 31: CG contracts with International Paper Company (IPCO) for 10-year use of a newbuilding Lighter Aboard Ship (LASH) vessel.

December 15: CG contracts with Uraga Heavy Industries Ltd. for construction of the world's first LASH ship, Uraga Hull #918, a 43,000-DWT vessel carrying 83 barges. Vessel is named MV *Acadia Forest*.

December 31: Consolidated Total Assets: $47,900,629. Consolidated Net Worth: $5,514,326.

1968 January 9: CG contracts with Equitable-Higgins Shipyards, Inc. for construction of the first 233 LASH barges for use with MV *Acadia Forest*.

August 31: CG and Mosvold Shippping contract with Sumitomo Heavy Industries Ltd. (formerly Uraga Heavy Industries Ltd.) for construction of the second LASH ship, Hull #928, a 43,500-DWT barge carrier,

a sister ship of the *Acadia Forest* to be named MV *Atlantic Forest*. An additional 150 barges are ordered from Equitable-Higgins for use with the *Atlantic Forest*.

November: Richard M. Nixon is elected U.S. president.

1969 March 25: Andrew E. Gibson is appointed U.S. maritime administrator.

September 27: World's first LASH vessel, MV *Acadia Forest,* sails on maiden voyage.

October 5: After delivering empty cargo containers to Puerto Rico and lifting aboard first group of loaded barges for IPCO at Panama City, Florida, *Acadia Forest* is greeted in New Orleans by anonymous labor pickets who impede vessel's operations and spoil maiden voyage festivities.

November 12: *Acadia Forest* labor dispute is settled with agreement on working rules with the International Longshoremen's Association. CG applies to Maritime Administration for Construction Differential Subsidy and Operating Differential Subsidy for three new 89-barge capacity LASH vessels to be constructed in the U.S. for U.S.-flag operation.

1970 April 4: Founding director Dr. Joseph C. Morris dies suddenly while visiting New York City.

June 21: MV *Atlantic Forest,* Uraga Hull #928, the second LASH ship, is delivered by Sumitomo and sails on her maiden voyage.

October 21: Nixon signs amended Merchant Marine Act, providing construction subsidies for qualified U.S. ships.

December 23: CG withdraws application for ODS but continues to process application for CDS and Title XI Insurance financing for three new LASH vessels for operation under U.S. flag.

1971 June 8: CG orders first 89-barge LASH vessel from Avondale Shipyards, New Orleans, for operation under U.S. flag, based upon the award of CDS and Title XI guarantee for financing. CG has option to order two sister ships.

June 30: Consolidated Total Assets: $65,143,403. Consolidated Net Worth: $10,934,426.

October 4: CG and Associated Companies agree to merge with TransUnion Corporation.

November 17: Gen. L. Kemper Williams, director of Central Gulf Steamship Corporation, dies.

December 21: Merger with TransUnion takes effect.

December 22: Niels F. Johnsen, founding director, past president and past chairman of CG and Associated Companies, retires. Niels W. Johnsen becomes chairman of the board and chief executive officer. Erik F. Johnsen is elected president. William B. Moore and D.A. Kuzmicki are elected assistant secretaries. Hugh Evans and J.M. Jones Jr. resign as directors. J.W. van Gorkum, chairman of TransUnion; W.B. Browder, vice president of TransUnion; Erik F. Johnsen, and S.E. Morrison, treasurer of CG and Associated Companies, are elected directors. Niels W. Johnsen is elected to the board of directors of TransUnion.

1972   February 29: CG contracts with Avondale Shipyards, Inc. for construction of the two optional U.S.-flag LASH vessels, and orders an additional 640 LASH barges.

June 30: Central Gulf Steamship Corporation certificate of incorporation is amended to change name to Central Gulf Lines, Inc. (CGL).

July 7: Robert J. Blackwell is appointed U.S. maritime administrator.

August 31: First Cape-size newbuilding, a 117,400-DWT named MV *Mosfield,* is delivered by Sumitomo Shipyard.

November: Nixon is re-elected U.S. president.

December 31: Consolidated Total Assets: $99,812,719. Consolidated Net Worth: $15,103,947.

1973   U.S.-flag ships carry more cargo than any time in 25 years.

July: Newbuilding MV *Mammoth Pine,* 32,600-DWT log/bulk carrier, is delivered by Kanasashi Shipyard.

July 31: William J. Toomey, vice president, operations and loyal employee since 1947, dies.

August: Newbuilding MV *Mammoth Fir,* 32,600-DWT log/bulk carrier, is delivered by Kanasashi Shipyard. (Both log/bulk carriers were time-chartered to Sanko Steamship Corporation for 10 years.)

U.S. completes pullout of troops from Vietnam.

October: Second Cape-size newbuilding, a 117,400-DWT bulk carrier named MV *Mosnes,* is delivered by Sumitomo Shipyard.

1974   June 23: Niels F. Johnsen, chairman emeritus, dies.

August 9: President Nixon resigns, is succeeded by Vice President Gerald R. Ford.

September 6: First U.S.-built, U.S.-flag LASH, SS Green Valley, Hull #1952, is delivered to CG by Avondale Shipyards, New Orleans.

September: MT *Amoco Trinidad,* 151,400-DWT newbuilding tanker, is delivered by Mitsubishi Kobe Shipyard.

December 10: Second U.S.-built, U.S.-flag LASH, SS Green Harbour, Hull #2257, is delivered to CG by Avondale Shipyards.

1975   January: MT *Amoco Cairo,* 151,400-DWT newbuilding tanker, delivered by Mitsubishi Kobe Shipyard.

February 25: Third U.S.-flag LASH, SS *Green Island,* Hull #2258, is delivered to CG by Avondale Shipyards.

April 30: South Vietnam officially surrenders to North Vietnamese troops.

June: Suez Canal reopens after eight-year closure.

July: MT *Amoco Whiting,* 151,400-DWT newbuilding tanker, is delivered by Mitsubishi Kobe Shipyard.

1976   November: MV *Hemlock,* new 29,255-DWT geared bulk carrier, is delivered by Oppama Shipyard. Jimmy Carter is elected U.S. president.

1977   February: MV *Holly,* new 29,255-DWT geared bulk carrier, is delivered by Oppama Shipyard.

June 8: Mammoth Bulk Carriers Ltd. (Mammoth), new associated company, contracts with Sumitomo Heavy Industries, for construction of two float-on/float-off LASH feeder vessels, Hull #1063 (named MV *Oak*) and Hull #1064 (named MV *Willow*), for adjusted contract price of 1,535,050,000 yen, or approximately $6,140,200 each.

1979   May 14: International Shipholding Corporation (ISC) spin-off from TransUnion is effected. TU shareholders receive one ISC share for each five TU shares, and independent ISC board is elected. TU retains Mammoth Bulk Carriers Inc. and certain subsidiaries.

December 31: ISC's Consolidated Total Assets: $161,165,000. Consolidated Net Worth: $26,771,000.

July 19: Samuel B. Nemirow is appointed U.S. maritime administrator.

Interest rates rise from 11½% to 15¼% at year-end. Rising energy prices increase company's fuel cost by $7.8 million over 1978.

Political unrest erupts in Iran and Afghanistan. U.S. embargoes grain shipments to the Soviet Union.

1980   March: Maritime Administration approves bare-boat charters of LASH vessels SS *Green Valley,* SS *Green Harbour,* SS *Green Island,* 450 LASH barges and six LASH support vessels (FLASH and SPLASH) for 12 years to Waterman Steamship Corporation.

November: Ronald W. Reagan wins U.S. presidential election.

December: Prime interest rate peaks at 21½%.

1981   February: CGL signs 22-year contract with Seminole Electric Cooperative Inc. to transport coal from Indiana to Florida by barge via Ohio and Mississippi rivers.

September: ISC concludes agreement with a consortium of banks to borrow $41 million;

proceeds are used to pay off TransUnion financing at spin-off.

October: Harold E. Shear is appointed U.S. maritime administrator.

1982   October: First bargeload of coal is loaded for Seminole.

November: Material Transfer Inc., coal transfer facility in Gulf County, Florida, is dedicated for use under Seminole contract.

1983   December: Waterman declares bankruptcy.

1984   February: ISC purchases Rodriguez Sons Company, Inc., a chartering brokerage company.

November: Reagan is re-elected U.S. president.

December 31: Consolidated Total Assets: $193,714,000. Consolidated Net Worth: $40,848,000.

1985   Newly acquired ice-strengthened multipurpose vessel renamed MV *Green Wave* begins an initial 4½-year time charter to Military Sealift Command (MSC) with one voyage to the Antarctic and one to the Arctic, to be followed by similar service.

November 26: John A. Gaughan is appointed U.S. maritime administrator.

1986   CGL contracts with Toyota and Honda to carry 4,000/5,000 fully assembled automobiles on each voyage from Japan to U.S. in two new Central Gulf roll-on/roll-off vessels, the first such ships registered U.S. flag. These two new vessels are named MV *Green Lake* and MV *Green Bay* upon delivery in 1987 from two Japanese shipyards.

1987   January: ISC purchases Forest Lines from a subsidiary of IPCO.

October: CGL contracts with Hyundai Heavy Industries, Ltd., to build a 4,800-car capacity Pure Car Carrier, MV *Cypress Pass,* to be delivered in 1988 for charter to carry Hyundai automobiles from South Korea to U.S.

October 26: MV *Green Lake* arrives in Baltimore on maiden voyage with the first shipment of 5,000 new Toyota automobiles from Japan to arrive in U.S. on a U.S.-flag Pure Car Carrier.

November: MV *Green Bay* arrives in Long Beach, California, on maiden voyage with first shipment of 4,800 new Honda automobiles from Japan to be delivered to U.S. on a U.S.-flag Pure Car Carrier.

1988   January: CGL orders sister ship of *Cypress Pass,* MV *Cypress Trail,* from Hyundai Heavy Industries.

October: ISC signs letter of intent to purchase Waterman Steamship Corporation, including its three U.S.-flag LASH vessels, supporting equipment and ODS contracts. ISC's common stock is listed on NASDAQ under the symbol INSH.

November: George H.W. Bush wins U.S. presidential election.

1989   March: ISC concludes acquisition of Waterman.

September: Toyota introduces Lexus and begins shipping the new model to U.S. on MV *Green Lake.*

October 11: Warren G. Leback is appointed U.S. maritime administrator.

November: Demolition of the Berlin Wall begins. Collapse of Communism in East Germany and Soviet Union follows.

1990   August: Operation Desert Shield begins following Iraq's invasion of Kuwait.

December 31: Consolidated Total Assets: $473,582,000. Consolidated Net Worth passes $100 million mark, reaching $110,789,000.

1991   January 17: Operation Desert Storm begins with objective of liberating Kuwait and defending Saudi Arabia. Company's U.S.-flag fleet participates in the movement of military support cargo to and from Saudi Arabia.

October 30: Company's common stock (ISH) is registered on New York Stock Exchange. First trade is at $21.25. First day's trading volume is 17,375.

1992   May: LITCO, new LASH intermodal facility at Memphis, is opened.

May 15: ISC subsidiary signs 15-year contract to transport molten sulphur from a port on the Mississippi River to Tampa, Florida, and orders construction in a U.S. shipyard of Hull #294, MV *Sulphur Enterprise,* a 27,241-DWT molten sulphur carrier, for delivery in mid-1994.

August 12: ISC signs stock purchase agreement to acquire American Overseas Marine Corporation (AMSEA), a wholly owned subsidiary of General Dynamics Corporation, subject to U.S. Navy approval.

October 14: Two-year LASH barge fleet refurbishment program is completed at cost of $88.4 million.

November: Bill Clinton wins U.S. presidential election.

1993   June-August: Company issues $100 million Par Value 9% Senior Unsecured Notes due 2003 and sells 427,500 shares of new-issue common stock at $20 per share. Proceeds are used to prepay debt and redeem all preferred stock for total of $80.895 million.

September 14: Albert J. Herberger is appointed U.S. maritime administrator.

1994   March: Molten sulphur carrier MV *Sulphur Enterprise* (Hull #294) is launched.

May: ISC subsidiary signs 11-year contract with further options, with Freeport-McMoRan Copper and Gold, Inc. to provide ocean transportation services for supplies for mine on Indonesian Island of Irian Jaya.

May 6: ISC and General Dynamics Corporation mutually agree to terminate, without liability to either party, the proposed stock purchase agreement signed August 12, 1992, since the acquisition of AMSEA by ISC had not yet been approved by U.S. Navy.

October: CGL contracts to purchase SS *Energy Independence,* a U.S.-flag bulk coal carrier equipped with conveyor belt system for self-unloading, together with 15-year time charter to New England Power Company.

1995 September 28: SS *Energy Independence,* a 38,164-DWT conveyor belt-equipped coal carrier, is delivered and renamed SS *Energy Enterprise.*

December 31: Consolidated Total Assets: $647,580,000. Consolidated Net Worth: $166,261,000.

1996 August 15: Eleventh LASH vessel in fleet is renamed MV *Atlantic Forest* (after the second LASH vessel built in Japan) and delivered at Singapore.

October 8: Maritime Security Act of 1996 is signed, providing a new subsidy program for up to 47 U.S.-flag vessels. Seven company vessels qualify.

November: Clinton wins re-election as U.S. president.

December 31: Consolidated Total Assets: $661,596,000. Consolidated Net Worth: $172,407,000.

1997 ISC becomes largest operator of LASH vessels, with Waterman Steamship Corporation a principal subsidiary.

June 18: ISC subsidiary purchases 12th LASH ship, a 1987 Ukrainian-built 41,000-ton vessel, sister ship of MV *Atlantic Forest,* at auction in Rotterdam District Court. Vessel is renamed MV *Willow.*

December 31: Consolidated Total Assets: $618,204,000. Consolidated Net Worth: $172,805,000.

1998 January: ISC subsidiary purchases 13th LASH vessel, a 1989 Ukrainian-built 48,093-ton sister ship to MV *Willow.* Newly acquired ship is renamed MV *Hickory.* ISC issues a new series of $110 million par value 7¾% Unsecured Senior Notes, due 2007.

August 6: Clyde Hart is appointed U.S. maritime administrator.

December: ISC acquires 37½% interest in Belden Cement Carriers, owners of a growing fleet of specialized cement carriers.

December 15: Seminole Electric Cooperative Inc. unilaterally terminates the 22-year coal contract that had six years left to run. Negotiations begin for financial settlement.

December 31: Consolidated Total Assets: $689,804,000. Consolidated Net Worth: $177,108,000.

1999 April: Cape-Size Pool is formed with two major European shipowners. MV *Amazon* joins nine similar-size vessels in the pool.

August: CGL settles litigation over unilateral termination of the Seminole Electric contract. Seminole pays Company approximately $23 million.

First LASH vessel, MV *Acadia Forest,* is retired after 30 years of service and sold at book value for demolition in India.

December 31: Consolidated Total Assets: $735,003,000. Consolidated Net Worth: $182,484,000.

2000 Interest rates (Libor) fall below 2%.

4th Quarter: Contract with Freeport Indonesia Mining Company is restructured to be serviced by one multipurpose vessel, a small tanker, and two container ships, releasing MV *Banda Sea* and MV *Bali Sea* for conversion to carry standard-gauge railroad cars. These vessels are transferred to the U.S. Gulf for regular service between Mobile, Alabama, and Coatzacoalcos, Mexico.

November: George W. Bush wins U.S. presidential election.

December 31: Consolidated Total Assets: $695,176,000. Consolidated Net Worth: $181,532,000.

2001 September 11: Terrorists crash four hijacked planes into the World Trade Center and the Pentagon, killing nearly 3,000.

October: ISC writes down book value of LASH fleet, MV *Amazon,* and certain other assets by

$81 million and suspends payment of dividends. Assets written down are held for sale.

December 6: Captain William G. Schubert is appointed U.S. maritime administrator.

December 31: Consolidated Total Assets: $460,403,000. Consolidated Net Worth: $114,905,000.

2002   January: Laurance Eustis, longtime board member, dies at 88.

May: ISC acquires 12½% interest in four newly built Cape-size bulk carriers, each about 170,000 DWT, operating in the Cape-Size Pool. Pool grows to 20 vessels owned and 15 to 20 vessels chartered.

December 31: Consolidated Total Assets: $406,752,000. Consolidated Net Worth: $115,227,000.

2003   March 19: Operation Iraqi Freedom begins. ISC vessels participate in carriage of supplies. Coalition armies rout Iraqi army but civil unrest continues.

April: Erik F. Johnsen succeeds Niels W. Johnsen as chairman of the board. Niels M. Johnsen replaces Erik F. Johnsen as president.

May: ISC sells Material Transfer, Inc., a coal transfer terminal facility previously used with the Seminole contract, for approximate book value.

July: US Gen New England, Inc. (USGenNE), successor to New England Power Company, an indirect subsidiary of PG&E, files petition for bankruptcy protection under Chapter XI. This causes a default under the SS *Energy Enterprise* financing, which accelerates the maturity of principal and interest on the SS *Energy Enterprise* notes of about $17 million as well as a "make-whole" prepayment penalty and a write-off of deferred charges totaling approximately $2.6 million, which the Company pays in full to cure the default. USGenNE continues to perform time charter without interruption.

September: USGenNE requests extension until 2004 to submit its reorganization plan. ISC secures new financing of $91 million to repay and consolidate outstanding debt on three vessels.

December 31: Consolidated Total Assets: $382,451,000. Consolidated Net Worth: $121,367,000.

2004   March: H. Merritt Lane III elected to ISC Board of Directors.

November: George W. Bush is re-elected U.S. president.

2005   August 29/September 24: Hurricanes Katrina and Rita hit Louisiana, Texas and Mississippi Gulf coasts. New Orleans is seriously flooded and vast areas devastated. ISC Poydras Center offices are closed and staffs dispersed to Mandeville, Baton Rouge and Houston.

November 15: Company reopens its New Orleans office.

December 31: Consolidated Total Assets: $449,507,000. Condolidated Net Worth: $178,268,000, including $37,554,000 in exchangeable preferred stock

2006   June 26: Board approves plans to relocate its corporate headquarters and CG Rail operations to Mobile, Alabama, due to Hurricane Katrina's effect on the Mississippi River Gulf Outlet.

4th Quarter: Company sells its interest of 26.1% in the expanded fleet of Belden Cement Carriers for a gain of $27,581.000.

2007   April 21: ISC moves into new headquarters in RSA (Retirement Systems of Alabama) Battle House Tower Office Building in Mobile, Alabama.

April 24: ISC holds first Board of Directors and Stockholders meeting at new headquarters in Mobile, Alabama. Eric F. Johnsen retires as Chairman, is succeeded by Niels M. Johnsen. Erik L. Johnsen becomes President.

Not For Widows
And Orphans

SS *Green Wave* (ex *Horatio Allen*), first ship purchased by Central Gulf. EC-2 Liberty-type built in 1943, 10,844 tons total deadweight, bale capacity 475,000 cubic feet, length overall 441 feet, beam 50 feet and speed 11 knots.

CHAPTER I

In the beginning...

Since the window of opportunity was open to acquire ships under the Merchant Ship Sales Act of 1946, my father, my brother Erik and I decided to form a shipowning company to buy a war-built vessel to operate under the United States flag. We had only modest personal savings, but we had friends in New Orleans and elsewhere who were potential investors. Over the next 12 months, we planned and sought co-investors. Positive interest developed slowly, but by the end of 1946, we had assembled about 20 prospective investors willing to put up a total of $225,000. We were still short of what we needed to meet the financial requirements to purchase one Liberty vessel using the credit terms afforded by the Merchant Ship Sales Act (25% cash on delivery, with the remainder paid over 15 years in equal annual installments at an interest rate of 3½%). We needed $250,000 to meet the financial requirements set by the U.S. Maritime Commission. Finally by April 15, 1947, we had 29 investors committed to purchase shares in the new company for a total of $252,500. The Company then issued 2,500 shares of 6% preferred stock and 2,500 shares of $1.00 par value common stock to these founding shareholders in packages of $100 worth of preferred stock (one share) and $1.00 worth of common stock (one share). The average amount of each investment was about $8,700. The largest single initial investment was about $51,000. The Company was ready to apply for its first ship.

Having raised this $252,500, we incorporated Central Gulf Steamship Corporation on April 19, 1947, and delivered the initial shares to the investors. The new company promptly filed its application with the Maritime Commission to purchase a war-built Liberty ship. The purchase price was $544,506, payable $136,506 cash on delivery, and the balance of $408,000 in annual installments of $25,500 from 1948 to 1963 at 3½%

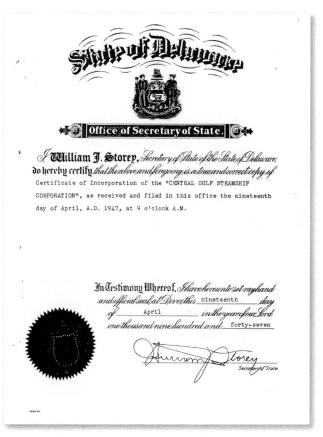

Central Gulf Steamship Corporation's certificate of incorporation, April 19, 1947.

interest. We thought that all we had to do now was select the ship. However, a few days after we submitted our application, the Maritime Commission surprised us. We were told, "Sorry, the minimum net worth requirement for deferred payment has now changed to 50% of the purchase price." Instead of the initial investment of $252,500 we had raised, we now needed $275,023 (an additional $22,523) to meet the revised equity and working capital requirements for our application to be approved. We thought we had already scraped together all the money we could for this project. Prospects for raising additional funds appeared

Central Gulf Steamship Corporation board members and founding shareholders with two senior officers of Hibernia National Bank in the engine room of the *Green Wave* before her maiden voyage. Left to right: Leonard Phelps, the ship's chief engineer; Niels F. Johnsen, president; James H. Kepper, vice president, Hibernia National Bank; Dr. Joseph Morris; Gary Gillis Jr., and Wallace Davis, the bank's president.

grim. We were close but still faced what seemed at the time an enormous gap. Fortunately, Dr. Joseph C. Morris, one of the Company's initial investors, saved the day. Dr. Morris raised the extra funds in a few days and agreed to purchase immediately an additional 223 shares of preferred stock at $100 per share, plus 223 shares of common stock at $1.00 per share. We were therefore able to amend our application accordingly. We were now in business.

On June 6, 1947, the Maritime Commission nominated the *Horatio Allen* as the vessel for Central Gulf to purchase. After inspection we accepted this war-built Liberty ship, signed Maritime Commission Contract MCc-60303 and decided to take delivery of the vessel immediately. On June 8, we became owners of the *Horatio Allen* and renamed her *Green Wave*. "Green Wave" was the name of the Tulane University athletic teams in the Company's hometown of New Orleans. The *Green Wave*'s first captain and first chief engineer were, respectively, Adolph M. Ringen and

Leonard E. Phelps, two of our founding shareholders.

So began the history of Central Gulf Steamship Corporation and its ultimate parent, International Shipholding Corporation. The first *Green Wave* was followed in later years by three replacement vessels to carry the same name: a C-2, a C-4 and an ice-strengthened multipurpose motor ship that traded for about 10 years between ports in the United States and bases in the Arctic and Antarctic, carrying military and scientific cargoes. This is the story of a ship-owning company that began with a single ship in 1947, total assets of $820,737 and a net worth of $275,023. It grew over a span of 60 years to ownership of 35 sophisticated cargo ships and related equipment with an asset value of over $700,000,000.

The strategy of the Company from its formation has been to own and operate a fleet of modern ocean-going vessels to service a highly credible customer base. We hope to show in this volume that our strategy is working.

Board members and shareholders have lunch aboard the *Green Wave* before her first voyage in 1947. Left to right: Captain Adolph Ringen, the ship's master; Joseph M. Jones; Niels F. Johnsen; L.D. Estes; and Wallace M. David and James H. Kepper of Hibernia National Bank.

Aboard the *Green Wave* in 1947. Left to right: William Dreux, partner, Jones Walker (attorneys for Central Gulf); Erik F. Johnsen, vice president; Leonard Phelps, the ship's chief engineer; Gary Gillis Jr.; Niels F. Johnsen (with napkin to face); Wallace M. Davis and James H. Kepper of Hibernia National Bank; Henry B. Bradford and Robert Labry.

New Orleans, Louisiana

April 15, 1947

SUBSCRIPTION TO CAPITAL STOCK

We, the undersigned, hereby mutually agree each with the other and with the corporation hereinafter named, to be formed severally and not jointly, to subscribe the number of shares set opposite our respective signatures hereto, of the preferred capital stock of the par value of One Hundred ($100.00) Dollars per share of a corporation to be organized under the laws of the State of Delaware, or any other state under the name of CENTRAL GULF STEAMSHIP CORPORATION or any other appropriate name, for the purpose of engaging in general steamship business; the corporation to be organized shall have an authorized capital stock of 5,000 shares of preferred capital stock of the par value of $100.00 per share, and 500,000 shares of common no par capital stock.

It is understood by the undersigned that each subscriber to the preferred capital stock shall receive shares of the common capital stock in the proportion of his subscription to the preferred capital stock; it is also understood and agreed by each of the undersigned that N. F. Johnson and assigns shall receive 20% of the common capital stock of this corporation remaining unissued for special services rendered by him.

This subscription agreement is conditioned upon the procuring of subscriptions for $250,000 worth of the preferred capital stock of the corporation to be organized and should this amount of preferred capital stock not be subscribed within two (2) months from the date appearing hereon, then the persons subscribing thereto shall be under no further duty or obligation.

The subscriptions hereby made shall be deemed to be accepted by the corporation immediately upon the filing and recording of its Articles of Incorporation in the manner prescribed by the laws of the state of incorporation. Payment for the stock hereby subscribed to shall be made immediately upon demand after the filing of the Articles of Incorporation as heretofore stated.

The first board of directors upon incorporation of Central Gulf Steamship Corporation was:

Niels F. Johnsen
Niels W. Johnsen
Robert S. Labry
Henry B. Bradford II
Dr. Joseph C. Morris
Gary E. Gillis Jr.
Joseph M. Jones

The first elected officers were:

Niels F. Johnsen	president
Niels W. Johnsen	vice president
Dr. Joseph C. Morris	second vice president
Robert S. Labry	secretary-treasurer
William B. Dreux	assistant secretary-treasurer

Separate copies of this agreement may be signed with the
same force and effect as though all of the signatures were appended to
one original subscription.

SIGNATURES	ADDRESSES	NUMBER OF SHARES
Wm. B. Dreux	847 Canal Bldg	$5000.00
GILLIS-HULSE INSURANCE AGENCY, INC.	839 Union St.	$10,000.00
	2010 Palmer Ave.	$1000.00
Henry F. Lafargue	935 N. Solomon St.	$1500.00
W.V. Howland	1747 Canal Bldg.	$5000.00
W.A. Williams	1323 Whitney Bldg	$10,000.00
J. Hulse	4618 Dart St.	$1,000.00
Norman Rau	420 Poydras St	$5000.00
James H. Gillis	5024 Prytania St.	$1000.00
W.A. Wagner	714 American Bank Bldg	$5000.00
J.C. Morris	1254 State St	$25,000.00
H. Vance Greenslit	1524 State St.	$5,000.00
Hugh McC. Evans	1520 Toledano St	$5000.00
E. Davis McCutchon by Mrs. E. D. McCutchon	233 Joseph St.	$3000.00
C. Marcel Chauviere	318 Magazine St.	$1000.00
Alton Ochsner	1547 Exposition Blvd	2000
	7537 Willow St	150
Henry B. Bradford II	1224 St Charles Ave	100
Walbert M. Salomon	3127 State St Drive	50
Leonard E. Salomon	5418 South Galvez St	50
Henry Oppenheim	213 N. Peters St	50
L. E. Phelps	2127. Esplanade Ave Chief Eng. Covington La.	100
N.W. Johnsen	509 Independence St.	100
S.V. Massimini	1403 Broadway St	100

The founding shareholders were:

H.B. Bradford II
C. Marcel Chauviere
William B. Dreux
Henry Dreyfus
Hugh Evans
G.E. Gillis Jr.
J.H. Gillis
Gillis Hulse Insurance Agency
H. Vance Greenslit

W.V. Howland
J.I. Hulse
E.F. Johnsen
N.F. Johnsen
N.W. Johnsen
Nanna Johnsen
Joseph M. Jones
R.S. Labry
E. Davis McCutchon
S.V. Massimini

Dr. Joseph C. Morris
Alton Ochsner
Norman Rau
A.M. Ringen
Leonard Salomon
Walbert Salomon
William A. Wagner
Gen. L. Kemper Williams
Leonard Phelps
F. L. Lafargue

<u>MINUTES OF FIRST MEETING</u>

<u>OF INCORPORATORS</u>

OF

<u>CENTRAL GULF STEAMSHIP CORPORATION</u>

* * * * * *

The first meeting of incorporators of the CENTRAL
GULF STEAMSHIP CORPORATION, was held at 317-325 South
State Street in the City of Dover, State of Delaware,
at ten o'clock in the forenoon on the 19th day of April,
1947, pursuant to a written waiver of notice signed by
all of the incorporators, fixing said place and time.

The following incorporators were present in person:

> E. G. Salmons
>
> E. R. Steele, Jr.
>
> G. F. Bowdle

being all of the incorporators named in the Certificate
of Incorporation.

On motion unanimously carried, E. G. Salmons was
elected chairman, and E. R. Steele, Jr. secretary of the
meeting.

The secretary presented the waiver of notice of the
meeting signed by all of the incorporators and it was
filed as part of the minutes.

Minutes of Central Gulf Steamship Corporation's first meeting, April 19, 1947 (3 pages).

The chairman reported that the Certificate of Incorporation of the corporation was filed in the office of the Secretary of State of the State of Delaware on the 19th day of April, 1947, and a certified copy thereof was filed for record in the office of the Recorder of Deeds in the County of Kent, on the same date, and a copy of said Certificate of Incorporation was ordered to be inserted in the minute book as part of the records of the meeting.

The secretary presented a proposed form of By-Laws for the regulation and management of the affairs of the corporation, which was read, article by article, and unanimously adopted and ordered to be made a part of the permanent records to follow the Certificate of Incorporation in the minute book.

Motions were then declared by the chairman to be in order for the nomination of directors of the corporation to hold office for the ensuing year and until their successors are elected and qualify, and the following persons were nominated:

    N. F. Johnsen
    N. W. Johnsen
    R. S. Labry
    H. B. Bradford,
    Dr. Joseph C. Nole
    J. E. Gillis, Jr
    Joseph M. Jones

No further nominations having been made, a ballot was taken and all of the incorporators having voted, and the ballots having been duly canvassed, the chairman declared that the above named persons were elected directors of the

corporation by the unanimous vote of all the incorporators.

Upon motion duly made, seconded and unanimously carried,

it was

> RESOLVED, that the Board of Directors be and it
> hereby is authorized in its discretion to issue
> the capital stock of the Corporation to the full
> amount or number of shares authorized by the Cer-
> tificate of Incorporation in such amounts and for
> such considerations as from time to time shall be
> determined by the Board of Directors and as may be
> permitted by law.

There being no other business to be transacted, the

meeting was, upon motion duly made, seconded and carried,

adjourned.

_____
Secretary of Meeting

CENTRAL GULF STEAMSHIP CORPORATION

Statement of Income

For the Period from Incorporation (April 19, 1947)
to November 30, 1947

Voyage revenue (3 terminated voyages - June 6, to October 17, 1947)		$ 339,764
Voyage expense, excluding depreciation		229,606
Gross profit from shipping operations, before overhead and depreciation		110,158
Overhead (administrative and general expenses and taxes):		
Officers' salaries	$ 19,368	
Legal and accounting fees	4,750	
Rent, heat, light, and power	135	
Communication expense	635	
Office supplies, stationery, and printing	328	
Entertaining and soliciting	12	
Traveling	191	
Taxes	2,869	
Insurance and bond premiums	28	
Postage	31	
Miscellaneous	13	28,360
Gross profit from shipping operations, before depreciation		81,798
Depreciation - floating equipment		16,503
Gross profit from shipping operations		65,295
Interest paid:		
First Preferred 3½% Mortgage Notes	6,945	
Sundry notes payable	332	7,277
Net profit before taxes on income		58,018
Provision for federal taxes on income		22,047
Net Profit (Surplus)		$ 35,971

First Central Gulf income statement, November 30, 1947.

CENTRAL GULF STEAMSHIP CORPORATION

Balance Sheet

As of November 30, 1947

ASSETS

Current Assets:		
Cash in bank		$ 244,798
Accounts receivable:		
Traffic	$ 11,297	
U. S. Maritime Commission	2,332	
Miscellaneous	712	14,341
Prepaid expenses (unexpired insurance premiums, - $29,509)		29,704
Total Current Assets		288,843
Vessel and Equipment:		
Vessel - at cost	544,506	
Vessel betterments	2,081	
	546,587	
Less Reserve for depreciation	16,503	
	530,084	
Furniture and fixtures	244	530,328
Organization Expense		1,566
		$ 820,737

First Central Gulf Steamship balance sheet, November 30, 1947.

LIABILITIES

Current Liabilities:
 First Preferred 3½% Mortgage Note - June
  6, 1948 maturity $ 25,500
 Accounts payable and accrued expenses   10,764
 Provision for federal taxes on income $ 22,047
 Less U. S. Treasury Notes Tax Series
  C held for payment of federal taxes on
  income - at cost   12,500 9,547

     Total Current Liabilities   45,811

First Preferred 3½% Mortgage Notes maturing
 $25,500 annually 1948 to 1963   408,000
Less 1948 maturity included in current liabilities   25,500 382,500

Deferred Credit - unterminated voyage revenue,
 less expenses, $32,040   80,932

Capital Stock:
 6% cumulative preferred capital stock of $100
  par value per share; redeemable at $105 per
  share plus accrued dividends. Authorized
  5,000 shares; issued and outstanding 2,723
  shares   272,300
 Common capital stock of $1 par value per share.
  Authorized 500,000 shares; issued and outstanding, 3,223 shares   3,223 275,523

Earned Surplus   35,971

               $ 820,737

C-2 SS *Green Wave* (ex *Santa Mercedes*), acquired April 5, 1960. DWT, 11,000; bale cubic capacity, 543,539 cubic feet; speed, 15 knots. This was the second Central Gulf ship to bear the name *Green Wave*. (Photo from Captain James McNamara)

The *Green Wave* successfully performed 12 voyages carrying bulk cargoes (coal and grain) in transatlantic trades between June 1947 and June 1949. Then the Board of Directors decided it was time to purchase a second and more advanced vessel. In preparation for this event the board resolved to raise $190,284 in additional capital and to offer existing shareholders the opportunity to purchase their pro-rata shares. In addition, to provide the funds to pay off the $408,000 Maritime Commission mortgage on the *Green Wave,* the board authorized management to borrow $275,000 from the Hibernia National Bank of New Orleans to supplement cash in the Company. The bank loan was to be repaid over two years in approximately equal quarterly installments at 4% interest. A first mortgage on the *Green Wave* was given as collateral.

After clearing our indebtedness to the Maritime Commission, we were ready to apply under the Merchant Ship Sales Act to purchase a second war-built vessel. We decided to apply for an AP-2 Victory vessel,

more sophisticated and, at 15 knots, faster than the 11-knot Liberty ship. The statutory sales price of an AP-2 was $879,157, payable $219,790 (25%) cash on delivery and the balance of $659,367 in equal installments over 15 years at 3½% interest. The net worth of the Company in June 1949 was about $460,000, which met the government's requirement of 50% of the purchase price to qualify for deferred payment. Later that same month, the Maritime Commission allocated the AP-2 *Ouachita Victory* to the Company for purchase under Contract MCc-62246. Central Gulf Steamship Corporation promptly acknowledged the nomination.

Before deciding to take delivery of the *Ouachita Victory,* the Company management had to satisfy itself that it was possible to alter structurally an AP-2 Victory to meet certain of our trading requirements. We expected to use the vessel to carry bulk cargoes such as grain, coal and fertilizer as well as lumber and bagged commodities. Standard Victory ships were built with multiple 'tween decks in the three holds forward of the midship section. In order to stow bulk cargoes and lumber efficiently, we wanted to remove the lower 'tween decks from the forward holds. Also, to make loading or discharging bulk grain more efficient, by permitting the bulk grain to flow easily between the upper and lower holds, we determined it was possible to cut manhole-size openings in the 'tween decks aft of midship and to fit them with grates. Once we had satisfied ourselves and the regulatory agencies that the structural changes could be made, we were in position to accept delivery of the ship. We renamed her *Green Valley* and she became the second ship in the Central Gulf fleet. She operated in tramp trades for several months until August 9, 1950, when we time-chartered her to the Military Sea Transportation Service for the Korean War under Charter MST 177. It was our first contract (charter) with MSTS and its successor agencies.

Central Gulf in the early 1950's

Subsequently, in October 1950, we accepted an offer from a third party to purchase the *Green Wave*. The price was $512,500, payable $256,250 cash on delivery (October 9, 1950) and the balance of $256,250 payable $56,250 on November 15, 1950, plus five semiannual installments of $40,000, beginning on January 1, 1951, secured by a first preferred mortgage to Central Gulf as mortgagee on the *Green Wave*. The Company realized a gain of $270,365 on the sale of the *Green Wave*. We deposited this in a tax-exempt Construction Reserve Fund account, to be applied against the cost of a replacement vessel, reducing the amount to be depreciated on the new vessel.

By the time we received payment of the first note from the buyer of the *Green Wave,* the Company had already decided to purchase a replacement vessel. We applied to the Maritime Commission to buy another AP-2 Victory vessel under the Ship Sales Act. The statutory sales price was the same as the *Green Valley*—$879,157, payable $219,790 on delivery. The balance of $659,367 was payable in equal installments over 15 years at 3½% interest, secured by a standard Maritime Commission mortgage. We were able to make some of the payments with funds from the Construction Reserve Fund. The Maritime Commission allocated the *Cooper*

Union Victory to the Company. Central Gulf accepted the vessel under Contract MCc-62692 and she was delivered to our ownership on January 15, 1951. We renamed her the *Green Harbour*. We also removed her lower 'tween decks in holds one, two and three, and cut grated openings in her 'tween decks in holds four and five so that she matched her sister ship. The Company's fleet now consisted of two U.S.-flag AP-2 Victory vessels, the *Green Valley* and *Green Harbour*.

At the Company's annual meeting of stockholders held in New Orleans on October 1, 1951, the following stockholders were re-elected to the board of directors until the annual meeting in 1952:

Niels F. Johnsen
Niels W. Johnsen
Robert S. Labry
Henry B. Bradford II
Dr. Joseph C. Morris
Gary E. Gillis Jr.
Joseph M. Jones
Gen. L. Kemper Williams
H. Vance Greenslit
Erik F. Johnsen (joined the board after honorable discharge as U.S. Navy Lieutenant)

A Bad Market in 1953 — Hard Choices

In these early days of the Company, we employed the *Green Valley* and *Green Harbour* in bulk cargo trades or on time charter to cargo liner operators. The results of their operations depended upon spot or current open-market charters. Our objective, however, was to employ the small fleet on more stable longer-term business from consecutive voyages. In the interim we had to take short-term business as available in the marketplace. Through the fiscal year ending March 31, 1953, the *Green Valley* and the *Green Harbour* generated sufficient revenue to provide the Company with modest net profits while providing for depreciation at the rate of 20% per year. However, by the end of fiscal year March 31, 1954, net losses had depleted any earlier earned surplus, although accrued depreciation had retrieved all but approximately $553,000 of the two vessels' $1,890,000 original cost (including the cost of the deck changes). Consequently, management could see that the marketplace was slightly out of balance in favor of the cargo interests—slightly more ships than cargoes were available, forcing rates downward. The Company faced a continuing downward trend in revenues. From this perspective, management had to review continuously the alternative deployment of its small fleet of two Victory ships. While management was still optimistic about the future of ship owning, we realized the importance of keeping those shareholders who were not active in the day-to-day business closely informed of economic conditions facing the Company. Consequently on November 30, 1953, at a special meeting of the stockholders of the Company held in New Orleans, N.F. Johnsen, president, gave a full report on the difficult markets in which the *Green Valley* and the *Green Harbour* were then operating. Whereupon Dr. Joseph C. Morris, seconded by G.E. Gillis Jr., offered the following resolution, which was unanimously adopted.

> "WHEREAS the management of the company and the directors have heretofore given serious consideration to some of the very acute problems confronting the company, specifically the necessity of providing the company with the best available tools with which to work, i.e. vessels – modern, efficient and of the latest construction design – to the end that the fleet may not suffer from the inefficiencies resulting from obsolescence, and further that the mounting costs incident to operation of vessels under the American Flag gives cause to consider the transference, if legally permissible, of a vessel or vessels to foreign registry, or the disposal of a vessel or vessels now owned by the company and the rechartering on a bareboat basis of such vessel or vessels and the utilization of all or part of the proceeds therefrom to enable the acquisition of a vessel or vessels under foreign registry, and to do any and all other things which might in general terms effectuate the purposes hereinabove outlined. AND, WHEREAS, the management and the directors are also quite mindful of the fact that it may be that a stockholder or stockholders might consider that because of economic or personal reasons such a program would not appeal to him or to them, and that the directors desire that any shareholder or shareholders not desirous of participating in such a program be given for a limited period of time the opportunity to receive his or their original investment and also be permitted to receive payment for his or their common stock at a price to be fixed by the Board of Directors, subject to the feasibility of arranging such a program with full consideration being given to the tax consequences.

> NOW THEREFORE BE IT RESOLVED THAT the stockholders of Central Gulf Steamship Corporation, at a meeting duly called subject to the terms and provisions of the company's charter and by-laws, on Monday, November 30th, at three o'clock, at 1547 National Bank of Commerce Building, do hereby authorize, in a permissive sense, the management and the directors to sell either one or both of the vessels presently owned by the company, to charter said vessel or vessels on a bareboat charter basis and to acquire other suitable vessels, either American or foreign. The management and the directors are also hereby authorized to take any and all steps that are deemed proper to secure the transfer of a vessel or vessels to foreign registry. The terms and considerations of each of these steps being matters which are left to the judgment and discretion of the management and directors of the corporation, it being recognized that in negotiations of this character time is of the essence and that sufficient authority is required in order to satisfactorily conduct the necessary negotiations and that it is impractical to call successive stockholders' meetings. However, insofar as it is practical to do so, it would be the intention of the management and the directors to submit the basis of any transaction to the stockholders for their information. Alternatively, the management seeks the permissive authority to secure, subject to compliance with all of the regulations of the Maritime Administration, an interest in foreign flag vessels through the media of acquiring a stock interest in a company either organized or to be organized which will own such foreign vessels.

> FURTHER, be it provided that any shareholder or shareholders may acquire the money, which he has originally invested in the company, provided he is prepared to also divest himself of his common stock at a price to be fixed by the Board of Directors. Such rights shall subsist for a period of sixty (60) days from the date on which the directors have fixed the figure at which the stock can be acquired and also from the date of the opinion from the company's legal counsel and auditors as to the legal permissibility of such an arrangement. It is agreed and understood that none of the steps authorized under the terms of this resolution are directives but solely permissive authority which is now granted by the shareholders."

At this difficult time and often over the ensuing years that N. F. Johnsen was president of Central Gulf, he reminded the shareholders, "Ship owning is a very risky business: not for widows and orphans." Nevertheless, only six of the original 29 shareholders asked the Company to repurchase their shares. They each received in payment slightly over $100,000, or 3½ times their original investment.

U.S. Flag/Foreign Flag

As part of our ongoing efforts to reduce our operating costs to remain competitive in the international bulk cargo markets, we decided to acquire a Liberty vessel eligible for transfer from U.S. to foreign flag. In October 1954 we purchased the *Peach Tree State* from States Marine Corporation for $500,000, transferred her to the Netherlands flag and upon delivery, renamed her *Zuiderzee*. We formed a new subsidiary in the Netherlands, Overzeese Scheepvaart Maatschappij N.V. (OSM), to own the vessel. We then formed another new company, Compania Maritima Unidas S.A. (CMU), to time-charter the *Zuiderzee* from OSM in order to retain profits, if any, in a foreign country. A few months later, in June 1955, we added to our foreign-flag fleet the Panamanian *Susan*, a C-2, which we purchased for $1 million and renamed *Noordzee*.

The *Noordzee* had a speed of 14 knots, compared to the 11 knots of the Liberty. Its steam-turbine engine was almost twice as powerful as the Liberty ship's lower-horsepower steam reciprocating engine. We financed 100% of the purchase price of the *Noordzee* with a loan of $1 million from the Chemical Corn Exchange Bank of New York. We used as collateral the charter hire generated by her first employment, a time charter to Continental Grain Company for about 15 months, plus a mortgage on the vessel. As with the *Zuiderzee,* we registered the *Noordzee* in the Netherlands, under OSM ownership and time-chartered her to CMU. A few months later we sold the *Zuiderzee* and shortly thereafter in 1957 replaced her by purchasing the AP-2 Victory *Black Dragon* from Isbrandtsen Company for $2 million ($500,000 cash and the balance of $1.5 million in deferred notes). We renamed her *Tappanzee,* registered her in the Netherlands under OSM ownership and time-chartered to CMU. The AP-2 Victory was also a more competitive vessel than the Liberty with a total deadweight of about 10,700 tons and a 6,600 horsepower steam-turbine engine capable of producing a speed of 15.5 knots.

Both the *Noordzee* and the *Tappanzee* operated profitably under the Netherlands flag for several months until the freight market for foreign vessels crashed in 1957. Since the market for U.S.-flag vessels offered better opportunities and we had completed previously arranged contract voyages, we sold the two ships to their sisters' owning company, Central Gulf, in December 1958, for transfer to U.S. flag. We renamed *Noordzee* the *Green Bay* and *Tappanzee* the *Green Island*. We then owned four competitive U.S.-flag vessels.

Company Opens Independent Offices

Having arrived at this point, it became increasingly important that the company be organized on an independent basis. The management felt it important to be able to take prompt advantage of any opportunities that presented themselves.

Therefore, in September 1956 Niels F. Johnsen, Erik F. Johnsen and, shortly thereafter, Niels W. Johnsen resigned from States Marine Corporation in order to devote full time to the development of Central Gulf Steamship Corporation and its associated companies. While there were a number of good reasons for Central Gulf to have its own offices we also resigned from States Marine, with which we had been associated for several years, to avoid any possibility of a conflict of interest. States Marine was at that time contemplating accepting an Operating Differential Subsidy from the U.S. Maritime Administration for its U.S.-flag cargo liner services and we did not wish to be in a position that might impede its negotiations with the Maritime Administration or Central Gulf's independent action.

Central Gulf established independent offices in the Hibernia Bank Building in New Orleans and 19 Rector Street in New York City in October 1956. Even before this date we were actively engaged in the ship and cargo markets. Concurrent with establishing Central Gulf's own offices, we also formed N.W. Johnsen & Co. Inc. in New York City to act as cargo and shipbrokers for Central Gulf and its associated companies. The first contract that the new brokerage company handled was fixed in May 1956 with States Marine Corporation for six cargoes of coal for shipment from Hampton Roads (Norfolk), Virginia, to Japan.

AP-2 SS *Green Valley*
(ex *Ouachita Victory*),
acquired June 1949, before
lengthening. DWT, 10,800;
bale cubic capacity, 495,000
cubic feet; 15 knots.

AP-2 *Green Harbour* (ex *Cooper Union Victory*), sister ship of *Green Valley,* acquired January 15, 1951, before lengthening. DWT, 10,800; bale cubic capacity, 495,000 cubic feet; speed, 15 knots. Watercolor on silk by T. Hagiwara, Yokohama, Japan, 1965, depicting the vessel circa 1955.

CHAPTER 2

The Coal Contracts

Our decision to open independent offices in New Orleans and New York coincided with a significant international development that had the effect of dramatically increasing freight rates. Dispute over control of the Suez Canal culminated in Egypt's nationalization of the canal in July 1956. The dispute escalated when Israel invaded the Sinai Peninsula and war broke out between Israel and Egypt. The United Nations sent in troops to stabilize the situation in the autumn of 1956, but the Suez Canal was closed to ship traffic. Ships that normally transited the Suez to proceed between the Indian and Atlantic oceans had to make the much longer voyage via the Cape of Good Hope. The effect was a substantial tightening of the supply of ships and a dramatic increase in freight rates worldwide. In a matter of weeks, rates rose by more than 50%. This exceptional shift in the tone of the market opened opportunities for which we had been waiting: The rise in freight rates coincided with increased volumes of coal exports from the United States to the Far East and Europe. As a result we booked the following contracts up to the capacity of our owned- and time-chartered fleet.

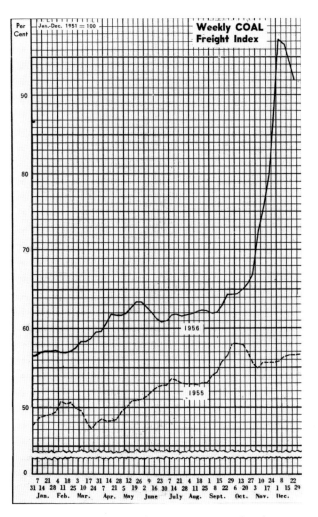

Weekly Coal Freight Index shows jump in rates after closure of Suez Canal in 1956. Courtesy of *Chartering Annual 1956,* Maritime Research Inc., New York.

IMPORTANT COAL CONTRACTS

- SIX CARGOES (NWJ#2) coal Hampton Roads (Norfolk, Va.,) to Japan, shipment one per month, each 9,000/10,000 tons, January 1957 through June 1957, freight rate $18.75 per ton. Fixed May 10, 1956. Charterer: States Marine Corp.

  Notional ship allocations (6 cargoes):

  Green Valley, 9,500 tons, 10% for cargo, first cargo January 1957, second cargo April 1957.

  Green Harbour, 9,500 tons, 10% for cargo, first cargo February 1957, second cargo May 1957.

  Green Island (ex *Tappanzee*), 9,500 tons 10% for cargo, first cargo March 1957, second cargo June 1957.

- NINE CARGOES (NWJ#3) coal Hampton Roads to Japan, shipment one per month, each 9,000/11,000 tons, July

1957 through March 1958, freight rate $19.25 per ton. Fixed June 1, 1956. Charterer: States Marine Corporation.

Notional ship allocations (9 cargoes):

Green Valley, 9,500 tons, 10% for cargo, first cargo July 1957, second cargo October 1957, third cargo January 1958.

Green Harbour, 9,500 tons, 10% for cargo, first cargo August 1957, second cargo November 1957, third cargo February 1958.

C-2 *Green Point* (ex *Santa Alicia*), acquired December 8, 1960. DWT, 10,645; bale cubic capacity, 559,000 cubic feet; speed, 15 knots. (Photo from Captain James McNamara)

Green Island (ex *Tappanzee*), 9,500 tons, 10% for cargo, first cargo September 1957, second cargo December 1957, third cargo March 1958.

- FIFTEEN CARGOES (NWJ#12) coal, Hampton Roads to Antwerp/Hamburg range, shipments fairly evenly spread May 1957-August 1958, each 9,000/11,500 tons, freight rate $9.50 per ton. Fixed January 12, 1957. Charterer: B.D. Blumenfeld, Hamburg. (See comment below on freight rate originally fixed. *)

Notional ship allocations (15 cargoes):

Green Bay (ex *Noordzee*), 9,000 tons, 10% for cargo, one cargo per month beginning May 1957 through April 1958 (12 cargoes).

Fernleaf, 11,000 tons, 10% for cargo, 11,000, 10% for cargo, three cargoes May through August 1958.

- TWELVE CARGOES (NWJ#58) coal, Hampton Roads to Rotterdam, shipments fairly evenly spread over the period September 1958 through August 1959, freight rate $9.50 per ton, each 9,000 to 11,500 tons. Fixed August 13, 1957. Charterer: B.D. Blumenfeld (Actually we loaded only the first, fourth and fifth cargoes on sub-chartered vessels *Atlantic Countess, Island Mariner* and *Othon.* Because the market was so depressed, the charterer asked for the remaining nine cargoes to be canceled, by mutual agreement, with the charterer paying the Company $615,994 (about $6.22/ton) for the 99,000 tons canceled.

* On the same day, August 13, 1957, the Company agreed to accommodate the charterer by adjusting fixture NWJ#12's freight rate from $11.35 to $9.50.

Notional ship allocations (12 cargoes):

Fernleaf, 11,500, 10% for cargo, eight cargoes, over September 1958 through May 1959.

Milross, 11,500, 10% for cargo, four cargoes, June 1959 through August 1959.

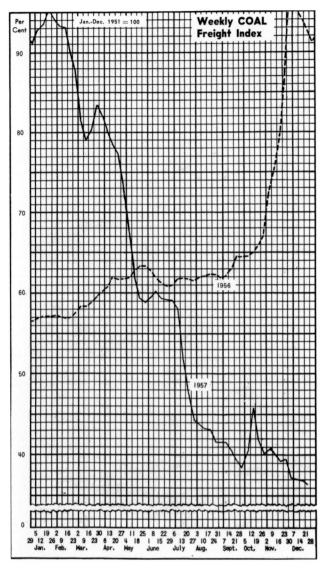

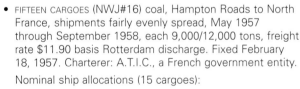

Weekly Coal Freight Index plunged after the Suez Canal reopened in 1957. Courtesy of *Chartering Annual 1957*, Maritime Research Inc., New York.

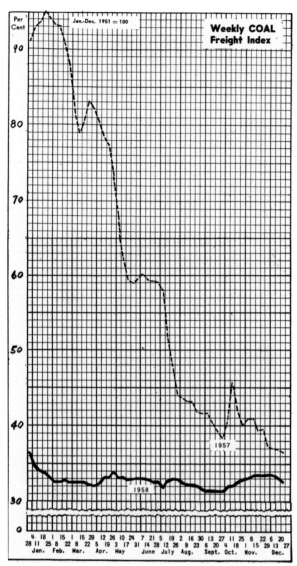

This chart shows how rates remained depressed through 1958. Courtesy of *Chartering Annual 1958*, Maritime Research Inc., New York.

• FIFTEEN CARGOES (NWJ#16) coal, Hampton Roads to North France, shipments fairly evenly spread, May 1957 through September 1958, each 9,000/12,000 tons, freight rate $11.90 basis Rotterdam discharge. Fixed February 18, 1957. Charterer: A.T.I.C., a French government entity.

Nominal ship allocations (15 cargoes):

Thais Hope, 11,000 tons, 10%, 11 cargoes, May 1957 through May 1958.

Milross, Four cargoes, June 1958 through September 1958.

We were fortunate by mid-1957 to have fixed 57 Liberty-ship size cargoes (9,500 to 11,000 long tons, the standard cargo size at the time) for shipment over the next couple of years. These commitments to carry about 600,000 long tons of coal produced an estimated gross

revenue for the Company of about $7 million. Then followed another dramatic shift in the market. Although unrest continued, the Suez Canal reopened to traffic in April 1957, sharply increasing the number of ships available for hire and causing the freight market to crash.

Freight Market Crash and Our Response

Before the market crashed, freight rates for coal cargoes of 9,000/10,000-ton Liberty-size ships from Hampton Roads to Rio de Janeiro, Brazil, were $14 per ton. By December 1957, they had declined to $4.75 per ton. During 1957 cargoes from Hampton Roads to Japan fell from $22 to $9.25 per ton, and from Hampton

21

Roads to Rotterdam from $14.15 to $3.50 per ton. Bulk grain cargoes from the U.S. Gulf to Rotterdam fell from $17.25 to $4.75 per ton. Throughout the market, rates collapsed to a level at which even vessels with the lowest operating costs could no longer afford to carry these cargoes. Owners began looking for lay-up berths to take their foreign-flag ships out of service rather than operate them at losses. Our reaction to the collapse of foreign-flag rates was to charter several foreign-flag vessels at reduced market rates to carry some of the contract cargoes we had booked at higher rates before the market collapsed. This move also enabled us to use our U.S.-flag vessels to book U.S. government-sponsored preference cargoes, which were becoming available for U.S.-registered ships.

Of the previously cited notional ship allocations, we only carried eight of the 57 cargoes booked under these contracts in the Company's owned- and time-chartered vessels—one cargo each in the *Green Bay* (ex *Noordzee*), *Green Valley*, *Green Island* (ex *Tappanzee*), *Ante Topic*, *Milross* and *Thais Hope*, and two cargoes in the *Fernleaf*. The remaining 49 cargoes were carried on ships we chartered for single voyages, or in the case of eight cargoes under contract NWJ #58, mutual agreement was reached for the charterer to pay a cancellation fee of $615,994 in lieu of our nominating vessels to actually carry these cargoes. Assuming we broke even on the eight cargoes carried by our own and time-chartered vessels, the Company realized a gross profit of approximately $1,761,000 (including the cancellation fee of $615,994) on the 49 cargoes that we sublet or canceled. These contracts obviously were of critical benefit to the Company. They enabled us to bridge the roughly two years of the bear charter market and to use our own and chartered fleet of U.S.-flag vessels to take advantage of cargoes reserved for U.S.-flag vessels, and as will be discussed later, to develop our Persian Gulf liner service.

We had been able to book these contracts because of the work we had done with States Marine and Harold Rodriguez, principal owner of Rodriguez Sons Company, Inc., cargo brokers for coal importers and exporters. The latter company was an offshoot of W.W. Battie & Co, Inc., cargo brokers for sugar importers established before World War I in Cuba by

Harold Rodriguez's father and his uncle, who came to the United States before the Castro revolution. W.W. Battie had major contracts with sugar exporting companies in Cuba and acted as brokers for most of the sugar exported to the United States from before World War II until Castro's takeover. Rodriguez Sons was set up to handle coal exports from the United States, a business they developed extensively with principals in Japan and Europe and major exporters in the United States. Niels W. Johnsen had established a reputation as an aggressive ship operator while working with States Marine. Rodriguez knew the market. With the establishment of Central Gulf Steamship Corporation and with N.W. Johnsen & Co., Inc. operating as broker, we were in a prime position to make the contracts.

While the contracts for the coal cargoes hedged the future employment of the Company's owned fleet, it was

CENTRAL GULF STEAMSHIP CORPORATION
Statements of Earnings (Loss)
Nine Months Ended December 31, 1957

Terminated voyage results:		
Revenue from vessel operations		$6,897,200
Expenses of vessel operations		6,657,801
Terminated voyage results, before depreciation		239,399
Depreciation of vessels and equipment	$134,451	
Administrative and general expenses	415,744	
Interest expense	37,775	587,970
		(348,571)
Other income:		
Interest and dividends	26,547	
Agency fees, commissions, etc.	23,298	49,845
		(298,726)
Adjustments applicable to prior years (net)		24,529
Net (loss)		$ (274,197)

Statement of Retained Earnings (Deficit)

Amount (deficit) at March 31, 1957	$ (134,522)
Net (loss) for the nine months ended December 31, 1957	(274,197)
	(408,719)
Dividend on preferred stock ($4.50 a share)	23,720
Amount (deficit) at December 31, 1957	$ (432,439)

ASSETS

Current Assets:

Cash		$605,384
Marketable securities – at cost:		
U.S. Government securities (quoted market, $164,045)	$163,900	
Bank stock (approximate market, $22,680)	11,100	175,000
Receivables:		
Traffic (U.S. Governmental agencies, $377,383)	943,521	
Other (insurance claims, $79,119)	170,859	
	1,114,380	
Less allowance for doubtful receivables	57,687	
	1,056,693	
Current maturities of notes receivable from associated company	130,000	1,186,693
Shipping inventories – at cost		13,459
Prepaid insurance premiums		92,362
Total current assets		2,072,898
Notes receivable from associated company, Compania Maritima Unidas, S.A. (secured by first preferred mortgage on S.S. *Noordzee*), maturing $65,000 semi-annually to March 31, 1961 [1]	455,000	
Less current maturities included in current assets	130,000	325,000
Investments:		
Cash surrender value of insurance policies of $425,000 on lives of officers	24,024	
Shares in steamship association	200	24,224
Vessels and equipment:		
Floating equipment (2 vessels) – at cost	1,895,149	
Less allowance for depreciation	1,657,025	
	238,124	
Office furniture and fixtures – at cost less depreciation, $7,159	11,263	249,387
		$2,671,509

LIABILITIES

Current liabilities:

Current maturities of first preferred 3-1/2% mortgage notes payable to Maritime Administration		$91,047
Accounts payable and accrued expenses		881,061
Associated company current account (Compania Maritima Unidas, S.A.)		300,035
Insurance proceeds reserved for repairs		14,335
Dividend payable		7,907
Total current liabilities		1,294,385
Net unterminated voyage revenue (excess of revenue, $1,981,156, over expenses of voyages in progress)		394,320
Long-term debt:		
Indebtedness to associated company, Compania Maritima Unidas, S.A., under unsecured note payable maturing December 4, 1959	$300,000	
First preferred 3-1/2% mortgage notes payable 1958/65 to Maritime Administration, less current maturities, $91,047, included in current liabilities	582,110	882,110
Stockholders' equity:		
Capital stock:		
6% cumulative preferred stock of $100 par value a share; Redeemable at $105 a share plus accrued dividends (dividends paid or provided for to December 31, 1957). Authorized 10,000 shares; issued 5,486 shares, whereof 215 shares in treasury, leaving 5,271 shares outstanding	527,100	
Common stock of $1 par value a share. Authorized 10,000 shares; issued 6,259 shares whereof 226 shares in treasury, leaving 6,033 shares outstanding	6,033	
	533,133	
Retained earnings (deficit)	(432,439)	100,694
Contingent liabilities [2]		—
		$2,671,509

1. Contingent liabilities:
   (a) $500,000 letter of credit issued by the Hibernia National Bank in New Orleans to guarantee the performance of certain time charter obligations on the M.S. Millross, secured by pledge of notes receivable from associated company, $455,000, together with the collateral security therefor.
   (b) Guarantee of note of an associated company, Compania Maritima

Unidas, S.A., issued in April 1957 in the amount of $1,500,000 for the purchase of a vessel.

2. At December 31, 1957, the company had six vessels under time charter which terminate on various dates from January 31, 1958, to September 22, 1959. The rentals for the period from December 31, 1957, to termination of the charters amount to approximately $4,600,000, of which $82,833 had been paid in advance at that date.

also becoming evident that the dry cargo markets were developing into specialized services. The market from the United States was dividing into one for U.S.-flag vessels and one for non-U.S. flag vessels. The foreign-flag market was further segmenting into bulk-carrier vessels and liner-type vessels. Owners began designing and building some dry-bulk carriers to carry ore and other close-stowing minerals, and some to carry coal. New oil tankers became larger and specialized to carry crude oil or refined petroleum products. We mention these developments to emphasize that when we made these coal contracts to hedge the employment of our owned and time-chartered fleet, we were unwittingly entering a period of structural change in ocean transportation of not only dry-cargo commodities but also oil and other liquid commodities.

The year 1957 marked the 10th anniversary of the Company. It also marked the beginning of a long bear market in bulk freight rates (see graphs). To survive and grow, we had to be able to make a profit at these low freight levels or cease to exist as a viable business. We had to take advantage of the cargoes available to U.S.-flag vessels under the U.S. government cargo preference laws. Our challenge was becoming clear. Not only did we have to maintain employment for the core fleet of conventional U.S.-flag breakbulk vessels in which we had invested over the preceding 10 years, but also we had to be prepared to take the risk of new ideas to compete effectively in a changing environment and grow the Company. We took the bit and ran with it.

CHAPTER 3

Service to Persian Gulf and South Asia

We decided that we would use the new low foreign-flag market rates to our advantage. We must:

1. Focus on the Public Law 480, Export-Import Bank, and Agency for International Development (USAID) cargoes for our U.S.-flag vessels;

2. Use these cargoes to form the basis for building up a U.S.-flag cargo liner service between U.S. Gulf and Atlantic Coast ports and ports on the Red Sea, Persian Gulf, India and Pakistan, designated under the 1936 Merchant Marine Act as Trade Route 18;

3. Increase our participation in the growing exports of consumer products from the U.S. to Middle Eastern countries that were spending more of their oil revenues;

4. Work with a Japanese shipyard to take advantage of the evolving technology that would gradually produce new ships that could compete effectively in the new market environment of low freight rates;

5. As we developed new cargo opportunities for U.S.-flag vessels, charter in U.S.-flag vessels to supplement our own;

6. Purchase additional U.S.-flag vessels as they became available for sale at attractive prices with favorable financing from other U.S.-flag shipowners (mainly subsidized) whose trade routes suffered from depressed economic conditions;

7. Maintain a position with the Maritime Administration that would protect our status as an unsubsidized operator on the trade route we had selected to develop, Trade Route 18.

Fortuitously, a major recipient of U.S. PL480 and USAID commodities was the Indian government, whose economy was being bolstered by U.S.-government programs. The commodities shipped under these programs were ideally suited for shipment on our U.S.-flag vessels in combination with the general cargo we were able to book destined for Eastern Mediterranean, Red Sea and Persian Gulf ports. The Indian government managed the shipment of these cargoes through its own agency, the India Supply Mission, in Washington, D.C. Our good friends Stanley Coron and Charlie Diamond, owners of Dyson Shipping Company, were ISM's exclusive agents in New York.

First U.S. Preference Cargo Bookings

In January 1957 we fixed the first India Supply Mission cargo reserved for U.S.-flag vessels. We allocated this cargo of 9,500 long tons of bagged rice to be carried from a U.S. Gulf port to Bombay on our bareboat-chartered AP-2 Victory ship *Bucknell Victory* (NWJ#1), later substituted by our AP-2 *Green Harbour*. The freight rate was $37.25 per ton (basis proceeding via Cape of Good Hope), or $4.00 per ton less if the vessel could proceed via the Suez Canal. The India Supply Mission became an important shipper of U.S.-flag reserved cargoes on our Trade Route 18 service in future months and years. In the early days of this service, after unloading in India, we would send the vessels in ballast to load a full cargo of ore from Durban, South Africa, home to Baltimore at a freight rate of $13 per ton. U.S.-flag vessels in our Persian Gulf cargo liner services performed many similar voyages in the coming months and years, carrying bottom cargoes of foodstuffs or mineral fertilizers from the United States to the Indian subcontinent, and returning to the U.S. with full cargoes of ore or other commodities from the Indian Ocean area.

After inaugurating the U.S.-flag service on Trade Route 18, we gradually increased the number of sailings. To protect our position against our competitors, we filed on February 25, 1958, an application with the Maritime Subsidy Board for Operating Differential

Subsidy to cover 36 to 48 voyages per year on Trade Route 18 (U.S. Gulf and Atlantic ports to Red Sea, Persian Gulf, Ceylon, and East and West Pakistani ports, including Indian ports). If we didn't get the subsidy, our objective was to prevent the Subsidy Board from awarding an ODS contract to a competitor, by convincing the board that additional sailings beyond ours were unnecessary. Our ploy worked. On September 23, 1960, the Subsidy Board offered Central Gulf an ODS contract for 24 sailings annually on Trade Route 18. Even though we declined the subsidy, no sailings were offered to any competing operators.

Risk

The foregoing contract fixtures and the Coal Freight Index, Weekly 1955-1958, showing ocean transportation rates on coal cargoes for this period, demonstrate dramatically the cyclicality and risk attendant to investment in shipping. When we made these fixtures, we, of course, could not predict that the market was going to crash within months. Obviously, neither could the charterers. After the passage of several decades and as we review our corporate history, we can attest to the A-1 credit quality of the customers with whom we did business then and continue to do so today. They all faithfully fulfilled their obligations. These coal contracts were an important contribution to the survival of our company, particularly at the critical time when we pursued the long-range objective of establishing a profitable cargo liner service between U.S. Gulf and Atlantic ports and the Persian Gulf/South Asia area. They served as a safety net while we concentrated on building this new U.S.-flag liner service, the first sailing of which was on October 7, 1957. The new service gained stability as it grew, covering the entire reach of Trade Routes 18 (U.S. Atlantic and Gulf/India, Persian Gulf and Red Sea) and 17 (U.S. Atlantic, Gulf and Pacific/Indonesia, Malaysia and Singapore) and continues as a main operation of the Company to this date. The coal contracts as well as other long-term charters in the ensuing years also contributed materially to our ability to finance new ship purchases. We used financing available through U.S. government-guaranteed Title XI loans and loans from the Export-Import banks of Japan and South Korea to borrow up to 80% of the cost of newbuildings secured by first preferred mortgages.

Dramatic Shift in Market Forces

In retrospect, as noted previously, a dramatic shift in market forces was taking place. Two distinct dry-cargo charter markets were developing: one for U.S.-flag vessels and one for non-U.S.-flag vessels. We focused on developing positions in both markets with emphasis on the U.S.-flag market, where we saw more opportunities to take advantage of U.S. government-sponsored export programs for U.S.-flag vessels. Before the abrupt downturn in the ocean freight market in 1957, U.S.-flag vessels could profitably compete with foreign-flag vessels. Once the market crashed, freight rates remained below remunerative levels for unsubsidized U.S.-flag ships. Meanwhile, as a result of the Marshall Plan and other U.S. government aid programs, the volume of business requiring U.S.-flag vessels was increasing. We therefore nominated chartered-in foreign-flag vessels to carry the coal under our contracts while we assigned our U.S.-flag vessels, owned and chartered, to transport U.S. government-impelled cargoes at rates profitable for unsubsidized U.S.-flag vessels.

A defining change in U.S.-flag shipping had occurred. Before World War II, operating subsidy had put U.S.-flag vessels on a par with foreign vessels. After World War II it didn't. The bifurcation of the freight market resulting from the market crash of the 1950s became a permanent condition that continues to this date. The U.S.-flag fleet has shrunk in size and competes only in the narrow market for cargoes reserved for U.S.-flag vessels.

The Operating Differential Subsidy, established by the 1936 Merchant Marine Act, came with benefits and restrictions. U.S.-flag companies who chose and were approved to receive ODS from the U.S. government (the so-called "Twelve Apostles"[1]) received subsidy pay-

---

1. The "Twelve Apostles": United States Lines, Moore-McCormack Lines, Grace Line, Delta Lines (Mississippi Shipping Co.), American Export Lines, Farrell Lines (American South African Lines), Robin Line, Lykes Bros. S/S Co., Prudential Lines, Pacific Far East Line, American President Lines, Bloomfield Steamship Corporation.

ments that helped to reduce their operating costs to close to the costs of their foreign-flag competitors. During a brief period before World War II, ODS payments achieved this objective. After the war, the gap between U.S.-flag and foreign-flag operating costs widened. New labor contracts that increased benefits to U.S. citizen crews were not matched by increased ODS contributions. Also, the terms of ODS contracts did not allow subsidized companies to shift from one trade route to another without Subsidy Board approval. This approval was usually granted, if at all, only after lengthy hearings. Their foreign-flag and unsubsidized U.S.-flag competitors were able to shift their port calls to meet cargo opportunities. Our company, unsubsidized, could follow U.S.-flag cargo demands from one trade route to another. The freight rates we obtained through this flexibility offset, to some extent, the absence of subsidy.

As we developed the Persian Gulf liner service in the third quarter of 1957, we were able to average the lower cost of newly chartered vessels with those of vessels chartered earlier at higher rates. In addition to the profits we made from subletting the aforementioned coal contracts to foreign-flag vessels on single voyage charters, the Persian Gulf liner service's positive results enabled us to expand our U.S.-flag owned fleet by further purchases or time charters of second-hand U.S.-flag vessels.

Overtonnage and Our Response

The supply of war surplus vessels that entered the commercial market under the Ship Sales Act, combined with the resumption of new ship construction in European and Japanese shipyards, finally caused overcapacity in the foreign-flag ship market at the same time a worldwide recession significantly reduced demand for ocean transportation. Events leading up to the nationalizing of the Suez Canal by Egypt in July 1956 briefly changed the picture. The threat of war involving France, Britain and Egypt altered market pressures. Freight rates stiffened in October of that year when the canal was closed. By March 1957, the picture changed again when the Suez Canal reopened; freight rates dropped sharply and stayed down through 1958 and beyond. The only exceptions

were cargoes available to U.S.-flag vessels under cargo preference laws that had been enacted before and after World War II. These laws covered military shipments and cargoes moving under the Marshall Plan and other government-sponsored programs such as Export-Import Bank loans and food shipments under Public Law 480. Hence it was strategic for us to concentrate on ownership and operation of U.S.-flag vessels.

By the beginning of 1957 our owned fleet consisted of the *Green Valley, Green Harbour, Noordzee* (later changed to U.S. flag and renamed *Green Bay* in December 1958) and *Tappanzee* (later changed to U.S.-flag and renamed *Green Island* in December 1958). Having fixed the aforementioned coal transportation contracts for "Vessels To Be Named," we time-chartered-in the following ships to supplement the capacity of our own fleet.

On January 24, 1957, we chartered the new motorship *Fernleaf* (Norwegian flag) at a time-charter rate of $8 per ton on 12,300-DWT carrying capacity ($100,000 per month or $3,000 per day), with delivery from the shipyard in Uddavalla, Sweden, April/May 1957. She had a speed of 14 knots, consuming 22 tons of heavy fuel oil per day. We chartered her for 22-25 calendar months, and renegotiated in June 1957 to extend her charter for 12 months at a reduced rate of $5 per ton.

We fixed the new motorship *Thais Hope* on time charter at $7.35 per ton on February 19, 1957 (NWJ#17). Delivery from Fujinagata Shipbuilding Co. Ltd, Osaka, Japan, (Hull #S55) was September 15–October 15, 1957. She was Liberian flag, 12,700 tons DWT. We chartered her for 24-26 calendar months. We also fixed in late 1956 the Norwegian-flag motorship *Milross* on time charter at $7 per DWT for up to 24 months. She was a 12,000-DWT newbuilding from Deutsche Werft, Hamburg. In addition, we bareboat-chartered three U.S.-flag AP-2 Victory ships (*Baylor Victory, Bucknell Victory* and *East Point Victory*) from the Maritime Administration.

The coal contracts hedged the cost of operating the aforementioned ships, but we soon began using them to provide the regular liner service between ports on the U.S. Gulf and Atlantic Coast and Eastern Mediterranean, Red Sea, Persian Gulf, India and Pakistan for which these ships (owned and chartered) were more suited.

Expanding the U.S. Flag Fleet—Persian Gulf Service

As 1957 unfolded we continued to operate the cargo liner service from U.S. Gulf and Atlantic ports to the Red Sea/Persian Gulf and Indian Subcontinent, using our four owned U.S.-flag vessels and an average of six chartered U.S.-flag vessels. The latter included C-1's (*Alcoa Pointer, Alcoa Planter, Alcoa Pilgrim* and *Alcoa Pegasus*), C-3's (*P&T Navigator* and *Mormacfir*), and C-2's (*Ocean Dinny, Ocean Deborah, Hastings, Afoundria, Hurricane* and *John C.*) The charter hire for each of these vessels was $56,000 to $63,000 monthly, about the same as the monthly operating cost of our owned U.S.-flag vessels. We were able to use the coal contracts to fall back upon if the liner service lacked cargo in any one position. As we fixed parcels of U.S.-flag preference cargoes for bottom stowage on which to build general cargo bookings, we covered our coal contracts by chartering foreign vessels on single voyages as required. Two years later, after we had profitably fulfilled the coal contracts, the liner service (part of Trade Routes 18 and 17) had taken hold and was profitable independent of the coal contracts. We had also extended the Persian Gulf service with our U.S.- and foreign-flag breakbulk vessels to include coverage of ports on the Bay of Bengal. From these ports we loaded burlap, jute and carpet backing for U.S. Atlantic and Gulf ports, providing homebound cargoes originating from the Trade Route 18 area—an improvement over sailing in ballast to South Africa to load ore for a U.S Atlantic Coast port.

As we time-chartered liner-type U.S.-flag vessels to supplement our own fleet, we were also able to purchase several secondhand liner-type U.S.-flag vessels at attractive prices with favorable credit conditions (100% deferred payment of the prices). For example, on April 5, 1960, we took title from Grace Line Inc., of the C-2 U.S.-flag *Santa Mercedes* (renamed *Green Wave*) for $770,000 (payable only $11,000 cash on delivery and the balance of $759,000 in 69 consecutive monthly installments of $11,000 each *without* interest.) On December 8, 1960, we took title to the U.S.-flag C-2 *Santa Alicia* (renamed *Green Point*) from Grace Line Inc. for $790,000 (payable only $11,794 cash on delivery and the balance of $778,206 to be paid in 66 consecutive monthly installments of $11,791.) On December 29, 1960, we purchased on the same basis the U.S.-flag C-2

William J. Toomey, vice president, West Gulf, and vice president, Mid Gulf Stevedores, Inc., before a painting of the SS *Green Valley*. (From *Port of Houston Magazine,* June 1965)

Santa Cristina (renamed *Green Cove*) from Grace Line Inc. for $790,000 (payable only $11,335 cash on delivery and the balance of $778,665 in 69 consecutive monthly installments of $11,285, with *no interest*). And on June 29, 1961, we purchased the U.S.-flag C-2 *Ocean Deborah* (renamed *Green Dale*) for $810,000 (payable only $11,670 cash on delivery and the balance of $798,330 in 69 monthly installments of $11,570, with *no interest*).

The monthly service to South Asia that began with conventional breakbulk cargo vessels in 1957 evolved into a highly sophisticated operation when Central Gulf Lines' innovative Lighter Aboard Ship (LASH) got into full swing 15 years later with new 45,000 DWT vessels. These vessels initiated the carriage of full cargoes of natural rubber homebound for Goodyear from Indonesia and Malaysia instead of jute products on the westbound service to the United States from the Bay of Bengal.

Subsidy

We received the following letter: (See page 29.)

To which Niels F. Johnsen, president of Central Gulf, replied on December 2, 1960, as follows: (See pages 30–31)

Thomas Lisi, secretary of the Federal Maritime Board, responded on December 13, 1960, as follows: (See pages 32–33)

Niels F. Johnsen replied on December 16, 1960: (See page 34.)

FEDERAL MARITIME BOARD
WASHINGTON D.C.

September 23, 1960

Central Gulf Steamship Corporation
Hibernia Building
New Orleans 12, Louisiana

Gentlemen:

With respect to your application of February 21, 1958, as amended on February 25, 1958 for operating differential subsidy on Trade Route 18, the Federal Maritime Board has directed that you be advised of its willingness to allocate to Central Gulf Steamship Corporation a maximum of 24 sailings per year, provided the Company, by December 1, 1960, submits evidence satisfactory to the Board of its ability to acquire three additional suitable vessels, and otherwise meets all of the financial and other requirements of Title VI of the Merchant Marine Act, 1936, as amended; and provided further that an operating-differential subsidy agreement is executed on or before December 31, 1960.

Should these conditions not be fulfilled by the dates stipulated, the allocation of these sailings to your Company will then be cancelled, and the application considered withdrawn and placed in the closed files. Please advise immediately whether you are willing to proceed on this basis.

Very truly yours,

/s/

James L. Pimper
Secretary

Letter from James L. Pimper, secretary of the Federal Maritime Board, offering ODS to Central Gulf, September 23, 1960.

CENTRAL GULF STEAMSHIP CORPORATION

HIBERNIA BUILDING
NEW ORLEANS 12, LOUISIANA

December 2, 1960

Mr. James L. Pimper, Secretary
Federal Maritime Board
Washington 25, D.C.

Re: Application for Operating Differential
Subsidy on Trade Route 18
(Your Reference: L25-23:640)

Dear Sir:

Referring to your letter of September 23, 1960, in connection with the above subject, we wish to confirm the information imparted to members of your staff by our Vice President, Mr. Niels W. Johnsen, during his visit to your office on November 29, 1960.

Since the date of your letter, we have purchased the C-2 Type vessel, "Santa Alicia" (to be re-named "Green Point"), for delivery to our Company about December 15, 1960. With this purchase, we own six U.S. Flag vessels – three AP2-Victory Type vessels and three C-2 Type vessels. We have received firm offers from other operators on two additional C-2 Type vessels for prompt delivery both at reasonable prices and fundamentally acceptable conditions. Copies of these firm offers were shown to the members of your staff. We think, therefore, that we have satisfactorily shown that we are able to acquire the additional suitable vessels referred to in your aforementioned letter.

We also confirmed to your staff that we are willing to sign an Operating Differential Subsidy contract on the basis of twenty-four sailings per year in this trade route, and we are confident that we would meet the net worth and working capital requirements to commence operating under this subsidy contract. However, we understand that, beyond the basic financial requirements, you will require a bank guarantee or similar security to substantiate the fact that funds will be available to meet the payments on the first flight of new construction if insufficient funds are generated by the Company in the interim period. Our financial advisors have cautioned us against committing our stockholders to such a guarantee, and we regret that we cannot agree to this stipulation.

With or without subsidy, we will continue our service on Trade Route 18 with our U.S. Flag vessels, offering at least twenty-four U.S. Flag sail-

Response to Federal Maritime Board from Niels F. Johnsen, December 2, 1960 (2 pages).

CENTRAL GULF STEAMSHIP CORPORATION

HIBERNIA BUILDING
NEW ORLEANS 12, LOUISIANA

Mr. James L. Pimper, Secretary
Federal Maritime Board
-2-   12/2/60

ings in this trade route each year. Consequently, we understand that
the Board will take our unsubsidized U.S. Flag sailings into consideration in arriving at the over-all voyages to be subsidized in this trade.

While we understand that our unwillingness to agree to the above-
mentioned bank guarantee may preclude awarding a subsidy to us at this
time, we wish to retain the privilege of reopening this matter at a future
date, should conditions and requirements warrant. In the meantime, we
presume that these voyages will not be awarded to any other operator in
view of our determination to continue without interruption our regular U.S.
Flag service in this Trade Route – at least to the extent of twenty-four
voyages per year.

Very truly yours,

CENTRAL GULF STEAMSHIP CORPORATION

N. E. Johnsen, President

NFJ/hc

b/c: NWJ,NY
b/c: JMJ – JCM, NO

31

OFFICE OF THE SECRETARY

L25-23:601

December 13, 1960

Central Gulf Steamship Corporation
Hibernia Building
New Orleans 12, Louisiana

Attn: Mr. N. F. Johnsen, President

Gentlemen:

This is to acknowledge receipt of your letter of December 2, 1960, in which you advise that your company is unwilling to meet the financial requirements of the Federal Maritime Board precedent to the execution of an Operating-Differential Subsidy Agreement.

Your attention is directed to the Secretary's letter of September 23, 1960, copy attached, which states the conditions under which the Board was willing to allocate twenty-four subsidized sailings per year to your company.

In view of your stated unwillingness to meet the financial requirements of the Board, you are advised that the allocation of twenty-four sailings per year to your company is hereby cancelled and the Board's commitment of September 23, 1960 is no longer binding.

In order that there will be no misunderstanding as to the position of the Board in this matter, you are advised that your presumption "that these voyages will not be awarded to any other operator in view of our determination to continue without interruption our regular U.S. Flag service in this Trade Route – at least to the extent of twenty-four voyages per year", as expressed in our letter of December 2, 1960, is incorrect, since under the circumstances the Board is free at any time to award

Reply from Federal Maritime Board, December 13, 1960 (2 pages).

voyages to any other operator who qualifies under the provisions of the Merchant Marine Act, 1936, as amended, provided such award is within the contracting authority of the Board as established by Congressional appropriations.

Very truly yours,

Thomas Lisi
Secretary

Attachment

CENTRAL GULF STEAMSHIP CORPORATION

HIBERNIA BUILDING
NEW ORLEANS 12, LOUISIANA

December 16, 1960

Federal Maritime Board
Washington 25, D.C.   Your L25-23:601

Dear Sir:

Re: Application for Operational Differential
Subsidy on Trade Route 18

We acknowledge receipt of your letter of 13th inst., received here this morning, December 16th. However we wish to make it abundantly clear that our unwillingness to meet the financial requirements verbally imparted to us by your staff, is because these requirements are considered excessive, having regard for the estimated return on the amount of capital invested and restricted for use in this venture. Our conservative financial judgment and that of our financial advisers can only reach the conclusion that we cannot recommend the acceptance of same to the Company's stockholders.

Insofar as your comments concerning the allocation of subsidy to any other operator on the trade routes we service, we fully realize your administration's authority under the Merchant Marine Act of 1936, but on the other hand we meant to convey in our letter of December 2nd that we, as an unsubsidized operator, fully intend to protect our rights and privileges under the law.

Very truly yours,

CENTRAL GULF STEAMSHIP CORPORATION

By:

N. F. Johnsen, President

NFJ/hc

b/c: Mr. J.M. Jones, N.O.
b/c: NWJ,NY

Response from Niels F. Johnsen to Federal Maritime Board, December 16, 1960.

At the stockholders' meetings of Compania Maritima Unidas and Central Gulf Steamship Corporation held in New Orleans on October 3, 1960, the chairman of the companies made the following reports:

COMPANIA MARITIME UNIDAS
N.F. Johnsen

REPORT AT STOCKHOLDERS MEETING—OCTOBER 3, 1960

The Compania Maritima Unidas, by September 30, 1960, should show profits ranging from $100,000 to $125,000.

By December 31, 1960, profits to Compmar should amount to about $180,000 to $200,000. For the last quarter of the fiscal year ending March 31, 1961, we expect, if the present trend continues, there should be a profit to Compmar of $300,000 to $350,000. The ships have sailed with full cargoes in practically every instance. The long itinerary leaves them open to hazards such as bad weather, strikes and congestion in ports, and it is only by the exercise of the greatest economy and cost control that we have been able to wring these profits out of the voyages. Needless to say, the revenues received from these vessels have been greatly helpful to Central Gulf in that we have been able to borrow cash to assist the American operations. Without the foreign-flag operations we, of course, could not have operated the American-flag vessels with the results which we have attained. However, if subsidy is granted upon our full qualification, this part of our business must be disposed of. Naturally we feel that the good-will of this branch of our service is very valuable, and this is a matter which we are bearing well in mind. Of course, any Line is as valuable as the know-how and hard work of the Management. A Line cannot progress or make money unless there is constant application and skillful handling in the most difficult markets today.

CENTRAL GULF STEAMSHIP CORPORATION
N.F. Johnsen

REPORT TO STOCKHOLDERS—MEETING: MONDAY, OCTOBER 3RD, 1960

Central Gulf Steamship Corporation's financial statements as of March 31, 1960, are on the table and available to the stockholders. It will be noted that the deficit after depreciation and amortization, as of March 31, 1959, was about $1,368,000, but that a year later the deficit had been brought back down to $1,311,000 after depreciation of nearly $400,000. The gross profit before depreciation was $922,000; the Administration expenses about $600,000, leaving a net profit of $322,000 profit on voyages before depreciation. The progress made during the last fiscal year is continuing by the exercise of the greatest cost control, since the freight rates have not advanced. As a matter of fact, in some cases they have been reduced, and the time in ports has been rather excessive during the first quarter of the present fiscal year, ending September 30, 1960, in that several of our vessels were caught in strikes in India which cost us in excess of $200,000. Nevertheless, on voyages terminated on September 30, there should be, after deducting overhead, a small net profit of $22,000 before depreciation. On voyages terminating December 31, 1960, on which cargo has been secured, some of it already loaded, we project a profit, after overhead, of

about $400,000 before depreciation and amortization. If this progress can be projected into the last quarter of our fiscal year, we expect Centraship to have a profit, after overhead and before depreciation, of about $500,000 on the American-flag vessels. It is therefore to be noted that by the exercise of strictest cost control we have been able to reverse the trend generally, and gradually are retrieving the losses from previous years. These losses, of course, are not entirely due to the depressed freight market, but since we had to completely rearrange our business from a full-cargo business to a liner service in order to survive, the deficit incurred is due to the pioneering efforts into the Mediterranean as well as the Persian Gulf and India business. In the long run we should consider these deficits as pioneering expenses, and we anticipate that an equivalent amount in good-will, which is saleable on the market, will offset.

In the current fiscal year we shall have completed twenty-six (26) voyages for the nine months ending December 31, 1960, and in the last quarter of the year we have projected seven (7) additional voyages, making a total of thirty-three (33) voyages in the fiscal year ending March 31, 1961. We are happy to report that since May or June of this year we have sustained no losses on our voyages, although in some cases the gross profit before overhead has been very slim. There is no doubt, therefore, that we have surmounted the most difficult shipping conditions that have been experienced in the memory of man, and naturally we feel confident that, barring an extended recession in the United States, we shall be able to continue, and improve, our position as we go along.

Our fleet now consists of three Victory vessels and two C-2s, and we have had under charter from two to three vessels additional, under different periods. We were offered by the Grace Line the SS Santa Mercedes at a price of about $770,000, payable in monthly installments of about $12,800 without interest, for a period of five years. Another similar vessel was subsequently offered to us, but at a price of $40,000/$50,000 in excess of what we paid, and this vessel was sold to others. We have presently under charter the SS Santa Alicia, also a Grace Line vessel, and have been offered this vessel at a price of around $810,000. We still feel that we should get this vessel at a lower price, and we are still continuing negotiations. In an enterprise such as ours, and during the present depressed state of the markets, we are laboring under great difficulties because of insufficient working capital. This is because the freights, and particularly governmental freights, are sometimes not paid for sixty or ninety days, or even longer after the cargo has been loaded and delivered. However, as we generate profits, even though small, the depreciation money will, of course, help in the working capital picture. Included in the profits for the Central Gulf we shall have close to $140,000 for management fees on the foreign-flag ships operated by our Panama affiliate. Since April 1, 1960, we have paid off in mortgages and loans in excess of $269,000, and our credit throughout has been unimpaired. Likewise, our reputation as first-class charterers is maintained throughout the world. This is evidenced by the fact that we can still obtain vessels in the market with our signature, whereas when we commenced in 1956, as you will recall, we had to put up a half a million dollars in the form of a Letter of Credit before we could charter tonnage.

We have now the most frequent service from the U.S. Gulf to Pakistan and India, and we have definitely established our place in this trade-route. The Federal Government, through the Federal Maritime Board, has noted our consistent progress through hard work, industry and now—two and a half years after we applied for subsidy—have finally offered us twenty-four (24) sailings per year in this trade-route for subsidy, provided we fulfill the requirements in connection with working capital, and the acquisition of two additional, suitable vessels. Needless to say, these matters have been most carefully looked into. Our Accounting Department as well as Management have carefully studied and projected in intricate calculations the earnings and position for the next fifteen years, and you will find on the table these elaborate reports. We must have all our financial requirements in order by December 1st, and be prepared to sign a contract before December 31, 1960. Additional capital of $1,400,000 will be required, but we feel that with our record and the equity in our vessels, totalling $1,100,000, based on the depressed standards of the Maritime Administration, that additional capital can be secured.

In concluding, we wish to state that the position of the Company as of 1958 and 1959, despite our equity in our vessels built up through frugality from the very beginning, was of great concern to the Management. Today we can say definitely that the stockholders' money has been safeguarded, and we can say further that if any of the stockholders should be inclined to dispose of their holdings, we are in a position to have the Company purchase the stock, or have interested present stockholders prepared to purchase the stock at reasonable prices, or certainly at face value. Whilst we are gratified about our ability, thanks to many fortuitous circumstances, to bring the Company back to what it is today, we wish again to remind our stockholders that shipping is and continues to be a most hazardous business, as you know, even under subsidy. With the contesting forces today—East and West—we shall progressively feel the impact of Communist competition in all markets of the world, including shipping. We say this so that we may have no illusions as to the future, and if there are any of our good friends who may wish to dispose of their holdings, partly or in full, we will do our utmost to help liquidate such holdings within the present stockholders of Central Gulf Steamship Corporation. It may be necessary to liquidate any holdings over a period of the next six months, on monthly payments. If we qualify for the Subsidy we undoubtedly will, during the next several years, build up large equities in the Corporation, as you will note from our projections on the table here, but then again we shall also be committing ourselves for two ships at the end of 1963 and four ships at the end of 1966, respectively. Under the circumstances, therefore, there can be no expectations of dividends to the stockholders for some years to come, but the equity should grow and the stock enhanced accordingly. We would also consider raising additional stock and making stockholdings liquid by placing it on the Stock Exchange.

We are now running the following American-flag vessels in our services to the East:

Owned Vessels:	D.W.	Cu. Ft. Bale	Speed	Cost per month
SS Green Bay (C-2)	10,270	539,620	15	$55,000
SS Green Wave (C-2)	11,000	543,539	15	55,000
SS Green Harbour (AP-2)	10,800	495,000	15	54,000
SS Green Island (AP-2)	10,800	495,000	15	54,000
SS Green Valley (AP-2)	10,800	495,000	15	54,000

Additionally, we have regularly on time-charter, three to four American-flag vessels, presently the following, on which the rate of hire is set out opposite each vessel:

Chartered American Vessels	D.W.	Cu. Ft. Bale	Speed	Cost per month (rate of hire)
SS Alcoa Pointer (C-1)	9,510	451,620	14	$50,500
SS Mormacfir (AP-2)	10,960	484,000	16	61,000
SS Robin Trent (C-3)	12,660	677,000	16½	72,000
SS Santa Alicia (C-2)	10,645	559,000	15	66,000

We have now been offered the SS Santa Alicia (a C-2 vessel) by Grace Line, for the price of $810,000, payable in equal installments of seventy (70) months, without interest; furthermore, any previous charter-hire to apply against the purchase price, so that in effect the "Santa Alicia" would cost about the same as the "Green Wave" ex "Santa Mercedes". We show below our outstanding vessel mortgage loans as of September 30, 1960:

SS Green Island – Bank of New Orleans	$400,000
SS Green Wave – Grace Line	704,000
SS Green Valley – U.S. Maritime Admn.	175,828
SS Green Harbour – U.S. Maritime Admn.	244,188
SS Green Bay – no loan – vessel free	
Total:	$1,504,016

Our average monthly cash balance in the last six months has averaged from $450,000/$500,000.

Employment:
Our shore staff now numbers fifty-six (56) and we are employing about 250 people on our own ships, giving employment to a similar number on the chartered American vessels. We are helping the economy in the U.S. Gulf ports by stevedoring and salaries amounting in excess of $2,000,000 per year in payrolls.

CHAPTER 4

Jumboizing Our Victories

On October 2, 1961, the Company contracted with the Deutsche Werft, a major shipbuilding yard in Hamburg, Germany, to lengthen the *Green Valley, Green Harbour* and *Green Island,* our owned AP-2 Victory ships, by inserting a new midbody 90 feet long to each hull forward of the engine room. For the *Green Harbour,* the price was $372,312.50 to be paid in 23 monthly installments of $16,187.50 with interest at 5%. For the lengthening the *Green Island* and the *Green Valley,* the price was $383,333.33 to be paid in 22 monthly installments of $16,666.66 plus one final installment of $16,666.81 with interest at 5%. For all three vessels, Central Gulf gave a first preferred mortgage on the ships as collateral. On December 28, 1961, we signed the promissory notes for the contract

prices. Within weeks after we took delivery from the shipyard, Congress passed a law requiring that ships built or converted abroad and brought under U.S. flag wait three years before becoming eligible to carry government-sponsored cargo. Our three vessels, however, were grandfathered and continued to be eligible for these cargoes. They returned from the German shipyard to our fleet as jumboized vessels before March 31, 1962. We then had a fleet of eight competitive U.S.-flag vessels (see list).

In addition to our owned fleet we had six U.S.-flag and three foreign-flag vessels on time charters that varied in number, depending upon our cargo commitments.

Larger U.S.-flag ships such as C-3's and C-4's were not available for purchase at that time. So we took

FLEET LIST AS OF MARCH 1962
FURTHER EXPANSION

Ship	Ex Name	Type	Year Built	Year Acquired	Speed	Capacity (DWT)	Capacity (Bale Cubic)	Cost $
Green Valley	Ouachita Victory	AP-2	1945	1949 June	15	10,800 *15,700	495,000 675,000	879,157 **383,333
Green Harbour	Cooper Union Victory	AP-2	1945	1951 January	15	10,800 *15,700	495,000 675,000	879,157 **372,312
Green Bay	Noordzee (Ex *Susan*)	C-2	1943	1955 June US flag '57 (Sold '58)	15	10,270	539,620	1,000,000
Green Island	Tappanzee (Ex *Black Dragon*)	AP-2	1945	1958 December US flag '57	15	10,800 *15,700	495,000 675,000	2,000,000 **383,333
Green Wave	Santa Mercedes	C-2	1944	1960 April	15	11,000	543,000	770,000
Green Point	Santa Alicia	C-2	1945	1960 December	15	10,645	559,000	790,000
Green Cove	Santa Cristina	C-2	1945	1960	15	10,012	546,900	720,889
Green Dale	Ocean Deborah	C-2	1944	1961	15	10,930	542,824	810,000

*After lengthening in 1962
**Cost of lengthening

AP-2 Victory ship SS *Green Valley* (ex *Ouachita Victory*) in 1962 after her capacity was increased to 15,700 tons with insertion of a 90-foot midbody just forward of the crew's quarters/engine room.

advantage of the attractive price and payment terms offered by the shipyard in Hamburg to lengthen the *Green Valley, Green Harbour* and *Green Island*. What we did was jump ahead of the pack (at least as far as U.S.-flag vessels were concerned). Because our ships were grandfathered under the new law that effectively closed the door on any further lengthening or reconstruction of vessels outside the United States, our three AP-2 Victories had a definite edge over other U.S.-flag vessels with which we were competing. Ships built or rebuilt outside the United States would still be eligible to carry military cargo, but too few military charters were available to make the costs of such rebuilding financially viable. U.S. shipyards hoped that their business would be stimulated by the three-year waiting period for carrying government-sponsored cargoes in foreign-built or -rebuilt ships. These hopes were in vain. The cost of doing the same work in a U.S. shipyard without construction subsidy (which was not available) was prohibitive. In fact, U.S. shipyards were competitive for commercial shipbuilding only if they could receive construction subsidy.

By choosing Deutsche Werft we capitalized on a weak shipbuilding market, obtained a relatively low price for the work, and negotiated favorable payment terms spread over more than two years. We were thus able within about 5½ months to add 5,000 revenue tons of carrying capacity to each voyage. The jumboized *Green Valley, Green Harbour* and *Green Island* operated profitably in our liner service for another nine years. Ultimately we sold them for scrapping as we replaced our breakbulk U.S.-flag vessels with new U.S.-flag LASH ships.

For the nine months ending December 31, 1965, the Company's 10 owned vessels and an average of seven chartered vessels operating on our U.S.-flag cargo liner service (U.S. Gulf and Atlantic ports to and from the Mediterranean Sea, Persian Gulf and South Asia) produced a total of about $21 million in gross revenue, yielding a gross voyage profit of just over $3 million. In addition, the Company operated an average of five foreign-chartered vessels during this period, producing revenue of just over $2 million and a gross profit of about $190,000.

CHAPTER 5

Newbuildings in Japan Begin

Having strengthened our U.S.-flag breakbulk fleet by lengthening our three war-built Victory ships and acquiring four war-built C-2's, we were ready to acquire new ships suitable to operate profitably in the foreign-flag market, despite its low freight rates. The bear market in ocean freight rates that began in December 1957 also had an impact on shipbuilding order books. Shipyards worldwide were desperately seeking newbuilding contracts—in some cases just to keep the doors open.

In the early 1960's the Japanese government, in order to aid its shipbuilding industry, provided incentives to attract new ship construction to its nation's shipyards. The Japanese established a program with the Export-Import Bank of Japan that allowed Japanese shipyards to sell newly built ships on attractive credit terms for export to foreign buyers. This opportunity came at a fortuitous time for us. We needed new ships at prices

and financing that enabled them to compete profitably in the prevailing bear market.

While investigating the interest of Japanese shipyards to build bulk carriers for our account, we identified a shipyard that had been established in 1897, had built ships before and during World War II for the Japanese Navy and that after the war was building ships commercially for Japanese shipowners. This yard was Uraga Dockyard, in Uraga, a port near the entrance to Tokyo Bay. Uraga also owned a shipyard at nearby Yokosuka. Both shipyards were the predecessors of Sumitomo Heavy Industries Ltd., which today is one of Japan's major shipbuilders. In 1997 they consolidated their shipbuilding activities into one huge facility at nearby Oppama and changed the name to Yokosuka Shipyard.

After World War II, Uraga had also built ships for non-Japanese shipowners before we contacted them. We were able to check with one or two of these foreign-

Captain Warren Leback, vice president, Central Gulf (hands together), and Jerome Goldman, naval architect (in dark glasses) inspect Uraga Shipyard in 1963 before ordering Hull #858, later christened MV *Baron Holberg*.

MV *Baron Holberg* under construction in 1965.

flag shipowners on the quality of Uraga's commercial ships. We satisfied ourselves that they would deliver an acceptable newbuilding. Over the next couple of years, discussions ensued with Uraga executives and marine architects. The shipyard was keenly interested in working with us. At this time the largest dry-bulk carriers being built were mostly less than 45,000-DWT carrying capacity. Uraga gave us a proposal to build a gearless bulk carrier in this size range at an attractive delivered price of $4,818,200. Japan's Export-Import Bank program enabled the shipyard to offer us favorable payment terms of 20% of the purchase price in cash on delivery of the ship, and the 80% balance to be paid in approximately equal installments over eight years. A very competitive interest rate of 5% was all the added stimulus we needed to go forward with a newbuilding program. Uraga's technical efficiency and the detailed specifications of the ship were approved by our naval architect, Jerome Goldman of New Orleans, whose expertise was known to our president for many years. As a result Niels F. Johnsen, president of the Company, signed the contract with Uraga Heavy Industries Ltd. for construction of the vessel, which when delivered was to be one of the largest dry bulk carriers afloat, with a 48,000-DWT carrying capacity. The contract for this, our first postwar newbuilding, designated Uraga Hull #858, was signed in December 1963. The contract included options for us to order a second and third vessel (either a dry-bulk carrier or a tanker) with similar fixed prices and the same financing package. With sufficient time available to consider these flexible options, they became valuable tools for us to exercise.

Mammoth Bulk Carriers

Upon ordering Hull #858, we decided to form a new operating company, which we called Mammoth Bulk Carriers, Ltd. Our objective was to use this new company to own or operate our new foreign-flag bulk carrier, together with any future newbuildings. Uraga Hull #858 was launched on April 13, 1965. Julia Anita Winchester Johnsen (wife of the president of Central Gulf), acting as sponsor, christened her *Baron Holberg* in memory of the bark of the same name owned by shipowner Nils Olsen of Larvik, Norway. We registered the *Baron*

Holberg in the International Ship Registry of Norway, where the ship could operate efficiently in the bear markets that we faced and still have access to qualified officers and seamen, who were not yet readily available in other parts of the world. It was important to have this large new ship with its modern technology sail under the registry of a recognized maritime nation, under the command and control of experienced officers and seamen rather than one of the "flag of convenience" registries. The latter generally lacked a pool of experienced seamen at that point in the post-war development of the world merchant fleet. To further implement our plan, Mammoth made an operating management agreement in 1965 with A/S Mosvold Shipping Company of Kristiansand, Norway, a Norwegian shipowner with whom we had had an operating agreement on another vessel the *Valetta,* renamed *Mosfield.* The owners of Mosvold were Torrey Mosvold, his son Martin Mosvold and other members of their family. A new Norwegian company was formed called A/S Mosgulf Shipping Company, owned 60% by Mosvold and 40% by Mammoth. The ship was chartered back to Mammoth so that Mammoth would realize the benefits of ownership. On delivery from Uraga Dockyard in August 1965, the *Baron Holberg* was bareboat chartered by Mosgulf to Mammoth for 18 years at a rate fixed to amortize the cost of the vessel over the period of the charter. Mammoth contracted for Mosvold to perform certain ownership functions as management agents. As other newbuildings followed, the same pattern of ownership/operation was followed.

As their association matured, in 1967 Mammoth and Mosvold expanded by establishing another jointly owned company, Allied Shipping Company Ltd., incorporated in Liberia. Allied was owned 60% by Mammoth and 40% by Mosvold's nominees. The bareboat charter on the *Baron Holberg* was amended to provide for the ship to be chartered by Allied instead of Mammoth. Subsequently, as new ventures were established, two more jointly owned Norwegian companies A/S Mosbulkers and A/S Moslash, were organized to work with their Liberian counterparts. (Chart on page 113 shows the corporate structure in 1972 of the international shipping group of which Mammoth was the core when TransUnion Corporation became parent of

MV *Baron Holberg* slides down the shipway into Tokyo Bay, April 13, 1965.

Julia Anita Winchester Johnsen, wife of President Niels F. Johnsen, cuts the ribbon to launch Hull #858 at Uraga Dockyard, and names the vessel *Baron Holberg*. In background are Torrey Mosvold and Niels F. Johnsen. Assisting Mrs. Johnsen is the shipyard's president.

Uraga Dockyard representative presents Julia Anita Winchester Johnsen, sponsor, and Niels F. Johnsen, shipowner, with traditional gifts in celebration of the launching as Torrey Mosvold, Norwegian shipowner partner, observes.

MV *Baron Holberg* being prepared for delivery at Uraga Dockyard.

MV *Baron Holberg* on her maiden voyage, August 1965. 48,520 total deadweight; bale 2,180,328 cubic feet; LOA 718 feet 6 inches; beam 104 feet; service speed 15.5 knots on 52 tons heavy fuel plus 2.5 tons diesel oil.

Mammoth, Central Gulf and associated companies.) Mammoth operated in the worldwide dry-bulk cargo and tanker markets. It generally followed a policy of employing the predominant portion of the fleet on long-term charters or contracts of affreightment with fixed income and cash flow to support repayment of the loans under which the ships were purchased and mortgaged. Mammoth also provided ocean shipping services with non-U.S.-flag vessels in a variety of ways, including the LASH liner system (to be discussed later), bulk-cargo contracts of affreightment, time chartering in and out and bareboat chartering in and out. Most of the charters had provisions for escalation in freight rates to offset increases in operating costs, thereby hedging the cash-flow income. Mammoth's policy of fixing long-term contracts provided a conservative and expanding base from which it continued to grow. In financing its expansion, Mammoth used medium- to long-term loans from the Export-Import Bank of Japan and U.S. and European banks or other financial institutions. Equity funds as required, ranging from 20%

to 25% of the capital costs, were supplied either from retained earnings or later through direct investment in Mammoth by TransUnion.

Mammoth later owned and operated new vessels directly under Liberian or other flags for its own account. Through Netherlands Maritime Agencies, its own organization in Rotterdam, Mammoth was able to obtain competent European and/or Asian crews. Mammoth also had a fully qualified shore staff in Rotterdam, headed by Captain N.W.J. Valkenier, an employee of the group for more than 20 years. This staff was capable of providing efficient management of vessel operations. Mammoth also had a fully staffed accounting organization under the name of Adrian Shipping, Ltd., in Bermuda. Mammoth had access to the best available business contacts through its New York brokers, N.W. Johnsen & Co. Inc., and its Western Hemisphere agents, Central Gulf Lines, Inc., with offices in New Orleans and New York. After Mammoth merged into Trans-Union in 1972 it had access to additional equity capital needed for continued growth.

1967—More War-Built Ships Purchased

By the end of 1967, Central Gulf and its associated companies had survived the severe market conditions that prevailed during the 1950's and early 1960's. The group owned a fleet of 11 war-built U.S.-flag liner-type vessels (three lengthened Victories, two C-2's, one C-3 and five of the six C-4's) as well as six newly built foreign-flag vessels (five dry-bulk carriers and one tanker).

Total assets had grown to $47.9 million by December 31, 1967. The combined net income for the group for the nine months ending December 31, 1967, was about $1.472 million. At the same time we placed the order for the *Baron Holberg* and the following five new-buildings in Japan, we also continued to acquire second-hand U.S.-flag war-built vessels for operation in our cargo liner service between U.S. Gulf and Atlantic ports and South Asia.

For example, in July 1964 we purchased the C-3 *Hawaiian Educator* for $1 million and renamed her *Green Ridge*. After operating her for about six years, we sold her for demolition for $236,460 in May 1970. In October 1964 we purchased the C-3 *Mormacport* for $940,000, renamed her *Green Port* and in June 1967 sold her for $1,150,000. As we acquired C-3's and C-4's we disposed of our smaller C-2's, such as the *Green Bay* and

the *Green Lake*. The sale of the *Green Port* was an exception to our plan because we had operated her profitably in our liner service for only slightly over two and a half years and took advantage of the opportunity to add a profit on the sale to her operating earnings.

Ship Exchange Act

In October 1964 the Maritime Administration began promoting a new program to upgrade the American merchant fleet, the Ship Exchange Act. We chose to use this act to exchange two of our remaining smaller C-2-type vessels, the *Green Bay* and *Green Point,* for two war-built C-4 vessels that had been outfitted during construction as troop carriers for use in the possible military invasion of Japan but were never put into service. As these C-4's were completed and outfitted, they were placed in the Reserve Fleet and maintained in virtually new condition until they were made available for sale or trade to private commercial operators. Two of the C-4's nominated to Central Gulf as trade-outs were the *Ernie Pyle* and the *Marine Marlin.* The price paid by the buyer for these C-4's consisted of the cost (1) to remove the troop accommodations, (2) to

C-3 SS *Green Port* (ex *Mormacport*) before her sale in June 1967. LOA 492 feet; beam 69 feet; deadweight 12,348 tons; bale cubic feet 677,000; speed 17 knots. (Photo by Eric Johnson)

SS *Green Forest* (ex *General W.M. Black*), a C-4 that Central Gulf converted from a WWII troop ship to a breakbulk carrier. TDW, 15,348 tons; bale cubic capacity, about 670,000 cubic feet. (Photo from Captain James McNamara)

C-4 SS *Green Springs* (ex *Marine Carp*) was acquired in 1967 under the Ship Exchange Act. (Photo from Captain James McNamara)

refit the vessels for commercial use and (3) of the appraised value of the *Green Bay* and *Green Point* or the relevant exchange vessel traded in. The trade-ins were transferred to U.S. government ownership and placed in the Reserve Fleet. The final computed sale prices for these two ships amounted to $1,884,000 and

$1,915,000. We changed the name of the *Ernie Pyle* to the *Green Lake* and the *Marine Marlin* to the *Green Bay*. Luckily, we delivered the C-2 *Green Bay* to the Maritime Administration on September 8, 1965, just two days before Hurricane Betsy hit New Orleans with winds of 140 miles per hour. The *Green Bay* had been made fast to the dock with extra lines, but because she had no cargo her hull was high in the water. She therefore took the full force of the hurricane, causing her mooring lines to snap. With only one watchman aboard, she was buffeted about the river, and even forced upstream against the current at 10 knots. Fortunately, the end result was no serious damage. One of our other vessels in New Orleans at the time suffered damage from the hurricane, even though she had not budged from the dock. She was hit by other vessels that were being knocked about the port.

Subsequently the Maritime Administration awarded our company four additional former troop ships. In acquiring these additional C-4's, we also used the Ship Exchange Act and were able to use four small obsolete ships we had bought at bargain prices as trade-ins. We traded in the *New Bedford* (purchased for $82,500) and the *Utica* ($45,000) for the C-4's *General C.G. Morton* (acquired in March 1967 and renamed the *Green Wave*) and the *General W.M. Black* (also acquired in March 1967 and renamed the *Green Forest*). Subsequently in July 1967 we acquired also under the Ship Exchange Act our last two C-4's, the *General S.D. Sturgis,* which we renamed the *Green Port,* and the *Marine Carp,* which we renamed the *Green Springs.* We traded in two obsolete vessels, the *Astoria* ($52,500) and the *Knickerbocker* ($57,500), which we had bought at bargain prices for that purpose. After the trade-ins and conversion costs, the final adjusted delivered prices for all six C-4's, which we booked as of June 30, 1970, financial statements were as follows.

Green Bay	$1,884,000
Green Lake	$1,915,000
Green Port	$2,561,000
Green Forest	$2,585,000
Green Wave	$2,625,000
Green Springs	$2,596,000

Having acquired these C-4's, by the end of 1969, the Company owned a U.S.-flag fleet of 12 competitive and relatively new vessels. These ships were profitably employed until we took delivery in the mid-1970's of the technologically revolutionary LASH ships.

After conversion of the six C-4's to commercial cargo liners, we time-chartered them to the Military Sea Transportation Service for periods of approxi-

mately five years. In their early operating years they were engaged in service to the U.S. military during the Vietnam War. During this service the C-4 *Green Bay* was lost to enemy action on August 17, 1971, when Viet Cong frogmen attached explosives to the hull of the vessel while she was docked in the military port of Qui Nhon. The explosion tore a hole in the hull under the waterline, which our agent was able to have patched to keep her afloat in order to be towed to Hong Kong for inspection. However, the sabotage was so extensive that the vessel was declared a constructive total loss.

Foreign-Flag Newbuilding Fleet Expansion — Baron Holberg, Sterling, Strathearn

Concurrent with our U.S.-flag operations, we began to rebuild our foreign-flag fleet, starting with the delivery of the newbuilding 48,250-DWT *Baron Holberg* in 1965. Our second newbuilding also came from Uraga Dockyard. She was a 57,897-DWT oil tanker (Uraga Hull #868), launched January 7, 1966, and named the *Sterling,* with Grace Morris breaking the champagne bottle on her bow. The tanker was one of the two optional ships that we had included in the *Baron Holberg* building contract. We were able to exercise this option in 1964 when Shell International Marine Ltd., the global oil company, came in the market for tankers to be taken on long-term time charter. Even though Shell required payment of the charter hire in pound sterling and despite the risk of devaluation of the pound, we decided aggressively to seek the business. We were successful in concluding a 12½-year time charter, with Shell taking delivery from the shipyard on March 30, 1966. We financed 100% of the cost of the vessel ($5,378,000 U.S. currency) with Teachers Insurance and Annuity Association New York. We agreed to repayment terms of equal installments at a fixed interest rate over the 12½-year life of the charter. As it turned out, this charter was considerably more risky than we had contemplated. About halfway through the charter, the pound sterling was devalued from about $5 to about $2.80.

Despite the drastic reduction in the U.S.-currency equivalent charter hire, we kept the ship running, supported by earnings from other ships. Also, from time

Grace Morris, wife of Dr. Joseph Morris, cuts the ribbon to launch Hull #868, the MT *Sterling,* a 57,897-DWT tanker on January 7, 1966.

Dr. Joseph Morris and Mrs. Grace Morris receive traditional gifts from the shipbuilder after the launching of the MT *Sterling*.

MV *Strathearn,* newbuilding bulk carrier, slides down slipway at Uraga, Japan, at launching on December 20, 1966. Total dead-weight tons, 54,685; LOA, 223 meters (735.9'); 32.2 meters (106.25'); draft loaded, 11.55 meters (37.125'), speed, 15.7 knots.

Dr. Joseph Morris is congratulated by the president of Uraga Dockyard.

Mrs. Edna Lee Johnsen, late wife of Erik F. Johnsen, cuts ribbon to launch MV *Strathearn* at Uraga Shipyard, Japan, on December 20, 1966.

MT *Sterling* is delivered on a 12½-year time charter to Shell International Marine, Ltd., March 30, 1966. LOA, 738.9'; gross tons, 30,683; net tons, 21,441; deadweight tons, 57,897; draft, 38'11".

Watercolor of the *Strathearn,* one of Captain Nils Olsen's sailing ships, for which the MV *Strathearn* (right) was named.

Millicent M. Johnsen cuts the ribbon at Uraga to launch Hull #884, named MV *Mostangen,* in October 1967.

to time, Shell granted modest *ex gratia* increases in hire to owners such as ourselves who operated in U.S. currency. In about the 11th year of the charter, the tanker market boomed. The opportunity to recover the operating losses from devaluation of the pound sterling had arrived! We sold the *Sterling* to an enthusiastic buyer for a price (paid in U.S. currency) slightly *in excess of the original purchase price.* In addition, the buyer took over the balance of the Shell charter. What started out as a purchase, financed 100% with borrowed money, turned sour in the middle of the term, but ended quite profitably.

Within 12 months of signing the contract to build the tanker *Sterling* we signed a new contract with Uraga Dockyard in June 1965 for construction of a second Panamax dry-bulk carrier (Uraga Hull #878), originally intended to be 48,000 DWT but later increased to 54,685 DWT, at a delivered price of about $5,564,500. This order was the second newbuilding option provided in the *Baron Holberg* contract with Uraga. The *Baron Holberg* was delivered to the Company in August 1965. Uraga Hull #878 was launched December 30, 1966, and named the *Strathearn,* with Edna Lee Johnsen splashing the champagne bottle on her bow. The *Strathearn* also was named after one of Captain Nils Olsen's sailing ships. By the time she was delivered in March 1967, she had been altered with the addition of a gantry crane for dry-bulk cargo handling. We had contracted for a ship

to carry full cargoes of bulk sulphur from the U.S. Gulf to Antwerp, returning in ballast to Florida to load bulk phosphate rock to Mexico for a new chemical fertilizer plant in Coatzacoalcos. The *Strathearn* operated on this business for about 10 years until we sold her to a Mexican buyer.

Baron Holberg Operation

After fixing long-term charters for the *Strathearn* and the *Sterling,* we had an opportunity to fix the *Baron Holberg* on time charter to one of the major grain trading companies, Bunge Corporation. One of the charterer's conditions to fix this vessel on this long-term time charter was that we change the name of the vessel. Bunge had just built a new grain-exporting terminal on the St. Lawrence River near Montreal, in the province of Quebec. Bunge wanted to publicize its new facilities by naming the ship it chartered to carry its exports. As much as we hated to lose use of the name *Baron Holberg,* we could not overlook the advantages of having

MV *Mostangen* being launched at Uraga Dockyard.

MV *Mostangen,* craned bulk carrier launched October 1967, delivered January 1968. Total deadweight, 28,110 tons; LOA, 167 meters (511.1'); beam, 24.8 meters (81.84') draft, 35 feet 11⅜ inches; 1,275,000 grain cubic feet.

the ship time-chartered at an attractive rate to one of the major international grain trading houses. We agreed to change the name of the *Baron Holberg* to *Quebec.*

CG/Mosvold Operations—Sea-Land

In March 1966 we ordered together with Mosvold four approximately 28,000-DWT dry-bulk carriers, each equipped with four 25-ton-capacity Haaglund revolving cranes. We placed these four newbuilding orders with Uraga Dockyard for construction at their Yokosuka Shipyard. They were designated Uraga Hull numbers 881, 882, 883 and 884. Each ship cost $3,840,000. Hull #881 was named *Mosbay,* as she was launched April 1967 by Lillian Mosvold. Hull #882 was named *Mosgulf,* as she was launched February 1967 by Ruth Mosvold. Hull #883 was named *Mosengen,* as she was launched March 1967 by Ingrid C. Johnsen. Hull #884 was named *Mostangen,* as she was launched October 1967 by Millicent M. Johnsen. These four sister ships were delivered and operated together as a package. All four were owned by A/S Mosgulf Shipping Company (60% Mosvold, 40% Mammoth) and bareboat chartered to Allied Shipping Company, Inc. (60% Mammoth, 40% Mosvold.) One of the interesting charters we were able to arrange for them was a time charter to Sea-Land Service, an evolving new container ship operator.

In those days, for a company to compete in the domestic coastwise trade or between U.S. territories and the mainland it had to hold an Interstate Commerce Commission certificate, an instrument not readily available. Malcom McLean, a trucking company operator from North Carolina, was seeking an ICC certificate for a container ship operation he planned between U.S. Gulf and U.S. Atlantic ports. Waterman Steamship Corporation was available for purchase and had a subsidiary, Pan-Atlantic Steamship Company, that had an ICC certificate. McLean bought Waterman and later changed Pan-Atlantic's name to Sea-Land Service. As part of its expansion, Sea-Land began a new service from U.S. East Coast ports and North Europe, using 35-foot containers. For this purpose Sea-Land time-chartered our four "Mos Ships" for a short period. We had the cranes temporarily removed to facilitate carrying containers on deck. These were therefore among the first ships to carry containers in the trade between the U.S. East Coast and North Europe. Each of these ships carried about 300 twenty-foot containers. The container carrying capacity of these ships was minuscule compared to the specially-built container ships operating in international trade today, where a 2,500-TEU capacity ship is considered small. Some of the container ships operating in the so-called "line haul" services today exceed 8,000-TEU capacity!

51

After cutting ribbon to launch the
MV *Mosengen,* Ingrid C. Johnsen,
daughter of Niels W. Johnsen,
observes the ship sliding into
Tokyo Bay at Yokosuka Shipyard,
Uraga, Japan.

Launching of MV *Mosengen,*
October 1967

MV *Mosengen* on one of her early employments, a charter to Sea-Land to carry 35-foot containers, mainly on deck, for transatlantic service. The ship's cranes were temporarily removed to accommodate containers. (Photo from Captain James McNamara)

Late 1960's Decisions—Newbuildings/Specialized Vessels

By the late 1960's the Company realized it had to consider options to replace its aging breakbulk fleet of C-2's, C-3's, C-4's, and lengthened Victories. Our war-built vessels were reaching the end of their physical and economic lives. We had used them to build up the trade to and from South Asia and the U.S. Atlantic and U.S. Gulf. At that time there were no better U.S.-flag vessels available to be purchased or enhanced to enable us to take advantage of the markets. We had to consider innovative vessel replacements. In the meantime, we focused on increasing our participation in the bulk-cargo markets. Globally, the ocean transportation industry was entering a period whereby specialization was becoming more important. Bulk cargoes, dry or liquid, would be carried increasingly in larger vessels, their size determined by the trade route in which the ship would be involved, the port and water-draft limitations and other factors that limit the size of the cargoes. The goal, however, always was to carry the maximum size cargo that could be economically transported. The same considerations were beginning to apply to the movement of general cargo, which was then directed toward the type of ship that could be most effective in handling unitized packages or cargo that may be rolled on, stowed and lashed, and rolled off. Other specialized types were beginning to appear on the shipbuilding berths and in operation. They included liquefied petroleum gas carriers, molten-sulphur carriers and cement carriers.

When we formed Central Gulf in 1947, the Liberty ship was the standard for cargo size (about 9,500 long tons). Before taking delivery of Uraga Hull #858 and the two optional bulk carriers (a tanker and a dry bulk carrier), we used the age-old practice of achieving best possible loading of our existing war-built breakbulk vessels on the Persian Gulf/India Service—"full and down." We took advantage of the closer-stowing bulk or bagged cargo available to the Indian subcontinent to combine with the high-cubic-stowage general cargo to the Persian Gulf, and in many cases, we used the deck space on these vessels to maximize profits. Now, as we contemplated newbuilding replacements, we had to consider that the evolution in oceangoing vessels was tending toward increased deadweight carrying capacity for bulk cargoes and innovative stowage and carriage of general cargo. Some method of increasing the unitized and carrying capacity for general cargo was in the talking stage.

Persian Gulf Outbound/India-USA Inbound

As noted in Chapter 4, starting in the mid 1950's we developed a close working relationship with Stanley Coron and Charlie Diamond, the two principal officers of Dyson Shipping Company, New York. Charlie and Stanley introduced us to the India Supply Mission in Washington, D.C. The India Supply Mission was an agency of the Indian government. Over the next 10 years or so, we became active in the transport of cargo contracted for by ISM and we got to know well each new director of ISM and other members of their staff. Our close working relationship enabled us to match base cargoes of grain, fertilizer and other suitable "base" cargoes outbound from the U.S. to the Indian subcontinent with general cargo for "top" stowage and sometimes with heavy-lift deck cargo, such as locomotives, to other destinations en route such as Pakistan and Red Sea and Persian Gulf ports. Most ISM cargoes were generated by the Commodity Credit Corporation (an agency of the U.S. Department of Agriculture), the U.S. Agency for International Development and the U.S. Export-Import Bank. These cargoes were required to be shipped on U.S.-flag vessels, at least to the extent of 50 percent of the total annual program. Our vessels carried an estimated 3 million tons of grain, fertilizer, and similar "base" cargoes on behalf of the ISM to principal ports in India over the 12 or so years that we operated the liner service with breakbulk vessels.

Beginning in early 1958 we also carried return cargoes from India to the United States (mainly jute, burlap and carpet backing) from Calcutta and to a limited extent from East Pakistan (now Bangladesh). One of the largest importers of carpet backing from Calcutta to U.S. South Atlantic ports was Ludlow Manufacturing and Trading Company of Needham, Massachusetts. To exploit the benefits of our mutual cooperation and offer Ludlow regular monthly service, we established a new shipping company, General Shipping and Trading Company, which was owned jointly by Ludlow and Central Gulf. This company operated successfully for several years and its cargo liftings per sailing were enhanced by the establishment on April 24, 1962, of another new company, Jute Importers, Inc., which was owned solely by Central Gulf. Jute Importers Inc. hired an experienced trader, Hans Tobiason, to manage the company with the clear understanding that he would buy these products only to cover firm purchase orders with importers in the United States. The price to the U.S. importer was to be the actual cost of the product FAS Calcutta, plus the conference freight rate for the ocean transportation and the actual insurance and other handling costs. Jute Importers Inc. was to ship its purchases on General Shipping vessels. Jute Importers Inc. did well for several years until one day we discovered to our surprise that Tobiason had violated the understanding that he should buy product only against firm purchase orders. He had been speculating in the futures market and he had sold short. When the Chinese army crossed the border into India in 1962, the market price for jute shot up and we found that instead of creating a profit for Jute Importers Inc. or breaking even, Tobiason had created a loss of some $600,000. Fortunately the Company had good relations with the Bankers Trust Company, which had helped finance these purchases and sales. The bank arranged for the Company to work off these purchases and minimize the loss. We were able to spread the loss, but the incident naturally dampened our enthusiasm for the jute business. Eventually we liquidated Jute Importers Inc. and General Shipping and Trading Corporation in 1962, suspending service from Calcutta. When our U.S.-flag LASH ships came into service about 10 years later, we replaced Indian jute products for the return voyages with natural rubber from Malaysia and Indonesia, with only occasional parcels of jute products from Calcutta.

CHAPTER 6

Bombay Office Opened

Flashing back to 1955 when we bought the *Susan* from a Hong Kong Chinese owner, we little realized that we were about to take a step that a few years later would lead to the establishment of an office in Bombay, India.

First, the story of how we came to own the *Susan*. The ship's former names were *Fairhope* and *Winged Arrow*. Built in 1943, she was a C-2 owned by Waterman Steamship Corporation and operated under U.S. flag. On a voyage in the Pacific Ocean off Baja California, a quarrel had developed among the *Fairhope's* crew. Some members of the ship's crew were engaged in daily card playing. The chief steward got the reputation of being a regular winner, to the detriment of the others and particularly one able-bodied seaman. The latter seemed to be a regular loser. After a series of heavy losses, the AB confronted the chief steward, accused him of cheating and demanded the chief steward give his money back. The chief steward denied the accusation and refused to return the money. A couple of days later another member of the crew reported to the captain that the chief steward was apparently missing. The captain left the bridge in command of the third mate, who was on watch at the time, and went down to the crew quarters to investigate. The chief steward was indeed missing. His room was in disarray, with blood splattered everywhere. The AB allegedly later confessed that he had disposed of the chief steward by cutting up his body and stuffing the parts through portholes into the sea. While the captain was investigating the missing chief steward, the third mate who had been left in charge on the bridge had managed to beach the ship on Isla San Bonita. The grounding was serious enough for the vessel to be declared a constructive total loss by the surveyors of the underwriters, who paid Waterman the insured value of the ship. The underwriters then offered the ship for sale "as is, where is." A Hong Kong Chinese company bought the *Fairhope,* and the Maritime Administration granted permission for the vessel to be transferred to the Liberian flag. The new owners floated the ship off the beach, patched her up and had her towed to Japan for repairs. She was repaired in Japan and returned to "Highest Class American Bureau of Shipping Free of Outstanding Recommendations." The new owners then fixed her on a cargo to North Europe, where they put her on the market for resale. We had our engineers review the specifications for the shipyard work that had been done to return the vessel to "A-1 ABS," which confirmed the ship was repaired and placed in "first-class operating condition." For a vessel of this type to be available under foreign flag in those days seemed a bargain to us. As we mentioned before, she was in the category of preferred "liner-type" vessels, originally offered for sale under the Ship Sales Act only to U.S.-flag liner companies. Also, even though the vessel would operate under foreign flag, neither she nor the *Tappenzee* lost eligibility to carry U.S. government preference cargo if returned to U.S. registry. They did lose Jones Act coastwise privileges by having been registered under foreign flag, even for such a brief time. We bought the *Susan* for $1 million, subject to inspection. She passed muster, and we accepted delivery promptly thereafter in Rotterdam in "Highest Class ABS Free of Outstanding Recommendations." We renamed her *Noordzee* and fixed her on a 15-month time charter to Continental Grain Company. To pay for the ship, we borrowed $1 million from Chemical Bank New York. We assigned ownership to our recently formed Dutch Company, OSM, and changed her to the Netherlands flag. Through our agents in the Netherlands we began interviewing candidates for master and other officers. Of the applicants for master, the outstanding candidate was a 35-year-old Dutch captain, Nicholas W. J. Valkenier, who was considering a change of command from a Dutch company, Van Nievelt Goudriaan, operator of Dutch ships serving the North Europe/South America trade. We hired him as captain of the *Noordzee* (this was the first step to establishment of our Bombay office). With the cooperation of our agents, Captain Valkenier assembled a Dutch crew. We took ownership in June 1955, as the ship lay afloat in Waalhaven, part of the port of Rotterdam. A day or two later with the crew assembled aboard, the vessel stored and fuel taken on, she was set to sail on her first voyage. It was not a smooth start, as Captain Valkenier recently recalled:

> Ever heard of a vessel refusing to leave port? The *Noordzee* did! Moored in the Rotterdam Waalhaven she did her best to convince us that she liked Rotterdam too much to leave. Her wish materialized as follows: Three minutes prior to the ship's departure time—all things shipshape, vessel in seaworthy condition, harbor and river pilot on board—all the vessel's lights slowly, eerily faded away into pitch darkness. No electric current left anywhere onboard and no steam pressure remaining for propulsion. A startled chief engineer came to the wheelhouse to report that "he lost it all" and that now he needed "steam from shore." The American superintendent, Arthur Ivey, also came in and angrily confirmed the chief engineer's conclusion that only "steam from shore" could save us. The vessel's two high-pressure boilers could only provide steam commencing from a minimum available pressure. This minimum they could not provide themselves. In practice this meant that another steamboat had to come alongside to deliver steam as needed. Such a boat was available. It delivered the life-giving minimum pressure. After half a day marked by heated discussions on who/what was responsible for us "losing it all" and more so, on how to prevent such a calamity to ever occur again, a new departure time was set. Not so by the crabby *Noordzee*. Again, from roughly three minutes from the scheduled departure time we returned to square one again, ending dead in the water. To make a long story short, after four fruitless attempts to get the vessel moving, three American engineers were flown in to teach the Dutch how to get the engine room under control. They did and, moreover, they proved it was not difficult at all. The subsequent search for responsibility was also not difficult. The Dutch hiring

agency had selected engineers on the strength of their performance in Dutch engine rooms. However, European engine rooms were diesel-oriented, nothing on steam. American propulsion systems ran on steam, not on diesel engines. Cause of the difference: American labor unions demanding sky-high surcharges to be paid to engineers and crews for maintenance work performed on diesel engines.

> Of course, during the *Noordzee's* first voyage, a transatlantic crossing, the Dutch engineers' capability to perform had to be established without doubt or dispute. Thus, after the first few days of close guidance and teaching, I asked the American advisors to try to gradually change from "hands on" to "hands off" supervision. They did, and fully one week prior to arrival U.S.A., the Dutch ran the engine room without American intervention. This gave me the confidence to suggest to cut substantially the planned three months' supervision. It was agreed, and henceforth the *Noordzee's* engine and auxiliaries ran like clockwork, no more guidance needed.

Thereafter the *Noordzee* under the command of Captain Valkenier operated satisfactorily on time charter, carrying successive cargoes of grain transatlantic between North America and Europe. Captain Valkenier, in recalling his service on the *Noordzee,* also mentioned a particular voyage he made for Continental Grain to the port of Churchill in the Hudson Bay to load a full cargo of grain. The Hudson Bay is usually icebound or its approaches impeded by floating ice for about eight to nine months of the year. It was during the short ice-free period that Captain Valkenier navigated the *Noordzee* in through Baffin Bay and Hudson Bay to load a cargo at Churchill. He reported that for at least 10 days he had only catnaps, and then only while still on the bridge. He said that most of the time into and out of Hudson Bay they had fog and could proceed at no more than three or four knots to avoid colliding with an iceberg. The only way that he could detect that the ship might be in the vicinity of an iceberg was to constantly measure the temperature of the water. Cooler water meant unseen icebergs nearby. He was fortunate to have navigated safely around icebergs, successfully load a full cargo of grain and complete that harrowing voyage. Usually we do not permit our vessels to trade in these high latitudes unless they are "ice classed." If they are not so classed and navigate outside

SS *Green Bay* (ex *Noordzee*, ex *Susan,* ex *Fairhope,* ex *Winged Arrow*), a C-2 built in 1943. LOA 468 feet; beam 63 feet; total deadweight 11,330 tons; bale cubic capacity 540,000 cubic feet; speed 15.5 knots.

the "Institute Warranty Limits," costly extra insurance premiums for hull coverage are required. I do not recall that we had another occasion to send a ship into Hudson Bay, (although, we had a specialized ice-strengthened vessel which we acquired later and named *Green Wave* to service the Arctic and Antarctic on charter to the U.S. Navy for more than 10 years). Captain Valkenier commanded the *Noordzee* for two or three more years. He then took over command of the *Zuiderzee* for a short period. He took command of the *Tappanzee* when we bought her in 1957 and remained on board her until she arrived in New Orleans on January 4, 1959. On that date Arthur Ivey, the Company port engineer, came on board the vessel with the message to Captain Valkenier that all the officers and crew were to be paid off and repatriated. The Company had decided to transfer the vessel back to U.S. flag and rename her *Green Island*. Captain Valkenier was asked to report immediately to Niels F. Johnsen, president of the Company. The meeting concluded with Captain Valkenier

being assigned to be the Company's representative in the Persian Gulf/South Asia area (this was the second step toward establishment of the Bombay office.) His mission was to expedite discharge of our cargo liner vessels in the various ports in this area to minimize delays caused by growing congestion. He packed his bags, returned to Rotterdam and, with his wife, proceeded to Calcutta in March 1959. At first he operated out of the offices of our agents in various ports including Karachi, Bombay and Calcutta. He worked this way for about two years but ultimately determined that we needed our own office and that it should be in Bombay. (This was the final step made on establishment of the Bombay office.)

Formed Central Gulf Lines Agency (India) in 1963

The decision to locate our new office in Bombay was in part attributable to good communications with New Delhi but also because Bombay was becoming India's most congested port. Valkenier's main activity became building up good relations with the Indian government agencies supervising the importation of India Supply Mission cargoes. He also had to establish strong working relationships with port authorities at the main and subsidiary ports along the Indian coast. He had to become aware of facilities available in other ports in order to induce receivers to accept a substitute port for Bombay, or agree to assign our vessel to another port at which the cargo could be transferred to a less expensive vessel. That vessel could then wait for a discharge berth to become available. Port authorities in Bombay had also developed a system of priorities. When our ship arrived, our agent would register with the port authorities its arrival time at or off the port. Our ship would then be given its position in the queue. At this point Valkenier might ask the receivers to agree to transfer the cargo into a chartered vessel that would cost less to wait. That vessel would take our ship's position in the queue, ultimately to dock and discharge. Our ship would then be free to go on to its next employment. Another option Valkenier often arranged was to discharge cargo at a port where facilities were more fluid than Bombay. None of these steps enabled us to completely solve the problem of congestion for our U.S.-flag breakbulk cargo liners. They did, however, reduce the cost somewhat. Congestion in South Asian ports required constant vigilance and gave us the incentive to seek a less costly and more efficient solution. After a couple of hectic years Valkenier asked for the Company's agreement to engage his replacement as manager of the Bombay office. He and his wife were eager to get back to Europe, and the Company agreed to this well-deserved request.

Enter Hugo Hansen

Valkenier had become friendly with Hugo Hansen, manager of ship operations of the Bombay office of Danish East Asiatic Company. He had met Hansen upon visits to Karachi, Pakistan, and Calcutta, where Hansen represented EAC at those ports. When Hansen transferred to Bombay in 1960, Valkenier had occasion to meet him more frequently as each pursued his duties of expediting the movements of his company's vessels

through South Asian ports. They gained mutual respect for each other's expertise in ship operations. It was only natural when Valkenier wished to move back to Europe that he recommend Hugo Hansen to the Company as his likely replacement. Without knowing whether this idea would be acceptable to Hansen or the Company, he made noncommittal inquiries with Hansen. When he received positive vibes that Hansen might be interested in the position, Valkenier suggested that the Johnsens should interview him.

Hansen made a trip back to Copenhagen in 1964 for discussions with officers of EAC in their headquarters. His objective was to determine whether EAC offered him a bright future with promotions and increased remunerations or whether he should seek opportunities elsewhere. Hansen got no encouragement from EAC on this visit to Copenhagen. He returned to Bombay, where he promptly met with Valkenier. Their meeting resulted in Valkenier encouraging Hansen to travel to New York and New Orleans at the Company's expense to be interviewed by the Johnsens and hopefully receive a proposal to join Central Gulf to replace Valkenier as manager of its Bombay office. A weekend was selected on which Hansen could get the required air transportation. He did so and made the trip from Bombay to New Orleans through New York and back to Bombay between Friday evening and Monday morning. The trip included a roundtrip hop from New York's Idlewild Airport (now JFK), by single-engine Beechcraft Bonanza to Red Bank, New Jersey, on Sunday to meet with Niels W. Johnsen. The outcome of these meetings was that Valkenier was authorized to engage Hansen as the Company's representative in the Bombay office. Hansen joined Central Gulf and its associated companies in May 1965. Valkenier and his wife packed their belongings and left Bombay for Istanbul. He operated out of our agent's office there for a couple of years until he moved back to Rotterdam to prepare for the introduction of the LASH system transatlantic service. Hugo Hansen took over from Valkenier the daily grind of keeping Central Gulf ships moving through the ports of South Asia, from Suez to Singapore (and sometimes farther east).

Hugo Hansen was born in 1930 in the small Danish town of Hjortespring. His father and grandfather had a

Hugo Hansen, right, with Niels W. Johnsen after Hansen assumed charge of our Tokyo office in 1968.

Hugo Hansen, left, 36 years later, as owner of his own company in Rotterdam, meeting with Niels W. Johnsen in 2004.

farm and botanical garden. As a boy he often accompanied them to the flower market in Copenhagen where they sold the products of their farm. He had the opportunity to observe his father making appropriate inquiries to determine what the going prices were on the flowers and other produce of the farm. He got his early education from the village elementary school. It was a two-classroom school with one man and one woman as teachers. He felt that the teachers made special efforts to give the boys and girls attending the school a broad education that included languages, art, music, etc. After completing his elementary school education, he attended middle school and upon graduating won a scholarship from the local government to attend university. While attending school in his hometown he also worked part-time on the farm. He was interested in languages. He actually joined an English church in Copenhagen and became a member of the St. George's Society in order to become fluent in English. His first job after finishing his education was with a bank in London.

He was most interested, however, in seeing the world. He enjoyed visiting the harbor and inhaling the aroma of the products imported and exported, and decided that working in a bank did not suit his ambition. He went back to Copenhagen and applied for an assignment overseas with the Danish East Asiatic Company. He had an interview with the personnel officer of EAC, submitted his *curriculum vitae* and requested that he be given an assignment overseas. He was particularly interested in South America but the personnel manager thought it would be more likely that he would be sent to South Asia. The personnel manager told Hansen that he would have to meet with the managing director, who had the final decision of whether he would get the job. Hansen remembers having a pleasant interview with the managing director. At the end of the interview the managing director asked him, "Do you play football?" Because he had participated in sports, including football, at school his reply was, "Yes sir." The managing director's immediate response was, "You start work tomorrow." Hansen heard that another young man had had an interview with the managing director just after his interview. The managing director asked this young man the same question toward the end of their interview, "Do you

Judith Hansen, wife of Hugo Hansen, sponsors launching and naming of 30,000-DWT carrier *Sankograin* on behalf of Mosvold Shipping Company, Christiansand, Norway, April 4, 1970, at Sanoyasu Dockyard Company Ltd., Japan.

play football?" The young man's reply was also "Yes sir." The managing director went one step further and asked, "How many goals did you score?" The young man's reply was, "None." The interview apparently ended at that point and the young man got up to leave. As he approached the door he made one parting comment to the managing director, "However, sir, I played goalie." He also got a job.

Hansen was actually assigned to the EAC office in Karachi, where he arrived in 1953 after a 30-hour trip via propeller-driven SAS aircraft from Copenhagen. He worked out of the EAC Karachi office as their shipping man, handling everything from arranging discharging and loading docks, to distributing imports to receivers and booking exports. In 1955 EAC sent him to East Pakistan for the purpose of developing exports, mainly jute products, to Europe. He needed to live there for several months to accomplish this objective. Living conditions in Chittagong, even in the Chittagong Club, were austere. His breakfast usually was a banana and a cup of tea. In 1956 he moved over to Calcutta where he became the joint general manager for shipping, controlling the Bay of Bengal area. In 1957 he moved back to Karachi to head up the EAC shipping office. While in Calcutta he met Judith Henderson. Judith was the daughter of the CEO of Hindustan Motor Company, which had the license to produce the British Morris

motorcar in India. After receiving the blessing of the EAC management, the couple married in Oxford, England, after Judith finished school in Switzerland. When Hansen moved back to Karachi, he also negotiated a joint service with two other Scandinavian liner companies that operated under the trade name of United Liners. EAC Karachi became agents for this new joint service.

It was at this time, in 1956, that Hansen met Valkenier. By 1960 Hansen had moved to Bombay to be in charge of the EAC and United Liner Company office there. Valkenier formed Central Gulf Lines Agency, Ltd. in 1963. The subsequent meetings between Valkenier and Hansen led to Hansen's weekend journey to the United States and his appointment as Valkenier's replacement as director of Central Gulf Lines Agency, Bombay, in May 1965. Hansen then took over the day-to-day activities of expediting our cargo liner vessels serving the India subcontinent. His duties became more demanding when we joined the Calcutta/USA Conference to participate in the export of jute, burlap and carpet backing to the U.S. East and Gulf coasts. As a participant in this service, Central Gulf Lines vessels had to meet the "Due Date" each month. This requirement was established by the Conference in order to meet the exporter's requirements for a regular monthly availability of shipping space and sailing date within the first half of each month. For this reason each monthly sailing of our vessels had to arrive Calcutta before the end of the preceding month and load not later than the seventh day of the current month. The congestion in other ports to which our vessels were destined to discharge inbound cargo obviously created a problem each month in meeting the Calcutta/USA Conference Due Date requirement. It is plain to see that not only did Hugo have to be concerned about expediting the discharge of our liner ships coming to ports in India and elsewhere to minimize the cost of delays (which could run for 30 days or longer) but he also had to be concerned about "meeting the Due Date" (ship in port before end of month, bill of lading dated before 7th) in order to preserve the outbound bookings from Calcutta.

In addition to the rough-and-tumble operation of the inbound and outbound sailings from South Asia Hansen had the responsibility for ships that we began

Twins?

Typical mailing circular Central Gulf used in 1965 to advertise the addition of two new C-4's to the fleet.

CENTRAL GULF STEAMSHIP CORPORATION AND
ASSOCIATED COMPANIES
Combined Income Account

Nine Months Ended December 31, 1967

Terminated Voyages
    Revenue $23,965,171
    Expense   17,279,678
        Gross Profit From Terminated
          Voyages $6,685,493
Administrative and General Expense   1,467,705
    Profit before Depreciation $5,217,788
Vessel Depreciation   2,856,695
    Net Operating Profit $2,361,093
Other Income & (Expense)
    Interest Income (Expense) Net   ($1,186,883)
    Other   137,097
         ($1,049,786)

    Net Income before Federal
     Income Taxes $1,311,307
Provision for Federal Income Taxes   371,029
Net Income, before Special Credits $940,278
Special Credit Gain on Sale of Vessels
        GREEN WAVE and GREEN PORT
        (Net of Taxes on Gain)   499,186
Net Income, After Special Credit $1,439,464
Change – Minority Interest (Increase)/Decrease   33,105
Combined Net Income $1,472,569

CENTRAL GULF STEAMSHIP CORPORATION AND
ASSOCIATED COMPANIES
Combined Balance Sheet
December 31, 1967

ASSETS

Current Assets:
    Cash $2,070,069
    Other   5,585,812
         $7,655,881

Investments in Subsidiaries at Cost or
    book value, whichever lower,
    Not combined -
    Central Gulf Lines Agcy. (India), Ltd.
      (Cost, March 1967)   ($53,560)
    Danish Corporation $15,000
    Allied Shipping Company, Ltd.   ———
    A/S Mosbulkers   ———
         ($38,560)

Vessels and Other Property
    Vessels at Cost $48,085,370
    Less – Allowance for Depreciation   10,717,979
         $37,367,391
    Other Property, Net of Depreciation   75,694
         $37,443,085
Construction Work in Progress $2,217,511
Other Assets and Deferred Charges $622,712
         $47,900,629

LIABILITIES AND NET WORTH

Current Liabilities (excluding Current
      Maturities on Long-Term Debt) $3,027,172

Unterminated Voyage Revenue Less Exp.   4,404,929

Long-Term Debt, including Current
      Maturities   31,943,487

Reserves   2,888,757

Minority Interest in Mosgulf Shipping Co.   (29,979)
Minority Interest in Mosbulkers   24,033
Minority Interest in Allied Shipping Co.   127,904
         $121,958

Net Worth
    Capital and Paid-in Surplus $649,187
    Retained Earnings   4,865,139
         $5,514,326
         $47,900,629

CENTRAL GULF STEAMSHIP CORPORATION AND ASSOCIATED COMPANIES
Vessels and Allowance for Depreciation
December 31, 1967

	Year Built	Year Acquired	Cost	Allowance for Depreciation	Net Book Value
Victory type					
GREEN HARBOUR	1945	1951	$941,945	$1,183,288	$332,248
Lengthening	1961	1961	573,591		
GREEN ISLAND	1945	1959	2,004,248	2,080,752	490,868
Lengthening	1962	1962	567,372		
GREEN VALLEY	1945	1949	932,159	1,190,925	322,979
Lengthening	1962	1962	581,745		
C-2 type					
GREEN COVE	1945	1960	720,889	507,655	213,234
GREEN DALE	1944	1961	738,904	551,373	187,531
C-3 type					
GREEN RIDGE	1945	1964	1,014,518	576,036	438,482
C-4 type					
GREEN BAY	1945	1965	1,884,411	1,132,440	751,971
GREEN LAKE	1945	1965	1,914,576	1,217,969	696,607
GREEN PORT	1944	1967	2,381,429	23,991	2,357,438
GREEN FOREST	1944	1967	2,671,920	126,302	2,545,618
GREEN WAVE	1944	1967	2,704,710	182,783	2,521,927
Norwegian Flag					
BARON HOLBERG (48,250 DWT)	1965	1965	5,062,640	667,898	4,394,742
STRATHEARN (54,685 DWT)	1967	1967	5,800,000	241,650	5,558,350
MOSBAY (28,006 DWT)	1967	1967	3,930,000	215,350	3,714,650
MOSGULF (28,100 DWT)	1967	1967	3,930,000	156,200	3,773,800
MOSENGEN (28,187 DWT)	1967	1967	3,930,000	119,800	3,810,200
Liberian Flag					
STERLING (57,897 DWT)	1966	1966	5,800,313	543,567	5,256,746
			$48,085,370	$10,717,979	$37,367,391

to send into Southeast Asia as the demand increased for military and other economic support cargo to Vietnam. He also had problems to solve there. In March 1966 the Company asked Hugo to fly to Saigon, South Vietnam, to expedite the discharge of the *Green Harbour,* one of our lengthened Victories that was scheduled to arrive with a full cargo of fertilizer and military supplies. We had received a pessimistic report from our agents, Saigon Shipping, that the vessel faced a long wait before obtaining a dock at which to discharge. Hugo met with the agents, got them organized, then met with the military people and the receivers of the fertilizer. He was able to arrange for lighters to be brought alongside the ship while at anchorage to receive part of the cargo until a dock became available to complete the discharge. This enabled the ship to avoid a substantial loss of time. Hugo recommended to the Company that the Saigon Agency be "shored up." After going back to Bombay he made a second trip to Saigon in July 1966. His long association with EAC enabled him to work with EAC people in Saigon. He got to know Nguyen van Minh, who was their shipping man. Hansen was able to bring Minh into the Saigon operation by arranging with Minh to have EAC agree to let him set up a separate entity called Vietnam Shipping Company, owned 60/40 by Minh and one of his friends. He then felt comfortable that there would be an efficient agency representing the Company when the next ships came into Saigon. Unfortunately, during this visit to Saigon, Hugo Hansen became deathly ill. Happily, he had become friendly with some of the local people in Saigon, including one Ian Bradley with Bank of America. If it had not been for this individual's help Hansen (a Danish citizen) would not have been admitted to the U.S. Seventh Army Hospital to receive

the emergency care of Dr. Cohen. To this day no one knows what ailment he had, but it was described as "fever of unknown origin." Severe headaches and fever had made him become dangerously dehydrated. On August 8, 1966, Judith Hansen arrived in Saigon to take him home. He had miraculously survived. He even went back to Saigon in December to further supervise operations there at Christmas time. It was a very trying period for all of us in the Company and for his family as Hansen fought this serious disease. Fortunately he is now fully recovered.

Hansen and his family spent two more years in the Bombay office. His objective was to prepare that office for his transfer to another company post. Captain Dadi H.B. Patell was told that he would take over as manager of the Bombay office when Hugo left. Manik Shahani had also been hired for the Bombay office mainly to supervise ship and/or barge repairs. In 1968 Hansen left Bombay for Tokyo. He had been told by the Company officers that he was needed to be a listening post in Japan because it was becoming a more important focus of our activities, including our vessel newbuilding program. When Hugo arrived in Japan with his family, we had already begun a newbuilding program. Seven of the newbuilding ships ordered from Japanese shipyards, beginning with the *Baron Holberg,* had been delivered by the time of his arrival in Tokyo in the beginning of 1968. Hansen spent the first weeks of his arrival in Tokyo visiting potential customers to introduce the Company. He also had to find suitable office space. He had some help from Sumitomo Shipyard and its associated companies. After about six months he made a breakthrough when he met Mr. Tanaka of Sumitomo Metals Corporation, who was helpful in introducing Hansen to other customers in the Tokyo market.

CHAPTER 7

Crossroads—Port Congestion

As Central Gulf Steamship Corporation marked its 20th anniversary, it had already begun a program of fleet renewal. By the end of 1967 the Company had combined assets of about $47.9 million and a net worth of about $5.5 million. Despite these somewhat modest resources, the Company continued its plan for further expansion. By adding and substituting ships, we had built up our owned fleet to 19 vessels: 12 war-built breakbulk cargo liners (six C-4's, one C-3, three Jumboized Victories and two C-2's), two newbuilding dry-bulk carriers (the *Baron Holberg*, 48,250 DWT, and *Strathearn*, 54,685 DWT) and one newbuilding oil tanker (the *Sterling*, 57,897 DWT). In 1967 we had also received delivery from the shipbuilder of three of our four newbuilding dry-bulk carriers, each geared and approximately 28,000 DWT, that we owned together with Mosvold. Additionally, at any one time we had between four and six cargo liners on time charter. Fleet growth had been steady and diversified by type of vessels. Our strategy was to strive for a competitively productive fleet capable of servicing our customers of prime credit standing.

According to U.S. Maritime Administration statistics, by 1963 Central Gulf's breakbulk cargo liners were carrying more cargo in the trade between U.S. Atlantic and Gulf ports and the Red Sea, Persian Gulf, Pakistan, and India than any other American-flag line. Later in the 1960's and early 1970's the U.S. Navy also required the charter of some of the Company's fleet during the Vietnam engagement. At the same time the Company's breakbulk cargo liners continued to operate regularly in its liner service. The ships were full and the balance sheet was steadily improving. The sky seemed the limit. The World War II-built fleet, however, was aging. Ships had a useful life of about 25 years and that point was at hand. In addition, our cargo liners were incurring cost

overruns and scheduling problems: Congestion at South Asia ports caused our ships and cargo to wait in queues for berths. Central Gulf had arrived at a crossroads. If we intended to continue our services on these hard-won trade routes, we needed to replace these aging vessels. If we replaced them with larger conventional breakbulk or container ships, we still would face the problems caused by congested ports. New, larger vessels of the same type were not the solution. We had to develop "smarter" ships.

Congestion

As noted in earlier chapters, our conventional war-built cargo liners serving the trade routes between U.S. Gulf and Atlantic ports and Mediterranean, Red Sea, and South Asian ports (Maritime Administration designated Trade Routes 18 and 17) were plagued by ship delays, mainly at ports in India, such as Bombay (now Mumbai) and Calcutta. There were also delays because of congestion at other ports en route to India, for example on the Red Sea and the Arabian Gulf. We needed ships that could circumvent these delays and get in and out of port quickly after delivering or receiving cargo. Container ships were not suited for our service because these ports were not yet equipped with up-to-date container handling cranes and there was no indication that dock areas would be expanded or upgraded in the near future. In addition, the infrastructure inland from the ports was not yet ready to handle standard cargo containers. Building larger conventional breakbulk ships were also not the answer. Were we ready to pioneer the development of a new system of ocean transportation? If so, could we finance such a venture? Were we ready to take the risk of investment in some untried revolutionary ship type? The board of directors faced these challenges.

The economic and political times were unpredictable. On the one side, new technology promised to unlock unlimited potential: The United States had succeeded in putting its first astronaut, Alan B. Shepard Jr., into space in 1961. Scientific progress fed efficiency and growth in business. Although the Cold War continued, the threat of nuclear attack seemed to fade in 1962 when the Soviet Union removed its missiles from Cuba. However, as the decade unfolded, the economy showed early signs of inflation. Meanwhile, the number of American combat troops in Vietnam increased. The mood in America was uncertain and apprehensive.

Crossroads—How We Decided

Before we could consider building a totally new ocean transportation system, we obviously needed to be assured of its technical and economic utility. Accordingly, we met and began discussions with Jerome Goldman, the well-known naval architect in New Orleans whom Erik F. Johnsen, the Company's vice president, had previously engaged for technical supervision of the Company's new ship construction in Japan: the *Baron Holberg,* the *Sterling,* and the *Strathearn.*

Goldman agreed with our conclusion that container vessels would not solve our problem at these underdeveloped ports with limited infrastructure. Compared with U.S. and European ports, South Asian ports had not yet modernized to the point that standard cargo containers could be handled efficiently. There was not enough dock and warehouse space for the growing volume of shipping. A vessel needed to dock to load or unload cargo, usually with ship's booms and winches. A container ship would have to wait in the queue for a dock to discharge containers just the same as a breakbulk carrier. Delivering or collecting cargo was further impeded by undeveloped highway and railroad systems to and from the ports. Consequently, a container vessel at these ports would face the same delays we were suffering with our breakbulk vessels: not the answer for newbuilding replacements.

In the 1960's, 15 to 20 years after the end of World War II, South Asian countries were still in dire need of importing materiel for rebuilding their economies, infrastructure and ports and importing foodstuffs to feed a growing population. Imports had to move through ports that had seen little expansion or redevelopment after the war. These port facilities, built for a lesser volume of trade and smaller vessels, were not equipped to handle efficiently the increased flow of imports and exports. The rail and highway distribution system from the ports to the interior had not kept pace with the increased volume of freight. Congestion in the ports threatened commercial expansion. South Asian countries had to choose between using their limited financial resources to expand ports or to develop highways, railroads, and other industrial facilities. They had chosen the latter, which meant that little had been done to improve port facilities. Port congestion was an ongoing reality. It was a case of not being able to afford all the things they needed, and yet the cargo had to move.

Congestion—Reasons, India

Relatively shallow water in Indian ports added to the congestion. Ship-draft limitations required us to use numerous smaller ships instead of a few large ships to carry the same amount of cargo. It would have been an enormously expensive undertaking to dredge ports such as Bombay to enable 50-foot-draft vessels to navigate safely. Shipping into Calcutta was also limited by the depth of water in the Hooghly River, a delta tributary of the Ganges River, which constantly silted up. The Indian government had developed a new port, Haldia, near Calcutta at the mouth of the Hooghly River, where up to 28-foot drafts (today 32 feet) were available, but Haldia in the 1960's had only limited facilities. Other South Asian ports had similar limitations. As we pondered the type of vessel to replace the aging breakbulk war-built ships serving this part of the world, we recognized that the ship had to be large enough to carry sufficient cargo to make the voyage economically viable but not too deep for these shallow-draft ports. This combination seemed impossible. In addition, the ship had to find a way to "leapfrog" congestion. One consideration: Existing within some Indian and other ports were shallow-draft areas at docks used only by relatively small craft. Could these unused or barely used spaces help leapfrog congestion? If a shallow-draft vessel could be designed to fit into these spaces, the answer would be "yes."

CHAPTER 8

LASH—The Solution

Naval architect Jerome Goldman's answer was to propose a new ocean transportation system that he thought would solve the overall problem of congestion and offer an improvement over container ships for ports such as those we were serving. Whereas container ships required either a highway or railroad connection to complete cargo delivery to final destination, Goldman proposed instead using the world's waterways. His revolutionary proposal was for a "mother" vessel to carry its cargo loaded in a set of matching standard barges instead of containers. The vessel would make its ocean crossing and, upon arrival outside a designated port, use her shipboard gantry crane to lift the barges off the vessel and place them in the water. The vessel would then proceed on her voyage without delay. Meanwhile, the barges would be towed into the port to be unloaded or loaded. Ideally. the most effective use of the barges would be for them to be loaded and unloaded at river or harbor areas inaccessible to deep-draft vessels. Goldman called his design the "Lighter-Aboard Ship" (LASH) system.

You might say that the LASH system held the potential to increase the capacity of certain ports without the cost of building new facilities. Perhaps we could take advantage of unused or underused shallow-draft docks to berth and unload one or two barges at a time. We could then tow the empty barges back to a fleeting area, where they would remain at anchor until reloaded or picked up empty by the next mother vessel for the homeward voyage.

The concept of bringing barges rather than an oceangoing vessel into a dock had another advantage. Customs clearance often caused port congestion and delay. If a cargo required clearance before being moved out of the port area to an inland destination, it could remain in the barges until clearance was obtained. The barges would then serve as temporary floating storage until a suitable dock became available. Meanwhile, the large and costly mother vessel would be free to continue on her voyage, without having to wait for dock space, warehouse space or customs processing. The LASH system looked promising.

Convinced that LASH barges would enable us to overcome port congestion, we needed to address the engineering challenges. We needed proof that it was feasible to construct a mother vessel that could carry enough loaded LASH barges to justify the financial investment. Goldman's initial design was for a mother vessel to carry about 73 LASH barges. Each loaded barge would weigh about 500 tons, comprising a total weight (cargo and barges) of about 36,000 tons. Constructing a ship able to carry this volume and weight under deck and/or on deck would be a pioneering innovation in naval architecture.

To put the LASH system into historical perspective, the reader should know that at this time, the late 1960's, there was an effort to replace aging breakbulk vessels with container-ship technology. Purpose-built container ships designed to carry containers in cellular holds were just beginning to be used on international routes. We also looked hard at this relatively new technology. Stowage on breakbulk ships had been designed to receive relatively small cargo units—for instance, individual bags of rice or pallets containing numerous bags of rice. Container ships were now being built to stow larger cargo units or "containers"—steel boxes on the scale of truck trailers, each loaded, for instance, with hundreds of bags of rice. Larger and larger container ships were being built to carry more and more container units. The largest container ships in the early 1970's were capable of carrying more than 1,000 TEUs (a capacity

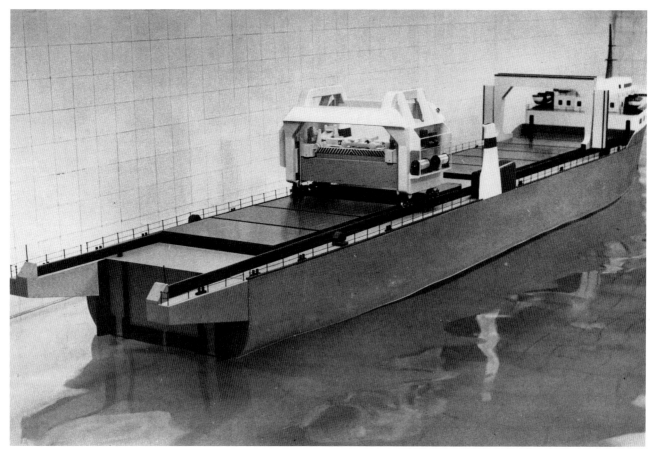

Model of LASH design being tested in tank.

small by today's standards.) Even a container ship capable of carrying the weight of 1,000 loaded containers did not approach the structural strength required of the proposed LASH mother vessel with a complement of 73 loaded LASH barges as well as the specially designed crane to lift the LASH barges. A loaded 20-foot container weighs about 20 tons. A loaded 40-foot container weighs about 40 tons. A loaded LASH barge, in contrast, would weigh about 500 tons. The empty LASH barge alone was going to weigh in the neighborhood of 80 to 90 tons.

After determining the deadweight carrying capacity that the proposed LASH ship would need to accommodate sufficient cargo to justify the financial investment, we needed to know if it was possible to build such a ship.

At the same time Goldman was promoting the LASH system to us, he was attempting to interest other shipowners to build this type ship instead of container ships. Our company was a better candidate to employ the LASH system than some of our competitors. We believed that the LASH system offered a preferable alternative to container ships on trade routes such as ours, where ports are connected to river systems, at least at one end of the trade route, but preferably at both ends. The LASH system also had decided benefits in serving shallow-draft and underdeveloped ports.

In addition to satisfying ourselves that the proposed vessel met all the technical requirements for a strong ship, it was also important that we be confident that the ship would perform economically at relatively high speeds (22 to 23 knots).

As our research progressed we determined that a LASH ship, to be financially viable, would have to have a speed of at least 18 knots and accommodate about 45,000 tons of cargo in 80 LASH barges. A ship designed to carry this load stowed in its holds would have been enormous, unwieldy, costly to build and difficult to operate. Technology did not exist (nor does it today) to construct such a ship with framing and

General Arrangement
of
M.V. ACADIA FOREST

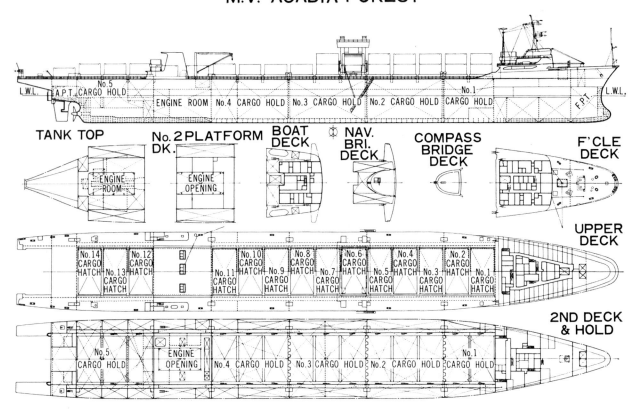

decks strong enough to hold this amount of weight. Stability was also a factor. It became clear that in order to handle the volume of cargo intended, we would need to stow barges partly in its holds and partly on deck. This distribution was feasible because LASH barges themselves were designed to be individually watertight units. What was unique about the proposed LASH system was its capability to stow about 38% to 40% of its cargo on the weather deck. We knew from experience that it was possible to stow heavy-lift cargo on the weather deck, above closed hatches, as long as the cargo could withstand the elements and the vessel had a safe stability factor. The LASH system was to accommodate a new record for "on-deck" cargo weight.

LASH Crane

A LASH ship, in order to bypass port congestion, had to be independent of the port's dock facilities. Instead of lifting barges on and off the mother vessel at a dock, the LASH system contemplated performing this function at an anchorage or mooring nearby but outside port congestion. This led Goldman to develop a shipboard crane capable of lifting each loaded LASH barge, with a weight of just over 500 tons. In order to place or lift a LASH barge at each of the stowed positions on board, this customized crane would be installed on deck to straddle the hatches and run on rails fore and aft for the full length of the open deck. The LASH crane operator places the crane on the port and starboard sponsons to position it over the barge at the stern. The crane also had to be of sufficient height to travel above LASH barges stowed both in the holds and on the weather deck. This plan allowed the LASH mother ship to carry up to four barges, stacked on top of each other, below deck in each of its multiple holds, and an additional two LASH barges on the weather deck, above each of its multiple hatches. Goldman located the engine room as far aft as possible to minimize the length of the tail shaft. The crew/officers' quarters and navigating bridge were located as far forward as possible to provide unobstructed views fore and aft and to reserve the entire weather deck for LASH barge stowage.

To accomplish our goal of carrying the maximum number of loaded barges on deck, as well as under deck, Goldman continued to work on the structural requirements of this innovative vessel. The weight of the on-deck cargo we contemplated loading on the LASH vessel would be extraordinarily heavy compared to that normally carried on the weather deck of an average breakbulk vessel. This required pioneering technology. In early designs Goldman indicated a capability of carrying fewer barges and therefore less cargo than what we needed to make the investment financially viable. We asked for more capacity. After further study, analysis and revision, Goldman (later in conjunction with Dr. Naonosuke Takarada, senior naval architect for Sumitomo Heavy Industries Japan) achieved the design of a vessel that could safely stow about a third of the loaded LASH barges on the weather deck and about two-thirds under deck yet still be stable and structurally sound. Our ultimate aim was to use this new type vessel on the trade routes between U.S. Gulf and Atlantic ports and ports on the Mediterranean, Red Sea and Indian Ocean (Maritime Administration-designated Trade Routes 18 and 17.)

Meantime Goldman was also proposing the LASH system to Prudential Lines and Pacific Far East Lines, two U.S.-flag operators receiving ODS for the new replacement vessels they were required to build under their subsidy contracts. They chose the smaller LASH ship, which the Maritime Administration designated as C-8 type, designed to carry 67 to 70 barges. They also opted to have the capability of carrying a significant number of standard containers as well as up to 60 barges. Their vessels would be equipped with both a container-handling gantry crane and a LASH barge crane. Ultimately Prudential Lines and Pacific Far East Line ordered 11 C-8 types from Avondale Shipyard in New Orleans for delivery in the early 1970's. As you will read later, we had already ordered two larger LASH vessels, our *Acadia Forest* and *Atlantic Forest,* which had been operating for over two years before the Avondale C-8 types were delivered. As the LASH system continued to take hold, by the mid-1970's, Avondale built the larger C-9 LASH vessels for Central Gulf, Delta Line and Waterman. Delta elected to add the container crane, but Central Gulf and Waterman chose the pure LASH barge-carrying C-9 vessel.

Our intended employment focused instead on carrying cargo in LASH barges only. There was no need to incur the capital cost of installing and maintaining a second crane for containers. In our LASH system the LASH barge becomes the ocean carrier, an issuer of bills of lading from and to upriver ports, inland waterway ports and/or shallow-draft ports.

CHAPTER 9

LASH—The IPCO Contract

While our research and analysis with Goldman had convinced us that the LASH system would meet the objectives of our U.S.-flag ship replacement program, there were still other concerns of equal importance to address.

For our intended service we needed a vessel built and registered in the United States for operation under U.S. flag. Reason: The cargoes being shipped from the United States to the ports we were serving on Trade Routes 18 and 17 were predominantly U.S. government preference cargoes, such as Public Law 480, the U.S. Agency for International Development, the Export-Import Bank and U.S. military supplies. These programs continue today and still require U.S.-flag vessels to be employed, at least to the extent of 50% and in some cases 100% of the shipments.

Why U.S.-built? A foreign-built vessel or a vessel that had operated under foreign-flag and later transferred to U.S. registry could not immediately qualify for the carriage of the aforementioned preference cargo. Any foreign-flag vessel brought under U.S. flag, or any U.S.-flag vessel that was built or modified in a foreign shipyard, had to wait three years until it became eligible to carry preference cargo. (See Chapter 4.) This impediment to U.S.-flag vessel ownership, which dated to when we lengthened three U.S.-flag Victories in Germany in 1961-62, was later modified when Congress passed the Maritime Security Act in 1995. The financial burden of waiting three years was an overwhelming penalty. It meant a foreign-built LASH vessel after 1962 and before 1995, even if registered under U.S. flag, would not be eligible to carry these cargoes reserved for U.S.-built vessels until three years passed. A foreign-built vessel could be used only to transport commercial cargoes and, in limited cases, military shipments. Commercial cargoes were available to certain countries on

these trade routes, such as Saudi Arabia, Iraq and Iran that could use their oil revenues to import manufactured goods such as automobiles and household appliances. Other countries on these routes depended on U.S. government programs for food and fertilizer imports. Homebound commercial cargoes such as jute, burlap and natural rubber were available to any flag vessel, but a successful voyage depended on the right combination of commercial and U.S. government-impelled cargoes outbound and inbound to utilize efficiently each vessel's deadweight and cubic carrying capacity. Between 1962 and 1995, this required the ship to be U.S.-built and remain U.S.-registered.

Another hurdle: The Construction Differential Subsidy through the Maritime Administration for building in a U.S. shipyard was available at that time only to U.S. shipping companies with Operating Differential Subsidy contracts. We were not then subsidized. Furthermore, guaranteed financing under the government's Title XI program was not available to unsubsidized companies without a change in the law.

Having arrived at this point, it appeared that these problems were going to delay indefinitely our introduction of the LASH system. U.S. government policy needed to be changed. Our efforts to introduce a new, revolutionary system of ocean transportation had hit the wall unless we could find new business that did not require U.S.-built ships—a major challenge—or U.S. government policy changed.

IPCO Contract—SERENDIPITY

Luckily, in seeking this alternative business we found a large U.S. company that exported its own products from the United States to Europe, using foreign-flag vessels. Coincidentally, their major trade route was also between river ports. Might they be a candidate for LASH? How we found them was pure serendipity.

Harry Smith, a shipping broker with offices in Washington whom I had known for some years, reacted to our description of the LASH system. He said, "You should meet with Lawrence Arthur Renehan, who has just recently joined International Paper Company and is in charge of logistics for IPCO's export shipping." Renehan was a graduate of the U.S. Merchant Marine Academy at Kings Point. He had sailed as a ship master on Farrell Lines' U.S.-flag vessels, then came ashore to become vice president of operations in Farrell's New York headquarters, in the same building as our office. Consequently, I'd often run into him in the building before he joined IPCO. After Harry Smith's suggestion, I had several lunches and meetings with Smith and Renehan at the Whitehall Club in New York and in our respective offices to develop IPCO's needs.

IPCO exported mainly wood pulp and linerboard in bales and packages from mills at Natchez and Vicksburg, Mississippi, on the Mississippi River, as well as from Pine Bluff, Arkansas, on the Arkansas River. Their importers in North Europe were located on rivers and waterways—a ready-made fit for the LASH system at both ends. When we met with IPCO, their method of handling these exports was to load them into river barges at the mills for movement in tows down the Mississippi River to New Orleans. There, longshoremen unloaded the river barges and placed the cargo on a wharf pending the arrival of an oceangoing breakbulk vessel. Upon the ship's arrival, longshoremen moved the cargo from the storage area on the wharf and loaded it with ship's gear into the breakbulk vessel that then sailed across the Atlantic Ocean to a seaport in North Europe. There, longshoremen unloaded the cargo and placed it on a dock temporarily, pending transshipment by river barge, rail or highway to its ultimate destinations. A number of IPCO customers were located on the Rhine River and other waterways in North Europe. IPCO was an obvious candidate for the LASH system to replace the multiple handling (at least five times) of their exports.

With LASH, their cargo could be loaded once into the barges at their mills on the Mississippi and Arkansas rivers. It would remain in the LASH barges as they were towed down the Mississippi River then lifted intact onto the LASH mother vessel to sail, with her full complement of loaded LASH barges, directly to Rotterdam or another safe port where the LASH barges would be lifted off the vessel with the LASH crane. The cargo, still intact in the barges, would then be delivered directly to waterside receivers. The cargo would be handled only once onto LASH barges at IPCO mills and once off LASH barges at destination. IPCO would thereby substantially reduce the expenses of multiple handling, minimize the potential for damage to its products and expedite delivery to its customers.

We got a positive reaction to the concept from Renehan. He asked us for a price. The sequence of events on which we based our pricing was as follows. The empty LASH barges would be towed to IPCO mills at Natchez and/or Vicksburg and/or Pine Bluff. They would then be loaded at IPCO's expense, towed downriver to New Orleans, and placed on the mother vessel, which would sail from New Orleans to Rotterdam. At Rotterdam the loaded barges would be lifted off the mother vessel. The barges would be towed intact from the mother vessel to their customers up the river and connecting waterways. We offered IPCO the option of handling the towage themselves on the rivers and waterways of the U.S. and Europe or having us include it in our freight charges. What finally developed was that we gave them an all-inclusive river/ocean freight cost from their mills on the Mississippi and Arkansas rivers to their customers on the Rhine River and other waterways of North Europe. After negotiations extending through the summer and into the fall of the year 1967, we reached a mutually agreeable contract to carry IPCO exports from Natchez and Vicksburg to North Europe. This contract for consecutive voyages over 10 years for the capacity of one LASH vessel became a living document over the ensuing years. The contract ultimately had 36 amendments. It was signed originally on October 31, 1967, by Niels W. Johnsen, vice chairman, on behalf of Central Gulf Steamship Corporation, and Judson Hannigan, vice president and later president and chairman of the board of International Paper Company.

Following are the main terms and conditions of this contract, the partial text of which appears in the Appendix.

Duration: 10 years

Owner (Central Gulf) provides the vessel and initially a fleet of 233 LASH barges necessary to sustain the system and carry the cargo provided by Shipper (IPCO).

Shipper will pay a lump sum of $264,260 per voyage plus other charges for IPCO's account.

Description of vessel and barges as per Exhibits A & B.

Outline specifications of the LASH vessel.

Barge delivery points: Panama City, Vicksburg, and Natchez.

Number of barges: 73 (later increased to 76) per sailing.

Barge destination points:

Range 1: Port or ports within the Bordeaux/ Hamburg/United Kingdom range.

Range 2: Port or ports on the west coast of Italy range.

Lump sum freight per voyage

Range 1: $213,160 plus $51,100 (if no other cargo is carried for owner's account eastbound or westbound) = $264,260.

Range 1 plus Range 2: $282,510 plus $51,100 (if no other cargo is carried for owner's account eastbound or westbound) = $333,610.

Cost of loading/stowage/discharge of cargo in/from barges was for IPCO's account.

Towage of barges arranged by Owner for Shipper's account while barges are in Shipper's custody plus Shipper pays cost from and to vessel's side or under LASH crane at vessel's stern.

This contract with IPCO called for freight payment to be a lump sum FIO (Free In and Out) per voyage based on the owner providing a LASH mother vessel capable of carrying 73 LASH barges per voyage and a fleet of 233 LASH barges for the system (one set aboard vessel, one set at loading area and one set at unloading area = 219 plus 14 cushion: total barges 233).

The contract also provided that the vessel owner could use the remaining spaces aboard the vessel for its account. Those spaces included side tanks and additional barge capacity, namely 10 more eastbound barges (to total 83) and the entire 83 barges westbound. IPCO was later given use of this added carrying capacity if they paid fair market rates for its use in addition to the lump sum freight for the 73 barges.

MV *Acadia Forest,* the world's first LASH vessel, slides down the building way at Sumitomo Heavy Industries, Uraga, Japan, April 3, 1969. Total deadweight, 43,517 long tons; LOA, 262 meters (859.57 feet); beam, 32.5 meters (106.6 feet); draft, 11.25 meters (36.9 feet); speed, 20.4 knots powered by a 9SD90 Sulzer engine with 22,100 normal horsepower. Gantry crane capacity, 500 tons; barge-carrying capacity, 83 LASH barges. Classed by Det Norske Veritas.

CHAPTER 10

LASH—The First Ship

Having signed the IPCO contract, based only on Jerome Goldman's plans, we still had to have the ship and barges built. We opened discussions with Sumitomo Heavy Industries, Uraga, Japan. After lengthy negotiations, we and Goldman reached agreement with the shipyard on price and detailed plans and specifications. We then signed a contract with Sumitomo on December 15, 1967, to build the world's first LASH vessel. Since Sumitomo had already built our first newbuildings, we were confident that the ship they built would be a strong and sturdy vessel for this historic venture. While excited to be pioneers, we were nonetheless aware that implementing a revolutionary ocean transportation system presented risks reminiscent of the stormy voyages that sailing ships like the *Baron Holberg* faced a hundred years earlier.

During the design and building of the LASH vessel, we received excellent cooperation and technical input from the shipyard (particularly Dr. Takarada, Sumitomo's senior naval architect) as we worked with Goldman to bring his idea to life. The result, some two years later, was delivery of the world's first LASH ship at a price of $10 million, including supervisory fees and ancillary expenses. The financing was provided by a loan from the Export-Import Bank of Japan in the amount of 80% of the contract price, repayable over eight years at an interest rate of 5½%. The remaining part of the vessel's cost came from Company resources.

Norwegian Flag

We decided to register our first LASH ship under the Norwegian flag so that she would operate within that part of the world fleet known as "national-flag carriers" as opposed to "flags of convenience" vessels. We had previously decided on Norwegian-flag operation of our non-U.S.-flag fleet to have access to experienced officers and crews to man our new highly sophisticated ships when in September 1965 we took delivery of the 48,000-ton bulk carrier *Baron Holberg,* the first of the series of bulk carriers built for us in Japan earlier in the 1960's. Essentially, we were continuing the arrangement already in place with A/S Mosvold Shipping Company of Kristiansand, Norway.

Sumitomo Shipyard launched the world's first LASH ship on April 3, 1969, and we named her *Acadia Forest,* after one of the forests in Eastern Canada owned by IPCO. Mrs. William Hinman, wife of the chairman of International Paper Company, christened her with a champagne bottle broken on her bow, sending the 859 foot, 6⅞ inch ship down the ways into Tokyo Bay. The new ship returned to the shipbuilder's yard for outfitting.

In the meantime, we needed to have the LASH barges constructed. We decided the 233 barges would be built in the United States and registered in New Orleans. We put the order out for bids accordingly. The lowest bidder was Equitable Equipment Company, owned by Captain Neville Levy. Their yard was located on the Industrial Canal in New Orleans and had covered workplaces that had been used during World War II to construct the famous Higgins PT boats. Captain Levy and his colleagues were convinced that Equitable could fabricate the 233 LASH barges in an assembly-line fashion for just under $20,000 each.

We awarded the contract to Equitable at a fixed price, and they promptly began ordering the steel and organizing an assembly line to construct the barges. Because barges intended for this type of service had never been built before, we insisted on employing shipbuilding inspectors recommended by Goldman to be stationed at the yard to be sure that the workmanship was up to standards. In addition to our inspectors, representatives

CENTRAL GULF STEAMSHIP CORPORATION
ONE WHITEHALL STREET   •   NEW YORK, N. Y. 10004

cc: Mr. E.F. Johnsen   } 12/12/69
     Mr. George Denegre

December 12, 1969

Mr. Lawrence Arthur Renehan
Director of Export and Marine Services
International Paper Company
220 East 42nd Street
New York, New York 10017

Re: M.V. "ACADIA FOREST"
        CONTRACT OF AFFREIGHTMENT DATED OCTOBER 31, 1967

Dear Sir:

Pursuant to the L A S H Contract of Affreightment dated October 31, 1967 Section 4 "CONTRACT PERIOD", this is to confirm that the M.V. ACADIA FOREST was tendered to you for sailing on her first voyage under this Contract at Panama City, Florida on October 28, 1969 and accordingly the Contract Period commences from that date. Furthermore, the 73 barges for use on the first voyage under the Contract have been tendered in accordance with Appendix 1 of the Contract.

If you find this agrees with your records, kindly sign and return to us the enclosed copy of this letter.

Very truly yours,

CENTRAL GULF STEAMSHIP CORPORATION

By

N. W. Johnsen
Vice Chairman

NWJ:mf
cc: Central Gulf Steamship Corporation - New Orleans, La.
AGREED:
INTERNATIONAL PAPER COMPANY

By _____   Date: _Dec 12_____ 19 69

Letter from Central Gulf to IPCO confirming that MV *Acadia Forest* was tendered for her first sailing under the IPCO contract.

Left to right: Martin Mosvold, Erik F. Johnsen and Torrey Mosvold view a model of MV *Acadia Forest*.

pendent, privately owned company, we could also establish a separate single-purpose company, CG Barge Company, to own the LASH barges. We organized CG Barge Company as a subchapter "S" corporation, which enabled us to pass tax benefits through to its shareholders, similar to a partnership but with limited liability. The partners of CG Barge Company were Niels F. Johnsen, Niels W. Johnsen, Erik F. Johnsen, George Denegre, Susan Jones Lane and Joseph Merrick Jones Jr. With this structure in place, we financed the construction cost of the barges with Teachers' Insurance and Annuity Association (TIAA). The two officers of TIAA with whom we arranged the financing, Harry Brown and Bruce Bent, had also worked with us to finance our second newbuilding delivered in Japan in 1966, the 57,897-ton tanker *Sterling*. With the foregoing structure, CG Barge Company was able to borrow 100% of the capital cost ($7.1 million including supervisory fees, etc.) of the 233 LASH barges for use with the *Acadia Forest* to perform the IPCO contract. Harry Brown and Bruce Bent subsequently retired from TIAA and in 1970 established the world's first money market fund, the Reserve Fund. Harry and Bruce asked Niels W. Johnsen to serve on the board of the Reserve Fund as one of its founding directors. This was a new venture with nothing to do with the shipping industry but, as

from the classification society, the American Bureau of Shipping, were also overseeing the construction.

Building the barges in the United States at that time qualified us to receive certain income-tax benefits, including an investment tax credit of 7½% applicable to new equipment. The barges also were eligible for accelerated depreciation (five years), a further income-tax benefit. Because Central Gulf was then an inde-

Mrs. William Hinman, wife of the chairman of International Paper Company, cuts a ribbon to launch MV *Acadia Forest*, April 3, 1969, at Uraga Shipyard, Japan.

MV *Acadia Forest* after delivery from Japan to the U.S. Gulf and ready for her maiden voyage loaded with a full complement of LASH barges containing International Paper Company's initial cargo.

it turned out, the Reserve Fund flourished and is today one of the leading money market funds in the United States.

As construction of the LASH barges progressed, we received reports from our inspectors that the welding was not meeting specifications. In spite of our complaints through the inspectors to the managers in the yard, no steps were being taken to rectify the problem. One day by surprise Captain Levy appeared at Erik Johnsen's office in New Orleans, threw the balance sheet of his company on the desk and said, "Here's your shipyard."

Erik responded to Captain Levy that we were not interested in owning a shipyard; we were only interested in getting our barges constructed in accordance with the

plans and specifications. Captain Levy admitted that he had underbid the job by not recognizing the intricacies of the specifications and that he was convinced his yard would go bankrupt if we continued to press for our rigorous inspections. After much discussion Erik suggested to Captain Levy that he let us designate the yard superintendent and our chief financial officer so that the responsible Neville Levy workers would report to our yard superintendent and our CFO would control the finances. We then would agree to let him break even on the job. Erik told Levy that we would also need to have complete access to his accountants and, of course, free rein in his yard. This obviously was an unprecedented approach, but we assured Captain Levy that we wanted completed barges, not his yard. He

Dimensions of standard LASH barges:

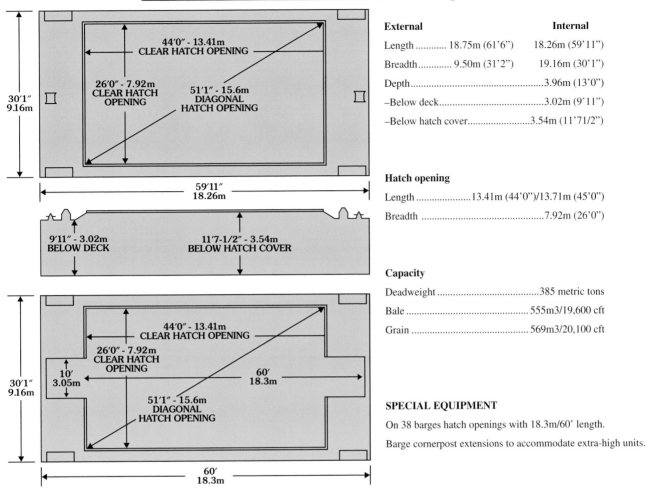

External		Internal
Length .... 18.75m (61'6")		18.26m (59'11")
Breadth .... 9.50m (31'2")		19.16m (30'1")
Depth		3.96m (13'0")
–Below deck		3.02m (9'11")
–Below hatch cover		3.54m (11'71/2")

Hatch opening

Length .... 13.41m (44'0")/13.71m (45'0")
Breadth .... 7.92m (26'0")

Capacity

Deadweight .... 385 metric tons
Bale .... 555m3/19,600 cft
Grain .... 569m3/20,100 cft

SPECIAL EQUIPMENT

On 38 barges hatch openings with 18.3m/60' length.

Barge cornerpost extensions to accommodate extra-high units.

agreed to our proposal, and we drew up a memorandum of understanding. In the end Equitable delivered all the barges on time and in accordance with specifications, but the final price was $25,000 per barge plus supervisory and other fees.

Another complication developed during the construction of the LASH barges at Equitable. Our attorneys reported that foreign steel, when imported into the United States, was subject to duty. However, if it were imported into a Free Trade Zone, constructed into a barge and the barge registered under U.S. flag, there would be no duty on the steel or the barge. Since Levy was having difficulty maintaining the budgeted price for constructing the barges, we approached him about converting Equitable Equipment's yard into a

Free Trade Zone. He saw the benefit and agreed to do it. Ultimately we had a Free Trade Zone, but because the approval process took time, some of the foreign steel had already been imported.

We learned that U.S. Customs was assessing us about $500,000 in duty against the steel already received at the yard for the project. We wanted to get that penalty canceled. Erik visited the local Customs director, who expressed appreciation of our situation but advised that the only way we could get the duty canceled was "by an act of Congress."

Erik talked to Ed Merrigan, our Washington, D.C., attorney, who agreed to assist. He also spoke with U.S. Senator Russell Long and Representative F. Edward Hebert of Louisiana. Both agreed to submit an

MV *Acadia Forest*, stern view during loading. The ship's crane prepares to lift a 500-ton LASH barge from the water. The crane then will move on deck rails to position the barge on board the mother ship. The operation will be reversed at the discharge port.

MV *Acadia Forest*'s 500-ton crane lifts a LASH barge from the water.

appropriate bill to Congress to get the duty waived. When the House Judiciary Committee called for public hearings, Erik went to Washington. He, together with Hebert and Merrigan, attended the Judiciary Committee hearing, where there were about 10 to 15 representatives of the Treasury Department, and of course, only our three representatives proposing the bill. Hebert, whose eyesight was failing, tried to read the bill but was unable to do so and turned it over to Merrigan, who read the three- or four-line bill. The chairman of the Judiciary Committee, after hearing our arguments concerning the need for the bill, turned to the chief Treasury representative, and asked if they had waiver authority without having to go through an act of Congress. The Treasury Department representative stated that they did, whereupon the chairman turned to Erik and asked if we would settle for $150,000 duty. Erik said we would. The chairman then turned to the Treasury Department representative and asked if he would agree to that adjustment. After some discussion among their group, he responded affirmatively.

At that point the chairman said, "Mr. Johnsen, would you therefore withdraw the bill and settle the matter with the Treasury Department?" Erik told him that indeed he would. At that point one of the representatives of the Judiciary Committee came down to congratulate us on the settlement, and introduced himself as Representative Edwin Edwards from Louisiana. He stated that he had recused himself when the issue came up and had encouraged the chairman to offer a compromise to us. This was the first time that we met the now well-known Edwin Edwards, who later served four terms as governor of Louisiana.

Some 20 years later Erik got a telephone call from a family member of Captain Levy, telling him that Captain Levy was gravely ill at the Public Health Service Hospital on State Street in New Orleans and would very much like to see Erik. The following day Erik visited him at the hospital. On Erik's arrival he noted Captain Levy was being administered oxygen from under an oxygen tent. Captain Levy pulled the tent away and expressed pleasure in Erik visiting him. After the usual greetings, Levy said he had very much wanted to see Erik before he died because he had on his mind these many years the problem that his yard experienced in constructing our LASH barges. He said he wanted Erik to know that if he had had our company in the situation that he was in, he would have "crushed" us, and that he was still amazed that we "took our foot off his neck" (his expression). Erik told him once again that he should have recognized then and should recognize now that our interest was only in completing the contract. In any event, he said he was relieved to get the thoughts off his chest, and after a pleasant chat Erik departed. Captain Levy died two days later.

CHAPTER II

LASH—The Second Ship

Before launching the *Acadia Forest* in April 1969, we had already had discussions with IPCO about the idea of dividing their monthly shipments into two parcels, thereby offering them two transatlantic sailings per month, approximately two weeks apart. We had not yet received a firm commitment from IPCO that they agreed to proceed with this plan. However, we had encouragement from Mosvold that they would like to order a sister ship to the *Acadia Forest* for time charter to Central Gulf. As we got closer to the date when the *Acadia Forest* would go into operation, we explored opportunities to employ a sister ship in tandem with the *Acadia Forest* in the transatlantic service. The question was whether IPCO either had additional cargo to ship or was interested in dividing its monthly shipments into two lots. We concluded that regardless of IPCO's response there was sufficient interest from others to warrant building a second LASH vessel for that trade route. Also, with two LASH ships operating, only about one and a half sets of LASH barges (150) were needed to be added to the three sets of LASH barges in the fleet built for the *Acadia Forest* alone. Consequently, our average capital cost would be reduced having two sister ships in service as opposed to only one. On August 31, 1968, Mosvold and Central Gulf made the firm decision to order from Sumitomo a sister ship to the *Acadia Forest*. Her keel was laid November 24, 1969, and she was launched March 9, 1970, and delivered July 21, 1970, (approximately 10 months after the *Acadia Forest*). During this period we had further discussions with IPCO, and before the delivery of the *Atlantic Forest* we signed a contract with them on March 17, 1970, for the carriage of up to 60 LASH barge loads on each sailing. The *Acadia Forest* contract was amended to, in effect, divide IPCO monthly shipments between the two sailings fairly

evenly spaced. This was in keeping with our plan. We intended to book cargo with other shippers to fill the balance of the barges and other space on the two vessels. This plan was an expansion of what we had under consideration when we stipulated in the first IPCO contract, that the owner had the right to carry cargo in the *Acadia Forest* for others or for their own account in addition to the IPCO cargo. Renehan left IPCO and joined American Union Transport, a cargo freight forwarder. Ted Przedpelski moved from American Union Transport to IPCO, taking Renehan's place. On August 31, 1978, we reached an agreement with IPCO to assign the *Acadia Forest* contract to International Navigation Ltd. (INL), a wholly owned subsidiary of IPCO. Next INL notified Central Gulf (owners) that they wished to exercise the option to use all of the barges and spaces on the *Acadia Forest* as well as the *Atlantic Forest*. In other words, they were booking up the capacity of both ships on a spot booking basis rather than having to

Madame Kjell Bondevik, Norwegian minister of education, was sponsor for the launching of the world's second LASH vessel, MV *Atlantic Forest,* on March 9, 1970. The vessel went into service in July 1970, joining her sister ship, MV *Acadia Forest.* Madame Bondevik's son was prime minister of Norway in 2004.

MV *Atlantic Forest*, launched March 9, 1970, and delivered July 21, 1970, at Uraga Shipyard, Japan. Total deadweight, 43,517 long tons; length overall, 262 meters (859.57'); beam, 32.5 meters (106.6'); draft, 11.25 meters (36.9'); speed, 20.4 knots; 22,100 normal horsepower; gantry crane capacity, 500 tons; barge capacity, 83 LASH barges. Classed by Det Norske Veritas.

Outfitting the foredeck of MV *Atlantic Forest* after her launching.

Traditional Japanese dance at MV *Atlantic Forest* launching party.

MV *Acadia Forest* loaded about 1,000 empty containers on deck with shoreside cranes in Yokohama. She delivered these containers to Puerto Rico after her maiden voyage from Japan before she entered her consecutive-voyage contract with International Paper Company.

contract for the space firmly in advance. Central Gulf agreed to their request, subject to sufficient notice. This was their second attempt to become a common carrier (a non-vessel-operating common carrier, or NVOCC). In the meantime we advised IPCO that we intended to file with the Federal Maritime Commission a tariff for booking cargo as a common carrier on these vessels. We did so because the FMC had given us its agreement that we could consider IPCO cargoes contract cargo and we would be free to be a common carrier for third-party cargo in the rest of the space. When INL came to us with the request to subcharter the barges and spaces on the two ships to another IPCO subsidiary, LASH Line Inc., we agreed, subject to FMC approval, in order to demonstrate our cooperation with them. The FMC denied approval for this operation. The use of LASH Line Inc. was therefore withdrawn. However, INL still maintained that it wanted to operate a common-carrier service. INL also

had claimed that it had the right to tow our LASH barges to loading points other than the so-called "barge delivery" points, Natchez, Vicksburg and Panama City. We finally came to the conclusion that a friendly arbitration of issues in dispute should be held. In the fall of 1973, the arbitration panel consisting of Messrs. George T. Stam, A.C. Valentine and Nicholas J. Healy heard the positions of each party and ultimately issued its decision on December 20, 1973. The decision was voluminous but the end result was that the parties reached an amicable settlement on January 25, 1974.

After the shipyard delivered the *Acadia Forest* on September 27, 1969, the *Acadia Forest* shifted to Yokohama, where she took on a full load of empty containers (about 1,000) for account of Sea-Land, the container ship operator to which we had previously chartered our "Mos" ships, and sailed from Japan to Puerto Rico. She delivered the empty containers in Puerto Rico and proceeded to Panama City, Florida, to begin service

MV *Acadia Forest* on her maiden voyage through the Panama Canal with deck load of containers for delivery to Sea-Land in Puerto Rico.

MV *Acadia Forest* transits a Panama Canal lock on her maiden voyage from Japan to Puerto Rico. Her 32.5-meter beam (106'6") enabled her to squeeze through the locks with only slight abrasions to her hull side paint.

LASH vessel MV *Atlantic Forest* on her trial voyage off Japan in July 1970.

under the IPCO contract. After lifting part of the 73 barges loaded with IPCO cargo at Panama City, she shifted to New Orleans to lift onboard the remaining barges waiting there.

We had invited guests at New Orleans to visit the world's first LASH vessel prior to sending her off on her maiden voyage. Festivities were planned. Instead, we had a surprise. After the *Acadia Forest* docked in New Orleans on October 30, 1969, anonymous pickets of unidentified affiliation appeared alongside the vessel. The longshore labor, in keeping with their traditional practice, refused to cross the picket line. We were unable to begin lifting the barges onboard with the ship's LASH gantry crane. The gangway had been lowered but the picket lines prevented our guests from boarding the ship. Instead of having a gala reception aboard the *Acadia Forest,* the Company was forced to substitute a chartered Mississippi River paddle steamer for the occasion. So our guests could only view the new LASH ship from her river side.

Earlier in 1969, weeks before the *Acadia Forest* was to begin service under the IPCO contract, Erik F. Johnsen

had had a number of meetings with the local International Longshoremen's Association leaders, Al Chittenden and Clarence "Chink" Henry. After these discussions, Erik had what he thought was a mutually satisfactory contract between the ILA and our company for the working of the LASH system. Erik held the signed originals of the contract in his office. When the ship reached Puerto Rico, we began to hear rumors that the longshoremen and the U.S. seamen's union were going to strike our company. The *Acadia Forest* was flying the Norwegian flag, and therefore had a foreign crew. The seamen's union, it was rumored, would be attacking us with a view to getting us to change her registry to U.S. The ILA wanted to conclude a national contract for the stevedore work, ignoring what had been signed by the local labor leaders.

Because the New Orleans Steamship Association had an existing contract with the ILA, Erik had private conversations with Jim Howell, president of the association, and Jim Smith, president of T. Smith & Sons, our stevedores. While they were having these discussions, Erik received a telephone call from Chittenden, who stated that he and Chink Henry were in a room at the Royal Orleans Hotel and very much wanted to talk to him.

Erik asked Jim Smith to accompany him to meet the gentlemen waiting in a private room on the 5th floor of the hotel. Chittenden and Henry were most agitated and asked Erik to return the signed contract. They stated that they had advised Teddy Gleason, who was then national president of the ILA, that they had no signed agreement with us and that if Gleason learned otherwise, they would be in great difficulty with their local union members. Erik told Chittenden and Henry that he would not give back the contract, but that we expected them to assist us in working with Teddy Gleason to settle this labor stoppage and reach a national agreement. If they did so, we would not make our contract public. They promised to do so. Erik then told them that we were going to stand on the fact that there was an existing national labor contract that encompassed the vessel, and we were going to seek an injunction against their striking.

Jim Howell took action the very next day in court, seeking an injunction under the Taft-Hartley Act. The judge immediately issued the injunction. However, the unions had planned their reaction well. Each day as a new injunction was issued, they came up with a new picketing group—one from the ILA, then by the U.S. seamen, then by the wives of the U.S. seamen, then by the friends of the U.S. seamen, etc. Meanwhile Erik went to New York to meet with our labor attorney, Peter Lambos, together with Teddy Gleason and his national union officials, and representatives of the U.S. seamen's unions, the National Maritime Union and the Marine Engineers Beneficial Association. We finally reached a new agreement with the ILA in November. While we were negotiating with the ILA, the seamen's unions continued their efforts to force us to re-register the *Acadia Forest* under the U.S. flag. They asked if we had a signed contract with the local longshoremen's union. All of this we resisted. Simultaneously with our activity in New York vis-à-vis the ILA and the seamen's unions, we continued our legal action in the court in New Orleans without success. The final settlement, when it came, called for two gangs of 18 men each on the mother vessel as it lifted barges on and off the vessel and a 10-man gang on the barges

as they were loaded or unloaded. Additionally we were assessed a royalty payment for the benefit of the ILA. Erik remembered it as $2.00 per ton of cargo handled. During this period, the ILA was also negotiating labor issues with container ship operators. In spite of the fact that we continued to tell the ILA that the LASH system was entirely different from the container-type operation, we could not (in the early days) convince them that we were literally saving work for them because longshoremen would continue to be required to load and discharge the LASH barges. We believe that our straightforward approach with the unions and the fact that the LASH system provided continued work for longshoremen finally softened the unions' attitude toward the LASH system.

The strike ended on November 12, 1969. This wildcat strike against the Company negatively impacted relations with our customers and bankers. It cost the Company more than $160,000 in lost time. Had we not reached a resolution, the Company faced insolvency and even liquidation. When the settlement finally removed the threat, we naturally breathed a sigh of relief. The longshoremen, having achieved their objective of negotiating working conditions in the port of New Orleans for this new-technology LASH system, went back to work. They operated the ship's crane to lift onto the *Acadia Forest* the remainder of the 73 barges loaded with IPCO cargo that had been waiting in the port. They also loaded six empty LASH barges to be carried for Owner's account for prepositioning in Rotterdam or Medway (UK) to be loaded with cargo for the ship's next westbound sailing.

The *Acadia Forest* departed New Orleans on November 16, 1969, on her maiden voyage to Rotterdam under the IPCO contract. IPCO paid freight of $264,260 lump sum FIO, in accordance with the contract. After delivering 73 barges loaded with IPCO cargo to Rotterdam and dropping off the empty barges at Medway, she returned to New Orleans without cargo or barges. On her second voyage eastbound to Europe she again carried 73 barges with IPCO cargo, plus three additional barges (for a total of 76) with cargo booked by IPCO for which IPCO paid freight of a lump sum of $264,260 and $8,760, respectively. On her second westbound voyage we picked up cargo that

MV *Acadia Forest* loads LASH barges with her crane while bulk soybean meal is poured into her side tanks from a floating elevator in the Mississippi River.

had been loaded for the U.S. in the barges that the *Acadia Forest* brought to Rotterdam on her maiden voyage. Thus we began the Eurogulf Lines Service with a cargo of 73 loaded LASH barges that produced FIO net revenue of $139,699. Because the contract stipulated that if owners carried other than IPCO cargo either eastbound or westbound in addition to the 73 barges used by IPCO, owners would share with IPCO up to $51,100 of the net revenue. In the case of Voyage #2 westbound IPCO earned the full refund of $51,100. Beginning with Voyage 4 eastbound, March 4, 1970, we agreed with IPCO to increase the number of barges contracted to IPCO by three barges to 76 barges. The freight revenue was increased by $3,620 per barge to

$275,120. Additionally on this voyage we carried 5,000 tons of bulk soybean meal, which had been loaded in the side tanks by a floating elevator alongside the vessel at Destrehan on the Mississippi River, near New Orleans. The bulk soybean meal carried a freight rate of $8.50 per metric ton. It was loaded in the side tanks at the same time the vessel was lifting onboard with the ship's LASH crane part of the 76 barges previously loaded at Natchez, Vicksburg and Panama City. The entire cargo of 76 loaded LASH barges and 5,000 tons of bulk soybean meal was loaded in 3½ days at the aforementioned three ports and unloaded at Medway and Rotterdam in three days. On Voyage 4 westbound the *Acadia Forest* loaded 73 barges in one extra day. This

MV *Atlantic Forest,* with a complement of LASH barges, operating in the Forest Lines service between New Orleans and Rotterdam.

LASH barges being loaded with heavy-lift cargo by a floating crane in the Mississippi River.

cargo, booked by Eurogulf Lines, generated revenue of about $137,653.

We were gradually moving toward the LASH vessels' full carrying potential. When we negotiated with Sumitomo Shipyard the specifications for the construction of this sophisticated new vessel, we had to be sure the vessel could conservatively carry the 73 barges we had committed to IPCO under the contract. No other vessel of this type had ever been built. It was truly a pioneering venture for all parties involved. We made sure the shipbuilder had incorporated the necessary strength and stability into the ship's structure to handle the weight and volume of cargo booked but also a safe additional margin. We would conservatively test this additional margin after the vessel entered service. As it turned out, the vessel was constructed and classified to be capable of carrying safely up to 10 more barges than we had booked with IPCO, plus the weight of about 5,000 to 6,000 tons of bulk grain in the side tanks. Without knowledge at the time as to what the vessel would be capable of after she was ready for service, we provided for the contingency that more carrying capacity could become available. We stipulated in the IPCO contracts that any revenue earned on cargo carried in addition to the 73 (later 76) barges allocated for IPCO cargo would be for owner's account/benefit.

In August 1970 the sister ship of the *Acadia Forest,* the *Atlantic Forest,* arrived in New Orleans to join her sister in sailings every two weeks between New Orleans and Rotterdam. We continued to carry 76 loaded barges on each eastbound and westbound sailing together with occasional 5,000-ton bulk grain parcels in the side tanks until May 1972. We then strapped each vessel to enable it to carry safely another seven loaded barges for a total of 83 barges on each sailing.

After about six or eight years had passed, Erik had breakfast one morning in New Orleans with the ILA's Teddy Gleason, who told him that he was convinced that we had a contract with the local ILA when the *Acadia Forest* arrived in New Orleans in September 1969. Gleason added that the ILA would never forget that we had protected two of their local labor leaders, who would have been in very awkward positions had we exposed the contract we held private. On a number of occasions since then we have been able to obtain concessions from the ILA, which we still believe resulted from our straightforward and determined position when the *Acadia Forest* first entered New Orleans and was at the mercy of the ILA. This later attitude of the ILA was a small balm to the wound they had inflicted on the Company when the *Acadia Forest* arrived in New Orleans on her maiden voyage.

Loading of helicopter depicts the capability of LASH barges to carry unusual and sensitive cargoes from point to point, fully protected in a sealed LASH barge.

CHAPTER 12

LASH Operation—New Orleans and Rotterdam

Our preparations for the LASH system's operation began while the LASH vessel and barges were under construction. Our New Orleans office was busy planning the loading of the IPCO cargo in the LASH barges at the IPCO mills on the Mississippi River and the barges onto the mother vessel at New Orleans. At the same time we began working to select the port in North Europe that was the most advantageous to deliver the inbound barges, unload them or coordinate their distribution to cargo receivers or shippers on inland waterways. We not only had to decide the best port in North Europe for the mother vessel to perform its operations but also the best facilities at which to fleet the barges—that is, to hold them alongside docks or at anchor—after delivering IPCO cargo. We had to determine the best port from which to distribute empty barges for reloading with export cargo from Europe to the Mississippi River and adjacent waterways.

Captain Valkenier had turned over the management of the Company's Bombay office to Hugo Hansen in 1965. From 1965 to 1967 Captain Valkenier supervised the unloading of our conventional breakbulk vessels at ports on the Mediterranean while he was temporarily stationed in Istanbul. Since Rotterdam was his home, it was logical for us to transfer him there in anticipation of the forthcoming LASH service. He and his family moved back to Rotterdam in 1967 and set up a temporary office. He began his survey of ports at which the LASH system could be efficiently handled. In addition to Rotterdam, he visited Antwerp, Belgium; Bremerhaven, Germany; and Sheerness, England, as likely candidates. Adequate depth of water and ease and safety of access were of course important considerations. Port charges, stevedoring costs, harbor and river towing costs were also important. Acceptability of the LASH

system by the local port authorities and port labor was necessary. When he finished his survey, he concluded that Rotterdam best met our requirements. The Dutch port was always open for navigation to the LASH mother vessels without having to contend with locks for entry into the inner port areas as would have been the case at Antwerp and Bremerhaven. The LASH barges were capable of entering and loading or unloading at all of these ports. Captain Valkenier, however, had to conduct lengthy negotiations with port and waterway authorities to receive agreement that the LASH barges could be safely towed and navigated on these waterways. He had to reach agreement on the number of barges allowed in a tow. To meet the Rhine River Authority's requirements, he created a portable raked bow equipped with an anchor. He also had to reach agreement with the stevedores on the minimum manpower required on the tow. Also, as in New Orleans, he had to agree on the number of longshoremen in the gangs for lifting the barges on and off the mother vessel as well as the number of gangs needed in the respective ports for unloading and loading the individual LASH barges. Because the Rotterdam port authorities recognized the prestige of becoming the center of LASH shipping in Europe, they were very cooperative in meeting the requirements of this new system and eager to accommodate Captain Valkenier.

A most important need was to find a place where the LASH mother vessel could be safely moored for lifting barges off and on. Captain Valkenier found a dock area in Rotterdam called Waalhaven, conveniently located in protected water off the south bank of the Rhine (Maas) River, only about 20 miles from the river's entrance at the Hoek van Holland off the North Sea. Towage was available at competitive rates for handling both the mother vessels and the LASH

Linerboard stowed in a LASH barge that MV *Acadia Forest* will carry to Rotterdam. The barge then will be towed to an International Paper customer up the Rhine River or on a shallow-draft waterway in North Europe. Each barge can hold up to 150 of these rolls of linerboard.

Aerial view of LASH barges integrated with standard-sized river barges being pushed by a Mississippi River towboat.

LASH barges were discharged and fleeted in the Port of Rotterdam's Waalhaven area (center of map).

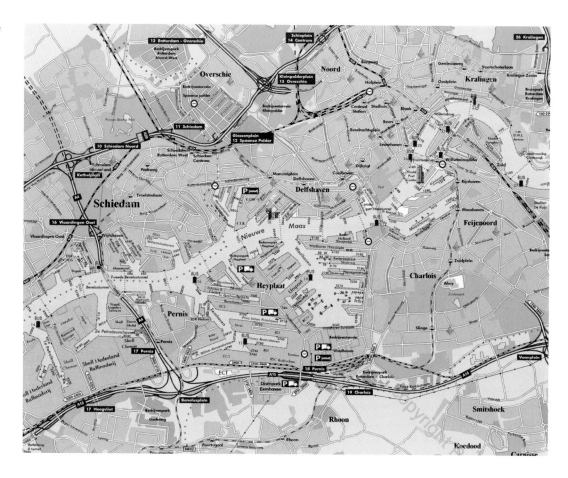

Central Gulf's introduction of LASH attracted wide attention. The innovation was featured in *The Journal of Commerce,* October 28, 1969.

SS *Robert E. Lee,* U.S-flag, U.S.-built LASH ship passing New Orleans skyline, circa 1989, with full complement of 89 LASH barges on and under deck to be discharged with vessel's 500-ton capacity LASH barge gantry crane.

barges. A large water surface area was available for fleeting the LASH barges. The barges could be easily accessible from and to the mother vessel and positioned for efficient mooring while waiting to be distributed to IPCO customers on the Rhine and other waterways and subsequently reloaded with home-bound cargoes from ports on connecting waterways. Container vessels, because they normally require docks equipped with container handling cranes, could not utilize areas of the port of Rotterdam like Waalhaven. The LASH mother vessel, however, with its own gantry crane, was self-sufficient so that shore side facilities were not necessary.

After concluding that Waalhaven in Rotterdam was the appropriate place for the LASH system in North Europe, Captain Valkenier established the Company's office in Rotterdam to supervise the operation and registered a new company, called Netherlands Maritime Agencies. We were then ready to receive the *Acadia Forest* on her first voyage from New Orleans to Rotterdam with IPCO cargo. Waalhaven is still used today for the Company's transatlantic LASH service.

CHAPTER 13

LASH Operation—Westbound Service

We had the eastbound cargo under contract with IPCO. We needed the return (westbound) cargo to make the venture profitable. We soon discovered that the major export out of North Europe to the United States at that time was semi-finished steel. In the late 1960's, this cargo was being carried mainly in bulk carriers or breakbulk ships. The prevailing freight rates were at a level such as to encourage us that our LASH system could be competitive. We therefore began contacting major exporters of steel to obtain the base cargo for the westbound leg of the LASH system. At first we were successful in booking one or two cargoes from Antwerp to New Orleans, but to provide the desired continuity, what we needed was to secure consecutive voyages of westbound steel or comparable cargo. Fortunately we attained this objective when we met Jean Brion. Brion was operating a number of services from Antwerp under the trade name of Contramar, an affiliate of Continental Lines; one of these services was to U.S. Gulf ports. Contramar was not a shipowner, but functioned as a freight forwarder with close relationships to a number of large steel exporters. Contramar would agree to carry their cargo and then charter 'tween deckers or bulk carriers for a voyage or a period of time to transport the cargo to its destination. Brion later told us the story of how he became the sole owner of Continental Lines.

Continental Lines was founded in 1923 by a certain Mr. Albert Schoutissen who inherited a large amount of money from an aunt. He had the money and didn't know what to do with it. Someone suggested, "Why shouldn't you become a shipowner?" So he bought two small ships of about 1,000 tons each and decided to start a freight service between Antwerp and London: therefore the name Continental Lines. It was mainly meant for the British that would give their cargo. At that time there were 12 lines running between London and Antwerp, all with the same type of ships. Ships made the round trip in a week's time. That means that two ships could offer regular sailings every week. Because the freight rates were so high, a 1,000-ton ship did not need to get a full cargo and was profitable even with 300 tons of cargo. So he entered into that trade saying to himself, "I have no expertise so I will quote 10% less than the other lines." All the others were quoting about the same rate. He was quickly able to fill the ships and get the support of forwarders and traders who were very pleased to have someone new in the trade, an outsider. As he was a man with a fantastic knowledge of languages, he could attract cargo from Germany because he was speaking German, he could speak Swiss, Dutch, whatever dialect they were speaking. Schoutissen was a tremendous linguist. He was Belgian. And so after two years, he had made a fortune with these two ships. Then he got a visit from all 12 British owners who came to him and said, "Sir you have done a fantastic job, but you have no right to come to England, you are not British. England rules the waves; the North Sea is an English sea. You have nothing to do, and we want you to quit." He said, "Well what do you suggest?" They said, "We know what you paid for the ships, we will repay you. We know that you have earned more than what you paid for these

Jean Brion, chief executive and principal owner of Continental Lines of Antwerp, Belgium, in recent photograph.

Westbound cargoes of
steel from Europe to
the United States were
important during the
early years of LASH
operations.

ships. We will pay you that amount. We will even pay you half more than what you paid but you must sign a contract that for 25 years you will nevermore come in England." All the other lines had gotten together and came to him and said this. His reaction was that he wanted to think it over. They said, "You have a week, but we want a definite reply. Otherwise you will have a freight war and you will be out." So he thought it over. And then he decided he would change and with that money he would do something different. He had learned a lot about shipping during these two years. He stated that, in fact, in all the companies there was a boss but the boss was doing nothing. He would have a good manager to do the deals. Schoutissen decided to become freight forwarder because his contacts were mainly with forwarders. He took on four forwarders as managers and offered them twice the amount the man was earning in the past and Continental Lines became a very important freight forwarder. The deal was done in such a way that everyone was satisfied. The guys got a better salary than they got in the past. And all these forwarding companies were not Belgians; they were Dutch, French and Swiss and some British, too. So for them the way of working in that time, in the years 1920 and 1921, just after the First World War, was quite different than it is now. His business flourished. He was an active man. He had four managers working for him when the war started in 1940, when the Germans came into Belgium. Belgium was occupied and the port of Antwerp was closed. There was no relationship and the company was in fact dead. No activity at all: There was nothing more. During this time he even left Antwerp and went to a place in the Ardennes, where he retired. He tried to go to England, where he still had a lot of friends, but he couldn't escape so he remained in contact with London through some channels. You may remember that Antwerp was the first port freed after the Allied landing. And that is why all the traffic came to Antwerp again. Once Antwerp was liberated, Schoutissen returned and, with his connections and other relations, got all transportation for the British army first, then for the American army. Once Antwerp was freed, he tried to attract people to work for his company, but some former members of his staff were too old and two died during the war. It was difficult for him but he immediately believed the company could awaken and start again.

It was in 1947 that I (Jean Brion) came into the picture purely by accident. I had started to study law in Brussels during WWII. After three months the Germans closed the university, and I had the possibility to go to the University of Louvain, dating from 1478, one of the oldest and biggest universities on the Continent. But I lived with my mother, my sister, my aunt and a cousin, all ladies. I felt responsible for them. I had lost my father when I was 7, so going to Brussels was a possibility but going to Louvain—I would have had to stay there overnight, so I decided to do something different. So I went to another

LASH barges proved ideal for heavy and oversized cargoes such as generators.

school in Antwerp which was not a law school but a school for diplomacy, a foreign service school, but also commercial. When I finished my studies, I was designated to be secretary of a commercial mission. After the war our government, like all governments, tried to rebuild trade relations. They organized commercial missions to all parts of the world. So I was designated secretary of a big mission where 300 businessmen from my country would go to Argentina and Brazil and all Central America.

One month before the departure of that mission, the minister called me and said, "Mr. Brion, I am very sorry but the mission will be delayed. There is opposition in Parliament. The Socialists are saying that all these missions are only a way for people to accrue money for themselves and not for the benefit of the state; that they are traveling there but without giving the benefit of their work to the nation. So there will be a delay of six months at least, maybe nine months." So I asked what I should do in the meantime. He said, "Well we cannot pay you so you will do nothing but you are living in Antwerp, an excellent place to learn. Why shouldn't you enter into a shipping company and try to find out in practice what you learned in theory, and that will help you in your future career tremendously." So I felt frustrated but I knocked on doors and someone said, "You should go to Continental Lines, they are starting again. The owner is an active man with a lot of ideas and you will be pleased." So I went to see Schoutissen, who at that time was about 60 years old, and he said, "Okay, you start tomorrow." But I told him it was for only six months because I will follow my career. I must say that the work of freight forwarding was an interesting job and I liked also the mentality after the war. There was such a spirit of building: I found it attractive. Then after six months I told him that I would leave the company in a month. He said, "Jean, you can't do that. Give me another chance. Ask if there is not another mission." So I said, "Well I will try, just to please you, but I am not sure that I will be successful." I went to Brussels and asked if there was eventually another mission. They said, "Yes, there is another one to China but it is in one-year's time." I said, "Okay. You just cancel my role on the Latin American—China is also an interesting mission." So I went back to Antwerp and said, "Just to please you I have changed and will go on a mission to China." Six months later he came to me and said, "Brion, you are not a guy to become a diplomat. You are a businessman. Why shouldn't you stay in the company?" I said, "What do you propose?" He said, "I have a son." This son had been doing the same studies I had done. He said, "You will work with him and I am ready to give you 25% of the shares of the company and you stay with us as a partner." I said, "It is a nice proposal and I must think it over." Then a week later I went to him and said, "I have thought it over and I am sorry but I won't accept." He said, "Why?" I said, "I see no future in the forwarding business. You know I am afraid that everybody knows what you earn: You said 2½%, 5% . . ." At that time we were working for 100 different breweries, 50 cement factories, all small entities. I said, "They will come together, there will be consolidation and they will create their own cement export companies and forwarding for them." He said, "What do you suggest?" I replied, "You must have your own materiel—either lorries or planes or ships or barges—but something where nobody can discuss your cost price." "Now it is my time to think it over," he said. Two days later he said, "I thought it over and you are probably right." So he gave me a blank check and told me to do something with it. I was at that time 25—I am just the age of the company, so it is easy. And then he died sometime later, and his son, maybe you have met younger Albert Schoutissen—he was a very clever guy, a very nice man, but he had very bad health. He came to the office two days a week and was always sick and it was a real disaster and he died 10 years later at the age of 48. So, at that time I became the only owner of Continental Lines. He left it all to me, because he had no family.

After demonstrating to Brion the advantages of the LASH system, we reached an agreement to form a new company, Eurogulf Lines Inc., owned 50/50 by Continental Lines and LASH Carriers, Inc. (our subsidiary). The plan was for Eurogulf to charter the LASH barges from LASH Carriers Inc. for the westbound voyage from Antwerp or other ports to New Orleans. The charter rate was set at a level to be sufficient to cover the capital costs of the LASH barges. Brion's organization would then book cargo to fill the barges. The profit Eurogulf made on the difference between the charter hire paid to LASH Carriers Inc. and freight rates charged by Eurogulf would be earned by the owners of Eurogulf based on the 50/50 ownership. This service created additional revenue for LASH Carriers Inc. over and above what would have been earned had the LASH vessels returned to New Orleans with empty barges. In 1975, however, the U.S. government imposed a penalty tariff on imported steel in response to demands by the American steelworkers union. The effect was to drastically reduce the volume of steel moving westbound from Antwerp to U.S. Gulf ports.

CHAPTER 14

LASH Operation—Triangular Service/Jeddah

While steel shipments from Europe to the U.S. Gulf had fallen off, the port of Jeddah, Saudi Arabia, was exploding with imports from Europe and the U.S. Gulf. More ships and cargoes were arriving at Jeddah than could be effectively handled: Jeddah became another seriously congested port. However, we saw this as an opportunity to demonstrate the flexibility of the LASH system and its ability to leapfrog port congestion. Eurogulf shifted its focus to this opportunity.

Jeddah, on the Red Sea, has been one of Central Gulf's regular ports of call in its freight service of Trade Route 18 (U.S. Gulf and Atlantic ports to ports on the Red Sea, Arabian Gulf, and Indian Ocean) since the 1950's. It was also an important destination for Contramar service from Antwerp, Belgium. Saudi Arabia's oil revenues were being spent on the country's infrastructure to accommodate the huge number of Muslim pilgrims visiting Mecca each year. As imports flooded in, they overtaxed a port accustomed to a more moderate flow of cargo. Waiting for a berth at Jeddah had become so costly that neither Contramar nor we could afford to service the port with our breakbulk vessels. Conventional and container vessels operated by our competitors were being delayed for 60 days or longer before they were able to come alongside a dock to discharge their cargoes. These cargoes originated in the United States and Europe.

Together with Contramar we agreed to employ the LASH system in this trade by establishing our own facility in Jeddah as part of a triangular service. Erik and Valkenier went to Saudi Arabia to convince the port authorities in Jeddah that we would make a substantial contribution to the efficiency of the port if they allowed us to position our own deck barge in the port of Jeddah, at a place where it was too shallow to dock

large vessels. We proposed to lift our LASH barges from the mother vessel at an offshore anchorage from where they would be towed into the port. Port officials agonized but ultimately granted permission. Contramar chartered to Eurogulf its submersible barge *Contilift I* (about 200 feet by 60 feet with a loaded draft of about 11 feet). We transported it to Jeddah, built a ramp to connect it to the land and equipped it with eight mobile cranes with which to unload the LASH barges onto heavy-duty trucks for transport to a safe place ashore. Because there was inadequate warehouse space, the Jeddah port authorities also granted permission for us to stack some of the cargo, such as bagged flour, on tarpaulins laid out on the adjacent desert floor pending their distribution to receivers. Upon completion of discharge of the LASH barges, they would be towed back to the mother vessel for return to New Orleans or held in a fleeting area to be picked up by a following mother vessel or to be returned to the next loading area.

On the first leg of this triangular service the *Acadia Forest* and *Atlantic Forest* carried the IPCO contract cargoes from the Mississippi River to Rotterdam as well as cargoes for Jeddah. After discharging IPCO cargo, instead of loading the empty barges with steel from Antwerp directly back to New Orleans, Eurogulf loaded various types of general cargo into LASH barges at Antwerp destined for Jeddah. The freight rates were attractively high for this cargo. It was possible for Eurogulf to obtain these rates because it could give quick delivery of the cargo in Saudi Arabia with the *Contilift I* operation. Eurogulf was able to provide this expedited service because Contramar, working together with LASH Carriers Inc., had in effect constructed a new port at Jeddah to accommodate the shallow-draft LASH barges. Meanwhile Eurogulf's competition was forced to wait for a dock in the port, costing millions of dollars in ship's time and lost revenues, or use extreme methods to deliver urgently needed cargo. Some even resorted to lifting cargo out of ships offshore by helicopters in large sling loads, an unorthodox alternative both expensive and dangerous. Eurogulf continued its service to Jeddah for a couple of years until it virtually cleared the congestion at Jeddah. Ironically, by solving the congestion, Eurogulf's *Contilift I* operation became surplus and it was redelivered to Contramar. Eurogulf service on the westbound transatlantic LASH operation then resumed until August 1982, when an International Shipholding Corporation subsidiary purchased the LASH *Bilderdyk* (renamed *Rhine Forest*) from Holland America Line together with a fleet of LASH barges and, as part of the package, a five-year contract to carry westbound cargo of semi-finished steel from Antwerp to New Orleans.

LASH Competitors/Combi Line

When two of our competitors in the transatlantic service learned that we were building the *Acadia Forest* and *Atlantic Forest* in Japan for use principally by International Paper Company, they apparently reached the conclusion that the LASH system was the newest advance in ocean shipping technology, and they were able to get the plans for the LASH ship and barges from Jerome Goldman. Of course, we had not made any stipulation with Goldman that we had exclusive use of his plans, and we recognized the fact that he would continue to sell the system to others, including our competitors. Consequently, we could do little to prevent Holland America Line and Hapag-Lloyd from going forward with a plan to build sister ships to our LASH vessels. Therefore we learned that in 1972, shortly after

the *Acadia Forest* and *Atlantic Forest* went into service for LASH Carriers, Inc. the aforementioned competitors had gotten delivery of the *Bilderdyk* and the *München* from Cockerill Werft in Hoboken, Belgium, together with a fleet of LASH barges, and began transatlantic service. These companies formed a jointly owned company, Combi Line, to operate the service of LASH ships between the U.S. Gulf and North Europe.

They operated jointly in competition with us until a startling event on December 12, 1978. Over the news ticker we heard that the *München* had disappeared without a trace en route from Bremerhaven, Germany, to Savannah, Ga., while on her 62nd voyage. There was not even an SOS. A lifeboat was found floating in the vicinity she was last known to be, in the North Atlantic near the Azores. The mystery as to what happened to her has never been solved. The consensus is that she sank after encountering a giant rogue wave or waves of unknown origin. These occurrences had not been known to happen often in the Atlantic. The loss of the *München* obviously disrupted the operation of the Combi Line service. The owners of Combi Line decided that they would not continue the transatlantic service with only one vessel, and Holland America Line offered to sell the *Bilderdyk* to us. Even though a third LASH vessel in our transatlantic service would slightly overtonnage the operation, we agreed in 1982 to buy the ship and barges, provided that Holland America Line sublet to us all the cargoes of steel remaining to be loaded under its westbound contracts for the next five years. The income from this additional business, at least for the time being, justified the purchase. We went ahead with the acquisition of the *Bilderdyk,* paying $22 million for the LASH vessel and 247 LASH barges. We changed her name to *Rhine Forest*. She continues to operate in this service to this day.

CHAPTER 15

LASH—U.S. Flag

While Hull #918 (eventually launched in April 1969, and named *Acadia Forest*) was under construction at Sumitomo Shipyard in Japan, Jerome Goldman continued to promote his LASH system with two subsidized U.S.-flag shipowners, namely Prudential Lines Inc. and Pacific Far East Line. Prudential operated a general cargo service between U.S. Atlantic Coast ports and Mediterranean Sea ports. PFEL operated a general cargo service between U.S. Pacific Coast ports and ports in the Far East (Japan/Singapore range) and Australia. Goldman acted as coordinator with the Maritime Administration in winning Marad's acceptance of the LASH system as replacement vessels for continued subsidized operations by these companies. As the date approached to sign the International Paper Company contract, information had leaked that we were negotiating a contract and that we were going to order a LASH vessel in Japan.

Without knowing the detailed specifications of the LASH ship we were having built, the Maritime Administration approved construction subsidy for 11 C-8 LASH vessels, five for Prudential Lines Inc. and six for Pacific Far East Line. These two subsidized U.S.-flag operators decided to build LASH ships as the replacement vessels they were required to build under their subsidy contracts. The C-8 version of the LASH was smaller than the Japanese-built *Acadia Forest* and the LASH ships we later had built in the United States. The design that Prudential and PFEL chose also was equipped with a container crane and carried a significant number of standard containers as well as up to 60 barges. The companies requested bids for construction, and Avondale Shipyards in New Orleans won the competition to build all 11 vessels. As the LASH system continued to take hold, by the mid-1970's, Avondale built the larger C-9 LASH vessels for Central Gulf, Delta Line and Waterman. Central Gulf and Waterman chose the pure LASH barge-carrying C-9, but Delta elected to add the container crane.

We, of course, signed our contract with International Paper Company at the end of October 1967 and placed our order with Sumitomo Heavy Industries in Japan in December 1967 for the construction of the world's first LASH vessel, to be named *Acadia Forest*. Our ships had already made several transatlantic voyages by the time the first C-8 LASH vessels began operation in 1970. In addition to being the first, our two Japanese-built LASH vessels were purely barge carriers, not a combination of barges and containers. The *Acadia Forest* and *Atlantic Forest* had capacities of 83 barges, while the C-8 carried between 49 and 58 LASH barges and 128 to 356 containers. The LASH barges were all standard size for all LASH ship operators.

Avondale had the advantage of serial construction, so that by the early 1970's they had already built the 11 ships for Prudential and PFEL and had reached the point in the learning curve where they could start making a profit on any further orders. All the LASH ships built by Avondale received Construction Differential Subsidy. It was therefore logical, when we decided in the early 1970's to order the three LASH ships for our U.S.-flag service on Trade Routes 18 and 17 (between the U.S. Gulf and South Asia), that we should negotiate with Avondale.

The estimated delivery dates and prices after subsidy for the LASH vessels built before our orders of new U.S.-built LASH vessels are shown on page 104.

LASH SHIP	OWNER	OPERATOR	BUILDER	DELIVERY	PRICE $
Acadia Forest (Hull#918)	Moslash Shipping Co.	Central Gulf	Sumitomo	9/27/1969	9,585,000
Acadia Forest (Hull#928)	Moslash Shipping Co.	Central Gulf	Sumitomo	7/21/1970	9,680,000
LASH Italia (C-8-S-81b)	Prudential-Grace Lines	Prudential	Avondale	11/1970	Prudential-Grace
LASH Turkiye (C-8-S-81b)	Prudential-Grace Lines	Prudential	Avondale	2/1971	Average per ship: 10,065,872
LASH Espana (C-8-S-81b)	Prudential-Grace Lines	Prudential	Avondale	4/1971	50,329,360 (Net of subsidy)
LASH Atlantico (C-8-S-81b)	Prudential-Grace Lines	Prudential	Avondale	7/1972	
LASH Pacifico (C-8-S-81b)	Prudential-Grace Lines	Prudential	Avondale	10/1972	
Thomas E. Cuffe (C-8-5-81b)	Pacific Far East Line	PFEL	Avondale	7/1971	
Golden Bear (C-8-S-81b)	Pacific Far East Line	PFEL	Avondale	9/1971	
Pacific Bear (C-8-S-81b)	Pacific Far East Line	PFEL	Avondale	11/1971	
Japan Bear (C-8-S-81b)	Pacific Far East Line	PFEL	Avondale	2/1972	Pacific Far East Line
China Bear (C-8-S-81b)	Pacific Far East Line	PFEL	Avondale	5/1972	Average per ship: 10,065,872
Philippine Bear (C-8-S-81b)	Pacific Far East Line	PFEL	Avondale	3/1973	60,395,232 (net of subsidy)

Our signing of the IPCO contract and our order of the first LASH vessel from Japan must have prompted the Maritime Administration to authorize the Construction Differential Subsidy for the C-8's that Prudential and PFEL ordered from Avondale. Because the *Acadia Forest* and *Atlantic Forest* were built in Japan, the U.S. government was probably also stimulated to change its shipbuilding and military preparedness policies. In 1970 President Nixon signed new legislation for promotion of the U.S.-flag Merchant Marine, making it possible for the government to award construction subsidy for ships to be built in the U.S. for operation under U.S. flag without the benefit of Operating Differential Subsidy. Furthermore, those ships could now be built with construction subsidy and also financed with the aid of loan guarantees under an existing law, Title XI of the Merchant Marine Act of 1936.

Title XI insurance works in the following manner. A shipowner who intends to acquire a new ship applies to the Maritime Administration for Title XI Insurance. This insurance permits the shipowner to negotiate a loan from a commercial financial institution. The U.S. government guarantees the repayment of the loan for a modest fee, usually 0.75% added to the interest rate. The shipowner in effect becomes "AAA"-rated credit. This enables the shipowner to qualify for interest rates and repayment terms that are available only to such a credit.

Title XI insurance had been in effect for some time and could be used by unsubsidized as well as subsidized companies. However, there was no incentive to build ships in the United States for unsubsidized international trade because it was not economically viable. The cost of U.S.-flag operation made it impossible to recover the capital investment in a U.S.-flag newbuilding at unsubsidized building costs. With new technology like the LASH system and building costs in a U.S. shipyard reduced by construction subsidy to nearly approach foreign shipbuilding costs, it became economically sound for us to own and operate a ship under U.S. flag without operating subsidy as long as we were eligible to carry U.S. government preference cargoes. We therefore promptly ordered one C-9 LASH ship from Avondale, for operation under U.S. flag without Operating Differential Subsidy, but with the option to order one or two sister ships. We later exercised options for the two additional ships.

In 1971, when we reached the decision to build three LASH ships (*Green Valley*, *Green Harbour* and *Green Island*) in the United States at a cost of about $26 million each, the U.S. government provided a construction subsidy so that our net cost came down to about $12 million each. This price was still higher, even after

Signing contracts with the Maritime Administration in June 1971 in Washington for construction of one U.S.-flag LASH vessel, with options for up to two more, to be built using Construction Differential Subsidy and Title XI insurance financing. Contract resulted in delivery in September 1974 by Avondale Shipyards, Inc., of Hull #1952, named MV *Green Valley*. Seated left to right: Niels W. Johnsen, vice chairman, Central Gulf Lines, Inc.; Erik F. Johnsen, president, Central Gulf Lines, Inc.; Andrew Gibson, U.S. maritime administrator; Zac Carter, president, Avondale.

construction subsidy, than the roughly $10 million each we had paid to construct the *Acadia Forest* and the *Atlantic Forest* in Japan. However, it was advantageous for us to have the new ships under U.S. flag because it also qualified them to carry U.S. government-sponsored cargo, such as PL480 foodstuffs, Export-Import Bank-financed projects and military cargo.

Having established the LASH technology first with the two newbuilding non-U.S.-flag LASH ships under

contract with IPCO and then by ordering one new U.S.-flag LASH ship, we looked forward to applying the LASH system to alleviate congestion in our U.S.-flag cargo liner service between U.S. Atlantic and Gulf ports and South Asia. To continue the Company's growth, we needed new equity financing resources. Our options to obtain these resources were to offer shares to the public or merge with an existing public company.

CENTRAL GULF STEAMSHIP CORPORATION
Statement of Income and Expense
Quarter Ended June 30, 1971

Terminated Voyages

Revenue	$7,702,864
Expense	6,727,041
Gross Profit	$975,823
Administrative & General Expense	$485,090
Profit before Vessel Depreciation	$490,733
Vessel Depreciation	630,492
Net Operating Profit	($139,759)
Net Income (Expense)	
Miscellaneous Income	$132,405
Miscellaneous Expense	(16,138)
Interest Income	108,692
Interest Expense	(74,058)
(Expense) Net	$150,901
Net Income before Federal Income Taxes & Extraordinary Items	$11,142
Provision for U.S. & Foreign Income Taxes (March 31, 1971, includes Investment Tax Credit of $122,968)	(26,045)
Net Income before Extraordinary Items	($14,903)
Extraordinary Items Net of Taxes	
Adjustments to Prior Years' Income	27,202
Gain on Sale of Vessels Net of Tax	-0-
Net Income	$12,299

CENTRAL GULF STEAMSHIP CORPORATION
Balance Sheet, June 30, 1971

<u>ASSETS</u>

Current Assets
Cash	$1,000,689
Traffic Receivables	1,553,374
Due from Affiliates	9,736
Miscellaneous Accounts Receivable	2,181,001
Unexpired Insurance	797,298
Inventories, Advances and Other Prepaid Vessel Expense	1,353,228
Construction Reserve Fund: Cash	287,648
Total Current Assets	$7,182,974

Investments In Other Companies, At Cost
Mid-Gulf Stevedores, Inc.	$50,000
Central Gulf Lines Agency (India) Ltd.	70,469
Sterling Tankers Corporation of Delaware	2,000
A/S Mosgulf Shipping Co.	27,975
A/S Mosbulkers	56,020
A/S Moslash Shipping Company	28,005
Total Investment in Other Companies	$234,469

Non-Current Receivables
Notes Receivable	$6,392,596
Total Non-Current Receivables	$6,392,596

Vessels and Other Property
Vessels	$17,782,504
Less Allowance for Depreciation	16,267,842
Book Value of Vessels	$1,514,662
LASH Barges (Net of Depreciation of $465,972 and $369,421, respectively)	4,175,820
Other Property (Net of Depreciation of $114,405 and $110,515, respectively)	35,912
Total Net of Depreciation	$5,726,394

Other Assets and Deferred Charges	259,545
	$19,795,978

LIABILITIES AND CAPITAL

Current Liabilities
Accounts Payable and Accrued Liabilities	$4,800,974
Federal Income Taxes Payable	758,460
Total Current Liabilities	$5,559,434

Current Maturities on Long-Term Debt
Notes Payable	84,810
Mortgage Notes	2,628,700
	$2,713,510
Total Current Liabilities and Current Maturities	$8,272,944

Unterminated Voyage Revenue Less Expense	$1,415,417

Long-Term Debt
Vessel Mortgages (Less $2,628,700 and $3,067,350, respectively, included in Current Maturities)	$3,698,500
Non-Current Notes Payable	889,190
Non-Current Bank Loan	666,000
Total Long-Term Debts	$5,253,690

Reserves
Reserve for Claims	$650,622
Reserve for Deferred Federal Income Taxes	371,498
Total Reserves	$1,022,120

Capital Stock and Retained Earnings
Common Stock	
10-cents Par Value; 150,000 Shares Authorized; 103,719 Shares Issued and Outstanding	$10,372
Excess of Amounts Paid for Common Stock over Par Value	563,923
Retained Earnings	3,257,512
Total	$3,831,807
	$19,795,978

CENTRAL GULF STEAMSHIP CORPORATION AND ASSOCIATED COMPANIES
Vessel Cost, Net Book Value, December 31, 1970

	Year Built	Year Acquired	Cost	Net Book Value
Victory Type				
GREEN HARBOUR*	1945	1951	—	—
Lengthening	1961	1961	—	—
GREEN ISLAND	1945	1959	$2,034,736	$48,950
Lengthening	1962	1962	567,372	
GREEN VALLEY	1945	1949	—	—
Lengthening	1962	1962		
C-2 Type				
GREEN COVE	1945	1960	720,889	52,500
C-3 Type				
GREEN RIDGE	1945	1964	1,014,518	66,500
C-4 Type				
GREEN BAY	1945	1965	1,884,411	70,000
GREEN LAKE	1945	1965	1,914,576	70,000
GREEN PORT	1944	1967	2,561,195	666,849
GREEN FOREST	1944	1967	2,584,989	576,675
GREEN WAVE	1944	1967	2,624,989	531,391
GREEN SPRINGS	1944	1967	2,595,718	745,282
Norwegian Flag				
QUEBEC (48,520 DWT)	1965	1965	5,062,640	3,519,411
STRATHEARN (54,685 DWT)	1967	1967	6,319,143	5,042,261
MOSBAY (28,006 DWT)	1967	1967	3,926,000	2,907,935
MOSGULF (28,100 DWT)	1967	1967	3,926,000	2,955,410
MOSENGEN (28,187 DWT)	1967	1967	3,934,000	3,005,120
MOSTANGEN (28,110 DWT)	1968	1968	3,934,000	3,162,453
ACADIA FOREST (43,517 DWT)	1969	1969	10,128,818	9,488,837
ATLANTIC FOREST (43,541 DWT)	1970	1970	10,153,397	9,922,925
Liberian Flag				
STERLING (57,897 DWT)	1966	1966	5,800,313	4,327,242
Singapore Flag				
BENARITA* (7,600 DWT)	1946	1969	—	—
LASH Barges	1970	1970	4,361,599	4,361,599
Total			$76,049,303	$51,521,341

*Sold during 1970

Construction in Progress:

Hull 958 (Mosfield)				$621,371
Hull 959 (Mosnes)				$2,200,000
Total Construction in Progress				$2,821,371

CENTRAL GULF STEAMSHIP CORPORATION
Summary of Voyage Results
For Terminations During Nine Months Ended December 31, 1970

Vessel	Voy. Ended	Voy. No.	Revenue	Expense	Gross Revenue Profit (Loss)
Owned Vessels					
SS GREEN VALLEY	4/27	94	$736,260	$717,523	$18,737
SS GREEN VALLEY	7/15	95	281,042	276,006	5,036
SS GREEN VALLEY	9/8	96	618,278	397,314	220,964
SS GREEN VALLEY	12/4	97	441,683	423,020	18,663
Total SS GREEN VALLEY			2,077,263	1,813,863	263,400
SS GREEN HARBOUR	7/20	94	780,205	737,356	42,849
SS GREEN HARBOUR	10/23	95	578,028	507,928	70,100
Total SS GREEN HARBOUR			1,358,233	1,245,284	112,949
SS GREEN BAY	6/3	43	549,183	389,752	159,431
SS GREEN BAY	9/18	44	567,203	407,935	159,268
Total SS GREEN BAY			1,116,386	797,687	318,699
SS GREEN ISLAND	8/22	36	784,223	828,088	(43,865)
SS GREEN ISLAND	12/24	37	825,387	663,292	162,095
Total SS GREEN ISLAND			1,609,610	1,491,380	118,230
SS GREEN COVE	7/31	35	592,613	487,173	105,440
SS GREEN COVE	12/27	36	613,783	491,512	122,271
Total SS GREEN COVE			1,206,396	978,685	227,711
SS GREEN LAKE	6/19	27	429,998	343,179	86,819
SS GREEN LAKE	10/31	28	723,373	548,674	174,699
Total SS GREEN LAKE			1,153,371	891,853	261,518
SS GREEN RIDGE	7/24	19	535,756	434,477	101,279
SS GREEN RIDGE	9/28	20	308,880	245,842	63,038
SS GREEN RIDGE	12/28	21	425,139	311,549	113,590
Total SS GREEN RIDGE			1,269,775	991,868	277,907
SS GREEN WAVE	4/9	9	685,564	451,479	234,085
SS GREEN WAVE	7/20	10	539,696	365,294	174,402
SS GREEN WAVE	11/9	11	607,678	409,950	197,728
Total SS GREEN WAVE			1,832,938	1,226,723	606,215
SS GREEN FOREST	6/12	9	435,673	311,807	123,866
SS GREEN FOREST	9/19	10	536,873	381,306	155,567
Total SS GREEN FOREST			972,546	693,113	279,433
SS GREEN SPRINGS	4/3	8	551,919	348,043	203,876
SS GREEN SPRINGS	7/9	9	503,754	318,569	185,185
SS GREEN SPRINGS	11/13	10	686,498	450,297	236,201
Total SS GREEN SPRINGS			1,742,171	1,116,909	625,262

Vessel	Voy. Ended	Voy. No.	Revenue	Expense	Gross Revenue Profit (Loss)
SS GREEN PORT	5/9	8	553,346	361,095	192,251
SS GREEN PORT	8/12	9	485,105	338,689	146,416
SS GREEN PORT	10/29	10	422,309	280,133	142,176
Total SS GREEN PORT			1,460,760	979,917	480,843
Total Owned Vessels – 28 Voyages			$15,799,449	$12,227,282	$3,572,167
Chartered Foreign-Flag Vessels					
MV ACADIA FOREST	4/12	4	$418,173	$439,036	($20,863)
MV ACADIA FOREST	5/17	5	395,802	455,294	(59,492)
MV ACADIA FOREST	6/24	6	437,012	475,640	(38,628)
MV ACADIA FOREST	7/30	7	417,494	469,488	(51,994)
MV ACADIA FOREST	9/4	8	429,439	472,720	(43,281)
MV ACADIA FOREST	10/10	9	492,742	544,048	(51,306)
MV ACADIA FOREST	11/16	10	517,885	548,821	(30,936)
MV ACADIA FOREST	12/22	11	512,228	533,499	(21,271)
Total MV ACADIA FOREST			3,620,775	3,938,546	(317,771)
MV ATLANTIC FOREST	8/11	0	-0-	175,163	(175,163)
MV ATLANTIC FOREST	9/23	1	540,164	630,653	(90,489)
MV ATLANTIC FOREST	10/28	2	555,408	550,547	4,861
MV ATLANTIC FOREST	12/1	3	511,899	539,726	(27,827)
Total MV ATLANTIC FOREST			1,607,471	1,896,089	(288,618)
MV LEIV EIRIKSSON	4/9	8	98,739	78,125	20,614
MV LEIV EIRIKSSON	5/14	9	145,061	113,527	31,534
Total MV LEIV EIRIKSSON			243,800	191,652	52,148
MV MOSBORG	7/19	1	235,645	188,236	47,409
MV MOSBORG	8/25	2	138,552	115,978	22,574
MV MOSBORG	9/17	3	85,620	73,838	11,782
MV MOSBORG	10/22	4	125,100	110,490	14,610
MV MOSBORG	11/17	5	100,157	84,471	15,686
MV MOSBORG	12/14	6	99,663	86,750	12,913
Total MV MOSBORG			784,737	659,763	124,974
Total Chartered Foreign-Flag Vessels – 20 Voyages			$6,256,783	$6,686,050	($429,267)
Total – All Vessels – 48 Voyages			$22,056,232	$18,913,332	$3,142,900

CHAPTER 16

Enter TransUnion

In mid-1971, as we were reviewing our options for a stock offering or merger with a publicly traded company, the Chase Manhattan Bank introduced us to TransUnion Corporation (TU), headquartered in Chicago. J.W. van Gorkum ("Van"), chairman of TU, was the driving force behind his company's expansion through acquisitions. TU's corporate stock was publicly held, registered on the New York Stock Exchange and of stable and growing value. TU was using its stock to acquire new subsidiary companies. We were interested. TU was desirous of adding a shipping company to its conglomerate.

The principal subsidiary of TU was the Union Tank Car Company, UTLX, whose predecessor company was Star Tank Line, which was founded in Pittsburgh in 1866. In 1873 John D. Rockefeller's Standard Oil Company bought Star and changed its name to Union Tank Car Company. UTLX's business was the ownership, building and leasing of railroad tank cars to the petroleum and chemical industries. In 1968 UTLX created Trans-Union Corporation as its parent holding company. TU then began a plan of growth through acquisition of companies in diversified fields. It first acquired the Credit Bureau of Cook County. It developed a national consumer credit file, which became Trans Union Credit Reporting Online Network Utility System (CRONUS). TU then continued its expansion through acquisitions, using TU common stock in pooling-of-interests transactions. A list of these companies is on page 112.

One of TU's competitors, General American Tank Transportation Company, had acquired a bulk-carrier shipping company, Marine Transport Lines, Inc., in 1970, so TU decided to acquire a shipping company, too. In 1971 TU issued 600,000 shares of its stock in exchange for all of the shares of Central Gulf Lines,

Inc., Mammoth Bulk Carriers and subsidiaries (Central Gulf). The owners of Central Gulf thereby became pro rata owners of TU shares registered on the NYSE and gained liquidity for their shipping company shares. Additionally, the merger was recognized by the IRS as a tax-free exchange and a new, higher basis was attained for their shares without being subject to capital gains tax. The management of Central Gulf remained intact and Central Gulf became a division of TU. Niels W. Johnsen joined the board of TU and, together with Erik F. Johnsen, joined the executive committee of TU. The merger of Central Gulf *et al* with TU closed on December 21, 1971.

The Board of Directors of Central Gulf Lines Inc. and its officers elected after the merger were:

DIRECTORS
Niels W. Johnsen
Erik F. Johnsen
J.W. van Gorkum, Chairman of TransUnion Corporation
W.B. Browder, Vice President of TransUnion Corporation
S.E. Morrison

OFFICERS
Niels W. Johnsen, Chairman of the Board and
    Chief Executive Officer
Erik F. Johnsen, President
S.E. Morrison, Treasurer
William B. Moore of TransUnion, Assistant Secretary
D.A. Kuzmicki of TransUnion, Assistant Secretary

———

Simultaneously with the merger, Niels F. Johnsen, Founding Director, Past President and Past Chairman of CG and its associated companies, retired.
Hugh Evans and J.M. Jones Jr. resigned as directors of Central Gulf.

TU shares had a market value on the closing date of $42.50 per share, making the total market value of Central Gulf at closing $25.5 million in TU stock. The book value of Central Gulf stockholders' equity on June 30,

Year	Business	Principal Activity	# of TU Shares Issued
1973	Midwest Bolt & Supply, Inc.	Distribution of Fasteners	68,992
1972	Vennard & Ellithorpe Ltd.	Sulphur Handling and Conversion	98,750
1971	McKenzie-Ris Mfg. Co.	Manufacture Heat Exchangers	112,000
1970	Environmental Developers, Inc.	Multiple Family Housing Developers	515,000

1971, was about $11 million. The effect of this merger was that Central Gulf stockholders realized an increased market value of their equity without paying capital gains tax until they chose to sell TU stock. At the same time it fulfilled Central Gulf's financial objective of increasing its equity resources by merging with a publicly owned company whose board had the same view for further expansion in ocean shipping. We were therefore in position as the first new investment of the merged companies to contract with Avondale Shipyards Inc. for the construction of two additional U.S.-flag LASH vessels. The price for each vessel was $27,349,000, less 43% Construction Differential Subsidy, or a net price of $15,588,930 for each vessel. The Company used Title XI guarantees to finance the debt of 75% of the cost of these two U.S.-flag LASH vessels when they were delivered from the shipyard in 1975. The TU Board also approved the acquisition of 640 more LASH barges at a price of about $40,000 each, to be ordered from builders to be chosen later.

The merger with TU, followed by the orders for these high-technology new vessels to be built in the United States, advanced the Company's position as a major player in the international ocean transportation industry.

Preparing for Transition from Conventional Breakbulk Ships to LASH

Having reached the point where we had received delivery of two newly built Norwegian-flag LASH vessels and ordered for construction in the United States three U.S.-flag LASH vessels, we were ready to complete disposal of the older breakbulk ships remaining in our fleet. In 1964 we had traded the C-2's *Green Point* and *Green Bay* to the Maritime Administration for two C-4 former troop ships, which were renamed *Green Bay* and *Green Valley*. We sold the C-2 *Green Wave* in July 1966. During most of 1969 we still had in operation under U.S.-flag three jumboized AP-2 Victory ships (*Green Harbour, Green Island* and *Green Valley*), one C-2 (*Green Cove*), one C-3 (*Green Ridge*) and six C-4's (the converted troop ships *Green Bay* and *Green Lake*, and the *Green Port, Green Forest, Green Wave* and *Green Springs*). In November 1969 we sold the jumboized Victories, the *Green Harbour* and *Green Valley*, and in October 1971 we sold the *Green Island*, the last jumboized Victory in our fleet. We had also sold the last C-2, *Green Cove*, in May 1970 along with the *Green Ridge*. This left our fleet in the pre-LASH period with five C-4's, the C-4 *Green Bay* having been destroyed by enemy action in Vietnam in 1971. Our underwriters declared the C-2 *Green Dale* a total loss in June 1968 after it was in a collision. The Company's U.S.-flag fleet then consisted of three newly built LASH vessels upon their delivery from Avondale Shipyards and the remaining five C-4's on time charter to the U.S. Navy.

At the same time our international-flag fleet was growing with the addition of newbuildings.

TRANS UNION INTERNATIONAL SHIPPING GROUP
CORPORATE STRUCTURE, 1972

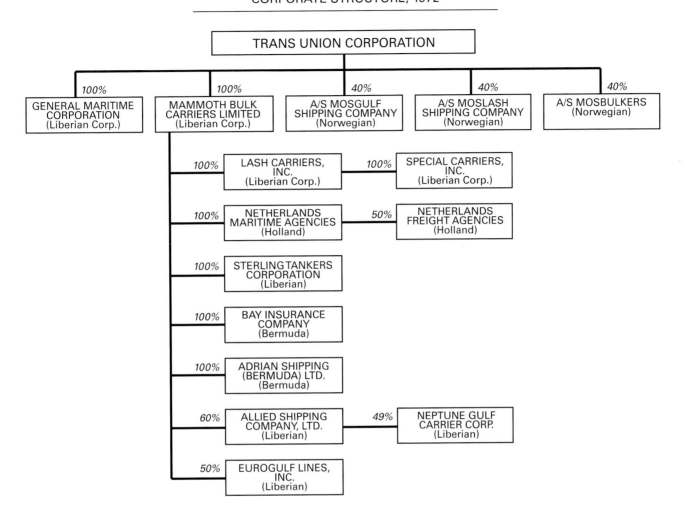

TRANS UNION INTERNATIONAL SHIPPING GROUP, 1972

MAMMOTH BULK CARRIERS LIMITED (MBC),
Monrovia, Liberia

Acts as holding company for other operating companies in the group. Also, will be the owner of "MAMMOTH PINE" and "MAMMOTH FIR", two (2) new about 32,600 TDW Log/Bulk Carriers. Has on order three (3) about 151,727 TDW Tankers from Mitsubishi Heavy Industries, Ltd., Japan (MHI) which will own upon their delivery. Also operates Dry Bulk Carriers and other type vessels on Time Charter as Contract Carrier in connection with cargo contracts concluded from time to time.

ALLIED SHIPPING COMPANY, LTD. (ALLIED),
Monrovia, Liberia

60% owned by MBC/40% by MOSVOLD's Nominees. Bareboat charters vessels from MOSGULF and MOSBULKERS. Owns 49% of Neptune Bulk Carrier Corporation, which is a company organized to operate a new 117,000 TDW Bulk Carrier (to be named "MOSNES") on joint-venture basis with Sumitomo Shoji Kaisha, Ltd., Tokyo (SSK).

EUROGULF LINES, INC. (EUROGULF),
Monrovia, Liberia

Operates Westbound Freight Liner Service from U.K./Continent to U.S. Gulf with LASH (Lighter-Aboard-Ship) vessels "ACADIA FOREST" and "ATLANTIC FOREST". Its 50% partners are Nominees of Continental Lines S.A., Antwerp, Belgium (CONTILINES), General European Agents for the LASH service.

STERLING TANKERS CORPORATION (STERLING),
Monrovia, Liberia

Owns and operates Liberian Motor Tanker "STERLING". This company will be merged completely into MBC in the near future.

GENERAL MARITIME CORPORATION (GMC),
Monrovia, Liberia

This company is now inactive, and its only assets are cash. It is in the process of being merged into MBC so that its cash assets can be reinvested.

LASH CARRIERS, INC., Monrovia, Liberia

Its sole activity is to act as Bareboat Charterer of the Lighter-Aboard-Ship (LASH), M.S. "ATLANTIC FOREST".

SPECIAL CARRIERS, INC., Monrovia, Liberia

Its sole activity is to act as Bareboat Charterer of the Lighter-Aboard-Ship (LASH), M.S. "ACADIA FOREST".

NETHERLANDS MARITIME AGENCIES (NMA), Rotterdam, Netherlands

This company acts as operating agent for the MBC fleet, and also as supervisory agents for the LASH operation in Europe. Its 50% owned subsidiary, Netherlands Freight Agencies (NFA), handles cargo bookings for the Westbound Service of the LASH vessels in conjunction with its 50% partner, CONTILINES, Antwerp, Belgium.

ADRIAN SHIPPING (BERMUDA) LIMITED (ADRIAN), Bermuda

This company acts as managing agents for the MBC fleet. It performs accounting and financial services for the companies in the group. All important transactions of the companies are approved by ADRIAN, and the chief executive officers of MBC and subsidiaries are located in ADRIAN'S Bermuda office. All principal meetings of MBC and subsidiaries are held in the offices of ADRIAN.

BAY INSURANCE COMPANY, Bermuda

This company was established in Bermuda to handle a limited share of the insurance requirements of the TransUnion Ocean Shipping Fleet.

NORWEGIAN OWNING COMPANIES

The following companies act solely as owners of respective vessels and bareboat charter these vessels out to subsidiaries of MBC:

A/S MOSGULF SHIPPING COMPANY, Kristiansand, Norway

Owns Bulk Carriers M.S. "QUEBEC" and M.S. "STRATHEARN".

A/S MOSBULKERS, Kristiansand, Norway

Owns Bulk Carriers M.S. "MOSBAY", M.S. "MOSTENGEN," M.S. "MOSGULF", M.S. "MOSTANGEN", M.S. "MOSFIELD", and M.S. "MOSNES".

A/S MOSLASH, Kristiansand, Norway

Owns M.S. "ACADIA FOREST" AND M.S. "ATLANTIC FOREST", two (2) Lighter Aboard Ships (LASH).

MAMMOTH BULK CARRIERS LIMITED AND
ASSOCIATED COMPANIES FLEET

Vessel/Registry	Year Built	Type	DWT	Speed	Owner	Bareboat Charterers
Sterling (Liberian)	1966	Tanker	57,897	15³/₄	Sterling	N.A.
Quebec (Norwegian)	1965	Bulk Carrier	48,520	15	Mosgulf	Allied
Strathearn (Norwegian)	1967	Bulk Carrier	54,685	16	Mosgulf	Allied
Mosbay (Norwegian)	1967	Bulk Carrier	28,006	15	Mosbulkers	Allied
Mosengen (Norwegian)	1967	Bulk Carrier	28,187	15	Mosbulkers	Allied
Mosgulf (Norwegian)	1967	Bulk Carrier	28,100	15	Mosbulkers	Allied
Mostangen (Norwegian)	1968	Bulk Carrier	28,110	15	Mosbulkers	Allied
Mosfield (Norwegian)	1972	Bulk Carrier	117,804	15	Mosbulkers	Allied
Acadia Forest (Norwegian)	1969	LASH	43,517	19	A/S/Moslash	Special
Atlantic Forest (Norwegian)	1970	LASH	43,517	19	A/S/Moslash	LASH

New Construction

Hull 959, TBN Mosnes (Norwegian)	1973	Bulk Carrier	117,400	14.9	Mosbulkers	Allied
Mammoth Pine, Hull 1040 (Liberian)	1973	Log/Bulk Carrier	32,600	14.8	Mammoth	N.A.
Mammoth Fir, Hull 1060 (Liberian)	1973	Log/Bulk Carrier	32,600	14.8	Mammoth	N.A.
Hull 1056 (Liberian)	1974	Tanker	151,427	15.9	Mammoth	N.A.
Hull 1057 (Liberian)	1975	Tanker	151,427	15.9	Mammoth	N.A.
Hull 1058 (Liberian)	1975	Tanker	151,427	15.9	Mammoth	N.A.

MAMMOTH BULK CARRIERS LIMITED AND ASSOCIATED COMPANIES
LONG-TERM CHARTER PARTIES AND CONTRACTS

Vessel	Charterer	Commencement Date	Duration	Net Monthly Time-Charter Hire
QUEBEC (Bulk Carrier)	Bunge Corp.	April 11, 1967	10 or 15 Consecutive Calendar Years	10 Years - $85,152.60; 15 Years - $85,152.60
STERLING (Tanker)	Shell International Petroleum Co. Ltd.	March 30, 1966	12½ Years	$109,000
MOSBAY (Geared Bulk Carrier)	Sea-Land Service, Inc.	Oct. 1, 1969	5 Calendar Years, option up to 1 additional Calendar Year	$88,500
MOSTANGEN (Geared Bulk Carrier)	Sea-Land Service, Inc.	Aug. 29, 1969	5 Calendar Years, option up to 1 additional Calendar Year	$88,500
MOSENGEN (Geared Bulk Carrier)	Sea-Land Service, Inc.	Oct. 6, 1969		$88,500
MOSGULF (Geared Bulk Carrier)	Sea-Land Service, Inc.	Jan. 19, 1970		$88,500
MOSFIELD (Bulk Carrier)	Yamashita Shinnihon	August 1972	7 Calendar Years	$230,370
Hull No. 959, TBN MOSNES (Bulk Carrier)	Sumitomo Shoji Kaisha, Ltd.	Oct./Dec. 1973	10 Consecutive Years	$293,500
MAMMOTH PINE (Log/Bulk Carrier)	Guaranteed Liberian Nominee of The Sanko Steamship Co., Ltd	June 1973	15 Consecutive Years Bareboat Charter	13 Years - $84,000; Last 2 Years - $67,200
MAMMOTH FIR (Log/Bulk Carrier)	Guaranteed Liberian Nominee of The Sanko Steamship Co., Ltd.	August 1973	15 Consecutive Years Bareboat Charter	13 Years - $84,000; Last 2 Years - $67,200

AFFREIGHTMENT CONTRACTS

Vessel	Charterer	Commencement Date	Duration	Net Monthly Time-Charter Hire
STRATHEARN (Geared Bulk Carrier)	Fertilizantes Fosfatados Mexicanos	Sept. 29, 1969	10 Consecutive Years	$55,357.57
STRATHEARN	Duval Sales Corp.	April 1971	5 Consecutive Contract Yrs, option additional 2 years	$3.60 per 2,240 Lbs. Per Ton Carried
ACADIA FOREST (LASH)	International Navigation, Ltd., Guaranteed by International Paper Co.	Oct. 28, 1969	10 Consecutive Contract Yrs, option additional 5 years	$275,120
ATLANTIC FOREST (LASH)	International Navigation, Ltd., Guaranteed by International Paper Co.	August 1970	10 Consecutive Contract Yrs, option additional 5 years	$275,120

CHAPTER 17

United States Lines in Play—We React

In March 1976 we received a booklet from investment bankers Dillon Reed and Company, New York, presenting details on United States Lines Inc. as a possible acquisition. United States Lines was a successor to International Mercantile Marine, established in 1901 by J.P. Morgan. It was widely known, of course, for its passenger liner *United States,* the flagship of the American Merchant Marine and the largest and fastest liner ever built in the United States for operation under U.S. flag. On her maiden voyage in July 1952 the *United States* captured the Blue Riband from Britain's *Queen Mary,* becoming the first American vessel to hold that title in a century. She crossed the North Atlantic in three days, 10 hours and 42 minutes at an average speed of 35.59 knots. The United States Lines had gradually replaced its war-built ships with new U.S.-built ships operating on subsidized voyages. The fleet by the early 1970's consisted of about 30 ships: eight Mariners, eight Lancers and 14 Challengers. The Mariners, built as breakbulk carriers, had been converted in early 1970 to carry approximately 1,000 TEU of containers. The Lancers, built as container ships between 1968 to 1973, carried 1,200 to 1,300 TEU. The remaining fleet of 14 Challengers were breakbulk ships that had been taken off regular liner service in the late 1960's and early 1970's and chartered to Military Sea Transportation Service.

Late in 1976, United States Lines became leaderless and a target for takeover. Malcom McLean, founder of container ship operator Sea-Land (which he had sold to R.J. Reynolds and Company in 1969), was looking for support from other operators who might be interested to join him in an attempted takeover. McLean had been in discussions with John J. McMullen, a well-known naval architect, but they were not able to get their act together in time. Walter Kidde and Company,

a conglomerate that had grown by acquisitions, launched a hostile takeover bid for 45% of United States Lines stock to ensure control. Kidde had no trouble in quickly accumulating more than 33⅓% of the company's shares by the middle of January 1977. At that point, despite a belated attempt jointly by Matson and U.S. Freight (which owned part of Waterman at that time) to outbid them, Kidde had gained control of United States Lines. While orchestrating this takeover, Kidde ironically had the alliance of John J. McMullen, who was still interested in getting involved with United States Lines.

Within a relatively short time Fred Sullivan, chairman and CEO of Kidde, decided that what he really wanted to do was to resell United States Lines, get a quick capital gain, and leave the business of owning American-flag vessels to others. Kidde made numerous attempts to sell the company, including one to R.J. Reynolds and Company. Because its purchase of U.S. Lines was frustrated by the Justice Department, R.J. Reynolds obtained an agreement from Kidde that Kidde would resell U.S. Lines and from the proceeds make a payment to RJR of $4.5 million. Another attempted sale was to WUI, a subsidiary of Western Union International (no connection to Western Union Telegraph Company). That also failed because WUI could not obtain the necessary financing without what the company considered to be onerous requirements of its bankers and the Maritime Administration. Sullivan continued to look for a buyer. It was then that we received the offering brochure and responded. We knew, of course, that the brochure had also been sent to others including Malcom McLean, who hovered in the background.

In the proposed sale to WUI, according to the lawyers for Kidde, the offering price of about

UNITED STATES LINES, INC
(wholly owned subsidiary of Walter Kidde & Company, Inc.)
AND ITS SUBSIDIARIES

Statement of Income and Deficit (in thousands)

	Year ended December 31, 1976	1975
Terminated Voyage Results:		
Revenue	$342,660	$291,147
Expense	$258,511	222,048
Voyage Results	84,149	69,099
Adjustment of Prior Years' Subsidy	—	3,621
Interest and other income	2,844	3,289
	86,993	76,009
Expenses:		
General and Administrative	40,361	35,718
Provision for Depreciation:		
Vessels	9,383	7,294
Containers, Chassis and Other Equipment	4,913	4,778
Interest	8,743	10,961
Other	1,436	1,928
	64,836	60,679
Income before income taxes	22,157	15,330
Provision for income taxes		
Federal	6,434	4,299
State and foreign	1,012	502
	7,446	4,801
Net Income	14,711	10,529
Deficit at Beginning of Year	(30,844)	(41,373)
Deficit at End of Year	($16,133)	($30,844)

Consolidated Balance Sheet (in thousands)

CURRENT ASSETS

	1976	1975
Cash	$2,959	$3,314
Marketable securities, at cost (approximating market)	34,055	20,128
Traffic and other receivables, less allowance of $1,513 in 1976 and $1,720 in 1975	39,034	34,151
Reimbursable terminal construction cost	125	944
Deferred income tax benefits	366	628
Shipping inventories ashore, at cost	1,963	1,555
Prepaid expenses	2,842	2,530
	81,344	63,250
Less – Estimated deposits to be made in Capital Construction Fund	7,000	3,000
Total current assets	74,344	60,250
Capital Construction Fund		
Cash and Marketable Securities	8,738	9,217
Estimated Deposits to be Made	7,000	3,000
	15,738	12,217
Property and Equipment, at cost		
Vessels, Less Depreciation of $85,446 in 1976 and $79,023 in 1975	157,575	163,957

	1976	1975
Containers and Chassis, Less Depreciation of $27,681 in 1976 and $24,840 in 1975	36,554	36,148
Terminal Property, Less Depreciation of $1,021 in 1976 and $646 in 1975	6,426	6,699
Other Property, Less Depreciation of $1,294 in 1976 and $914 in 1975	1,998	1,830
	202,553	208,634
Other Assets and Deferred Charges		
Insurance and Other Claims Pending	2,165	1,994
Investments	594	100
Deferred Financing Expense and Other Deferred Charges	722	901
Inventories, Deposits and Other Assets	2,584	2,405
	6,065	5,400
Total Assets	$298,700	$286,501

LIABILITIES AND STOCKHOLDERS' EQUITY

	1976	1975
Current Liabilities		
Current Maturities of Long-Term Debt	$7,492	$7,296
Accounts Payable	7,676	8,078
Accrued Voyage Expenses	12,293	10,568
Income Taxes	6,887	2,434
Dividend Payable	1,250	
Other Accrued Liabilities	23,232	24,199
Payable to Walter Kidde & Company, Inc.	1,223	2,264
Total current liabilities	$60,053	$54,839
Unterminated Voyage Revenue Net of Expense	9,861	7,784
Long-term Debt	89,096	100,493
Deferred Income Taxes	6,536	4,869
Other Non-Current Liabilities	20,072	17,868
Payable to Walter Kidde & Company, Inc.	7,085	8,112
Stockholders' Equity:		
Common stock, authorized and outstanding 1,000 shares without par value, at stated value	2,000	2,000
Capital Surplus	120,130	121,380
Deficit	(16,133)	(30,844)
Total Stockholders' Equity	105,997	92,536
Total Liabilities and Stockholders' Equity	$298,700	$286,501

UNITED STATES LINES, INC.
Owned Vessels – Data

	Year originally built/reconstructed	Owner's cost	Net book value	DWT	Cargo capacity
Leader Class					
American Argosy	1953/1970	$9,576	$5,381	15,402	1,0009 TEU's (4)
American Accord	1954/1971	$10,111	$5,864	15,402	1,0009
American Alliance	1954/1970	$9,795	$5,551	15,402	1,0009
American Legacy	1954/1971	$11,388	$6,342	15,402	1,0009
American Leader	1953/1970	$9,910	$5,652	15,402	1,0009
American Legend	1954/1971	$10,143	$5,856	15,402	1,0009
American Ace (1)	1953/1970	$9,727	$5,536	15,402	1,0009
American Archer	1954/1970	$9,780	$5,526	15,402	1,0009
Lancer Class					
American Astronaut	1969	$8,252	$6,821	20,484	1,272 TEU's (4)
American Lancer	1968	$8,836	$7,056	21,198	1,252
American Lark	1969	$9,884	$8,036	20,529	1,272
American Legion	1968	$8,527	$6,851	21,103	1,252
American Liberty	1968	$9,960	$7,946	20,444	1,272
American Lynx	1968	$9,845	$7,939	20,574	1,272
American Apollo	1970	$10,303	$8,804	20,014	1,302
American Aquarius	1971	$10,514	$9,096	20,014	1,302
Challenger Class I's					
American Challenger	1962	$5,510	$3,344	13,563	720,035 Cubic
American Champion	1963	$5,653	$3,508	13,563	720,035 Feet Bulk
American Charger	1962	$5,511	$3,372	13,566	720,035
American Chieftain	1963	$5,569	$3,472	13,578	720,035
American Corsair	1963	$5,221	$3,229	13,578	720,035
American Courier	1963	$5,364	$3,276	13,532	720,035
Pioneer Commander	1963	$5,360	$3,306	13,532	720,035
Pioneer Contender	1963	$5,336	$3,359	13,532	720,035
Pioneer Contractor	1963	$5,351	$3,347	13,532	720,035
Pioneer Crusader	1963	$5,335	$3,381	13,532	720,035
Pioneer Moon	1962	$5,645	$3,404	13,583	720,035
Challenger Class II's					
American Racer	1964	$6,063	$4,057	13,264	758,957 Cubic
American Ranger	1965	$6,062	$4,143	13,183	758,957 Feet Bulk
American Reliance	1965	$6,064	$4,185	13,164	758,957
Feeder Vessels					
American Mist	1972	$2,634	$2,259	2,200	172 TEU's (4)
American Main	1972	$2,634	$2,270	2,200	172
American Ming	1973	$2,635	$2,293	2,200	172
Total		$242,498	$164,463		
Adjustments (2)		482	507		
Total, Including Adjustments		$242,980	$163,957		

$110,750,000 consisted of a fair amount of "soft money" (such as the subordinated notes of United States Lines and United States Lines dividend payments to Kidde of roughly $7 million to $8 million.) The book value of United States Lines Inc. as of December 31, 1976, was about $106 million. U.S. Lines was making a little money. It reported a net income after taxes for 1975 of just over $10 million, and a net income after taxes in 1976, of about $14.7 million.

We reviewed the offering brochure, discussed it internally and conferred with the officers of TransUnion Corporation. We decided that despite its trials and tribulations, the company could have some use to us. We had been accustomed to acquiring two to four ships at a time as newbuildings or as secondhand vessels. For us now to purchase an entire company with its whole fleet at one time was a departure from our usual practice. In October 1976 we submitted an offer to Kidde through our financial advisers, Warburg, Parabas Inc. Our offer totaled $89 million, predicated upon getting 51% of the stock of the company. Kidde would retain 49% but we would have the obligation to redeem the value of Kidde's 49% at $12.25 million and also pay Kidde an option price of $18 million. After we made our proposal, time dragged on. Kidde made no decision. It was obvious from rumors flying around that Kidde was trying to get the best possible price and perhaps using others and us as stalking horses to nail McLean. In September 1977 the word was finally out that McLean was the successful bidder. Our attempt to capture United States Lines, with its fleet of 30 ships and the contracts that went with them, was not successful. We were never overly optimistic about our chances because the decision was a matter over which we had little control. All we could do was decide the price we would pay and that it was the best we were going to do. TransUnion endorsed our position. As it turned out we lost the bid. McLean won it.

After building large new container ships and launching a round-the-world service during a period of intense competition and low rates in the container trades, United States Lines' financial condition soon began to deteriorate. By the end of the first nine months of 1986, the losses reached $236 million. At this rate the company could not continue in business. On November 24, 1986, United States Lines Inc. filed for protection under Chapter 11 of the Bankruptcy Act.

In retrospect, one reason we were interested in acquiring United States Lines was its ownership of 30 recently built U.S.-flag vessels that replaced its war-built ships. We had been disposing of our war-built ships and needed new ships to replace them. We had ordered the three U.S.-flag, U.S.-built LASH ships but needed to do more. We had also built ships abroad for operation under foreign flag but still we saw an advantage in continuing to operate U.S.-flag, U.S.-built ships. United States Lines' fleet of 30 recently-built ships with ODS contracts attracted our attention. There is no hiding the fact that we were also impressed by the prestige of owning a company whose fleet included the flagship of the American Merchant Marine, and that held the transatlantic Blue Riband. We rationalized that with the 14 Challenger vessels chartered to the Navy, we would be able to operate them for some time to come, because the ships were only about 13 to 15 years old. The eight Mariners and eight Lancers could be chartered to a container operator, possibly even Sea-Land. Sea-Land at that time was still operated by R.J. Reynolds and Company. Although R.J. Reynolds was unable to purchase United States Lines, we felt that Sea-Land might charter some of the container ships, if not all of them, and the balance could be used by United States Lines or another U.S.-flag operator for the short term.

It was an interesting exercise, but in the final analysis we were not sorry that we had lost the bid to add United States Lines to our fleet.

CHAPTER 18

LASH—U.S.-Flag Newbuildings and the Fall of Saigon

The three U.S.-flag LASH vessels built for us by Avondale Shipyards in New Orleans were the *Green Valley* (Hull #1952), delivered September 6, 1974; *Green Harbour* (Hull #2257), delivered December 10, 1974; and *Green Island* (Hull #2258), delivered February 25, 1975.

Of the fleet of 640 new LASH barges under construction, enough were completed to provide one ship-load set per vessel so they could be loaded with their first cargoes prior to each mother vessel's delivery. The *Green Valley* on her first voyage carried 89 bargeloads of chemical fertilizer from Donaldsonville, Louisiana, for discharge at Saigon, Vietnam. She then proceeded via Chiba, Japan, and Pusan, South Korea, to pick up some of the LASH barges we had constructed in Japan. (This is a subject that we will cover in Chapter 21.) The

LASH SS *Green Valley* (Hull #1952), first U.S.-flag, U.S.-built LASH for the company, is side-launched at Avondale Shipyards, May 4, 1974. LOA, 893 feet; beam, 100 feet; deadweight, 46,890 long tons; capacity, 89 LASH barges; service speed, 22 knots, 32,000 SHP steam engine.

Mrs. Mary Johnson, wife of William B. Johnson, formerly chairman and chief executive officer of IC Industries, parent of Illinois Central Railroad, officiates at launching of SS *Green Valley* at Avondale Shipyards, New Orleans. From a 16 mm film of the May 4, 1974, side launching.

Green Harbour on her maiden voyage carried a set of 79 bargeloads of chemical fertilizer from St. Rose, Louisiana, to Saigon. She then also proceeded via Chiba to pick up empty barges constructed there. Both ships returned to the U.S. Gulf via Port Kelang in Malaysia to drop off empty barges for future use and then home via the Cape of Good Hope, since the Suez Canal was still closed. The *Green Island* on her first voyage carried 82 barges loaded with government-sponsored food cargo for Bangladesh. She also picked up empty barges constructed at Chiba and returned to the U.S. Gulf via the Panama Canal.

Ms. Karen Klara Johnsen, daughter of Erik F. Johnsen, smashing the traditional magnum of champagne against the bow of SS *Green Harbour*. Avondale President Edwin Hartzman assists the sponsor.

LASH SS *Green Harbour* (Hull #2257), second U.S.-flag, U.S.-built LASH for the company, being side-launched into Mississippi River at Avondale Shipyards, June 20, 1974. Vessel was delivered December 10, 1974. LOA, 893 feet; beam, 100 feet; deadweight, 46,039 long tons; gantry crane capacity, 500 tons; barge capacity, 89 LASH barges; service speed, 22 knots, 32,000 SHP steam turbine engine.

LASH SS *Green Island* (Hull #2258), third U.S.-flag, U.S.-built LASH for the company, is side-launched at Avondale Shipyards, September 28, 1974. LOA, 893 feet; beam, 100 feet; deadweight, 46,039 long tons; capacity, 89 LASH barges; service speed, 22 knots, 32,000 SHP steam engine.

Principals at launching of LASH SS *Green Island* at Avondale Shipyards. From left: Edwin Hartzman, president, Avondale Shipyards; Erik F. Johnsen; Robert W. Reneker, chairman of the board, Esmark, Inc., and director, TransUnion Corporation; Mrs. Robert W. Reneker, sponsor; Niels W. Johnsen; Robert Blackwell, U.S. maritime administrator, Senator J. Bennett Johnston, D-La.

Mrs. Robert W. Reneker smashing the champagne bottle on the hull of LASH SS *Green Island* on September 28, 1974, to officially launch the vessel. Avondale Shipyards President Edwin Hartzman assists.

Unloading bagged USAID cargo at Saigon in 1974 from LASH barges that had been towed up the Mekong River, which was too shallow for the LASH mother vessel to navigate. The mother vessel remained at the anchorage 40 miles downstream.

Vietnam Shipping Company

With our new U.S.-flag LASH vessels *Green Valley, Green Harbour,* and *Green Island* now calling at Saigon with shiploads of LASH barges, we were fortunate to have Nguyen van Minh handling the agency for our vessels. Since 1966 he had acted as agent for one or two of our jumboized AP-2's, discharging bagged goods and/or steel at one time or another from all of the C-4 former troop ships on charter to MSC.

A brief description of Minh's background and experience is worth recounting.

In 1948 Minh started working for a French shipping company in Haiphong, North Vietnam. He was associated with this French company through 1955, until the French army was defeated by the forces of Ho Chi Minh. The terms of the Geneva Conference that partitioned Vietnam required all French political and commercial involvement in North Vietnam to cease, so the company for which Nguyen van Minh worked was forced to withdraw from North Vietnam. Vietnamese citizens were given the choice of staying in North Vietnam with the Communists or leaving for South Vietnam. Minh chose to leave and the French company with which he was associated helped him resettle his family in Saigon. He stayed in Haiphong until the last units of the French military left for South Vietnam

aboard the last ship. Minh then joined his family in Saigon and continued to work for the same French shipping company. He was shortly promoted to operations manager, taking the place of a French captain. Minh asked the French company to increase his salary. His request was denied on the basis that the company's activity had been reduced. Minh resigned from the French company and accepted the position of shipping manager with a Danish company, the East Asiatic Company. Because Hugo Hansen had been employed by the East Asiatic Company before joining Central Gulf, it was natural for him to develop a relationship with Minh at EAC Saigon. Minh worked for EAC from late 1955 until April 1975, when the South Vietnamese government collapsed. During the time Minh worked for EAC, he (1) was sent to Copenhagen and other European cities for training; (2) returned to Saigon and enjoyed very pleasant relationships with Vietnamese local officials, mainly port authorities and the Ministry of Economy; (3) was elected secretary general of the Vietnamese Shipping Owners and Agents Association of Vietnam.

When the U.S. military began to be deployed in large numbers in 1965, the port of Saigon (as well as all South Vietnamese outposts) became heavily congested. Because priority had to be given to the vessels carrying military cargo, commercial vessels coming to Saigon would regularly have to wait at least three months at the outside anchorage for a space in the port and in the warehouses to discharge their cargo. Minh's solution was to provide shipowners whom his company represented with lighters he controlled, so their ships could discharge cargo at anchorage and proceed on their voyage. The cargo could be held at less expense in the lighters than aboard the ship. Sometimes the lighters could be docked between larger vessels and discharged if warehouse space was available. If not, the lighters had to wait for dock or warehouse space to receive the cargo, causing the shipping company to suffer heavy lighterage surcharges (demurrage). For this, Minh had a further solution.

He established a system under which his staff would contact every consignee personally to tell them when they could expect the cargo to be delivered. Once the cargo had been discharged into the lighters, he would ask for special authority from Customs to discharge the

SS *Green Island* loaded with LASH barges approaching anchorage area at entrance to river at Saigon, 1974.

cargo from the lighters onto the river bank without waiting for a dock to discharge. He asked the consignees to pick up the cargo there, directly from his lighters. The consignees were happy to receive their cargo sooner and not suffer the risk of loss from pilferage, sinking of lighters, rain or heat, etc. Minh saved plenty of money for his principals. That is one of the reasons Hugo Hansen approached Minh in 1966/1967 to ask if East Asiatic Company could take over the agency of Central Gulf Lines. Minh submitted Hugo Hansen's request to East Asiatic Company's head office in Copenhagen. The Danes at that time had adopted a policy of staying neutral in the war between the American forces and the North Vietnamese. Therefore East Asiatic Company was reluctant to get involved in American shipping, particularly American ships carrying U.S. military cargo. East Asiatic Company would not

allow Minh to accept the agency of Central Gulf Lines on its behalf. Hugo Hansen then suggested that Minh leave EAC and go to work for Central Gulf Lines. Minh replied that since he had been working for East Asiatic Company for so many years and wanted to stay loyal to that company, he did not want to leave their employ. However, Minh was willing to set up an agency, subject to EAC's approval, to handle Central Gulf Lines' business in Vietnam. Hugo agreed, so Minh asked EAC for permission to set up such an agency under his name to handle Central Gulf Lines' ships. They agreed, provided he also continued to attend to East Asiatic Company business. So Minh set up his own agency. It was very hard in the beginning, because the Vietnamese government required a $50,000 deposit as a guarantee for the repatriation of foreign currency to pay for the disbursement account as well as any cargo claims that the local receivers might have against his new company. One of Minh's friends offered to provide the necessary funds but asked for control of the company. Minh refused the money on those conditions. He would be responsible for all of the new company's affairs, so he wanted to be the major shareholder and in control. They had to accept that. So Minh controlled 60% of the new company and his friends had 40%. Minh set up Vietnam Shipping Company and started handling Central Gulf Lines' vessels.

The first of Central Gulf Lines' new U.S.-flag LASH ships to arrive at Saigon was the *Green Valley* on her maiden voyage in October 1974 with 81 LASH barges on board loaded with U.S. Agency for International Development (USAID) cargo of bagged fertilizer. Minh had already prepared the way for this vessel to unload her barges following the procedure he had adopted using the port's own lighters and the practice he was using when PFEL's LASH vessels called at Saigon. The *Green Valley* came into the Saigon River as far as Vung Tau, about 13 miles upriver from the sea buoy. There she anchored and began offloading the 81 LASH barges. The barges were promptly towed 40 miles further upriver to Saigon. If a suitable dock was available near warehouse space, the barges were placed there. Alternatively, they could be fleeted at buoys in the river to await discharge. The *Green Valley* off-loaded all her barges in less than 48 hours and proceeded on her voyage. She made other calls in the Far East and, to facilitate reuse of the LASH barges, returned to Vung Tau twice to pick up empty LASH barges that had been unloaded in the intervening month and a half. She brought some of the empties back to the U.S. Gulf and delivered others to Malaysia (Port Kelang) for future loading of inbound natural rubber cargoes. The operation at Saigon worked just as Minh had planned. The port authorities were elated that the introduction of the LASH system solved the congestion problem at Saigon.

The new U.S.-flag LASH ship *Green Harbour* arrived at Vung Tau on her maiden voyage in mid-January 1975. She carried 79 barges of USAID shipments of bagged chemical fertilizers, slightly less than a full load. The *Green Harbour* was also able to off-load her LASH barges in just over 48 hours. They were towed upriver to Saigon, releasing the *Green Harbour* to proceed on

her voyage. On voyage two, the *Green Valley* loaded another cargo for Saigon, where she arrived on February 22, 1975. She carried 81 LASH barges of USAID cargo, which she offloaded in 7½ days. After suffering some delay at Vung Tau, she sailed to Singapore and Port Kelang to pick up 54 LASH barges of natural rubber for U.S. Atlantic and Gulf ports.

The *Green Harbour* also loaded another cargo of USAID bagged chemical fertilizer for Saigon in 87 LASH barges. By the time she was scheduled to arrive in Saigon, about April 20–22, 1975, the threat of the Viet Cong entrance into Saigon was imminent. USAID elected to have us deliver their cargo to the nearest safe port. We chose Singapore, where she arrived on April 24, 1975.

Meantime, at the request of the U.S. forces, Minh had kept 16 LASH barges at Saigon into which the American Embassy was coordinating the delivery of various documents, personal effects and other items in anticipation of the total withdrawal of American personnel from South Vietnam. Minh had loaded 12 of the 16 LASH barges when the American Embassy and American logistics personnel ordered him to move all 16 barges out for departure with whatever was on board. At the same time, the *last* ship in the port of Saigon was our U.S.-flag C-4 *Green Wave*. She was also being held to take out of Saigon whatever last-minute items the U.S. government wanted to preserve. Minh had already sent his wife and six children out by air on April 21, on one of the last flights from Saigon. Minh assured his wife he would catch up to her. He was determined to remain until all 16 LASH barges were safely loaded onto a LASH mother vessel.

The Fall of Saigon

Minh had $10,000 in cash. He gave $5,000 to his wife when she left and kept $5,000 himself. He was forced to abandon his house, a collection of gold bullion pieces, and his Mercedes car parked on the street. He moved into the American Embassy compound. He used an official government car. He contacted New Orleans to inquire if Central Gulf had a ship in the vicinity to pick up 16 LASH barges. Fortuitously, the *Green Harbour* had arrived in Singapore on April 24, 1975, to deliver

Nguyen van Minh, center, on tug enroute from Vung Tau to Pagoda Point near entrance to Saigon River to meet one of the Company's ships with inbound cargo on June 23, 1973. At left: Captain D. T. Huy, harbor master, Vung Tau. Right: Major V. L. Trinh, deputy port director. Front right: son of Captain Huy.

barges of fertilizer originally intended for Saigon but now delivered at Singapore. She was only a day and a half away. We agreed to send her to Vung Tau to pick up the 16 barges. By this time, April 24, the port of Saigon was virtually empty. The only ship remaining was our *Green Wave* and the 16 LASH barges. Not only had all oceangoing ships departed but also all commercial tugboats were gone. Minh was able to obtain the services of two remaining tugboats owned by the U.S. Navy. These tugs had already gone downstream to the entrance of the river with a number of Vietnamese on board intending to leave the country. The Navy agreed to order the tugs back so they could tow the LASH barges to Vung Tau. Minh also arranged for whatever labor remained in the area to assist, and the two Navy boats towed the 16 barges (with each boat towing eight barges) from Saigon to Vung Tau to meet the *Green Harbour* on April 28.

Minh was preparing to go to Vung Tau to supervise the loading of the barges on the mother vessel. After supervising lifting and securing the barges on the *Green Harbour,* Minh intended to return to Saigon to join the *Green Wave.* Minh had earlier requested that Captain Weems of the *Green Wave* obtain permission from Central Gulf's home office for him to leave Saigon on his vessel. He expected the affirmative reply to come by radiotelephone. All written messages sent by teletype came into Saigon through the Vietnam Post Office and were monitored by the Vietnamese army. If the army had seen the message, Minh would have been subject to arrest. Unfortunately the staff in New Orleans was not aware of this. So when the permission arrived at the Post Office, Minh's only choice was to officially state he was staying in Saigon. Despite having responded to the teletype message from New Orleans by declining their invitation to leave on the *Green Wave,* Minh privately had an understanding with Captain Weems that he would go with them when they sailed, after the *Green Harbour* operation was completed. On the morning of April 26, as Minh was driving to his office on the docks with a U.S. government car, preparing to go to Vung Tau by Army helicopter, he saw the *Green Wave* in the middle of the river sailing downstream. His expected means of escape had sailed! When he got to his office, he called the captain by pilot walkie-talkie.

"Why have you left without me?" Minh asked.

"MSC (Military Sealift Command) officers came aboard at 4 a.m. today and ordered me to leave as soon as possible," the captain replied. "I said I should wait for Minh. They replied, 'I must leave. They will take care of Minh.'"

Minh had a sinking sensation and was on the verge of panic. He nevertheless was determined to evacuate the 16 LASH barges. He packed a small bag with $5,000 and over one million piastres (Vietnamese currency worth about $1,000), a tape recorder and walkie-talkie, the key to his Mercedes, and a handgun. The money was to pay bribes if his future movements were challenged; the pistol if the bribes were not effective.

The 16 barges had been safely towed to Vung Tau on April 27. The *Green Harbour* came as close to Vung Tau as she could safely maneuver without violating her war-risk insurance coverage. Minh arrived early the morning of April 28 by U.S. Air Force helicopter. Minh asked the helicopter pilot to land him on the shore at Vung Tau so he could go aboard the towboat to supervise the loading operation. The pilot refused. His orders were to stay aloft as Minh relayed instructions via walkie-talkie to the loading crew while the pilot maneuvered the helicopter as it hovered above the *Green Harbour.* There would be no landing on the ship either. Minh stayed aloft on the helicopter while the loading operation, with the ship's crew manning the LASH crane, took eight hours. A small local tug available at Vung Tau shifted the barges to the stern of the *Green Harbour*. Minh arranged with Captain Daronja of the *Green Harbour* to take with him Captain Huy, Vietnam Harbormaster at Vung Tau, together with his wife and two children, plus several other people from Minh's office. The *Green Harbour* sailed from Vung Tau April 28, 1975. Mission accomplished.

The pilot of the helicopter had orders to take Minh to the CIA airport at Saigon. When they arrived, Minh contacted the American officer in charge, who told him a C-141 cargo plane was waiting for him on the tarmac. Minh then handed over his pistol to the officer. The ground crew had already removed the ramp stairs from the aircraft, but the plane crew lowered a rope and told Minh to climb up to get aboard. He was still young and agile, so he clambered up the rope. Once aboard, the captain of the aircraft asked him to identify himself and state whether he spoke Vietnamese. He responded affirmatively. The pilot then told Minh to go to the rear of the aircraft and tell the passengers that it was absolutely essential for everyone to remain seated during the taxiing and takeoff. The runway had been pockmarked by enemy rockets, and the takeoff was to be risky and uncomfortable. When Minh opened the door to the rear section, he saw about 500 refugees sitting on the netting on the floor in the cargo bay. He relayed the pilot's warning: if the plane moves back and forth, you should not panic and move, otherwise we will all go down together. As the plane started to take off, two gunmen were stationed at the open cabin doors with hand-held heat-seeking flares to shoot down rockets that might be fired from the ground. The takeoff was risky and uncomfortable, as predicted, but they made it. Two days later on April 30, 1975, the Viet Cong entered the Imperial Palace in Saigon, and South Vietnam fell to the Communists.

After the plane was airborne, Minh learned that they were going to Guam, where some 70,000 Vietnamese refugees were being held temporarily. Minh assumed he would find his wife and children there. After going through the tedious process of registering, he was given a blanket and found a place to put his head down. Upon awakening at daybreak Minh was delighted to see his wife's face looking down at him. His wife and children were safe and they were all together again. They were alive, although they had been forced to abandon practically all of their worldly possessions.

The process of being released from refugee camps proceeded slowly. After about 14 days in Guam with all the other refugees, Minh and his family were transferred to Camp Pendleton in California. There the process continued. Through Hugo Hansen, Minh was assisted by Erik F. Johnsen, who secured the support of the Louisiana congressional delegation in expediting the admission of Minh and his family into the United States. Erik had also agreed to give Minh a job in our New Orleans office and helped him find a place to live. When Minh was ready to leave Camp Pendleton he discovered that the airfare was prohibitive, so he bought a secondhand station wagon. The family piled in, and they drove from California to Wilmington, Delaware, where one of his daughters was living. She had earlier come to the United States to study at the Massachusetts Institute of Technology. After Minh knew he had a job in our New Orleans office, he left Wilmington with his family for his new home in New Orleans, where he began working on July 27, 1975.

Central Gulf sent an invoice to the U.S. government in the amount of $1 million for the freight on the cargo carried in the 16 LASH barges from Saigon to Norfolk. The government refused to pay because there had been no signed contract covering carriage of the cargo. Central Gulf sued. At the trial in New Orleans, Minh testified. The judge asked Minh why there was no contract. He replied: "Your Honor, if the enemy was just across the river from New Orleans and you were forced to sail before the enemy captured your ship and vital cargo, do you stop to prepare a contract? Don't you act with all deliberate speed to depart and assume the owners of the cargo will pay for the transportation?" The court ordered the government to pay the freight invoice as presented, except that the government could deduct $60,000, the cost of using the Navy tug.

CHAPTER 19

LASH—Bareboat Charters to Waterman

In June 1975, after the end of the Vietnam war and the reopening of the Suez Canal, we were able to deploy our U.S.-flag LASH system, consisting of three mother vessels and associated LASH barges and feeder vessels, to the service for which they were intended. We aggressively marketed this service as a technological innovation to our established breakbulk liner service on its eastbound legs from U.S. Gulf and Atlantic ports to the Mediterranean/Red Sea/Persian Gulf and South Asia (Trade Routes 18 and 17). At the same time, we contacted Goodyear Tire and Rubber Company, as well as certain other shippers of westbound cargoes including natural rubber from Indonesia and Malaysia, to line up return cargoes. Having decided to forgo Operating Differential Subsidy for Central Gulf, we operated the LASH ships in these trade routes and for a short time on the triangular voyages via North Europe and Jeddah unsubsidized until 1980. Because Waterman Steamship Corporation had an operating subsidy contract for these trade routes, had room for additional sailings, and was interested in adding our ships to their service, we found it advantageous to open discussions with them. These led to an agreement, subject to the Maritime Administration approval, to bareboat-charter our three U.S.-flag LASH mother vessels, 450 LASH barges and six float-on/float-off LASH feeder vessels to Waterman for 12 years. On March 27, 1980, Marad granted Waterman the authority to include these ships and barges in Waterman's existing Operating Differential Subsidy contract. From our side, we achieved the same financial result by bareboat-chartering this fleet to Waterman as we would have operating it ourselves had we chosen to accept operating subsidy. Unfortunately, after about three and a half years into the bareboat charters, Waterman encountered financial problems related to its other business and was

compelled to declare bankruptcy in December 1983. In order to retrieve our LASH ships, barges and other assets, we petitioned the bankruptcy court for permission to terminate the bareboat charters. Of our three LASH mother vessels, Waterman had subchartered one, the *Green Island,* unsubsidized for about five years to the Military Sealift Command. This was one of the more positive developments of the Waterman bareboat charters. It demonstrated another unique feature of the LASH system—its military usefulness. The Defense Department was "sold" on the idea that LASH mother vessels could be used as floating armories. A LASH

LASH barge loading packaged natural rubber at shallow-draft Indonesian port before being floated on board *FLASH I* for towing to Singapore and lifting on board LASH mother vessel.

ship's 89 barges could be loaded with military supplies, stationed in this fully loaded condition at advanced places near potential hot spots, then moved to the nearest point for delivery of the barges and their contents—if necessary, over a beach or up shallow waterways. In the *Green Island*'s case, she was stationed at the Indian Ocean island of Diego Garcia, a British colony. We agreed to maintain this charter when we took the ship back from the bankruptcy court. The Military Sealift Command was interested in similar charters. By mid-1985 we were successful in chartering the *Green Valley* and the *Green Harbour* to MSC for 18 months pending their re-entry into liner service. In the meantime, our LASH vessels became important participants in Desert Shield/Desert Storm when the U.S. military took action in Iraq in 1991.

LASH—Natural Rubber Trade

Reflecting Goodyear's opinion of our LASH system, we recently received the following report from James N. Walsh, a Goodyear officer at the time we were active in the Trade Route 18 service of carrying natural rubber from Southeast Asia to the U.S. The report highlights the benefits of the LASH system to shippers of natural rubber.

In the early 1970's the natural rubber delivery system to the United States of America was very much different than what takes place today. The majority of consumers depended upon USA natural rubber dealers to sell them basis FOB USA port (normally New York or New Orleans), point being the dealers were the selectors of a great deal of the ocean carriage of natural rubber, most often with the ultimate buyer not knowing or not caring what carrier brought the natural rubber to the USA. To a great degree this process did not always encourage service improvement, because the dealers for the most part were only chasing rates. Some of the major USA manufacturers did in fact book ocean freight for some tonnage, but this side of the business, led by Goodyear, was to steadily increase as more and more direct buying (meaning bypassing the New York dealers) was taking place.

At the time Central Gulf arrived on the scene, the natural rubber shipping situation was a concern for the USA dealers and consumers. Breakbulk rates and services were erratic and containers overpriced, with limited access to natural rubber points of origin.

To address this situation the industry, led by members of the Rubber Manufacturers of America and the Rubber Trade Association of New York formed the non-profit, incorporated Natural Rubber Shippers Association. The objective was to secure reliable, ongoing, volume natural rubber ocean-carriage service contracts, at reasonable rates. At the outset there were mixed views as to how successful and effective this effort would be. The New York dealers were somewhat reluctant to participate, and had to be "urged," if you will, by a few major manufacturers to join NRSA. In my opinion, NRSA served its purpose, consequently becoming a very effective strategy factor in regards to putting the LASH service in place and thus providing the industry physical carrier characteristics that would make a positive impact on natural rubber shipping.

At the time LASH (Central Gulf Lines) entered the scene much natural rubber was still presented for shipment in 224- or 250-lb. bales. However, thirty 75 lb. bales placed in a six-sided wooden crate were coming into the market in larger volume. In turn Goodyear was experimenting with shrink-wrapped natural rubber to replace the fully crated package, the object with this type packaging being to reduce the contamination factor brought on by use of wooden crates.

Due to the nature of most Indonesia ports in Sumatra, much of the natural rubber from that country was being transshipped to Singapore for shipment from there. Obviously, this involved coastal shipping, and the many handlings involved oftentimes resulted in serious damage and additional expense. In turn, because of this situation, natural rubber processors located in Djambi, Sumatra, and other Indonesian outports were not on the same competitive level as those natural rubber processors who could ship direct FOB Belawan.

The introduction of the LASH system helped make major changes in the natural rubber world as related to the USA. LASH offered a whole new positive benefit to those who really understood the total natural rubber scene, from tree to factory.

To relate the advantages of LASH, I have to tell the story from the point of view of our Goodyear natural rubber supply group. First off, we had to encourage members of the NRSA, both dealers and other consumers, to use LASH. This was necessary in order to generate sufficient volume tonnage for each LASH sailing. This was accomplished by way of Goodyear making a direct con-

U.S.-flag LASH SS *Sam Houston* in Waterman homebound service from Malaysia and Indonesia to U.S. Atlantic and Gulf ports with capacity load of 89 LASH barges filled with natural rubber.

tract for LASH and then also participating in having the NRSA make a volume contract as well, which we also supported in various ways.

Prior to LASH we had surveyed the Djambi area, which was a major natural rubber production center but was handicapped by having to transship. We knew there was great potential in Djambi for quality upgrading—better factory housekeeping, introduction of shrink-wrap packaging and long-term natural rubber contracts. The key would be LASH, which would give natural rubber suppliers in Djambi the advantage of becoming an FOB port. The result of all this made a very significant contribution to our operation.

Seemingly, nothing worthwhile that represents significant positive change comes easy. In the case of Djambi there developed early on physical and political problems that had to be solved. The first attempt to bring barges into Djambi was denied because of a lack of "permits." Everyone played a part in solving that preposterous situation. I am sure people at Central Gulf will remember the

"at the coastal hook" arrangement put together to temporarily and monetarily solve the Djambi barge no entry dilemma. I'm sure my friend, Mr. Shahani, will. Manik Shahani was Operating Vice President of Central Gulf, formerly stationed in its Bombay office. In turn a barge-loading platform had to be anchored in the middle of the Batang Hari River. Then, too, not to be outdone by Singapore, Indonesia "set up" a "Port Authority in Djambi"! Eventually LASH also served the outport of Pontianak, Kalimantan, Indonesia, also a transshipment port, and other Indonesian locations.

There was a slight interruption in LASH service around 1980. The service was restored by way of Waterman Steamship Corporation entering the natural rubber business (after the Company bought Waterman when it came out of bankruptcy). While the activity described in Indonesia was taking place, Goodyear was also developing sources in Thailand, the prime reason being to try to secure more uniform rubber in large volume. However, Thailand also was a transshipment country in terms of shipping natural rubber to the USA. Initially the LASH service could not, due to draft limits, call directly at the East Coast Thailand Port of Songkala, nor the West Coast Port of Phuket, in terms of direct loading from pier to barge. The natural rubber had to be moved via water to the barge at anchor. However, this was solved by way of Goodyear and Teck Bee Hang determining that the river port of Kantang could offer a deep enough draft to provide direct pier-to-barge loading facilities. With this in place, large tonnage of Thailand natural rubber destined for Goodyear moved on barges from Kantang.

To be sure, LASH had problems. The large tonnage normally on board a given mother vessel was risky market-wise and supply continuity-wise when something happened to a vessel causing sometimes considerable delay. Needless to say this did happen from time to time. Also schedules were not, oftentimes, as advertised.

Toward the end of my time at Goodyear, with a lot of unknowledgeable people coming on the scene and a poor analytical process in place, the notion evolved that Waterman's LASH operation should and would be phased out, and containers used in place of LASH and other break-bulk carriers. Also at that time we (Goodyear) were deluged with container presentations, given by people who had never traveled beyond Chicago, expressing the glories of the container movement of natural rubber. Most of what was presented was sophistry or outright baloney, but I evidently was the only one who felt that way.

Waterman was then told in late Fall 1991 that their traffic would be considerably cut back, and replaced with containers. The short of it is LASH barge traffic was cut back until the container carriers, some months later, told Goodyear the rates were going up substantially. This made the LASH system look very good again, and Waterman once again obtained considerable tonnage from Goodyear and others.

In addition to the positive aspects provided by LASH as outlined above, LASH also helped Goodyear introduce metal box packaging in the late 1980's and into the 1990's. Another benefit was being able to go from a 30-bale package to a 36-bale package, which is a common size today.

Despite the proponents of Six Sigma nothing is ever perfect, but basically the LASH system was a blessing for the USA natural rubber consumer for many years.

CHAPTER 20

LASH—Introducing Feeder Vessels

As the Company continued to grow and establish its position in the trade between the U.S. Gulf and South Asia, and with the forthcoming introduction of our U.S.-flag LASH service, we decided to order six special-purpose vessels to act as feeders that would carry LASH barges. We placed orders with Sumitomo Shipyard in Oppama, Japan, for two self-propelled units, each capable of carrying 18 LASH barges in a float-on, float-off configuration. These "SPLASH" vessels were the *Mammoth Oak*, christened by Dolly Ann Johnsen, wife of Erik F. Johnson, president of the company, and delivered on March 30, 1978, and the *Mammoth Willow*, delivered May 12, 1978. Also included in the feeder vessels were one non-engined unit for 15 LASH barges (the *Mammoth Spruce*, delivered in December 1978) and three non-engined units, *Flash I, II* and *III*, that could carry eight barges each. An engine later was installed in the *Mammoth Spruce* to make her self-propelled.

The semi-submersible vessels were designed so that the LASH barges, which had a draft of nine feet, could be floated onto the main deck of the vessel through an open stern gate. After all LASH barges were safely aboard, the feeder vessel would use its pumping system to return to normal operating drafts. The semi-submersible process would be repeated at the discharging port. We used these units as feeder vessels for several voyages to enhance the efficiency of our LASH mother vessels on the service between U.S. Gulf and Atlantic ports and South Asia. Later, we also took advantage of opportunities to provide special services carrying cargoes for which only vessels of this size and configuration were suited. For example, we had one voyage in which the *Willow* carried two Nile River floatels from the port of Aalesund, Norway, where they were constructed, to Alexandria, Egypt. Later, both the *Oak* and the *Willow* were involved in a series of voyages carrying large-diameter pipe from North Europe to Italy, the

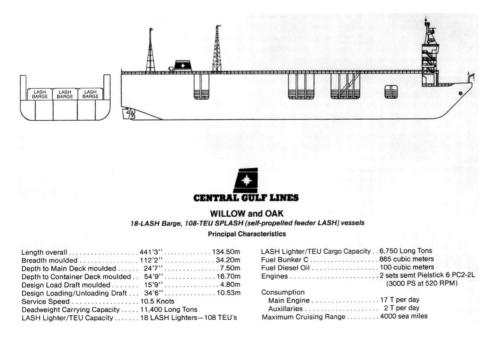

CENTRAL GULF LINES

WILLOW and OAK
18-LASH Barge, 108-TEU SPLASH (self-propelled feeder LASH) vessels
Principal Characteristics

Length overall . . . . 441'3" 134.50m	LASH Lighter/TEU Cargo Capacity . . 6,750 Long Tons	
Breadth moulded . . . . 112'2" 34.20m	Fuel Bunker C . . . . 865 cubic meters	
Depth to Main Deck moulded . . . . . . 24'7" 7.50m	Fuel Diesel Oil . . . . 100 cubic meters	
Depth to Container Deck moulded . . 54'9" 16.70m	Engines . . . . 2 sets semt Pielstick 6 PC2-2L	
Design Load Draft moulded . . . . 15'9" 4.80m	(3000 PS at 520 RPM)	
Design Loading/Unloading Draft . . . 34'6" 10.53m	Consumption	
Service Speed . . . . 10.5 Knots	Main Engine . . . . 17 T per day	
Deadweight Carrying Capacity . . . . . 11,400 Long Tons	Auxiliaries . . . . 2 T per day	
LASH Lighter/TEU Capacity . . . . 18 LASH Lighters—108 TEU's	Maximum Cruising Range . . . . 4000 sea miles	

Outline of particulars of SPLASH vessels *Mammoth Oak* and *Mammoth Willow*.

MV *Mammoth Oak* in March 1978 on sea trials off Japan prior to entering service shuttling LASH barges from shallow-draft ports to LASH SS *Green Harbour* and sister ships. LASH barge capacity, 18; total deadweight capacity, 11,400 metric tons; LOA, 134.5 meters (441' 3¼"); beam, 34.2 meters (112' 2½"); draft loaded, 4.8 m (15' 9"); speed, 10.3 knots on 19.8 metric tons HVF.

MV *Mammoth Oak* displaying her versatility to handle oversized cargo such as large-diameter steel pipe between North Europe and Italy and the Middle East.

Red Sea and Persian Gulf. Thereafter, we took the opportunity to employ these 18-barge-capacity units to carry LASH bargeloads of steel and other cargo from Japan to the Persian Gulf. Each ship could handle approximately 9,000 weight tons of cargo stowed in LASH barges.

Because the market to ship semifinished steel and other cargo from Japan to the Persian Gulf, mainly Iran, was strong in the late 1970's and early 1980's, it was quite profitable to use these vessels in this service. Our agent in Hong Kong, Herman Chen, booked some of this cargo. Mr. Chen's company collected the freight on the cargo he booked. He was supposed to remit these monies to our New Orleans office. Instead, it was discovered that Mr. Chen was submitting to our New Orleans accounting office "credit memos" for the freight revenue he had collected and deposited in his

Dolly Ann Johnsen, wife of Erik F. Johnsen, cuts ribbon to release festive streamers and balloons at MV *Mammoth Oak* naming ceremony on March 30, 1978, at Uraga Shipyard, Japan.

own bank account. After two or three months of not receiving money in lieu of the "credit memos," our treasurer, Stanley Morrison, hopped on a plane to Hong Kong. Purpose of mission: Find Mr. Chen and the roughly $600,000 in freight revenue that he owed the Company. When Morrison got to Hong Kong, he discovered that Chen had closed his office and was nowhere to be found. He was not in Hong Kong and no one knew where to look for him. To this day, Chen is still amongst the missing and perhaps enjoying a comfortable retirement at some luxurious spa in "Shangri La." The Company had to take the loss, which could not be recovered from any other source.

We thereafter terminated this service, making the *Mammoth Oak* and *Mammoth Willow* surplus to our operations. Enter the Mainland Chinese. They knew about these ships and, we later learned, needed them to carry oversized cargo from China to the Persian Gulf. They contacted us through a sale-and-purchase broker and offered to purchase both the *Mammoth Oak* and the *Mammoth Willow*. We sold both vessels to the Chinese and delivered them to these buyers in May and June 1983. The sale produced a total capital gain of $2.981 million for the two vessels. It was a profit that we considered better than could be obtained by continuing to operate the ships for our own account.

Having sold the *Mammoth Oak* and *Mammoth Willow*, the Company was left with the *Mammoth Spruce* and

MV *Mammoth Oak*, partially submerged to receive LASH barges floated aboard.

Aerial view of self-propelled feeder vessel MV *Spruce* with full complement of 15 LASH barges. This was typical of voyages performed between shallow-draft ports in Indonesia and Singapore as well as in the vessel's recent consecutive employment shuttling LASH barges between Rotterdam and the U.K. East Coast and Bremerhaven, Germany, working with the Forest Lines' trans-Atlantic service.

three non-engined feeder barges (*FLASH I, II* and *III*). After the spinoff from TU (to be discussed in Chapter 22) the *Mammoth Spruce* became simply the *Spruce*. When we determined that she could be better utilized elsewhere, we dispatched her to North Europe to act as a feeder ship for the *Acadia Forest* and *Atlantic Forest*. There she continues to improve the efficiency of handling imports and exports to and from Felixstowe, England, and Bremerhaven, Germany. The three non-engined feeder barges remained in Southeast Asia to service shallow-draft ports in Indonesia and elsewhere in that region.

For the operation of the FLASH units in Indonesian waters, special arrangements were required. Erik Johnsen had made several trips to the area without success until he heard of an intermediary in Indonesia. The intermediary turned out to be Bob Hassan, who arranged for us to appoint Karana Line as our agents. The arrangement was for us to pay Karana a special fee to operate our SPLASH vessels, to which we agreed. When that agreement was reached, all problems in Indonesia ceased and we were able to begin using the FLASH units to shuttle LASH barges loaded with natural rubber to Singapore, where they could be picked up by our mother vessels.

MV *Spruce*, self-propelled feeder vessel, with conventional barge being floated aboard loaded with miscellaneous cargo.

CHAPTER 21

International-Flag Newbuildings Continue to Join Our Fleet

Having filled out its LASH ship fleet by adding U.S.-flag newbuildings, the Company returned to its program of expanding its new international-flag bulk-carrier fleet. In June 1970, together with A/S Mosvold, we ordered the first of a series of Cape-size bulk carriers. These ships, as the name implies, were too large to transit the Panama Canal and needed to proceed via the Cape of Good Hope or Cape Horn between the Pacific and Atlantic oceans. We were stimulated to order this type vessel by our early involvement in contracting bulk cargoes of ore and coal from new loading installations in Australia, where emerging mines produced increasing quantities of coal, iron ore and bauxite. Our interest in this business stemmed from our earlier experience with ships carrying coal from Hampton Roads to Japan. It was becoming evident that coal exports from the United States were declining and being replaced from other sources.

The typical trading pattern for Cape-size ships would be to carry bulk coal or bulk iron ore from the Atlantic (loading either Hampton Roads or Brazil) to Japan, and returning to the Atlantic via Australia and the Cape of Good Hope. We signed a contract to build our first Cape-size vessel with Sumitomo on June 17, 1970. The keel for Hull #958 was laid at Uraga, Japan, on February 16, 1972. She was launched on May 12, 1972, with Lillian Knutsen, sister of Martin Mosvold, as her sponsor and named the *Mosfield*. She was delivered from the shipyard on August 31, and went into service carrying coal from Haypoint (a new coal-loading installation in northeast Australia) to Europe.

On December 9, 1970, less than six months after signing the construction contract for Hull #958, the Company signed a contract for her sister ship, Hull #959. She also was a 117,400-DWT bulk carrier, and was owned by A/S Mosbulkers, the joint venture between our Company and Mosvold. The prices for Hull #958 and Hull #959 were $12,415,000 each, delivered at the shipyard. The keel of Hull #959 was laid at Sumitomo on April 19, 1973. The *Mosnes* was launched in July 1973, with Mrs. Frank Naitoh as sponsor, and was delivered by the shipyard in October 1973.

Ordering Additional Ships, Including Tankers

In the fall of 1972 we contracted with Oriental Shipping Corporation, a subsidiary of Sanko Steamship Corporation, a large Japanese contract carrier, to time-charter to them two newbuilding bulk carriers of 32,600 DWT, designated as log/bulk carriers. The charterer employed these ships to carry huge newly harvested logs from the United States and Canadian Northwest to Japan, where the logs would be sent through

Lillian Knutsen, sister of Martin Mosvold, cuts the ribbon to launch the 117,400-DWT newbuilding bulk carrier MV *Mosfield* at Uraga Shipyard, Japan on May 12, 1972.

MV *Mosfield,* 117,400-DWT Cape-size dry-bulk carrier, being launched at Uraga, Japan, May 12, 1972. Vessels of this size were too large-beamed to go through the Panama Canal and had too deep a loaded draft to proceed through the Suez Canal. The ship navigated between the Atlantic and Pacific oceans via the Cape of Good Hope or Cape Horn.

MV *Mosfield* on her trial trip before delivery on August 31, 1972. 117,804 DWT; LOA, 256.04 meters (844.93'); beam, 40.26 meters (132.86'); draft, 16.917 meters (55.83'); 15 knots at 502.5 tons HVF.

sawmills. We received the export license for Hull #1040 in early November 1972 and for Hull #1060 in mid-November 1972. They were built at Kanasashi Ship-building Company in Shimizu, Japan. The price for each ship was 2,050,000,000 Japanese yen, equivalent at that time to $7,298,282. We named Hull #1040 the *Mammoth Pine* when she was delivered in July 1973. We named Hull #1060 the *Mammoth Fir* when she was delivered August 1973. The charterer, Oriental Ship-ping, handled their launching and sponsors. They were owned by Mammoth Bulk Carriers. We financed about 80% of each ship, one with Hambros Bank, London, and the other with Orion Bank, London. The remaining 20% was paid from the Company's cash resources.

While we were acquiring mainly new dry-bulk carriers, we also could not help but note the growing need for the United States to increase its crude oil imports. The considered opinion was that domestic production of U.S. crude oil would become insufficient to meet the growing demand in the United States. In fact, oil industry sources were predicting that imports of crude oil would rise to at least 50% of total daily requirements. One of the areas to which crude oil would be brought in from abroad was the U.S. Gulf, particularly to refineries on the Mississippi River,

where a relatively shallow-draft tanker would be needed. This was before the construction of the Louisiana Offshore Oil Port (LOOP). Because our home office was in New Orleans, we wanted to intro-duce the largest tanker capable of navigating the Missis-sippi River to refineries as far north as Baton Rouge. We discussed this project with Mitsubishi Heavy Industries, one of the major Japanese shipbuilders. MHI was keen to add us to their customer list. They designed a crude oil carrier that could handle 151,400 DWT on the relatively shallow draft of 51 feet. After discussions over several weeks, we received from MHI what we considered to be a favorable price. In early 1973 the tanker freight market was weak. Shipyards were anxious to receive building contracts. Mitsubishi quoted us a firm price of 6,463,000,000 yen, equal at that time to $22,918,500, for each of three tankers of this design, for delivery in September 1974, January 1975 and July 1975. The offer was too attractive to pass up. Even though we had no immediate business for these vessels, we decided to accept the offer for all three tankers to be added to the newbuilding fleet of Mammoth Bulk Carriers Ltd. The Board of Directors of TransUnion approved our decision and we therefore ordered Hulls #1056, 1057, and 1058 from the Mitsubishi Heavy Industries shipyard

Mrs. Blaine J. Yarrington, wife of Amoco official, sponsored MT *Amoco Trinidad,* Hull #1056, at Mitsubishi Shipyard, Kobe, Japan, May 31, 1974.

at Kobe, Japan, at the price and delivery dates aforementioned. Mrs. Blaine J. Yarrington, wife of an Amoco official, sponsored *Amoco Trinidad* (Hull #1056). Hull #1057 was christened the *Amoco Cairo* upon her launching by Mrs. Betty van Gorkum, wife of the chairman of TransUnion. Hull #1058 was christened the *Amoco Tehran.* After terrorists seized the American Embassy in Tehran, however, Amoco changed her name to a more benign designation, *Amoco Whiting.*

Why did we use the name "Amoco" in the tankers' names? Answer: Before the first vessel was delivered in September 1974, we had reached an agreement with an Amoco Oil Company subsidiary, Amoco Ocean Marine Company, to bareboat-charter all three vessels to them for 20 years. The charter rate for the entire charter period was $10,000 per diem "hell or high water" for each vessel, which under a bareboat charter all goes to the bottom line. Each vessel, at a cost of about $23 million, would generate $73 million net income over the 20 years. However as part of the deal,

MT *Amoco Trinidad* slips down the way at Mitsubishi Shipyard, Kobe, Japan.

MT *Amoco Trinidad* on trial trip in September 1974 prior to delivery on bareboat charter to Amoco Ocean Marine Company. 151,427 DWT; LOA, 280.02 meters (924.06'); beam, 53.65 meters (177.05'); draft, 15.139 meters (49.96'); 15 knots at 291 tons HVF.

we also granted Amoco the option to purchase Hull #1058 for $35 million if they exercised the option before delivery from the shipyard. The *Amoco Cairo* and *Amoco Trinidad* were delivered new as scheduled and went on charter to Amoco. Amoco exercised the option to purchase the third ship before delivery and paid us $35 million cash. The annual bareboat-charter hire on the *Amoco Cairo* was $3,650,000. The annual level (mortgage) payments of principal and interest on her loan were $2,298,836, leaving a net annual profit of $1,351,163 or a profit over 20 years of $27,023,269. The *Amoco Trinidad* profit over 20 years, calculated on the same basis, was $25,018,794. That made a total for the two ships of $52,042,064, to which we added a profit on the sale of Hull #1058 of $13 million ($35 million, less delivered cost of $22 million), for a total profit of $65,042,064 for the three ships. Our bold decision to order these tankers even before arranging employment was rewarded.

After Mammoth took delivery of the two tankers, we formed MBC Tankers, Inc. in February 1975. As a wholly owned U.S.-citizen subsidiary of Central Gulf, MBC Tankers Inc. complied with the financing policy of Teacher's Insurance and Annuity Association to invest only in U.S.-citizen entities. MBC Tankers Inc. therefore issued its 10% secured notes due October 1, 1994, and July 1, 1994, to TIAA for a total investment of $42 million. Mammoth supported these notes by issuing its notes in the same amount and form to MBC Tankers, Inc. This complicated mechanism allowed Central Gulf to finance 100% of the cost of both ships and TIAA to invest its funds at a favorable interest rate for 20 years, the life of the bareboat charters.

On March 16, 1978, Mammoth added another tanker to its fleet. It purchased from Sanko Steamship Company, Tokyo, the *Euroasia Monarch,* an 89,464 liquid-tons-deadweight oil tanker, and changed its name to the *Mammoth Monarch.* Sanko bareboat-chartered her

MT *Amoco Cairo* sponsor Betty van Gorkum, wife of Jerome van Gorkum, chairman of TransUnion Corporation with president of Mitsubishi Heavy Industries shipyard, at launching ceremony September 14, 1974.

At dinner party celebrating launching of MT *Amoco Cairo,* Jerome and Betty van Gorkum, with Niels W. Johnsen, admire gifts to sponsor.

MV *Hemlock,* ready for floating out of building dock, with assembled owners and shipbuilders, July 15, 1976.

MV *Hemlock* delivery celebration July 15, 1976. Seated: Erik F. Johnsen; Anne Johnsen Bailey, sponsor; Edie Lee Johnsen (Mrs. Erik F. Johnsen), the president of Sumitomo Shipyard, and Japanese performers. Standing: Erik L. Johnsen and Karen Johnsen Baldwin.

Japanese entertainment at MV *Hemlock* launching celebration.

back for 10 years. In May 1978, Neotank Carriers Ltd., a TransUnion subsidiary, took over ownership of the *Mammoth Monarch* and the bareboat charter from Mammoth Bulk Carriers and paid the contract price of $18 million.

At this time in November 1973, the demand for shipbuilding berths in which to construct large crude oil carriers was lively. We therefore considered ourselves fortunate to secure a building berth with Sumitomo Heavy Industries at Oppama to construct what amounted to a giant leap forward, one of the largest

MV *Hemlock* delivery celebration. Right to left: Anne Johnsen Bailey, sponsor; Edie Lee Johnsen (Mrs. Erik F. Johnsen); Erik F. Johnsen, and the president of Sumitomo Shipyard.

MV *Holly* on trial voyage. DWT, 29,255; LOA, 159.98 meters (527.93'); beam, 26.45 meters (87.29'); draft, 10.239 meters (33.45').

Festive display of ribbons and balloons as MV *Holly* is launched and named from graving dock at Oppama Shipyard, November 15, 1976.

MV *Holly* ready to float out from graving dock. The *Holly* is the exact sister ship of the MV *Hemlock*. DWT, 29,255; LOA, 159.98 meters (527.93'); beam, 26.45 meters (87.29'); draft, 10.256 meters (33.85'); 15 knots.

Marlene M. Johnsen, sponsor, and wife of Niels M. Johnsen, applauds as MV *Holly* is launched.

class of crude oil carriers in the world, designated an Ultra Large Crude Carrier (ULCC). In December 1973 we signed the contract to build Hull #1032, a huge 412,000-DWT-capacity turbine oil tanker, at the contract price of 21,950,000,000 yen ($78,400,000).

Nine months later, however, with unsettled political and economic conditions in the Middle East and before we were able to charter out this newbuilding, the tanker market collapsed. We faced substantial operating losses if this new tanker were built and delivered to us.

The shipyard had also underestimated its building costs. Fortunately for both buyer and builder, our good relations with Sumitomo enabled us to satisfy the financial needs of both parties to avoid these potential losses. We reached agreement to terminate the contract for Hull #1032 and substitute (1) contracts for two new craned dry-bulk carriers, Hulls #994 and #995, each 29,255 DWT, for delivery at Oppama in November 1976 and February 1977 at a price of 3.8 billion yen ($13.6 million) each, and (2) 400 LASH barges to be constructed by a Sumitomo affiliate, Oihama Ironworks, in Chiba City, Japan, at a price of about $40,000 each. Hull #994 was named the *Hemlock* and #995 was named the *Holly*. The *Hemlock* was launched on July 15, 1976, and sponsored by Anne Johnsen Bailey, daughter of Erik F. Johnsen. The *Holly* was launched on November 15, 1976, and sponsored by Marlene M. Johnsen, wife of Niels M. Johnsen. Neobulk Carriers Ltd., a new company, was formed in Liberia as a wholly owned subsidiary of TransUnion to own these vessels.

At this time we also ordered 40 new LASH barges to be constructed by the Union Tank Car Company, a first for this subsidiary of TransUnion. The total cost of the 40 barges was $1,600,000, which we financed by a loan from the Bank of New Orleans and Trust Company.

CHAPTER 22

ISC Spinoff from TransUnion

After substantially expanding our fleet during eight active years as a subsidiary of Trans-Union, Central Gulf and its associated companies arrived at a point where it became attractive both to TransUnion and Central Gulf to divide this fleet into assets more suitable to the investment policies of each company. A spinoff was in prospect. We could allocate to TransUnion the ownership of vessels that were already fixed on long-term contracts. Central Gulf would accept those ships operating in the spot market. With that general principle in mind, another subsidiary of TransUnion, International Shipholding Corporation, was formed in 1978 to be the spinoff candidate. The LASH operation and some of the other U.S.-flag vessels operated by Central Gulf in the spot market (see ISC Fleet List at Spinoff) were allocated to ISC. TransUnion retained Mammoth Bulk Carriers and its associated companies with ships on contracts (see MBC Fleet List). N.W. Johnsen and Co. Inc., an ISC subsidiary, agreed to continue operation of the Mammoth fleet as TransUnion's agent, while ISC took steps to restructure its organization.

In March 1979, ISC issued 2,385,100 shares of its common stock to TransUnion in payment for all of the stock of Central Gulf Lines Inc. and its associated companies. On the closing date of May 15, 1979, the 2,385,100 shares of ISC common stock were distributed to TransUnion shareholders of March 1979 (record date) on the basis of one share of ISC stock for each five shares of TransUnion stock owned by the TransUnion shareholder. At the same time, International Shipholding Corporation was registered as a public company with the Securities and Exchange Commission. ISC shares began trading over-the-counter. To provide ISC subsidiaries with adequate

financing so they could operate independently of TransUnion after the spinoff, TransUnion made the following loans: (1) to Central Gulf, $9,315,000, loan agreement dated March 31, 1979, with the principal amount repayable in 32 consecutive quarterly installments on the last day of each January, April, July and October commencing July 31, 1979, and ending April 30, 1987; (2) to LASH Carriers Inc., $26,000,000 (loan date, terms and conditions same as loan to Central Gulf).

TransUnion stipulated that interest on the loans would be payable at the prime rate plus an escalating "spread" to induce earlier repayment. We understood the message and promptly after the spinoff began discussions with our bankers to refinance. Within 24 months, on September 1, 1981, ISC had reached an agreement with a consortium of banks for a secured loan of $41 million, primarily from banks in the Eurodollar market. We used the major portion of this loan to repay the outstanding balance of the TU loan, about $32.7 million. We added the rest to our working capital. Hence ISC became a totally free entity, independent of TransUnion.

Through its affiliation with TransUnion, Central Gulf had achieved its objective of becoming a public company. It had expanded the fleet of Central Gulf and its associated companies. It had advanced the introduction of a sophisticated transportation system, LASH, to U.S.-flag ship construction and operation and it had provided the foundation for renewed growth. Additionally, it had acquired for TransUnion a fleet of modern vessels with solid employment that surely contributed to the value of TransUnion.

The Board of Directors and officers of Central Gulf Lines Inc. just prior to the spinoff in 1979 follow:

INTERNATIONAL SHIPHOLDING

BOARD OF DIRECTORS: Niels W. Johnsen, Erik F. Johnsen, Harold Grehan,
George Denegre, J.W. van Gorkum, W.B. Browder, S.E. Morrison.

OFFICERS:

Niels W. Johnsen	Chairman of the Board	Gerard D. Doyle	Vice President (sales)
Erik F. Johnsen	Senior Vice President	George Denegre	Secretary
Harold Grehan Jr.	Senior Vice President	S.E. Morrison	Treasurer
Hugo F. Hansen	Vice President	Gary L. Ferguson	Controller
E. C. Faerber	Vice President, Southwestern Division	William B. Moore	Assistant Secretary
Charles F. Monninger	Vice President (traffic)	D.A. Kuzmicki	Assistant Secretary
William B. Browder	Vice President of TransUnion	Robert B. Acomb Jr.	Assistant Secretary
Donald Romans	Vice President	Niels M. Johnsen	Assistant Secretary
Charles V. Wolff	Vice President	Mary A. Flannery	Assistant Secretary

MAMMOTH FLEET LIST

Vessels owned by Mammoth Bulk Carriers Ltd. and Its Affiliates, a Liberian corporation,
retained by TransUnion as of May 15, 1979, at time of spinoff

Ship	Type	Year Built	Capacity (DWT)	Fair Market Value* (Millions $)
Quebec	Bulk Carrier	1965	48,520	2.30
Strathearn	Geared Bulk Carrier	1967	54,248	7.00
Summit ex-Mosnes	Bulk Carrier	1973	117,400	0.65
Mammoth Fir	Log/Bulk Carrier	1973	32,600	2.90
Mammoth Pine	Log/Bulk Carrier	1973	32,600	1.80
Amoco Trinidad	Tanker	1974	151,427	9.80
Amoco Cairo	Tanker	1975	151,427	10.60
Sequoia	Bulk Carrier	1968	49,100	3.10
Hickory ex-Mostangen	Geared Bulk Carrier	1968	28,100	1.50
				Subtotal 39.65*
Holly	Geared Bulk Carrier	1977	29,255	13.60** (Yen 3.8 billion)
Mammoth Monarch	Tanker	1978	89,464	18.00**
Hemlock	Geared Bulk Carrier	1976	29.255	13.60** (Yen 3.8 billion)
				Subtotal 45.20**
				Total 84.85

*Net after allowing for payment of existing debt as per appraisal by the American Appraisal Company dated September 29, 1980.

**Gross value with no allowance for debt.

INTERNATIONAL SHIPHOLDING FLEET LIST

Vessels owned by International Shipholding Corporation's subsidiaries,
Central Gulf and its associated companies, as of the spinoff, May 15, 1979

Ship/Flag	Type	Year Built	Capacity (DWT)	Capacity (Barges)	Cost $ (Millions)
Green Harbour / U.S.	LASH	1974	46,039 LT	89	15.589
Green Island / U.S.	LASH	1975	46,039 LT	89	15.589
Green Valley / U.S.	LASH	1974	46,890 LT	89	15.346
Acadia Forest / Norwegian	LASH	1969	43,517 MT	83	9.585
Atlantic Forest / Norwegian	LASH	1970	43,517 MT	83	9.680
Oak / Liberian	SPLASH	1978	11,400 MT	18	6.140
Willow / Liberian	SPLASH	1978	11,400 MT	18	6.140
Spruce / Liberian	SPLASH	1975	8,660 LT	15	3.311
FLASH I / Liberian	FLASH	1974	5,956 MT	8	1.665
FLASH II / Liberian	FLASH	1975	5,956 MT	8	1.667
Pine Forest / Liberian	FLASH	1975	5,956 MT	8	1.666
				Cubic Feet	
1150 Barges / U.S.	LASH	Var.	450 MT each	20,000 each	46.001
Green Lake / U.S.	C-4	1945 converted 1969	15,500 LT	774,400	1.915
Green Port / U.S.	C-4	1944 converted 1969	15,500 LT	789,400	2.561
Green Forest / U.S.	C-4	1944 converted 1967	15,500 LT	789,400	2.585
Green Wave / U.S.	C-4	1944 converted 1967	15,500 LT	789,400	2.625
					Total 142.800*

★The original total cost of the vessels and barges in the ISC fleet at spinoff was $142.8 million, to which we added adjusted delivery costs of $4,121,000, for a total delivered cost of $146,921,000. Depreciation to the spinoff date of May 15, 1979, was about $35 million, making net total book value of vessels and barges $111,921,000 on the ISC balance sheet.

In September 1979 TransUnion received an offer from the Marmon Group, a Pritzker family conglomerate, to acquire for cash 100% of the outstanding common stock of TU. Shortly thereafter N.W. Johnsen and Co. Inc. ceased acting as agents for TransUnion's vessels, bringing an end to a pleasant and productive period in the life of ISC and its principal subsidiaries, Central Gulf and LASH Carriers, Inc.

The Post-Spinoff

In 1971, when TransUnion acquired Central Gulf and its associated companies (the principal subsidiaries later to make up ISC), the shareholders of those companies had received 600,000 shares of TU stock, valued at that time at about $25 million. When the International Shipholding Corporation spinoff took place on May 15, 1979, TransUnion Corporation delivered 2,385,000 ISC shares (adjusted later to 2,417,330 shares) to TransUnion shareholders on the basis of one share of ISC stock for every five TU shares held by the shareholder. The 2,417,330 shares had a book value of approximately $36,767,000. When ISC common stock began trading over-the-counter in 1979, the Johnsen family and certain other insiders, rather than retire from the Company as well as from TransUnion, began purchasing ISC stock as it became available for resale. Other TransUnion shareholders elected to sell their ISC shares for various reasons, including the fact that ISC shares were not then listed on the New York Stock Exchange nor did they pay a dividend. The shares were selling then in the neighborhood of $2.00 or $2.50 each. We bought sufficient shares of ISC to retain control of the Company. Within a short time Niels W. Johnsen held 426,735 shares and Erik F. Johnsen 427,198 shares. This represented a 17.7% percentage ownership by each Johnsen brother. All original shareholders of Central Gulf and its associated companies, of course, saw the value of their investment increase from some $25 million in December 1971 (at the TransUnion merger) to $5.5 million (the approximate market value of the ISC shares distributed by TransUnion) plus the value of the TransUnion shares they received when purchased by the Pritzker Group shortly after the spinoff. Those 600,000 Trans-Union shares then had a value of $55 each or $33 million or (for the two lots) a value of $38,500,000 when

the Pritzker Group acquired TransUnion later in 1979. At this point certain non-ISC TransUnion shareholders contended that the board of directors of TransUnion had accepted less than the fair market price from the Pritzker Group for the total shares of TransUnion, and initiated a class-action suit. The Supreme Court of the State of Delaware agreed and in 1985, in Smith v. Van Gorkum (TransUnion), awarded TransUnion shareholders an additional $1.05 per share to be paid by Pritzker.

At the ISC spinoff, TransUnion retained the assets of Mammoth Bulk Carriers and Associated Companies. ISC continued with the assets allocated and initially operated at a net loss. The fourth quarter results for ISC showed a loss of $6.513 million and a net loss for 1979 of $12,167,000. The results for the corresponding periods in 1978 showed a loss of $4,310,000 for the fourth quarter and a net loss of $2.976 million for the year. However, the capitalization of ISC at the spinoff was more than sufficient to absorb the 1979 losses and still maintain the Company's financial integrity (see Financial Statement as of December 31, 1978 and 1979). Factors that contributed to the losses in 1979 were: (1) post-closing information necessitated approximately $3.5 million in upward adjustments to reserves established in earlier years, principally to cover cargo damage claims and other insurance reserves. Almost half of those adjustments affected the fourth quarter of 1979; (2) the cost of fuel oil continued to escalate sharply in 1979, and even though we used about the same amount of fuel as in 1978, it cost $7.8 million more. We were able to recover only a part of the increased fuel cost by adding surcharges to our base tariff rates and applying escalation clauses in some of the Company's contracts; (3) at the beginning of 1979 the prime interest rate was 11½% and approximately $26 million of the Company's debt was at fixed rates averaging about 6%. All of this fixed-rate debt was converted to variable-rate loans as a result of the spinoff from TransUnion. By the end of 1979 the prime rate had soared to 15¼% and the Company's debt subject to floating interest rate was $36.3 million after the spinoff. As a result the Company in 1979 paid about $2 million more interest than it would have paid had its debt structure and interest rates remained unchanged from the start of the year. Because of stiff competition, practically none of this increased cost could be passed on to customers. We thus had the incentive, as mentioned earlier, to begin negotiating immediately with our bankers to convert as much debt as possible to lower rates based upon the contracts we held and the close banking relationships we had established. An extremely competitive market, exacerbated by overtonnaging on many of the trade routes we served, contributed to the 1979 downside year. Political upheavals in Iran and Afghanistan and the U.S. embargo of grain shipments to Russia disrupted trade patterns. In short, worldwide shipping conditions were unstable. The thrust of our efforts had to be to redeploy our ships, personnel and equipment to markets and trading areas that offered better returns and more stability.

Results of these endeavors were initially positive. We were able to fix employment for the *Atlantic Forest*, the second Norwegian-flag LASH ship we had built in Japan (a sister ship of the *Acadia Forest*), on a new contract with International Paper Company (with which we had made the initial contract to introduce the LASH system). This 10-year charter for the vessel and a fleet of LASH barges began in February 1980 and provided for increases in revenue to cover increases in operating costs for the entire charter period. Our next step was to negotiate with a U.S.-flag subsidized operator, Waterman Steamship Corporation, to bareboat-charter our three U.S.-flag LASH vessels and 450 LASH barges for 12 years. Maritime Administration approval for that charter was pending at the end of 1979 and was not given until the second quarter of 1980. The effect of the contract with Waterman was to change the employment of our five LASH vessels (the *Acadia Forest* and *Atlantic Forest* under the Norwegian flag, and the *Green Valley, Green Harbour* and *Green Island* under U.S. flag) from common carriers to contract carriers (with the exception of the westbound common carrier service of the two former Norwegian-flag vessels to make satisfactory round voyage employment). We continued the operation of our liner service between the U.S. Gulf and the Middle East and South Asia with conventional breakbulk ships. We tested the container market in this trade with chartered container ships. Our test convinced us that container ships were not for us.

INTERNATIONAL SHIPHOLDING CORPORATION AND SUBSIDIARIES
Summary of Consolidated Income, 1979

(All amounts in thousands except per-share data)

Revenues	$147,319
Voyage Expenses (Including Depreciation)	145,995
Administrative and General Expenses	10,144
Interest Expense (Net)	6,658
Equity in Net Income (Loss) of 50% Owned Companies	(76)
Income (Loss) Before Provision (Credit) for Income Taxes	(15,554)
Provision (Credit) for Income Taxes	(3,387)
Net Income (Loss)	($12,167)
Net Loss Per Common Share	($5.03)
Number of Common Shares Outstanding	2,417,330

INTERNATIONAL SHIPHOLDING CORPORATION AND SUBSIDIARIES

Consolidated Balance Sheets, December 31, 1979

ASSETS (all amounts in thousands)

Current Assets:	
Cash	$3,278
Temporary Cash Investments (Including $5,630 at 18.30% and $7,733 at 10.75% Invested with Trans Union Corporation at December 31, 1979 and 1978, Respectively; Rate Varies with Prime)	6,523
Accounts Receivable, Net of Allowance for Doubtful Accounts of $2,181 and $1,334 at December 31, 1979 and 1978, Respectively	
Traffic	18,749
Agents	6,139
Claims and Other Receivables	3,768
Trans Union Corporation	381
Refundable Income Taxes	4,007
Other Current Assets, Primarily Prepaid Insurance	2,376
Material and Supplies Inventory, At Cost	1,316
	46,537
Investments in 50% Owned Companies, At Underlying Equity in New Assets	97
Vessels and Other Property, At Cost	
Vessels and Barges	142,919
Furniture and Equipment	1,786
	144,705
Less – Accumulated Depreciation	(38,146)
	106,559
Other Assets	
Deferred Charges in Process of Amortization	1,671
Claims Pending	3,202
Other	3,099
	7,972
	$161,165

LIABILITIES AND STOCKHOLDERS' INVESTMENT

Current Liabilities	
Current Maturities of Long-Term Debt	$2,605
Accounts Payable and Accrued Liabilities	34,737
Payable to Trans Union Corporation	1,127
Deferred Income Taxes	—
	38,469
Billings in Excess of Income Earned and Expenses Incurred	7,412
Long-Term Debt:	
Bonds and Notes Payable, Less Current Maturities	70,251
Reserves and Deferred Credits	
Deferred Income Taxes	11,928
Deferred Investment Tax Credit	—
Claims	6,334
	18,262
Commitments and Contingencies	
Trans Union Corporation's Investment in ISC Operations	—
Stockholders' Investment	
Common Stock, $1.00 Par Value, 5,000,000 Shares Authorized, 2,417,330 Shares Issued and Outstanding	2,417
Additional Paid-In Capital	34,350
Retained Earnings (Deficit)	(9,996)
	26,771
	$161,165

CHAPTER 23

The Beat Goes On

Having contracted to sell one of the four war-built C-4 former troop ships remaining in our fleet at the spinoff, by May 1980 we sold the last three at a capital gain of $2.95 million. After disposal of these four C-4's upon expiration of the U.S. Navy Military Sealift Command charters, the door was open to do new MSC charters. We were successful in negotiating new time-charter contracts with the MSC for four U.S.-flag vessels for two years, with two ships to begin in February and March 1980, followed by the third and fourth in May. The MSC had the option of continuing the charters for further periods. To service these charters, we had secured options to purchase suitable ships to cover these contracts: the *Export Buyer, Export Builder, Export Bay* and *African Dawn* from Farrell Lines. With their employment in

place, we exercised the options, purchased the four ships, and put them against these new time charters. The charters also had escalation clauses to offset increases in operating costs. We gave the MSC the option to extend these charters in one-year increments, which they ultimately did. Prime interest rates for commercial bank loans had skyrocketed to *21½% per annum*. We found other credit available. To attract buyers, the sellers offered much better terms. We purchased the *Bay, Buyer* and *Builder* at a price of $2,725,000 each for delivery in February, March and April 1980. We paid for them by assuming the balance of their Title XI loans at an interest rate of 8.05%. The *Dawn* was delivered in the same period. The price was $3 million, payable $300,000 on signing the purchase contract, $200,000 on delivery, $1,096,000 by issuing a

C-3 SS *Buyer* (ex *Export Buyer*) in New Orleans after purchase and before delivery to Military Sealift Command in 1980. DWT, 12,832; LOA, 150.27 meters (495.89'); beam, 22.33 meters (73.69'); draft, 9.32 meters (32.74'); 18.5 knots on 222 tons OF.

C-4 SS *Dawn* (ex *African Dawn*), built June 1963, DWT, 12,932; LOA, 174.35 (575.35'); beam, 22.92 meters (75.64'); draft, 9.399 meters (31.02'); 20 knots on 407 tons OF.

LASH MV *Rhine Forest* (ex *Bilderdyk*) with full complement of 83 LASH barges on and under deck before delivery to Central Gulf in Rotterdam in August 1982. DWT, 44,799; LOA, 261.42 meters (862.69'); beam, 32.29 meters (106.56'); draft, 11.28 meters (37.22'); 18 knots at 585.5 tons HVF.

promissory note (repayable in 10 equal semi-annual installments of $109,600 each at 8.05% interest) and the balance of $1,404,000 by assuming obligation to pay the Title XI loan (in 16 semi-annual installments of $84,000 each with interest at 8.05%) plus one final installment of $60,000.

We expanded our LASH fleet by purchasing the surviving vessel of the Combi Line, the Dutch *Bilderdyk*, built in Belgium in 1972. She was modeled after the *Acadia Forest* and based upon the LASH designs of Jerome Goldman. The purchase price, which included a fleet of 247 LASH barges, was $22 million. The *Bilderdyk* was delivered to us in August 1982 to sail in our transatlantic liner service. We renamed her *Rhine Forest* and she continues to operate safely and efficiently today (2007) after 35 years of service.

When Erik negotiated the purchase of the *Bilderdyk* from Combi Line, Ari Lels of Holland America Line (one of the two operators of Combi Line), advised him that Combi Line was doing better westbound than our agents on the westbound service. To effectuate the sale, Lels prevailed upon our agent, Herfurth, to make a contract with us for five years based upon the higher return per barge. Armed with this contract, Lels came back to us and we then agreed to pay the $22 million for the *Bilderdyk*. Combi Line had contracted for this

cargo at favorable freight rates before the transatlantic steel market deteriorated. Part of this contract was for the carriage of steel to be used in the construction of an interstate highway and a bridge across the Mississippi River upstream from New Orleans. It was not clear how much of the steel for this highway and bridge had already been moved when we purchased the *Bilderdyk,* what part remained to be moved, or whether part of it was on board the *München,* her German partner that was mysteriously lost at sea while in the Combi Line service. This contract to carry semi-finished steel from Europe to the United States' East and Gulf coasts made the *Bilderdyk* purchase package attractive.

Meantime, as mentioned earlier, our operation of a container ship service was admittedly experimental. We wanted to make sure that we did not overlook a potentially profitable opportunity available on Trade Route 18. We time-chartered modern ships capable of carrying up to 1,000 TEU (20-foot equivalent units) of containers to start a monthly service between U.S. East Coast ports and Jeddah, Saudi Arabia, on the Red Sea. On the eastbound leg we carried mainly cases of bottled soft drinks and bagged food products packed in 20-foot containers. There were no return cargoes from the Saudi Arabia area, so we had to shift the vessels and containers to South Europe on the Mediterranean for homebound cargoes. There we picked up cases of Perrier bottled mineral water, which the shippers required to be stowed in 40-foot containers. This meant we had the expense of redelivering 20-foot containers in South Europe and rehiring 40-foot containers for the homebound cargo. We were obliged then to return the 40-foot containers after the cargo was delivered at U.S. East Coast ports and acquire a new supply of 20-foot containers to reload the eastbound (U.S. export) cargo. This operation turned out to be so expensive that the freight revenues were not sufficient to cover the multiple handling costs for containers and cargo. We concluded this container service was not worth maintaining. Therefore we redelivered the chartered container ships and promptly terminated the leases on the containers—also a costly process because we had to return the containers to lessors' yards and in many cases complete expensive repairs before stopping the lease hire. The losses we sustained in this experiment delivered the hard lesson: Concentrate on our breakbulk and LASH services.

We were able to assume two new vessel charters with the MSC after we contracted in September 1983 to purchase from United States Lines two U.S.-flag ships built in the late 1960's, the *Rapid* and the *Rover*. These were C-4-size combined breakbulk and roll-on/roll-off vessels for which we paid a total of $31.5 million. We financed part of this purchase by taking over the

remaining Title XI loans of $26.5 million and the balance of $5 million with available Company cash. The charter hire was sufficient to amortize the purchase price over the remaining four-year MSC charter periods, which began in March 1984. We subsequently agreed with the MSC to terminate the *Rapid's* charter in September 1987, in consideration of which MSC agreed to extend the *Rover's* charter for another four years. Upon termination of the *Rapid's* charter we sold the ship to the U.S. government for placement in the Reserve Fleet, for which we obtained a net of $4,350,000. After paying off the Title XI mortgage debt, the Company retained about $2 million. Upon termination of the *Rover's* charter in June 1993, we sold the vessel to a demolition yard in India at the approximate book value.

In December 1983, when Waterman was compelled to declare bankruptcy under Chapter XI, we promptly took steps to retrieve our LASH ships, barges and feeder vessels from the bankruptcy court. By March 1984 the *Green Island* was back in our fleet, together with the remaining 3½ years of a charter to the MSC that Waterman had fixed while the ship was on bareboat charter from our company. In June 1984 we regained charter-free control from the bankruptcy court of the other two LASH vessels, the *Green Valley* and *Green Harbour*, and were ready to redeploy them.

While we were adding ships and contracts to our fleet, we were also selling. We managed a fluid fleet with which we could take advantage of buying and selling opportunities as they became available. For example, as mentioned earlier, we sold our two SPLASH units, the *Oak* and the *Willow*, to the Mainland Chinese in May and June of 1983. The profit from the sale exceeded what the ships would have earned by continued operation for the foreseeable future.

In March 1984 the MSC redelivered the three C-3's (the *Bay, Buyer,* and *Builder*). We sold them for $1.6 million less than book value to the Maritime Administration, which placed them in its Reserve Fleet, ready to be mobilized by the U.S. government in future emergencies. The MSC extended the charter for the C-4 *Dawn* for another four years, after which we sold her to the Maritime Administration for $1.1 million more than book value. She was also put in Marad's Reserve Fleet.

C-4 type SS *Rover* (ex *American Rover*), purchased from United States Lines with her sister ship *Rapid* (ex *American Rapid*) in September 1983 for operation on time-charter to the Military Sealift Command.

In 1983 and 1984 our fleet operated in a charter market affected by reduced international trade, a strong dollar, a recession in Europe and a surplus of ships in almost every category of shipping. Our fleet fared well relative to the market because of our policy of concentrating in specialized trades and fixing medium- to long-term charters.

In this severe economic climate, two major liner operators in the trade between the U.S. and the Middle East/South Asia were forced into bankruptcy, including Waterman, whose bankruptcy obviously affected our operations.

One recent estimate placed the number of ships seized by creditors worldwide during 1983-84 at close to 300. Reflecting the depressed conditions in the bulk charter markets, a record volume of ship tonnage was sent to demolition yards in 1985—a total of 869 ships or 41.1 million DWT, compared with 29.3 million DWT in 1984. Of this tonnage, 30.3 million DWT were tankers and combination tankers/dry cargo carriers, including 72 very large or ultra large crude carriers. Most were only 10 to 12 years old. Many had seen very little employment since they were built and were sold to the scrap yards for about 10% of their original building price! Even after a record year of scrapping and inefficient use of operating vessels (for example, slow steaming), about 50% of the large-size tanker fleet was still laid up for lack of employment. More scrapping was needed. Obviously, this overtonnaged, depressed tanker market was a source of severe financial distress for many owners who had heavily invested in large crude carriers.

The world dry-bulk cargo market was also beset with surplus capacity, about 5% of the fleet, which kept rates depressed. World trade had not grown sufficiently to absorb this extra capacity. ISC policy remained unchanged: Serve particular water transportation needs of our clients with specialized vessels in selected trades with medium- to long-term contracts. The objective: level out what would have otherwise been wide swings in operating results.

Continuing our success in exploiting niche markets, in October 1985 we chartered our three U.S.-flag LASH vessels, the *Green Island, Green Harbour* and *Green Valley,* to the MSC for about 18 months as advance prepositioned ships. The Navy was convinced that these LASH vessels were ideally suited to be floating armories of high-priority military cargoes strategically placed near the front lines where an anticipated emergency might occur. They could be dispatched immediately fully loaded to the trouble spot to meet contingents of Army or Marine personnel flown in from Europe and/or the United States. The LASH ships stationed at Diego Garcia, an island lagoon in the Indian Ocean, were centrally located so as to be at or near a battlefront within a few days. As developments unfolded, the *Green Valley* was one of the first ships to arrive in Saudi Arabia in 1990 as part of Desert Shield/Desert Storm. The barges were quickly taken off the mother vessel and towed ashore where their contents, urgently needed military equipment and supplies, were dispatched to the troops.

In 1983 our friends John Hatleskog and Paal Caspersen contacted us with an investment opportunity in another niche market. Havtor, a Norwegian company they jointly owned, was promoting acquisition of a new type of combination bulk carrier. These 45,000-DWT newbuildings, equipped with a gantry crane to be self-discharging, were designed to be easily self-cleaning so that they could carry dry-bulk or liquid cargo, such as gasoline or other refined petroleum products, on successive voyages. The vessels were nicknamed "Probo" (Petroleum Bulk Ore Carrier). They were able to operate either as tankers or dry-bulk carriers as the market warranted.

Havtor had contracts with a South Korean shipyard to build four Probos for delivery in 1986. By the end of 1984 we had reached an agreement with Hatleskog and Caspersen to invest in two of the four ships then under construction at the Korea Shipbuilding and Engineering Company, in Pusan, South Korea. The plan was to establish a pool of up to eight sister ships for operation in A/S Bulkhandling, a ship pool that A/S Torvald Klaveness (another Norwegian company) would own and/or manage. Projections of the voyage results on typical itineraries were very favorable. However, the sea trials of the first vessel completed in this series indicated that the rudder design was not suitable for the configuration of the hull to enable the ships to make adequate turning ratios. Ultimately we found a solution

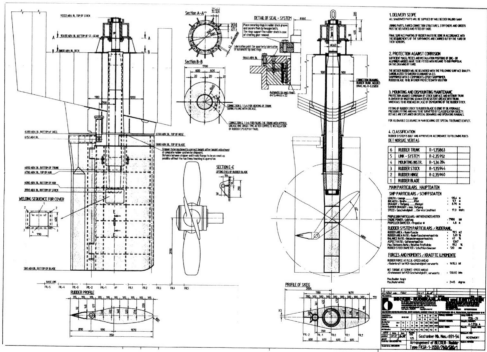

Photograph of a typical Becker Rudder, which we decided to have installed on the Probo ships to enable for them to meet specified turning ratio. The schematic drawing at right gives specifications and construction details for this unique rudder design.

which required the shipyard to fabricate a new, so-called "Becker designed" rudder (see illustration) that consisted of two steel panels operating on a hinge. This adjustment met the requirements for proper turning ratio. We then made the investment in two of these new ships (subsequently named *Probo Gull* and *Probo Hawk*) to match two owned by Havtor at a price of $23.6 mil-

lion each (of which $18.9 million each was a loan and $4.7 million each was equity), adjusted down from $28.4 million each to compensate for the rudder replacement. In 1985 we invested 50% in a third sister vessel, the *Probo Bangor,* with the A/S Torvald Klaveness group, which had also contracted with Hyundai Heavy Industries of Ulsan, South Korea, to build four Probos.

MV *Probo Gull,* one of eight sister ships that operated in the Bulkhandling Pool under the management of A/S Torvald Klaveness, of which we owned two. "Probo" is the acronym for "Petroleum Products Ore Bulk Oil" carriers, which are capable of carrying dry bulk or liquid cargo such as gasoline on successive voyages. Equipped with two 35-ton-capacity gantry cranes with grab buckets.

The adjusted price for each vessel was $22 million after the shipyard installed the new "Becker designed" rudder. The cost of our 50% share was $8.8 million (loan) and $2.2 million (equity).

Freight rates for petroleum products cargoes for handy-size tankers had increased. There was no certainty this market would continue to improve, but petroleum products were moving from and to new markets as new refineries came on stream in developing countries that were crude oil producers, and older and smaller refineries closed down in developed countries. Even though we had no fixed employment yet for these new vessels and could only speculate on the direction of the market, we considered the risk of buying this new type of petroleum/dry-bulk carrier worth taking, particularly since the Probo ships would operate in a pool of up to eight sister vessels.

We began 1979 with four war-built C-4's, which we had converted to dry-cargo ships from troop ships. These ships' charters to the MSC expired at the end of the year. We sold three of these older ships at prices substantially above their book value during 1979, and the fourth vessel in the fourth quarter of 1980 at a similar price. Operating results for 1979 thus reflected an $800,000 gain on the sale of one of these vessels, which we delivered to the buyers in 1979. The gains on the other three vessels were recognized in 1980.

In addition, before we sold the *Oak* and the *Willow* to Mainland China, we operated all three of our self-propelled SPLASH units as float-on/float-off carriers between North Europe and the Middle East. Their unique design enabled them to carry unusual cargoes such as "floatels" (floating hotels) from North Europe to the Nile River. They also carried dredges, cranes, sections of giant pipe and other outsize cargoes and offered the Company the capability to handle diverse cargoes in the future. With new business and gains on vessels sales on the books as a result of our aggressive efforts in the second half of 1979, we faced the future with optimism.

Our efforts to improve the Company's financial condition began to show progress in the fourth quarter of 1980, when we reported a net profit of about $637,000. However, despite the profit in the fourth quarter of 1979 and a first quarter 1980 gain of $2.5 million on the sale of three obsolete vessels, the Company ended 1980 with a net loss of $4.423 million. Of course, this was still an improvement over the losses of the previous year and showed that we were making progress restructuring our service and our organization. We would have seen slightly better results in 1980 had we been able to deliver the three U.S.-flag LASH vessels on bareboat charter to Waterman as originally contemplated in November/December 1979 and January

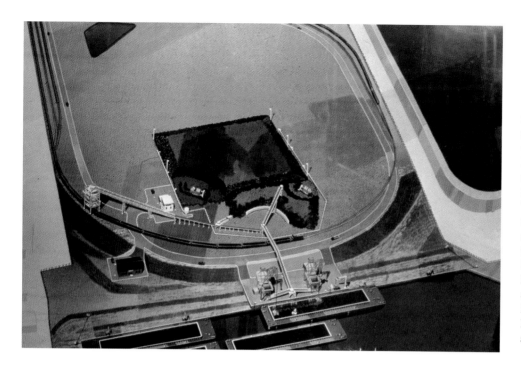

Artist's conception of Material Transfer Inc. in Gulf County, Florida. This facility was used in connection with the long-term contract to transport coal from mines in western Kentucky and southern Illinois via 3,000-ton capacity barges loaded at Mount Vernon, Indiana, and towed via the Mississippi River and Intracoastal Waterway. At Gulf County the coal was temporarily stored for transfer to shuttle trains operating to Palatka, Florida, where the Seminole Electric Cooperative generating plant is located. The Material Transfer Inc. facility handled 3 million tons of coal annually when in operation.

1980, but our wait for Maritime Administration approval held up delivery until March 1980. In the meantime our only choice was to continue their unprofitable operation until the LASH ships were delivered on charter to Waterman. In 1980, three chartered-in container ships also had unprofitable voyages leading us to terminate this service by mid-year. We consequently incurred additional expenses in 1980 for redelivering these vessels and containers.

As a result of the Company's actions taken almost immediately after the spinoff, we were able to boil our operations down to five profit centers built on medium- to long-term charters and contracts at acceptable rates. These five profit centers were: (1) our

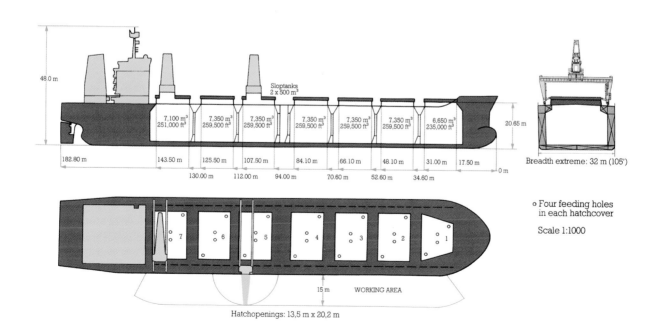

Probo Hawk, Probo Gull Vessel Specifications: Each 49,500 metric tons DWT; LOA, 182.8 meters (599', 8"); beam, 32 meters (105'); draft, 13.1 meters (43'); seven tanks/holds; service speed 14 knots on 35 tons HVF.

two Norwegian-flag LASH vessels, the *Acadia Forest* and *Atlantic Forest,* operating under contracts with IPCO in transatlantic service; (2) our three U.S.-flag LASH vessels, the *Green Valley, Green Harbour* and *Green Island,* together with 450 LASH barges and other feeder equipment, which began operation in 1980 on bareboat charter to Waterman; (3) our three self-propelled SPLASH ships, which profitably carried contract cargoes between North Europe and Saudi Arabia until we sold two of them to the Chinese; (4) our four newly acquired C-3's and C-4's, which were time-chartered to MSC and began operations on schedule in early 1980, and (5) our cargo liner service on Trade Routes 18 and 17, which we streamlined with vessels dedicated to carry breakbulk cargoes only.

The most troublesome problem the Company faced financially at the end of 1980 was high interest rates. Even though the prime rate reached a peak of 21½% in December 1980, we were successful in 1981 in arranging $41 million of new debt with a consortium of European banks at a lower floating rate to pay off the Trans-Union loan. This borrowing substantially reduced our interest costs and greatly improved our financial condition. We saw proof of the dramatic turnaround in our operations in 1981, when we reported pretax profit for the year of $6,065,000. The net tax credit of $1,586,000 brought the net profit of the Company for the year to $7,651,000.

The 1981 financials reflected the successful redeployment of our vessels, debt refinancing and the addition of a sixth profit center. One of the highlights of the year was signing a 22-year contract with Seminole Electric Cooperative Inc. of Palatka, Florida. The contract called for us to carry a total of more than 65 million tons of coal mined in western Kentucky and southern Illinois in 3,000-ton-capacity barges from Mount Vernon, Indiana (on the Ohio River), down the

Mississippi and across the Intracoastal Waterway to a facility that we had constructed in Gulf County, Florida, where it would be transferred into shuttle trains to Palatka, Florida. The contract provided for us to build and own the port facility at Port St. Joe, Florida, which we called Material Transfer, Inc. We completed it in October 1982 and the first coal shipments began later that year. In accordance with the Seminole contract, we arranged for the construction and financing of all the barges, towboats, rail cars and other equipment, including the transfer facility at Port St. Joe (dock, storage yard, cranes, conveyor belt, etc.). Leasing companies offered the most favorable financing opportunities because of the advantages available through accelerated depreciation, investment tax credits and off-balance sheet assets and liabilities. We therefore leased the barges, towboats and rail cars for the account of Seminole. We owned the transfer facility and used its financing for the tax benefits. We then charged Seminole a freight rate to cover the cost of the lease hire (which Seminole agreed to pay directly to the leasing company) and the operating expenses and profit.

The board of directors and officers of International Shipholding Corporation after the spinoff in 1979 were:

BOARD OF DIRECTORS
Laurance Eustis
Harold S. Grehan, Jr.
Erik F. Johnsen
Niels W. Johnsen
Raymond V. O'Brien, Jr.

OFFICERS
Niels W. Johnsen, Chairman
Erik F. Johnsen, President
Harold S. Grehan, Jr., Vice President
George Denegre, Secretary
Stanley E. Morrison, Treasurer
Gary. L. Ferguson, Controller

CHAPTER 24

Automobile/Truck Carriers

While international bulk-cargo freight rates for both dry- and liquid-cargo carriers remained depressed into the middle 1980's, we continued to search for other areas in which to expand our operation. When we began our cargo liner service in the mid-1950's with conventional breakbulk vessels, one commodity we handled in relatively large volume was unboxed automobiles. These were fully assembled new Chrysler and General Motors cars for shipment from the United States to the Middle East: Lebanon, Saudi Arabia and Iran. Shipping automobiles then right off the factory floor in conventional breakbulk ships meant lifting them on and off the vessels, using slings and stowing and lashing them in a rather awkward manner in the vessel holds. As a result, there was usually a considerable amount of damage in transit, which required us to set up a special repair service before delivery at destination. When Japanese and European car manufacturers began exporting automobiles to the United States, they used bulk carriers that carried bulk grain in one direction, then erected multiple portable decks in the holds to carry automobiles on the return voyage. This method of transportation also used slings for lift-on, lift-off of the cars, also risking damage to the cars in loading, stowing and unloading. The Japanese devised a more effective means of transporting fully assembled automobiles. They introduced what became known as "Pure Car Carriers," ships built with 10 or more decks and with loading and unloading ramps so that the cars could be driven on, parked and driven off the ship instead of being lifted on and off with slings. We watched this development unfold in the early 1980's.

At that point Japanese manufacturers such as Toyota, Honda and Nissan all shipped their fully assembled automobiles from Japan to the United States in foreign-flag Pure Car Carriers, i.e. third-country flag vessels, not exclusively Japanese. We saw this business as an opportunity to employ such specialized ships under U.S. flag. Despite the higher cost of U.S.-flag operation, we concluded that the productivity of these new ships would enable us to compete for this business with other flags if we used certain tax incentives available to U.S. taxpayers. We contacted the major Japanese car manufacturers in an effort to convince them of the political desirability of using U.S.-flag vessels to carry their cars to the American market. We emphasized that it would only cost slightly more, which would be *inexpensive* good public relations. Japanese exporters and importers had the policy of giving cargo preference to Japanese-controlled ships, either Japanese or third-flag vessels. The United States had cargo preference laws that required 50% (and in some cases slightly more) of government-sponsored cargoes to be shipped on U.S.-flag vessels. Even so, in most cases the U.S. permitted 50% of these cargoes to be shipped on non-U.S.-flag vessels.

Our initial marketing efforts to promote the transport of Japanese cars in U.S.-flag vessels were, to put it mildly, unsuccessful. We soon realized that we needed something more dramatic to stimulate these exporters to ship on U.S.-flag vessels. Because it was a political issue, the obvious place to look for assistance was the United States Congress. Negative balance of payments was a hot issue in Washington then. The climate was ripe for Congress to pass additional cargo preference laws to require a certain percentage of automobile exports from Japan (and, for that matter, other countries) to be brought in on U.S.-flag vessels. Since there never before had been cargo preference laws on commercial imports, this idea took some time to gain support in

Gretchen Johnsen Bryant, daughter of Niels W. and Millicent Johnsen, officially names MV *Green Bay,* at launching of the second Pure Car Carrier built for operation under U.S. flag for Central Gulf Lines Inc. at Mitsui Engineering & Shipbuilding Company in Tanamo, Japan, on July 15, 1987.

the Congress. At the same time we sought the aid of the U.S. Trade Representative, Ambassador Michael Smith. He was already seriously considering bringing before the Japanese car export associations the idea of voluntarily shipping fully assembled automobiles on U.S.-flag vessels. Smith stated that not doing so would encourage Congress to enact laws requiring at least 50% of these imports be shipped on U.S.-flag vessels. Some members of the congressional delegation from Louisiana (our home office being in New Orleans) were interested in helping U.S. companies to expand their operations. Congressman Bob Livingston, from the New Orleans area, and Senator John Breaux of Louisiana agreed to support such a bill. In the meantime, we

MV *Green Bay* slips down building way at Mitsui Engineering & Shipbuilding Company in Tanamo, Japan, on July 15, 1987, with streamers and balloons flying.

MV *Green Bay* on trial trip before delivery. Her cargo-carrying capacity was 4,000 fully assembled Honda automobiles driven on and off the vessel at loading and unloading ports respectively. LOA, 182 meters (597'); beam 30 meters (98.4'); speed, 18.3 knots on 32 metric tons HVF; gross tonnage, 38,000 tons. On long-term charter to Honda Motor Company.

also promoted the idea through the commercial representative in the U.S. Embassy in Tokyo as well as through Ambassador Smith.

We gradually began to get the message through in Japan that Congress was close to passing such a law. We then engaged as our exclusive agent in Japan a Japanese specialist in the car export market, Toshio Hotta, who owned a company called HBS Japan Limited. He became very helpful particularly because we soon found out that executives of the Japanese car exporters with whom we had to deal spoke very little English. With Hotta's assistance we made the point that we would build the Pure Car Carriers in Japan, and put them under U.S. flag, and that we then expected to contract with the Japanese car manufacturers to perform consecutive voyages from Japan to the U.S. Just as the bill was about to be passed by Congress, Hotta succeeded in setting up appointments for our representatives to meet the car manufacturers in Japan. Early in

1986, with Hotta's help we convinced the manufacturers that our knowledge of shipbuilding and ship operations qualified us to carry their cars. Toyota and Honda subsequently solicited offers for the charter of U.S.-flag Pure Car Carriers to ship their fully assembled automobiles from Japan to the United States.

As it turned out, both manufacturers requested offers to time-charter a ship for their exclusive use for 10 years—better than we had expected. Under such an arrangement, the charterer pays charter hire monthly whether or not it has cargo on board. After submitting our offers, the passage of time and further negotiations, the day finally arrived for us to sign time charters with both Toyota and Honda each for a Pure Car Carrier newbuilding to be delivered by a Japanese shipyard "to be named" in 1987. Toyota nominated Nippon Yusen Kaisha (NYK) as the time charterer to handle the operation of the new ship on its behalf. Honda nominated a company it had established a number of years before,

Gayle Denegre is congratulated by her husband, George Denegre, general counsel of the Company, and by the president of IHI Shipyard, Kure, Japan, after naming ceremony on July 24, 1987, for MV Green Lake.

MV Green Lake after floating out of building dock, being outfitted prior to delivery. Her capacity was 5,000 fully assembled Toyota automobiles.

Artist's conception of a cutaway of MV Green Lake showing typical stowage of vehicles after loading.

Partial view of Toyota automobiles on dock at Toyohashi, Japan, waiting to be driven on board MV *Green Lake* on her maiden voyage to Baltimore.

ACT Maritime Limited, to handle the operation of their time-chartered ship. Toyota also chartered a second PCC for U.S.-flag operation to be owned by Overseas Shipholding Corporation, and nominated Mitsui OSK Lines as the time-chartered operator. Honda took only our new ship. Nissan also got into the act and contracted to have a ship built for U.S.-flag operation and chartered to Nissan by Marine Transport Lines. Nissan nominated Kawasaki Shipping Company as the time-chartered operator.

We then solicited proposals from IHI, Sumitomo, Mitsubishi and Mitsui for building the new ships. We had aggressively sought the contracts to carry the cars before owning the ships needed to perform the contracts. It was therefore important for us quickly to acquire inexpensive yet quality ships. Fortunately for us, competition among the shipyards was strong. We were successful in accomplishing the mission. IHI agreed to build a Pure Car Carrier capable of carrying 5,000 standard Toyota cars to meet the shipper's requirements for $24,964,737, and to deliver the completed ship on September 28, 1987. We named her *Green Lake*. Mitsui agreed to deliver a new Pure Car Carrier capable of carrying 4,000 standard Honda cars to meet the shipper's requirements in October 1987 for $18,955,080. We named her *Green Bay*. We signed both building contracts and thus began our participation in the transportation of new automobiles from Japan to the United States in specialized Pure Car Carriers—a major breakthrough for the American Merchant Marine.

Niels W. Johnsen and Erik F. Johnsen with scale model of MV *Green Lake,* the first U.S.-flag Pure Car Carrier to transport 4,600 fully assembled Toyota automobiles from Japan to the United States, 1987.

Negotiations for the construction of the ship to fulfill the Honda contract resulted in rather intense competition between Sumitomo Heavy Industries and Mitsui Engineering and Shipbuilding Company. Mitsui finally won the bid with the best price and best delivery. The *Green Bay* was launched at the Mitsui Engineering and Shipbuilding Company in Tanamo, Japan, on July 15, 1987, and was christened by Gretchen Johnsen Bryant, daughter of Niels W. Johnsen. The *Green Lake,* chartered to Toyota, was christened by Gayle Denegre, wife of the Company's general counsel, as the ship floated out of her building dock at IHI Shipyard in Kure, Japan, on July 24, 1987, and was delivered to Central Gulf Lines Inc. on September 28, 1987. She had her first

MV *Green Bay* entering New York Harbor early 1988, to unload Honda automobiles from Japan.

full cargo of 4,600 fully assembled automobiles driven on board at Toyohashi, Japan, and sailed on October 3, 1987, for Baltimore, where her maiden voyage celebrations were held on October 26, 1987. The *Green Bay*, after delivery from the shipyard on October 29, 1987, shifted to the loading port for Honda automobiles and sailed on November 3, 1987, arriving in Long Beach, California, on November 17, 1987, for her maiden voyage celebration.

Continuing to build on our investment in the car carrier market, one of our international subsidiaries placed orders in October 1987 and January 1988 with Hyundai Heavy Industries Ltd. of Ulsan, South Korea, for two Pure Car Carriers, each with capacity of 4,800 cars, to be constructed for delivery in the first half of 1988. We time-chartered both vessels for 10 years to Hyundai Merchant Marine Ltd. in December 1987 and February 1988 to carry new Hyundai automobiles from South Korea to the United States and other destinations. We took delivery of the first, which Happy Grehan, wife of the Company's executive vice president, christened the *Cypress Pass* on March 9, 1988, and the second, which Ellen O'Brien, wife of a director of the Company

and chairman of the Emigrant Savings Bank of New York, named the *Cypress Trail* on June 17, 1988. Both operated under the Panama flag.

The Company reached another milestone when the stockholders' investment passed the $100 million mark in 1990. At the annual stockholders meeting in New Orleans on April 24, 1986, the shareholders voted to increase the number of authorized common shares from 2,500,000 to 10,000,000. The board then voted to declare a stock dividend of two shares of common stock for each share owned on May 15, 1986, payable on June 2, 1986. The total number of shares of common stock then outstanding became 3,373,407. The Company also acquired from the market 88,446 shares during 1985, bringing the total of shares in the treasury to 119,239. At the Company's annual meeting in New Orleans on April 23, 1987, shareholders approved an increase in the authorized preferred shares to 1,000,000 with $1 par value. To augment the equity base in anticipation of further new projects meeting our investment objectives, in October 1987 we completed the sale of 85,000 shares of the Company's preferred stock at a price of $200 per share, for a total of $17 million. Having this additional

Happy Grehan, wife of Central Gulf Lines Inc. Vice President Harold S. Grehan, Jr., cuts ribbon to name, float out and deliver Pure Car Carrier MV *Cypress Pass* in March 1988 at Hyundai Heavy Industries Ltd. Shipyard in Ulsan, South Korea.

Ellen O'Brien, wife of Raymond V. O'Brien, Jr., director of the Company and chairman of the Emigrant Savings Bank of New York, cuts ribbon to name, float out and deliver Pure Car Carrier MV *Cypress Trail* in June 1988.

MV *Cypress Trail* on her trial trip. The *Cypress Pass* and *Cypress Trail* each had capacity for about 4,800 Hyundai automobiles and were time-chartered to an affiliate of Hyundai Motor Company, Hyundai Merchant Marine Ltd., for about 10 years each for operation under international flag. LOA, 184 meters; beam, 30.6 meters; speed, 17 knots on 42 metric tons HVF; gross tonnage, 42,447 tons.

equity base also facilitated our bank borrowings, which we used to cover a substantial portion of the purchase price of both the U.S.-flag *Green Lake* and *Green Bay* and the international-flag *Cypress Trail* and *Cypress Pass*.

Flashing back to United States Lines, we got an overdue bonus from that company. By this time, U.S. Lines had filed for bankruptcy and had ceased operation. From the bankruptcy court we won the bid at $1,550,000 from the estate of U.S. Lines for all three approvals they had received from the Maritime Administration to purchase three new multipurpose cargo vessels to be constructed in a foreign shipyard for registration and operation under U.S. flag. These approvals, under Section 615 of the Merchant Marine Act, permitted the vessels to carry government-sponsored cargoes immediately after registration under U.S. flag rather than wait the required three years. With all of our other activity going on in the forward years, we didn't immediately use these approvals. We ultimately sold all three in 2002 to Liberty Carriers, Inc., headed by Philip Shapiro, for $1,650,000.

We sold the *Rapid* in September 1987 to the government for placement in the reserve fleet, in a sale for which we obtained net of $4,350,000. After paying off the Title XI mortgage debt the Company retained about $2,000,000 cash, the approximate book value.

We had an active year in 1988 following a busy one in 1987. New capital expenditures in 1988 were about $75 million, of which about $18 million was provided from internal sources and about $57 million from new borrowings. During the year we paid off almost $22 million of old debt. Our new capital investments of 1988 were made substantially in accordance with our policy of matching investment with medium- to long-term charters. The Company invested about $45.5 million in two new U.S.-flag Pure Car Carriers (the *Green Lake* and *Green Bay*) tied to period charters to Toyota and Honda. We also invested about $18.235 million in two ships employed on Military Sealift Command time charters. The balance of $11.265 million covered payments on the *Probo Gull* and *Probo Hawk*.

During 1988 our fleet continued to operate in specialized markets against the background of a strong world charter market, which had substantially improved from the doldrums of earlier 1980's. Both tanker and dry-bulk cargo rates maintained a steady to upward movement relative to the firm trend that had already been established in 1987. Freight rates in the dry-bulk cargo market increased in response to continuing large imports of grain by the Soviet Union coupled with increased grain sales to Mainland China, Taiwan and Japan. As 1989 began, those market forces continued to underpin world charter rates. The Soviet Union's grain harvest in the previous year fell about 40 million tons short of its target of 235 million tons. The Soviet Union therefore found it necessary to import some 45 million to 50 million tons of grain to compensate for this shortfall, a sharp increase from about 32 million tons of imports the previous year, and close to the a record 55.5 million tons of imports in 1985. The United States and the Soviet Union concluded a new agreement at the end of 1988 for further substantial grain imports from the United States. Overall imports of grain into the Soviet Union and other traditional markets in 1989 continued at about the same level as 1988.

Scrapping of obsolete tonnage continued in 1988 but at about half the rate of 1987. About 5.5 million deadweight tons of ships were scrapped in 1988. The reduced rate of scrapping was attributable to the firm charter rates and the shrinking fleet of idle ships available for scrapping. At the end of 1988, only 34 tankers of 3.1 million deadweight tons were laid up, whereas the year previously 61 tankers of about 10.16 million deadweight tons were in layup fleets. With the supply of ships about in balance with demand, a stable to slightly stronger charter market was expected in 1989. Indicative of the improved freight markets, an independent appraiser estimated the resale value of our fleet to be over $205 million, compared to the net book value of $168.3 million as of December 31, 1988.

In September 1988 the Company paid its first cash dividend of 5 cents per share on the common stock and followed up with quarterly dividends of this amount until June 30, 2001. At the annual meeting in April 1989, the stockholders elected to the Board of Directors Niels M. Johnsen, vice president of the Company and vice president of its principal subsidiary, Central Gulf, and Edwin Lupberger, chairman of the board and president of Entergy Corporation. The board now consisted of seven directors, of which three were outside directors.

MV *Green Lake,* U.S.-flag Pure Car Carrier, prior to delivery of the vessel on long-term time-charter to Toyota Motor Company. LOA, 180 meters (590.4'); beam 32.26 meters (105.8'); speed, 18.3 knots on 35.7 metric tons HVF; gross tonnage, 47,500; car capacity, 5,000 fully assembled automobiles.

ISC BOARD OF DIRECTORS AS OF MARCH 1989
Laurance Eustis
President
Laurance Eustis Company, New Orleans

Harold S. Grehan, Jr.
Vice President
International Shipholding Corporation
Executive vice president
Central Gulf Lines, Inc.

Erik F. Johnsen
President
International Shipholding Corporation
President
Central Gulf Lines, Inc.

Niels M. Johnsen
Vice President
International Shipholding Corporation
Vice President
Central Gulf Lines, Inc.

Niels W. Johnsen
Chairman of the Board
International Shipholding Corporation

Chairman of the Board
Central Gulf Lines, Inc.

Edwin Lupberger
Chairman of the Board and President
Entergy Corporation, New Orleans

Raymond V. O'Brien Jr.
Chief Executive Officer
Emigrant Savings Bank, New York

We were now ready to make another acquisition and opened discussions with Waterman Marine Corporation. Waterman had its origin in Mobile, Alabama, in 1919. John B. Waterman, founder along with two associates, was a native of New Orleans who moved to Mobile in 1902 and, until his death in 1937, was a prime mover in establishing Mobile as a major port. During World War II, Waterman Steamship Corporation was operating 125 vessels (37 of its own), with 450 employees located at shipping centers from the U.S. Gulf to the North Atlantic. In addition, 900 officers of the Merchant Marine worked on shipboard.

In May 1955, McLean Industries, Inc. purchased all of the capital stock of Waterman Steamship Corporation. McLean kept Pan-Atlantic Steamship Company, a Waterman subsidiary that held an Interstate Commerce Commission certificate for operation in the domestic coastwise trade. McLean did not want the international operations of Waterman, and put it on the market for sale. He contacted our company, among others. He never went further with us, assuming that we were not able to finance the purchase of Waterman at our company's young age. He sold Waterman's international unsubsidized fleet to the Walsh brothers, with support from U.S. Freight Company. The Walshes resigned from States Marine Lines, Inc., whose management had no interest in Waterman.

Ironically, 24 years after McLean apparently decided we were not financially capable of acquiring Waterman, we ended up purchasing it in March 1989. When Waterman declared bankruptcy in December 1983, we immediately began negotiations to get back our three U.S.-flag LASH ships, LASH barges and certain other equipment. We accomplished this by June 1984 with one exception: a FLASH vessel and an oceangoing tug continued to operate under charter to Waterman. Waterman had continued the operation of the Waterman fleet of LASH ships as "debtor in possession." Gradually our discussions with Waterman evolved to the subject of Waterman selling its ships and operations once it came out of bankruptcy. By October 14, 1988, we had signed a letter of intent to purchase Waterman's outstanding common and preferred stock. In addition to three U.S.-flag LASH vessels with about 450 LASH barges and three ro/ro ships on charter to the Navy, Waterman had Operating Differential Subsidy contracts on the LASH vessels. On March 30, 1989, ISC concluded the acquisition of Waterman and paid the purchase price of $34 million in cash, plus the fair market value of an investment portfolio having a market value of $2,612,518. On June 20, 1990, the Secretary of Transportation approved the Maritime Subsidy Board's decision authorizing Waterman's Operating

Differential Subsidy contract MA/MSB#450 to be amended in scope and adjusted in termination date by adding two years to December 1996 on Trade Routes 18 and 17. As a result of this decision and in order to ensure continuation of its liner service with efficient equipment, Waterman entered into contracts with shipyards in the New Orleans area to refurbish its fleet of LASH barges. On July 25, 1990, Sea-Land Service filed a complaint, asking the DOT to review its decision approving the Waterman sale to ISC. The DOT upheld the decision. At the Company board meeting in January 1990, the directors agreed that the acquisition of Waterman Marine Corporation was the most significant factor contributing to the increased gross profit in 1989.

The Company had approximately $2.3 million of investment tax credits available for use beyond 1989, primarily generated from the construction of the two new U.S.-flag Pure Car Carriers delivered in 1987. On April 11, 1989, we added to the equity capital of the Company by issuing 920,000 new shares of common stock to the public at $19⅜ per share. In July 1989 we issued 25,000 new shares of preferred stock, so-called "Series D", for $5 million. In March of that year we closed a private placement of $15 million in subordinated debentures. To finance the acquisition of Waterman, the Company had arranged for bridge financing for up to $27 million with the Chase Manhattan Bank. The bridge loan was paid off with the net proceeds to the Company after fees from the sale of the 920,000 shares of common stock, $16,431,200, and other financing. We had arranged to refund the bridge loan also by issuing long-term subordinated notes with institutional investors. The Company ultimately issued in 1993 $100 million face value of unsecured subordinated notes bearing interest at 9% and maturing in 10 years. Four years later, in January 1997, we issued another series of unsecured subordinated notes with a face value of $110 million, bearing interest at 7¾% and maturing in 2007. We used the proceeds to pay off other financing in the same amount.

INTERNATIONAL SHIPHOLDING CORPORATION
AND SUBSIDIARIES
Summary of Consolidated Income, 1987

(All amounts in thousands except per-share data)

Revenue	$136,004
Operating Expenses	
Voyage Expenses	97,099
Vessel and Barge Depreciation	10,889
Administrative and General Expenses	12,276
	120,264
Operating Income	15,740
Interest	
Interest Expense (Net)	6,180
Investment Income	(678)
	5,502
Gain (Loss) on Sale of Vessels and Barges	(79)
Equity in Net Income of Unconsolidated Subsidiaries	452
Income before Provision for Income Taxes	10,611
Provision for Income Taxes	
Current	765
Deferred	3,545
State and Foreign	60
	4,370
Net Income	$6,241
Less	
Preferred Stock Dividends	348
Accretion of Discount on Preferred Stock	64
Net Income Applicable to Common Shares	$5,829
Per Share of Common Stock Outstanding	$1.79

INTERNATIONAL SHIPHOLDING CORPORATION AND SUBSIDIARIES

Consolidated Balance Sheets, December 31, 1987

ASSETS (All amounts in thousands)

Current Assets	
Cash	$2,057
Temporary Cash Investments	31,264
Accounts Receivable, Net of Allowance for Doubtful Accounts of $1,495 and $1,438 in 1987 and 1986, Respectively	
Traffic	14,401
Agents	3,325
Claims and Other Receivables	841
Other Current Assets, Primarily Prepaid Insurance	930
Material and Supplies Inventory, At Cost	2,636
	55,454
Less – Deposits To Be Made to Capital Construction Fund	—
Total Current Assets	55,454
Capital Construction and Title XI Reserve Funds, Including Deposits To Be Made	9
Investment in Unconsolidated Subsidiaries At Underlying Equity in Net Assets	11,175
Vessels, Property and Other Equipment, At Cost	
Vessels and Barges	217,700
Other Marine Equipment	5,231
Coal Terminal	13,205
Land	2,126
Furniture and Equipment	2,179
	240,441
Less – Accumulated Depreciation	(86,874)
	153,567
Other Assets:	
Deferred Charges In Process of Amortization	21,021
Other	5,981
	27,002
Total Assets	$247,207

LIABILITIES AND STOCKHOLDERS' INVESTMENT

Current Liabilities	
Current Maturities of Long-Term Debt	$16,896
Current Maturities of Capital Lease Obligations	2,624
Accounts Payable and Accrued Liabilities	24,361
	43,881
Billings In Excess of Income Earned and Expenses Incurred	3,167
Long-Term Capital Lease Obligations, Less Current Maturities	3,258
Long-Term Debt Less Current Maturities	91,084
Reserves and Deferred Credits	
Deferred Income Taxes	27,961
Claims and Other	7,777
	35,738

COMMITMENTS AND CONTINGENCIES

Cumulative Redeemable Preferred Stock, $1.00 Par Value, 1,000,000 Shares Authorized, 85,000 Shares Issued and Outstanding at Dec. 31, 1987, Redemption Value	17,000
Less – Excess of Redemption Value Over Fair Value	(1,785)
	15,215
Stockholders' Investment	
Common Stock, $1.00 Par Value, 10,000,000 Shares Authorized, 3,373,407 Shares Issued and Outstanding at December 31, 1987 and 1986, Respectively	3,373
Additional Paid-In Capital	33,802
Retained Earnings	18,822
	55,997
Less – 126,739 and 119,239 Shares of Common Stock in Treasury, at Cost at Dec. 31, 1987 and 1986, Respectively	(1,133)
	54,864
	$247,207

CHAPTER 25

AMSEA Encounter

On August 12, 1992, Niels W. Johnsen, chairman of ISC, and James E. Turner Jr., executive vice president of General Dynamics Corporation, signed a contract for the purchase by ISC of all of the rights, titles, and interests in and to the outstanding capital stock of five General Dynamics subsidiaries: Concord I Maritime Corporation, Concord II Maritime Corporation, Concord III Maritime Corporation, Concord IV Maritime Corporation, Concord V Maritime Corporation (the Concord Sellers) and all of the rights, titles, and interests in and to the outstanding capital stock of American Overseas Marine Corporation (AMSEA), also a subsidiary of General Dynamics. The contract also provided for the purchase by ISC of all the rights, titles, and interests in and to all of the outstanding capital stock of the General Dynamics subsidiaries Braintree I Corporation, Braintree II Corporation, Braintree III Corporation, Braintree IV Corporation, Braintree V Corporation (the Braintree Shares).

The closing of the transaction was to take place no later than October 30, 1992. How we got to the point of signing this contract and what happened after the contract was signed is the subject of this chapter.

The Braintree Companies (Lessees) each bareboat charter one special-purpose vessel from Wilmington Trust Company (Lessor) and in turn sub-charter them to the Concord Sellers, which then time-charter the five ships to the U.S. Navy. These time charters represent the source of income to AMSEA, the operator of the ships for their respective lessees/charterers.

The five sister ships were built by General Dynamics in Quincy, Massachusetts, in 1985 and 1986. They were built specifically to be placed on long-term charter to the U.S. government for use as part of the Military Prepositioning Ships fleet, dedicated to providing the ready storage and supply of equipment and associated cargo for the Marine Corps. The General Dynamics' subsidiaries' ships are among 13 ships in this fleet. The MPS ships carry all the equipment needed for three Marine brigades, each composed of 6,500 U.S. Marines. Waterman, a subsidiary of ISC, operates three of these MPS ships. Five are operated by Maersk Line Ltd., a U.S. subsidiary of the Danish shipowner A.P. Moller. The other five are operated by the five subsidiaries of General Dynamics that are the subject of the aforementioned contract between ISC and General Dynamics. Each ship is time-chartered to the U.S. Navy for five periods of five years each (total 25 years). The Navy has the right to terminate each charter at the end of each five-year period upon payment of a stipulated termination amount, or continue for another five years at stipulated charter terms.

The story began on or about November 18, 1991, when Niels M. Johnsen received a telephone call from Joseph Zimmel, a partner in Goldman Sachs's New York City headquarters. The purpose of his call was to inform ISC that General Dynamics had decided to dispose of several of its subsidiary companies, including AMSEA. Zimmel wanted to know whether ISC or Waterman would be interested in the acquisition of this company. He was aware of Waterman's operation of similar contracts for the Maritime Prepositioning Ships vessels. We told Zimmel that we were interested but required more information. On November 20, 1991, Zimmel sent us a telefax giving us so-called cost data on the five MPS vessels. On December 3, Gary L. Ferguson, controller in the ISC New Orleans office, sent Niels W. Johnsen a telefax in which he stated that during November, Goldman Sachs had apparently contacted Rick Macmillan, an attorney with Jones Walker in New Orleans, long-time corporate attorneys for ISC and its subsidiary companies. Since Goldman Sachs

MV *2nd Lt. John P. Bobo,* a Military Prepositioning Ship with lift-on/lift-off and roll-on/roll-off capabilities. LOA, 673' 2"; beam, 105' 6"; draft, 32.1'; speed, 17.7 knots.

did not know whom to call at ISC, they called Jones Walker, because that name is on all of the Company's SEC filings. Zimmel had apparently contacted Jones Walker before calling Niels M. Johnsen in New York. During the week of December 16, 1991, Niels M. Johnsen received another telephone call from Zimmel to advise that they were assembling a complete package for our review and expected to have it in our hands "after the holidays."

On February 12, 1992, ISC received a confidentiality agreement from Goldman Sachs, which they would require ISC to sign prior to releasing further information on the AMSEA project. We advised Zimmel's assistant, Jill Johnson, that we would review the confidentiality agreement and get back to her as soon as possible. We did so within a day or two and told her we would sign

AMSEA MPS convoy passing Diamond Head, Hawaii, en route to Guam, 1987.

the agreement and deliver it to them in exchange for the information we requested at a meeting to be held in the New York offices of Goldman Sachs, on February 19. They agreed, and the meeting was held as scheduled. Present, in addition to Niels M. Johnsen and Niels W. Johnsen, were Leland B. Bishop II, president AMSEA, Joseph R. Zimmel, partner of Goldman Sachs, and Jill L. Johnson of the investment banking division of Goldman Sachs. Bishop presided at the meeting on behalf of AMSEA and went through a brochure containing some financial information on past and projected performance of the five AMSEA companies. He left a copy of the brochure with us for our further study. We then spent the next few days reviewing the data and concluded that additional information was required.

Several days after the meeting Niels W. Johnsen had a question on part of the information in the brochure and called Bishop for clarification. When speaking to Zimmel subsequent to this conversation Zimmel requested that we not contact Bishop again but restrict all discussions on the subject of AMSEA to Zimmel. On February 28, 1992, we wrote Zimmel requesting further material for our due diligence. On March 5, 1992, we received a telefax from Bishop answering some of the questions but deferring reply to other questions in our February 28 letter. In any case, we continued our review of the financial figures and decided that the best approach would be to advise Goldman Sachs what we considered to be the value of the companies and tell them that if that could be fixed, we would then proceed with the balance of our due diligence.

Over the next three weeks we had two or three conversations with Zimmel, the last one on or about March 27. All the telephone calls were initiated by Niels W. Johnsen. At that point we decided to advise Goldman Sachs what we considered to be the value of the companies. We told them the number and stated that our intention was to pay the price in two installments, approximately one half upon closing and the balance after the Navy declared the next five-year periods on each of the five vessels. Zimmel responded that the total price we suggested was "close" to their ideas, and he would get back to us. We then discussed the matter in confidence with representatives of the

Chase Manhattan Bank, Citibank, and the First National Bank of Maryland. All three banks stated that they were interested in financing our purchase of these companies and would work together as a syndicate. We had met with Chase officials on April 3. We spoke to Citibank officials by telephone and supplied them with an outline of the plan on April 8. We met with an officer of the First National Bank of Maryland on April 14.

Tom Gallagher, senior vice president and group executive of Chase, agreed to visit with General Dynamics on April 7, to advise them of our serious interest and let them know we were waiting for their reply to our proposal. On April 13, Gallagher said that he had spoken to Richard Johnson, treasurer of General Dynamics, and advised him of our interest in acquiring the AMSEA companies. Johnson commented during this discussion that it was possible General Dynamics would not sell the companies to anyone. On April 14, Gallagher received a telephone call from Joe Zimmel, complaining that Gallagher had contacted General Dynamics asking why the deal was going so slowly. Gallagher had the impression that maybe his visit was going to speed things up. Citibank also called on April 15 to find out whether any progress was being made. In any event, Gallagher's visit at least got the message to General Dynamics that we had financing standing by to do the project. Nothing further was heard from Zimmel during April.

Because Niels W. Johnsen expected to be traveling during much of May, he decided to call Zimmel to tell him that he would be out of the office and ask him what the status was before he left. Zimmel said that as a matter of fact, a presentation was being made that very morning to the General Dynamics Finance Committee connected with the sale of AMSEA companies. He said he expected to be able to get back to us later in the day or at least no later that noon on May 4. No call was received from Zimmel nor did Niels W. Johnsen hear from him for the balance of May. On May 28, Johnsen received a report that AMSEA companies and Maersk Line Ltd., the Danish-owned U.S. company already operating five of the Navy's MPS ships, had contacted the Military Sealift Command to determine whether the Navy would approve the sale of the AMSEA companies to Maersk. On May 29, we also received a copy

June 8, 1992

MEMORANDUM

TO: FILE

FROM: NIELS W. JOHNSEN

RE: AMERICAN OVERSEAS MARINE CORPORATION (AMSEA)

Following is a brief description of the ship operating companies involved in this transaction and their respective relationships with the Military Sealift Command (MSC):-

[1] **AMERICAN OVERSEAS MARINE CORPORATION (AMSEA)**

This company operates five Military Pre-Positioning Ships (MPS) under time charter to MSC. These charters are for five 5-year periods for up to a total of 25 years, each vessel. The company also operates some ships in the Reserve Fleet for the Maritime Administration, but they are not an important part of this transaction. The five MPS ships are each in the second 5-year cycle. If the ships are kept for 25 years, the charters would expire in the years 2010 and 2011. The current estimated annual charter hire paid to the company by MSC on the five ships is about $46.7 Million.

[2] **MAERSK LINE, LTD. (MAERSK)**

This company was established as a Delaware corporation by a Danish company, A.P. Moller (a.k.a. Maersk Line) we believe for the sole purpose of owning ships chartered to the U.S. Navy. The company, while Danish controlled, has taken advantage of the liberal laws for registration of ships under U.S. Flag and the minimum almost non-existent U.S. citizenship requirements for companies owning or operating vessels chartered to the U.S. Government for carriage of military cargo. Maersk were able in the early 1980's to transfer to U.S. Flag from foreign flag five RO/RO vessels surplus to their foreign flag operation, convert them and fix them on these long-term charters for use as MPS. The five MPS ships operated by Maersk are part of a 13 ship fleet of MPS ships all carrying strategic military equipment for the U.S. Marine Corps. The other eight MPS ships are operated five by AMSEA and three by Waterman. In addition to the five MPS ships, Maersk also has a RO/RO vessel built in 1980 which was also transferred from foreign to U.S. Flag and chartered to MSC (M/V "MAERSK CONSTELLATION"). Additionally, Maersk operates 18 Surveillance Ships (TAGOS). These vessels are equipped with sophisticated sonar gear (see attached clipping) and perform submarine surveillance duty for the Navy.

1

Niels W. Johnsen memo to file regarding AMSEA vessels, June 8, 1992 (2 pages).

Maersk's estimated annual revenue from MSC contracts is, as follows:-

5 MPS Ships	About	$ 47.6 Million
MAERSK CONSTELLATION	About	6.0 Million
18 TAGOS Ships	About	32.0 Million
Total	About	$ 85.6 Million.

Indicative of the huge interests the Maersk Group (A.P. Moller) has in foreign flag ships is a copy of a recent list (1990) of ships owned by the A.P. Moller companies. Of the about eighty-two ships on this list most are registered under Danish (Da) flag (flg) and a few under Singapore (Sg) flag (flg). Please note that the Chairman of the company as well as Directors are Danish.

[3] **INTERNATIONAL SHIPHOLDING CORPORATION (ISC)/WATERMAN STEAMSHIP CORPORATION (WATERMAN)/CENTRAL GULF LINES, iNC. (CGL)**

Waterman, a wholly-owned subsidiary of ISC, operates three MPS ships on charter to MSC of similar duration and terms as the ten operated by AMSEA and Maersk. As mentioned above, these thirteen MPS ships carry pre-positioned equipment for the U.S. Marine Corps. CGL, also wholly-owned by ISC, has three LASH vessels, two ice-strengthened vessels, and one RO/RO vessel on time charter to MSC. The estimated annual revenue paid to Waterman and CGL on the MSC chartered ships is about $69.8 Million.

Obviously, if Maersk were to get control of the AMSEA fleet, ten of the thirteen MPS vessels would be in the hands of a company with substantial foreign interests domiciled in Denmark, a small country with a potentially volatile political constituency. Witness, the recent result of the Danish vote in connection with the Maastricht Treaty. A further substantial share of the Defense Department's payments would be made to this foreign controlled company. Why should the U.S. Navy take the risk of foreign control of these assets when a U.S. citizen controlled company is ready to perform? It should be in the interests of the U.S. Navy for General Dynamics to sell AMSEA to ISC, a bona fide U.S. citizen.

NWJ:mf   Niels W. Johnsen

2

MARITIME

General Dynamics Weighing Sale Of Sealift Unit to Waterman

Reported Talks Ease Concerns

By MICHAEL S. LELYVELD
Journal of Commerce Staff

BOSTON — General Dynamics Corp. is considering a sale of its Military Sealift Command business to U.S.-owned Waterman Steamship Corp. in an apparent effort to ease concerns over foreign control of a Navy cargo fleet, sources said this week.

The reported talks with Waterman on the sale of General Dynamics subsidiary American Overseas Marine Corp. are believed to be in response to congressional pressure over a possible sale of the unit to Maersk Inc., a Danish-owned company, the sources said.

American Overseas, based in Quincy, Mass., operates one of three MSC squadrons of "prepositioning" cargo ships under Navy contract to support U.S. Marine operations. Maersk already operates a second squadron, and Waterman operates the third. The ships were crucial to U.S. supply operations in the Persian Gulf war.

Of the 13 ships in the prepositioning fleet, five are operated by American Overseas, five by Maersk and three by Waterman. A sale of American Overseas to either of the other lines would make it the dominant carrier in the fleet. Waterman is owned by International Shipholding Corp., based in New Orleans.

The ships, which are all American-flagged, are owned by U.S. banks and financial institutions, the MSC has said.

Last month, members of the Massachusetts congressional delegation petitioned then-Navy Secretary H. Lawrence Garrett III to delay approval of a sale to Maersk after concerns were raised about foreign control and a potential loss of jobs. The lawmakers included Sens. John F. Kerry and Edward M. Kennedy and Reps. Brian Donnelly, Gerry Studds and Nicholas Mavroules, all Democrats.

It should be noted, however, that although Maersk is Danish-owned, its New Jersey-based subsidiary operates as a U.S. company.

Last week, Sen. Kerry also wrote to General Dynamics Chairman William A. Anders, citing concern over the possible job loss and signaling his support for a buy-out by American Overseas managers. Sen. Kerry said the Navy had indicated that it "would be amenable" to such a plan.

But in his July 2 letter, Sen. Kerry left the door open to another possible bidder for the business saying, "of course, other potential buyers may also exist who might continue operations in Quincy. In either case, I hope General Dynamics can meet its requirements by selling this fine company to a purchaser who will maintain it in Quincy, Mass."

Kjeld Johansen, Maersk corporate secretary, said he could not comment on the reports. Joseph Sutherland, a spokesman for St. Louis-based General Dynamics, declined comment. Jim Ahearn, American Overseas director of administration, cited company policy against responding to reports of possible deals and Erik F. Johnsen, president of International Shipholding, could not be reached for comment.

Critics say that General Dynamics has refused to negotiate with American Overseas managers on a company buy-out and that Maersk would merge the operation into its Madison, N.J.-based headquarters at a cost of some 55 jobs. Backers of a buy-out plan say they have been unable to determine a reason for General Dynamics' apparent refusal to negotiate with the management group.

"I find it incredible that here they're backing off from Maersk and they won't even give their own managers a chance," said Kevin Costello, government affairs manager of the South Shore Chamber of Commerce, which has been lobbying against a sale to Maersk.

Sources said this week that the managers have received positive signs on financing from the Bank of Boston and could mount a competitive offer. They also indicated that it is unlikely that a bidding war for the business is under way, because the Navy contract is for a fixed amount.

While Mr. Costello's organization has been instrumental in bringing congressional pressure to bear on behalf of the local managers, he also indicated there could be support for a sale to Waterman if it means no loss of jobs.

"If they would guarantee they would keep the jobs here, that's obviously a step in the right direction," Mr. Costello said.

Article in *The Journal of Commerce,* July 9, 1992.

of an article from that day's *Boston Herald* indicating the same information. Niels W. Johnsen placed a call on the same day to Zimmel. No response from him. Also on May 29, Johnsen received a call from James Grubbs of Citibank, who had heard the same story from contacts in the industry. With the news already out about Maersk, Zimmel undoubtedly felt it time to return my call, which he did on the morning of June 1. By then the story had also appeared in *The Journal of Commerce.* When confronted with the fact that we knew about Goldman Sachs's activity with Maersk, Zimmel apologized for not getting back to us. He claimed he really did not know what to tell us, because the decision had been made by General Dynamics to proceed with Maersk since their proposed price was higher than ours.

Niels W. Johnsen told him that he was surprised that at no time had Zimmel told us that they were working with another potential buyer. Johnsen also registered surprise that General Dynamics would attempt to sell AMSEA Companies to Maersk, a Danish-controlled company that already had five of the MPS ships under operation, plus a substantial number of other ships chartered to the U.S. Navy. We told Zimmel we would have to take whatever steps we thought necessary to protect our position. Zimmel realized that we would have to do so. Johnsen told him that our contacts would be in the Navy and in Congress and perhaps elsewhere. He again said we would have to do whatever we thought necessary. The first step we decided to take was to make sure that the Military Sealift Command was aware that we had been contacted on the purchase of these companies and had indicated our strong interest in concluding the transaction. Joseph Farrell, vice president of our Waterman subsidiary,

The Journal of Commerce
and Commercial

MARITIME
Additional Maritime News
On Page 6B

International Shipholding Expected To Win the Military Supply Race

By ALLEN S. ROBERTS
Journal of Commerce Staff

International Shipholding Corp. appears to have overtaken A.P. Moller-Maersk Line in the $250-million-a-year business of running the 13 ships that supply U.S. Marines sent into battle, sources said Thursday.

International Shipholding and A.P. Moller-Maersk, which already operate seven of those "prepositioned" supply ships, have been wrestling over the remaining five. Run by American Overseas Marine Corp. (Amsea), Quincy, Mass., a division of General Dynamics Corp., St. Louis, Mo., those five vessels went up for grabs after the shipping company was targeted for spin-off by its troubled, defense-contracting parent.

Three squadrons of such supply ships, each stocked with enough food, ammunition, fuel and equipment to support a 16,500-person Marine brigade for a month, are posted in the Atlantic, Indian and Pacific oceans.

Because the prepositioned ships played a crucial role in supporting the first Marines sent to Operation Desert Shield, their fate has caught the attention of congressmen and admirals. Several had lobbied for International Shipholding, based in New Orleans, to be given preference over Maersk Inc., Madison, N.J., the U.S. subsidiary of A.P. Moller-Maersk of Copenhagen, Denmark, in bidding for Amsea.

After nearly a year of wrangling, International Shipholding apparently prevailed Wednesday by signing an agreement to buy Amsea's ships from General Dynamics. That would give International Shipholding control of both the Atlantic and Pacific squadrons, leaving Maersk only the Indian Ocean group.

The parties did not disclose a price. But International Shipholding could expect revenues as high as $100 million a year — at the government's standard daily rate of $55,000 per ship — for continuously operating Amsea's five supply ships on behalf of the Military Sealift Command. The buyer also would take over more modest revenues, which could not be immediately estimated, from Amsea's 12 Ready Reserve Force freighters in the mothball fleets of the Maritime Administration.

International Shipholding's goal, executives said, is to add stable, military business to the cyclical, commercial trades, which it serves under the names of Central Gulf Lines Inc., Forest Lines and Waterman Steamship Corp.

As the United States withdraws from its bases overseas, they said, it will increasingly rely on prepositioned ships to support its troops in foreign conflicts. "This is part of the overall strategy of the Defense Department," Niels W. Johnsen, chairman, said, "and we want to be part of it."

The transaction would bring International Shipholding "a fairly balanced operation between commercial and military, with the bias toward commercial," Mr. Johnsen said. Amsea's 17 military ships would complement International Shipholding's nine ships in government service and 19 in commercial markets.

Because International Shipholding is a publicly traded company and Amsea is a defense contractor, however, the deal may face hurdles at the Securities and Exchange Commission, the Defense Department and the Transportation Department. "Don't assume it's going to be quick," one government official said of the approval process. "It may or may not be."

Maersk officials could not reached for comment.

Article in *The Journal of Commerce*, August 14, 1992.

The Times-Picayune
Friday, August 14, 1992

International Shipholding beefs up fleet

By MIKE HUGHLETT
Business writer

International Shipholding Corp. has made a major addition to its fleet, agreeing to purchase a subsidiary of General Dynamics Corp.

The New Orleans shipping company announced Thursday that it plans to buy American Overseas Marine Corp., which operates five vessels under long-term charter to the Military Sealift Command.

The Sealift Command coordinates civilian-operated shipping for U.S. Armed Forces.

Neither International Shipholding, based in Quincy, Mass., or General Dynamics, based in Falls Church, Va., would disclose the price for American Overseas Marine. The purchase was made with cash and bank financing, ISC President Erik Johnsen said, declining to provide details.

International Shipholding had been negotiating with General Dynamics since February or March, Johnsen said. The deal, expected to be closed by the end of the quarter, requires approval by the Sealift Command and shipping regulators.

The acquisition will boost International Shipholding's fleet from 30 to 35 ships, and will give it an even bigger presence in the military sealift

The acquisition will boost International Shipholding's fleet from 30 to 35 ships, and will give it an even bigger presence in the military sealift business.

business.

The five ships operated by American Overseas Marine Corp., which are owned by financial institutions, are part of the Sealift Command's 13-vessel Maritime Prepositioning Force.

Those ships are always staffed with civilian mariners and loaded with equipment for U.S. Marines. They're rushed to potential combat sites when needed, and were used extensively in the 1991 Persian Gulf War.

Waterman Steamship, one of International Shipholding's subsidiaries, operates three of the other Maritime Prepositioning ships, while the U.S. unit of Denmark-based Maersk Inc. operates the other five. All

See FLEET, C-3

Fleet

From C-1

of those ships are on 25-year charters.

International Shipholding has about six other ships on charter to the Military Sealift Command. The company also operates purely commercial ships, including Waterman Lines' service to the Middle East and South Asia.

As part of the deal, International Shipholding will also acquire the management of 12 Ready Reserve ships. The Ready Reserve ships, also used extensively in the Persian Gulf War, are owned by the U.S. Maritime Administration and managed by private companies. They are staffed only in emergencies.

American Overseas Marine Corp. will become an International Shipholding subsidiary, and stay headquartered in Quincy for the immediate future, Johnsen said.

The location of American Overseas Marine's headquarters, which employs about 55, has been a prickly issue in Massachusetts. Congressmen had raised their eyebrows over the sale of American Overseas to Maersk, which was reportedly interested in the company.

International Shipholding closed at 20¼, down ¾, in trading on the New York Stock Exchange.

Article in *The Times-Picayune*, August 14, 1992.

made an appointment to see Admiral Francis Donovan, commander of the Military Sealift Command, to make sure he was aware of our involvement in this transaction and of our continued interest in acquiring the AMSEA companies. Joe at first was scheduled to see Admiral Donovan at 9:30 a.m. on June 1. However, Admiral Donovan was called out of town and postponed the meeting until 11 a.m. June 3. After Joe Farrell explained our involvement in this transaction he said the admiral told him he thought we were treated unfairly. The admiral also said that he and the MSC would be sensitive to the opinions of members of Congress. Admiral Donovan and his deputy Wally Sansone, who was also at the meeting, said they also had some concern that a company with substantial Danish control might add the AMSEA companies to an already substantial position of ships on charter to the Navy. The admiral also stated that he understood we might want to make our position known to members of Congress and others.

This chronology is set forth here in order to show the somewhat convoluted method of negotiating employed by Goldman Sachs and General Dynamics, and to indicate the presence and lobbying effort done by the Danish company, Goldman Sachs, and General Dynamics Corporation. After these series of events Niels W. Johnsen also had a telephone conversation on the afternoon of June 4, 1992, with Leland Bishop of AMSEA. He told Bishop that we had to let the Navy know of our involvement in this project since they had not previously been informed on the subject. Johnsen also asked Bishop if there was anything we could do to reopen negotiations at this time, or whether we had to take other action to protect our interests. Johnsen told him we did not want to go to Congress or any other parties without having had this conversation and giving him an opportunity to tell us whether we could make further progress now or would have to await further developments. Bishop's response was that in view of the fact that General Dynamics Corporation had decided to pursue the possible sale to Maersk, he could not see any opportunity for General Dynamics to change its approach at this time. He acknowledged, however, that the only event that would change their minds would be a turndown of Maersk by the Navy.

Bishop also acknowledged that we had to protect our interests and do whatever we consider necessary to get our message to the Navy. It would not be any surprise to AMSEA or General Dynamics Corporation if members of Congress support our position with the Navy and/or oppose the Navy's placing more vessels in the hands of a Danish-controlled company. Johnsen told him that ISC was sorry that the situation had developed to this point but that ISC would proceed without malice. Johnsen wanted Bishop to know that we were dealing completely in the open with him.

One of the points that Johnsen made with Bishop was that while Zimmel had told him that there was a "level playing field" in the material given to Maersk and to us, there was obviously not a level playing field in the manner in which Maersk arrived at its price and we arrived at ours. Johnsen told Bishop that the impression we had was that Maersk was just buying the contracts and not the companies. Bishop did not confirm this point, but his response indicated that our impression was correct. In other words, Maersk arrived at the value just for the contracts, while we were arriving at a number that included AMSEA overhead expenses each year, something Zimmel told us General Dynamics desired. Zimmel told us that General Dynamics wanted the buyer of the AMSEA companies to take over the overhead of the AMSEA companies, retaining the administrative staff.

We promptly made known to the relevant members of the U.S. Congress, the Navy and the Maritime Administration our concern that General Dynamics would consider selling these AMSEA companies to Maersk, a Danish-controlled company that already had a substantial position with the operation of U.S. Navy ships. Our activities with various branches of the U.S. government apparently bore fruit. On June 15, 1992, we received a telephone call from Zimmel asking us to set forth our revised estimate of the value and purchase price of the employment contracts (charters) applicable to the five Military Prepositioning Ships operated by AMSEA. This was in contrast to our previous price indication, which was based upon the purchase of the stock of each operating company subsidiary of AMSEA and included ISC taking over the costs of AMSEA overhead. We promptly sent a letter to

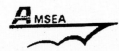

AMERICAN OVERSEAS MARINE CORPORATION

A General Dynamics Subsidiary

116 East Howard Street, Quincy, Massachusetts 02169 • (617) 786-8300

TELEX 174065   FAX (617) 770-4568

Leland B. Bishop, II
President

October 16, 1992
LBB/92-158

VADM Michael P. Kalleres
Commander
Military Sealift Command
Washington Navy Yard, Bldg. 210
901 M Street SE
Washington, DC 20398-5540

Reference: (a) MSC letter to AMSEA
                 Ser N104/01202, dated 5 June 1992

            (b) Braintree Companies letter to MSC
                 File No. JFO:rb/92-118, dated June 22, 1992

Dear Admiral Kalleres:

I was disappointed to learn from your 9 October letter that MSC would be unable to support an AMSEA sale closing date of 15 October which we had previously discussed in your office. Instead, you suggested I contact Jack Roche and establish a meeting to review certain issues. In accord with that request, I immediately got in touch with Mr. Jack Roche to establish the suggested meeting.

The meeting was held on Friday, 16 October at 10 AM and basically addressed the MSC proposal to renegotiate the present MPS contract. Based on the meeting, I believe it important to again address the subject of the sale closing and the MSC approval to switch the Guarantor.

Most of the MSC proposed renegotiation items had previously been presented to us on June 5th via Reference (a). Shortly thereafter (June 22, 1992) we responded, see Reference (b), stating that several of the items had definite merit and could be easily adopted. Some, however, were more complex and required a proposal from MSC to enable us to better understand the concept and appropriately comment. However, even after today's meeting focused to this subject, we have yet to receive the requested proposals.

Some of these issues require not just proposal concept agreement, but the development and agreement to ground rules which will definitely take some time to develop and agree on, based on past history. Accordingly, to hold up the AMSEA sale until this MSC proposed contract change is developed, negotiated, and consummated seems inappropriate, impractical and unbusinesslike, especially since one has nothing to do with the other.

On 12 August, we met to notify you of the proposed change in ownership of AMSEA. That was followed by formal letter notification on 17 August which requested your consent to and support and endorsement of the proposed transaction. Justice Department and other required consents were later requested and are now ready to support a sale closing. The banks financing which is in place is good until the 30th of October. Further, the sale agreement was based on a closing on or before 30 October 1992. However, before the closing can take place, we need the requested MSC endorsement. Accordingly, we again request MSC's agreement to the substitution of International Shipholding Corporation for General Dynamics as the Guarantor so we can close this sale before time runs out.

Your support is urgently requested.

Sincerely,

Leland B. Bishop

Leland B. Bishop, II
President

Letter from Leland B. Bishop II, AMSEA President, to Michael P. Kalleres, Commander Military Sealift Command, October 16, 1992.

TERMINATION AGREEMENT

This Termination Agreement ("Agreement") is made and entered into as of the 6th day of May, 1994 by and among GENERAL DYNAMICS CORPORATION, a Delaware corporation, ("GD"), CONCORD I MARITIME CORP., a Delaware corporation, CONCORD II MARITIME CORP., a Delaware Corporation, CONCORD III MARITIME CORP., a Delaware corporation, CONCORD IV MARITIME CORP., a Delaware corporation, CONCORD V MARITIME CORP., a Delaware corporation, INTERNATIONAL SHIPHOLDING CORPORATION, a Delaware corporation, ("ISC") and AM SEA ACQUISITION CORP., a Delaware corporation ("Am Sea").

The above parties entered into a Stock Purchase Agreement dated as of August 12, 1992 (the "Stock Purchase Agreement") and have subsequently entered into Continuation Agreements extending the "Close" of the transaction to dates ("Continuation Agreement(s)"), all of which have expired.

Since August 12, 1992 the parties have each complied with their pre-closing covenants as set out in Section 5 of the Stock Purchase Agreement except that although the parties have diligently sought the approval of the U. S. Government, Department of Navy, Military Sea Lift Command (hereinafter referred to as the "MSC") to the transactions contemplated by the Stock Purchase Agreement, they have been unable to obtain such approval. In view of the foregoing and the resulting frustration of the Agreement, the parties hereby agree as follows:

1. The parties hereto hereby confirm that the Stock Purchase Agreement, each provision thereof and all rights and obligations arising thereunder were terminated and revoked in their entirety as of the November 30, 1992, the date provided in the last Continuation Agreement.

2. Anything contained in the Stock Purchase Agreement or in any Continuation Agreement(s) to the contrary notwithstanding since November 30, 1992 and at all times thereafter, none of the parties hereto has been or shall be limited in any way in connection with any negotiations or discussions with the MSC regarding the contracts and vessels which are described in the Stock Purchase Agreement and Exhibits thereto and no party hereto has since that date nor will hereafter have any obligation to discuss or consult with any other party with respect thereto.

3. ISC and Am Sea will forthwith return to GD and or American Overseas Marine Corporation ("AOMC") all of the confidential material furnished by GD or AOMC pursuant to Section 5.3 of the Stock Purchase Agreement. The material shall be sent to:

> Mr. Leland A. Bishop
> President
> American Overseas Marine Corporation
> 116 E. Howard Street
> Quincy, Maine 02169

4. No person acting on behalf of any party or any of their affiliates or under authority of any of the foregoing is or shall be or will be entitled to any brokers' or finders' fee or any other commission or similar fee, directly or indirectly from any of the other parties hereto in connection with any of the transactions contemplated by this Agreement. In particular, without limiting the

Termination agreement between General Dynamics Corporation and its subsidiaries and International Shipholding Corporation and its subsidiaries, May 16, 1994 (2 pages).

above and foregoing, a fee payable Goldman Sachs, if any, is the responsibility of GD.

5. Each party will pay its own expenses and neither party shall have any liability to the other for such expenses. it is understood, however, that each party will pay Arthur Andersen & Co. one-half of the appraisal fee.

6. Each party shall jointly and severally indemnify and hold harmless the other parties and their respective directors, officers, employees and agents from and against any and all claims (contingent or otherwise) causes of action, losses, damages, costs, expenses (including, but not limited to attorneys' fees, and accountants' fees) and any liability whatsoever arising out of or in connection with any action or non-action on the part of such party pursuant to the Stock Purchase Agreement. Except as herein in this Section 6 specifically provided, it is understood that no party shall have any obligation whatsoever to the directors, officers, employees and agents of any other party.

IN WITNESS WHEREOF, the parties hereto have executed and delivered this Agreement in counterparts as of the date first written above.

CONCORD I MARITIME CORP.

By: _____
Its: Vice President & Secretary

CONCORD II MARITIME CORP.

By: _____
Its: Vice President & Secretary

CONCORD III MARITIME CORP.

By: _____
Its: Vice President & Secretary

CONCORD IV MARITIME CORP.

By: _____
Its: Vice President & Secretary

CONCORD V MARITIME CORP.

By: _____
Its: Vice President & Secretary

GENERAL DYNAMICS
CORPORATION

By: _____
Its: Executive Vice President

AM SEA ACQUISITION CORP.

By: _____
Its: Chairman

INTERNATIONAL SHIPHOLDING
CORPORATION

By: _____
Its: Chairman

James E. Turner, executive vice president of General Dynamics, setting forth our revised price. It was based upon Waterman, a longtime operator of U.S.-flag vessels and a subsidiary of International Shipholding Corporation, purchasing the value of the charters applicable to the employment and operation of the AMSEA companies' five MPS vessels. We stated that we assumed a closing date of June 30, 1992. We also assumed that, after stripping the five MPS charters from the AMSEA companies, all the other net assets and net worth would be retained by General Dynamics. We assumed that AMSEA would continue to operate its Ready Reserve Fleet and any other non-MPS business and own its main building and land in Quincy as well as the design plans for the *2nd Lt. John P. Bobo*. Then we set forth the price we would pay after taking into account the foregoing.

Over the next month, the pace of the negotiations quickened and we soon agreed to have a draft of the stock purchase agreement prepared. The financing for the transaction was approved by our banks and we were able to present General Dynamics with a copy of the financing plan. The lawyers then submitted the final draft of the stock purchase agreement for signatures. Signing took place on August 12, 1992, and *The Journal of Commerce* on August 14, published an article entitled "International Shipholding expected to win the military supply race."

After signing the stock purchase agreement on August 12, the parties immediately took steps to obtain the necessary regulatory approvals. The Justice Department certified that the proposed acquisition was legal and that the department had no opposition under the Hart-Scott-Rodino Act. The Maritime Administration endorsed the transaction. Everything proceeded according to plan with one exception: The Military Sealift Command, on behalf of the U.S. Navy, did not react favorably.

On October 16, Leland Bishop wrote a letter to Vice Admiral Michael P. Kallares, commander of the MSC, stating in part that he was disappointed to learn from Admiral Kallares' letter of October 9, that the MSC would be unable to support the AMSEA sale closing date of October 15, which Bishop and Kallares had previously discussed in his office. In his letter of October 16, Bishop also stated among other things, he had met with Admiral Kallares on August 12, followed by a formal letter on August 17, notifying him of the sale requesting MSC consent and support. The Justice Department and other regulatory agencies' approvals had been obtained in support of the sale closing. He also pointed out to Admiral Kallares that the bank financing was in place and valid until October 30. He further encouraged MSC to approve the sale, which had previously been based upon a closing of October 30, 1992.

There was no further response from MSC. So we decided to go to the Office of the Secretary of the Navy. Erik F. Johnsen wrote to Navy Secretary Sean O'Keefe on November 23, requesting a meeting to discuss the acquisition of AMSEA by International Shipholding. The letter was replied to by Gerald A. Cann, assistant secretary of the Navy, on December 17. He wrote, in part, that he understood that Niels W. Johnsen had met with Ronald Kiss, deputy assistant secretary of the Navy, other members of Cann's staff, and representatives of MSC on December 1, to discuss the acquisition. During that meeting Niels W. Johnsen was advised that the Navy was contemplating the purchase of some or all of the existing MPS ships and that until the Navy decided whether to pursue such a purchase, it did not appear to the Navy that action should be taken on ISC request for purchase of the AMSEA companies. Cann went on to say that he could not predict when or whether the Navy would buy the ships but they were seriously considering their purchase options. He expected to be able to provide an indication of the Navy's planned course of action within the next 120 days, which would have been about the middle of April 1993. He further stated that until the Navy made this determination it was not prone to act on ISC request for approval of the AMSEA purchase.

In the meantime, hoping that the Navy would act favorably on General Dynamics' and our request for approval of the AMSEA purchase by ISC, we had agreed with General Dynamics to a continuation agreement that extended the October 30 closing date to November 17, 1992. It was then again extended to November 30, and a third continuation agreement replaced the second, extending the closing date to April 16, 1993. We soon arrived at the middle of April 1993, and still no action by the U.S. Navy.

Since August 12, 1992, the parties had each complied with their pre-closing covenants as set forth in Section 5 of the stock purchase agreement. Despite the fact that the parties diligently sought the approval of the U.S. Government, Department of the Navy, to the transactions contemplated by the agreement, they were unable to obtain such approval. Consequently, it was becoming clear that the Navy had decided it was not going to allow General Dynamics to sell the AMSEA companies and that it was useless to continue extending the original stock purchase agreement. The transaction was frustrated.

So the parties to the frustrated agreement decided that it was best officially to terminate that agreement so that they could be free to operate in any manner consistent with their own policy. Thirteen years have gone by since the stock purchase agreement was signed. General Dynamics still owns AMSEA companies, still operates the five ships in the MPS and still has not altered its contracts with Navy (to the best of our knowledge, although we continue to hear rumors that the Navy still wants to buy the ships). Also the Navy still talks about buying other ships operating on military prepositioning contracts, including the three operating by Waterman. So far the Navy has been unable to agree on the purchase prices with the leasing companies that own the ships. The Navy has obviously declined to pay the termination prices stipulated in the leasing agreements and the lessors have apparently refused to reduce those prices.

Thus ended the AMSEA Encounter.

(For the record, a copy of the Termination Agreement dated May 16, 1994, between General Dynamics Corporation and its subsidiaries and International Shipholding Corporation and its subsidiaries is reprinted here.)

Post Mortem

On January 17, 2006, the U.S. Navy announced that it had purchased the *1st Lt. Jack Lummus*, *1st Lt. Baldomero Lopez* and *PFC Dewayne T. Williams* from the lessors of these AMSEA ships, Phillip Morris Credit Corporation, for $70 million each. Apparently AMSEA continues as the operating contractor for all three ships, pending U.S. Navy advertising for competitive bids.

Members of the Johnsen family, executives of the Company, standing forward of the raked stem of the LASH vessel SS *Austral Rainbow*, acquired from Farrell Lines in 1990. Left to right: Niels M. Johnsen, vice president; Niels W. Johnsen, chairman; Erik F. Johnsen, president; Erik L. Johnsen, vice president.

CHAPTER 26

More Value Added—New York Stock Exchange and Other Niches

We were disappointed that the U.S. Navy did not give its approval for us to acquire the AMSEA vessels. Still we did not let the government's failure to act distract us too long. We already had 10 ships (three LASH, three MPS, two ice-strengthened vessels and two others) on charter to the U.S. Navy Military Sealift Command. So the Navy's inaction obviously had nothing to do with our qualifications to operate U.S. flag vessels. The MSC had employed our ships for over 50 years. Other opportunities for continued growth were available, so we shifted our attention.

Despite a volatile ocean shipping market, our financial condition in 1990 strengthened. We recorded $15,065,000 net profit.

Instead of buying the AMSEA companies, the Company made other capital investments in 1990 totaling approximately $60 million. We purchased the *Amazon,* a 1981-built 148,000-DWT Cape-size dry-bulk carrier, for $32.760 million. We acquired the *Austral Rainbow,* a U.S.-flag LASH vessel, for $ 6.350 million. We began a LASH barge purchase and refurbishment program for $13.640 million. We also made a down payment of $929,000 on our share of a newbuilding 56,000-cubic-meter liquefied petroleum gas carrier. The cost of our international LASH mother vessel's life extension program came to $6.086 million. So our total capital investments for the year amounted to $59.765 million, which we financed with $43 million of new long-term loans and the balance from internal sources. Also during 1990, we paid off $27.129 million of old debt and refinanced approximately $14 million of old loans that came to the Company with Waterman.

In 1991 our capital investments were $44 million. Most of this, together with the $43 million spent in 1990, went to continue the program to refurbish our LASH barge fleet of approximately 700 barges, to purchase new LASH barges replacing older barges being scrapped, and for life extension work on the *Rhine Forest.*

Going back to the beginning of 1990, we recorded a gain of $6.171 million when we sold our one-half interest in the *Probo Bangor,* a Probo ship, which we had owned with our Norwegian partner, Torvald Klaveness. We retained one-half interest in the other two Probo vessels owned with A/S Havtor, which continued to operate in the Bulkhandling Pool managed by Klaveness from Norway.

At our request the U.S. Department of Transportation approved the consolidation of Waterman's Operating Differential Subsidy contract, to extend its termination date to December 1996. This contract covered subsidized operation of four U.S.-flag LASH vessels by Waterman on Trade Routes 18 and 17 (U.S. Gulf/ U.S. Atlantic ports to and from ports in South Asia with privileges to make calls en route.) Sea-Land Service filed a complaint against the DOT in the U.S. District Court for the District of Columbia, asking for a review of the decision, but later withdrew the complaint. In 1990 Waterman contributed to our improved results in its first full year as a member of our group. Completion of the LASH barge refurbishment program also enhanced Waterman's operations.

With the decision of the U.S. government in 1990 to send military forces into Saudi Arabia under the code name Desert Shield, our ships on prepositioning service to the Military Sealift Command began delivering their

MV *Amazon,* Cape-size bulk carrier, built Hyundai Heavy Industries, Ulsan, South Korea, November, 1981, acquired by Company from FedNav in July 1990 and time-chartered back for 10 years. DWT 148,629 long tons; LOA, 266.5 meters (878.45'); beam, 42.97 meters (141.8'); draft, 17.4 meters (57.1'); speed, 13 knots on 52 metric tons HVF.

military cargoes to that country. Additionally, the MSC used cargo space on Waterman's LASH liner vessels to deliver part of these cargoes. One of our roll-on/roll-off U.S.-flag Pure Car Carriers temporarily suspended the carriage of automobiles from Japan to the United States in order to assist in the movement of military vehicles from the United States to the Middle East.

The life extension program for our international-flag LASH vessels was completed in October with the return to service of *Rhine Forest.* This vessel also performed feeder service for Waterman on a temporary basis, replacing one of Waterman's U.S.-flag LASH vessels that was undergoing repairs in a Mediterranean shipyard after sustaining bottom damage from grounding near the southern entrance to the Suez Canal in September 1990.

The unfolding of dramatic events in Europe and the Middle East in 1991 also significantly shook up our market. Desert Storm directly affected our operations, but we were able to adjust our schedules to make available a substantial part of our ship capacity to carry military cargo to and from Saudi Arabia. The tearing

down of the Berlin Wall and sudden collapse of Communism in the former Soviet Union also created confusion in the world ship charter markets. For most of the year, shipments of grain to Russia and other countries of the former Soviet Union were "on-again, off-again," due to a temporary lack of funding to purchase these much-needed commodities and an inefficient distribution system in the recipient countries. Shipments, halted several times because Russia was delinquent in paying ocean freight charges, were ultimately resumed as the year ended and financing became available.

In the ocean ship market a near balance was developing between availability of vessels worldwide and demand for their use.

The Company ended 1991, another year of financial growth, with a profit of $15.233 million. We paid off $28.1 million of debt and $2.8 million of lease obligations during the year.

After having participated in the movement of military cargo for the MSC during Desert Shield/Desert Storm, our U.S.-flag Pure Car Carriers returned to

ISC Board and Management, on first day of ISC stock trading on NYSE, October 30, 1991. Left to right, Erik F. Johnsen, George Denegre, Laurance Eustis, Gary Ferguson. Back row: Niels M. Johnsen, Niels W. Johnsen, Raymond O'Brien, Jr., Edwin Lupberger, Harold S. Grehan, Jr.

LASH Intermodal Terminal, Memphis, Tennessee, opened in 1992 to receive loaded LASH barges inbound and deliver loaded LASH barges outbound.

MV *Sulphur Enterprise,* molten-sulphur carrier delivered August 6, 1994. Cargo capacity, 27,241 long tons; LOA, 524 feet; beam, 90 feet; draft, 37 feet; Wartsila VASA diesel engine, speed, 15 knots; Class, ABS; home port, New Orleans; builder, McDermott, Inc., Amelia, Louisiana.

MV *Sulphur Enterprise* at sulphur loading terminal at Galveston, Texas.

MV *Sulphur Enterprise* sponsor, Mrs. Joan Latiolais, wife of executive vice president of Freeport-McMoRan, viewing model with Erik F. Johnsen, president of the Company.

their regular service carrying automobiles from Japan to the United States. Our two international Pure Car Carriers continued uninterrupted during this period, carrying automobiles from the Far East to the United States and Europe.

Three of our U.S.-flag LASH vessels that had been on charter to the MSC for several years completed those charters during the third quarter of 1991. We successfully renewed time charters for each of them for 17 months with two 17-month extensions at the option of MSC. The three vessels operated by Waterman on long-term time charter to the MSC returned to their prepositioning service after operation in Desert Storm.

Our investment in A/S Havtor and A/S Havtor Management recorded a profit of $4.697 million in 1991. In 1992 this group lost $ 1.421 million—a swing of $6.118 million—because of a weakened market for LPG carriers. Even so, our original investment in these Norwegian companies held their appreciated value.

To broaden the market for trading in the Company's common stock, the Board decided to register its shares (symbol ISH) with the New York Stock Exchange. Trading began on October 30, 1991, at a price of $21.25 per share.

The next year, 1992, turned out to be a year of transition. Highlights were: (1) completion and financing of the renovation of our LASH barge fleet, (2) fixing new charters at improved rates, and (3) the opening of LITCO in Memphis. At the same time we were not

happy with the year's operating results. But considering the sluggish economic environment and the difficult trading conditions in ocean shipping markets, we were fortunate to have achieved even a modest profit of $3.281 million. We also continued to reduce long-term debt by repaying $35,596,000. We scheduled for long-term debt amortization payments in 1993 $39,865,000 and redeemed $1,750,000 of preferred stock.

During 1992 we concluded new charters with the MSC. Additionally the LASH *Atlantic Forest* transferred from foreign flag to U.S. flag under Waterman ownership, and was renamed the *Jeb Stuart,* and chartered to the MSC prepositioning service for 17 months plus two 17-month option periods. She was delivered to this charter on December 8, 1992. The halting recovery from recession in the United States, a subject of endless rhetoric during the U.S. presidential election campaign of 1992, and shrinking economies of Japan and Europe (coupled with the serious economic problems in the states of the former Soviet Union) presented a bleak background to the world ship charter market. Steel production declined by four percent in Europe and by more than 11 percent in Japan. This industry consumes two basic commodities, iron ore and coal, the backbone of the dry-bulk carrier market. Japan imported 112.6 million tons of iron ore in 1992 (down 13% from 1991) and 71.5 million tons of coal (down also from 1991.) The reduced imports of coking coal used in steelmaking by Japan were partially offset by an increase in import of steam coal for electricity generation, so that total coal imports by Japan remained virtually unchanged at about 111 million tons. Russia and the former Soviet states imported 11.8 million tons less grain in 1992 than 1991. Credit problems that delayed or frustrated grain shipments in 1992 continued. The recessions in Japan and Europe also reduced demand for liquefied petroleum gas, hurting the LPG freight market. About four million DWT of dry-bulk carriers were scrapped that year—more than the total tonnage scrapped in all of the preceding three years. About 11 million DWT of tankers and about 1.5-million DWT of combination carriers were also scrapped.

Material Transfer Inc., our domestic river barge system and coal transfer facility at Gulf County, Florida, handled about three million tons of coal in 1992 destined for Seminole Electric Utility in Palatka, Florida. In 1992 we also completed construction of our intermodal facility in Memphis. LASH Intermodal Terminal, LITCO, recognized by U.S. Customs as an official ocean port, was established to receive loaded LASH barges inbound and deliver loaded LASH barges outbound. The company was therefore able to offer its customers the facilities of its own port for reception and distribution of their products at an upriver facility, closer to the customer's markets and sources of exports. LITCO became an integral link in the LASH system. The terminal handled approximately 160,000 tons of cargo from its inauguration in May 1992 until year-end.

In May 1992 our wholly owned subsidiary Sulphur Carriers, Inc., signed a contract with Freeport-McMoRan Resource Partners providing for the construction in a United States shipyard of a 27,241-ton capacity U.S.-flag molten sulphur carrier to be used under a contract for 15 years in the U.S. domestic (coastwise) trade. We ordered Hull #294 to be built by McDermott, Inc. at Amelia, Louisiana, at a cost of $60 million. Joan Latiolais, wife of Freeport-McMoRan's executive vice president, named her Sulphur Enterprise at a festive ceremony in New Orleans in August 1994. The Sulphur Enterprise is the largest tanker of her type and the only one operating under the U.S. flag. The ship typifies our strategy of owning vessels that perform services in special market niches. She has operated well for over 10 years and has a profitable future in a unique

ocean transportation service. By the end of 1995 the Sulphur Enterprise had made 100 trips, carrying a total of 2.4 million tons of molten sulphur. In our domestic trades during 1995, our river barge fleet carried a total of 3.2 million tons of coal for Seminole Electric Cooperative from the Ohio River to Florida via the Mississippi River, Intracoastal Waterway, and our coal transfer facility, MTI, in Gulf County, Florida.

The capital cost of our LASH barge fleet refurbishment was substantially completed in 1992 and came to $88.4 million, of which we financed $82.5 million by a combination of bank loans, Title XI loans, and a sale/leaseback. After combining the LASH barge operations of Waterman and Forest Lines into one fleet, we sold 144 surplus LASH barges.

In late 1993 we consolidated our debt by issuing $100 million of unsecured notes maturing in 2003 and the exercise by holders of warrants for 427,500 shares of common stock at $10.12 per share yielding $4,326,000, or a total of $104,326,000. We used $80,895,000 of this new cash to prepay various other debts and redeem all of our preferred stock. Fees and other expenses in connection with the note issue amounted to $3,548,000. The remaining $19,883,000 was available for other investments, including part of the cost of Sulphur Enterprise.

After negotiating with the MSC on the charter terms for the three vessels operated by Waterman on prepositioning service, we mutually agreed to fix the period of these charters for the entire 25 years in consideration of Waterman reducing the future charter-hire payments, rather than have them subject to possible termination at the end of each five-year period. The three charters will now run uninterrupted through 2010.

The Cape-size bulk carrier Amazon ended her initial charter toward the end of 1993 when she entered a new charter for one year with options. The fact that she had just completed an extensive renovation helped generate interest by new charterers.

Material Transfer Inc., at Gulf County, Florida, again in 1993 handled just over three million tons of coal under the long-term contract with Seminole Electric.

In the same year LITCO had a total of 1,095 LASH barge loads, equivalent to 400,000 tons of export and import cargo, processed through its facility. Our goal was to increase throughput in 1994 to 500,000 tons annually.

ISC made a nominal profit in 1993 of $5,929,000 after paying $1,716,000 as the after-tax cost of prepayment penalties for early retirement of certain debt and preferred stock. We continued to focus on debt reduction. We also remained alert to new opportunities to expand our book of business. Despite uncertain world charter markets, our fleet ended 1993 well-positioned for the forthcoming year.

Our transatlantic LASH service, Forest Lines, continued to achieve improved results, ending the year with operating income higher than the previous year. We had expected to add the *Austral Rainbow* to this service as a third LASH vessel in early 1995. However, the MSC invited offers for a renewed charter, so we refixed her for another 17 months beginning in February 1995, with options for two additional 17-month periods.

While Waterman's service between U.S. Gulf and Atlantic ports and South Asia had an uptick in the last quarter of 1994, operations for the full year were down from 1993. LITCO handled the increased total of 1,300 LASH barge loads in 1994, equivalent to about 500,000 tons of export and import cargo. This year we purchased the two U.S.-flag LASH vessels *Robert E. Lee* and *Stonewall Jackson,* which had previously been on leases to Waterman. The MSC declared options to continue the charters of two of our other U.S.-flag LASH vessels for further 17 months each beginning December 1994. Three other vessels on medium-term charter to the MSC were fixed well into 1995, with one option declarable March 1995 and two declarable in the fourth quarter.

Also in 1994, our investments in the Norwegian company, A/S Havtor, and certain associated companies were merged into Havtor AS, a company listed on the Oslo Stock Exchange. As of December 31, 1994, the Company's interest in Havtor AS was approximately 12.6%, including direct and indirect holdings. The market value of our interest was then approximately $29,800,000, versus the book value of $13,200,000. Havtor AS owned a fleet of 26 liquefied petroleum gas carriers and seven dry bulk carriers and was joint owner with us of the two Probo vessels. In addition, the Company held a 14.2% interest in A/S Havtor Management, the Norwegian company that managed most of the vessels owned by Havtor AS.

Early in the next year, Havtor AS, A/S Havtor Management and Kvaerner signed a letter of intent whereby A/S Havtor Management and the gas carrier activities of Kvaerner were to be merged into Havtor AS. This resulted in Havtor AS having ownership interest varying from 10% to 100% in 46 gas carriers, six dry-cargo carriers, two Probo vessels and one petroleum product carrier in addition to other minor participations. As 1995 ended we sold our holding in Havtor AS for a gain of $11.3 million.

We acquired another special-purpose vessel in October 1994. The New England Power Company had contracted in 1983 to charter for a long term a ship to be built at the Quincy, Massachusetts, yard of General Dynamics. The design was for a 38,164-DWT bulk carrier qualified for Jones Act trade and equipped with a conveyor-belt system for self-unloading coal about 3,000 tons per hour. She had a steam turbine engine that fired its boilers with either stoker coal or fuel oil. This ship came into service at the same time we were employing an oceangoing barge of 30,000 DWT that we had constructed in Green Bay, Wisconsin, in 1981 to supply coal to New England Power Company at Brayton Point, Massachusetts. Our barge normally loaded at Norfolk, Virginia, and was towed by ocean-going tug boat to and from Brayton Point. She was a bulk-carrier type barge without cargo-handling cranes, so she needed shore cranes to unload at Brayton Point. The utility was anxious to discontinue use of shore cranes for environmental reasons (air pollution). When the new conveyor-equipped bulk carrier *Energy Independence* came into service in 1983, she virtually put our barge out of business. The *Energy Independence* was financed using a leasing company. Keystone Shipping Company of Philadelphia was her operator. New England Power Company had the option in the lease to purchase the vessel at a fixed price anytime during the lease period. Seeking a change of owners and operators, the utility company exercised the option and then offered the vessel for repurchase combined with a long-term time charter. We won the bidding to buy the vessel and took delivery on September 28, 1995, simultaneously time-chartering the ship to New Eng-

SS *Energy Enterprise,* conveyor-belt self-unloading bulk carrier, passing the Statue of Liberty, New York Harbor with a full cargo (35,000 MT) of bulk coal to be delivered to the electric generating utility at the Danskammer power plant at Newburgh, New York, on the Hudson River. The coal was unloaded using the vessel's own conveyor belt system for transfer to a shoreside conveyer belt system.

land Power Company for 15 years. We changed her name to *Energy Enterprise*. Then followed a period of about four months during which we had substantial shipyard work done at Bethlehem Steel Shipyard, Sparrows Point, Maryland (mainly steel repairs on the 12-year old ship), to return her to coastwise coal-carrying service. In February 1996 the shipyard work was completed. The *Energy Enterprise* shifted from Baltimore to Norfolk and loaded her first coal cargo to Brayton Point under our ownership to begin her 15-year time charter.

We provided interim financing with a bank loan. For permanent financing we formed a "bankruptcy remote" company, Energy Enterprise Company, to own the vessel. Then, using her charter to New England Power Company (a D&B-rated "A" security) as collateral, we sold secured notes to two prime insurance companies maturing in 15 years in order to obtain a fixed interest rate of 6% (a very attractive rate at the time). One covenant of the loan provided that a bankruptcy of the ship's charterer would constitute a default under our loan and trigger cross-defaults on our other loans, no matter how strong the borrower's or guaran-

tor's (ISC's) financial strength might be. New England Power Company was later sold to Pacific Gas and Electric Company, becoming its indirect subsidiary. California-based Pacific Gas and Electric Company subsequently declared bankruptcy that trickled down to its subsidiaries. To our surprise in 2004, New England Power Company also declared bankruptcy, creating a default on our *Energy Enterprise* loan. In order to prevent cross-defaults on our other loans, we had to pay off the balance of the *Energy Enterprise* loan, about $20 million including prepayment penalty (which would not be waived), and legal expenses. The *Energy Enterprise* remained on its time charter to New England Power Company. Next, Pacific Gas and Electric Company sold the charter to Dominion Resources, together with other assets of the utility and all its contracts. The ship became chartered to Dominion Resources until the time charter's maturity in 2010.

In June 1994 a subsidiary of the Company signed a contract with another Freeport company, Freeport-McMoRan Copper and Gold, Inc., to transport supplies required by its mines on the Indonesian island of

Irian Jaya. The contract, for 11 years, gave the mining company options for further years. To perform this contract the Company purchased in March and June 1995 two existing float-on/float-off vessels ("Dock Ships"), which we had lengthened by 33 meters resulting in a deadweight of about 22,800 tons each. We renamed these vessels the *Bali Sea* and the *Banda Sea* and had them converted in a Singapore shipyard to accommodate the carriage of 26 special-purpose barges each, in the float-on/float-off mode. We had the barges built in China. Each barge had the capacity to carry 1,588 tons of cargo. Float-on/float-off technology was well-suited to this operation, because the port for the mining company was up the Akijawa River, requiring a shallow-draft vessel not exceeding 22.5 feet.

About halfway through this contract, the mining company decided it wanted the supplies to arrive instead by breakbulk ships and container ships (one multipurpose vessel, a small tanker, and two small container ships). We agreed to restructure the contract to accommodate the customer. We chartered the replacement vessels and withdrew the *Bali Sea* and *Banda Sea* for reassignment.

Waterman LASH service between U.S. Gulf and Atlantic ports and South Asia had improved results in 1996 over a poor year in 1995. This service began the new year with a revised U.S. government assistance program. When the Operating Differential Subsidy contract ended for the four Waterman vessels on completion of their then-current voyages, the replacement program for ODS, enacted as HR 1350, the Maritime Security Act of 1996, became effective. The act replaced the expiring ODS with the Maritime Security Program, which provided annual U.S. government subsidy payments of $2.1 million per vessel for a total of 47 eligible U.S.-flag vessels. We made some operating cost savings to accommodate lower subsidy payments and keep Waterman competitive in this service. The new MSP also became applicable to three additional U.S.-flag vessels in the Waterman and Central Gulf fleets, which we later assigned to three car/truck carriers. This gave us a total of seven MSP-eligible vessels. MSP had more flexible operating requirements than the expired ODS contracts, so the seven vessels receiving MSP payments operated freely, trading worldwide.

Our four LASH vessels on charter to the Military Sealift (those not receiving MSP payments) were fully employed in the Military Prepositioning Service for 1997 and into the following year.

The *Green Wave* remained on charter to the MSC in service to the polar regions, having had her charter extended from the second quarter of 1998 for another

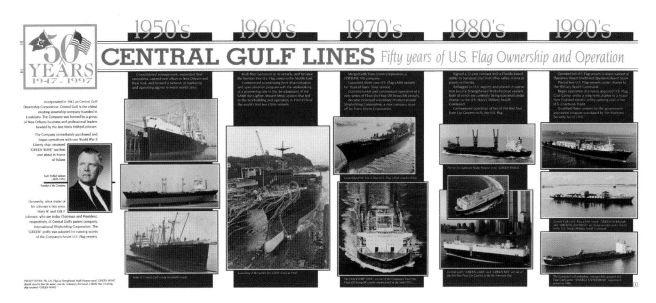

This illustrated timeline of the Company's first 50 years was printed in the 1997 annual report of International Shipholding Corporation.

17 months plus two 17-month options. We re-fixed our other ice-strengthened vessel, *Green Ridge,* on a new charter to the MSC for prepositioning in the Indian Ocean area. She entered this 17-month charter, with two 17-month option periods, in the third quarter of 1997.

The Cape-size bulk-carrier *Amazon* continued to operate in the spot market. Freight rates during 1997 were fairly steady for this type of vessel, and we were able to employ her on business that produced a positive cash flow. Some hope was gained from a forecast of fewer new-buildings scheduled for delivery in 1998 (15 vessels totaling 2.2 million DWT capacity) and potential for more scrapping of older dry bulk and oil bulk ore carriers).

The *Sulphur Enterprise* carried a total of about 2.4 million tons of molten sulphur during the year. The *Energy Enterprise,* in the coastwise coal trade along the Atlantic Coast, completed her first charter year and entered her second charter year in December 1996.

During 1996, our river barge system transported 3.1 million tons of coal from the Ohio River to our coal transfer facility at Gulf County, Florida, for ultimate delivery to Seminole Electric.

We took delivery on September 6, 1996, of a small container/breakbulk vessel, renamed the *Java Sea,* to replace a similar vessel we had on time charter. This vessel, together with the float-on/float-off *Bali Sea* and *Banda Sea* and associated barges, comprised the fleet serving our long-term contract with the Freeport Copper and Gold Mines facility on West Irian Jaya.

The *Green Bay*'s time charter to a Japanese car manufacturer was extended for a further multiyear period, which began in October 1997. The *Green Lake,* our other U.S.-flag Pure Car Carrier, had its charter renewed for a further multiyear period beginning in the first half of 1998. The other two car carriers in our fleet continued to operate satisfactorily on charter to Hyundai on contracts running into the year 2000.

As we came to the end of our 50th Anniversary Year, 1997, our gross revenue for the year had grown to $391,056,000 annually. Total assets were $618,204,000 and common shareholders' equity was $172,805,000, represented by 6,682,887 shares of common stock outstanding.

INTERNATIONAL SHIPHOLDING CORPORATION AND SUBSIDIARIES
Summary of Consolidated Income
Year Ended December 31, 1997

(All amounts in thousands except per-share data)

Revenues	$375,515
Subsidy Revenue	15,541
	391,056
Operating Expenses	
Voyage Expenses	301,084
Vessel and Barge Depreciation	34,569
Gross Voyage Profit	55,403
Administrative and General Expenses	25,454
Operating Income	29,949
Interest	
Interest Expense	27,654
Investment Income	(1,458)
	26,196
Income before Provision (Benefit) for Income Taxes and Extraordinary Item	3,753
Provision (Benefit) for Income Taxes	
Current	3,119
Deferred	(1,773)
State	252
	1,598
Income before Extraordinary Item	$2,155
Net Income	$2,155
Basic and Diluted Earnings Per Share	
Income Before Extraordinary Loss	$0.32
Net Income	$0.32

INTERNATIONAL SHIPHOLDING CORPORATION AND SUBSIDIARIES

Consolidated Balance Sheets, December 31, 1997

(All amounts in thousands)

Current Assets	
Cash and Cash Equivalents	$32,002
Marketable Securities	10,758
Accounts Receivable, Net of Allowance for Doubtful Accounts of $208 and $256 in 1997 and 1996, Respectively:	
Traffic	35,442
Agents'	7,128
Claims and Other	3,031
Federal Income Taxes Receivable	43
Net Investment in Direct Financing Leases	1,913
Other Current Assets	4,187
Material and Supplies Inventory, At Cost	13,296
Total Current Assets	107,800
Marketable Equity Securities	582
Net Investment in Direct Financing Leases	20,552
Vessels, Property, and Other Equipment, At Cost:	
Vessels and Barges	689,856
Other Marine Equipment	7,590
Terminal Facilities	18,377
Land	2,317
Furniture and Equipment	16,853
	734,993
Less – Accumulated Depreciation	(311,557)
	423,436
Other Assets:	
Deferred Charges, Net of Accumulated Amortization of $53,913 and $41,446 in 1997 and 1996, Respectively	38,960
Acquired Contract Costs, Net of Accumulated Amortization of $12,699 and $18,706 in 1997 and 1996, Respectively	17,826
Due from Related Parties	369
Other	8,679
	65,834
	$618,204

LIABILITIES AND STOCKHOLDERS' INVESTMENT

Current Liabilities	
Current Maturities of Long-Term Debt	$35,865
Current Maturities of Capital Lease Obligations	2,579
Accounts Payable and Accrued Liabilities	51,735
Current Deferred Income Tax Liability	171
Current Liabilities to be Refinanced	(22,511)
Total Current Liabilities	67,839
Current Liabilities to be Refinanced	22,511
Billings In Excess Of Income Earned and Expenses Incurred	5,903
Long-Term Capital Lease Obligations, Less Current Maturities	14,994
Long-Term Debt Less Current Maturities	271,835
Reserves and Deferred Credits	
Deferred Income Taxes	39,494
Claims and Other	22,823
	62,317
Commitments and Contingent Liabilities	
Stockholders' Investment	
Common Stock, $1.00 Par Value, 10,000,000 Shares Authorized, 6,756,330 Shares Issued at December 31, 1997 and 1996	6,756
Additional Paid-In Capital	54,450
Retained Earnings	112,794
Less – 73,443 Shares of Common Stock in Treasury, at Cost at December 31, 1997 and 1996	(1,133)
Accumulated Other Comprehensive (Loss) Income	(62)
	172,805
	$618,204

MV *Atlantic Forest* (ex *Aleksey Kosygin*) built in Kherson Shipbuilding Yards, Odessa, Ukraine, in 1984 and purchased by the Company on August 15, 1996, as the 11th LASH vessel in our fleet. This vessel has traded under both U.S. and international flags, depending upon her employment. LOA, 260 meters (852.8'); beam, 32 meters (104.96'); DWT, 48,093; draft, 11.65 meters (38.21'); speed, 18 knots; LASH barge capacity, 82. Vessel has two diesel engines and twin propellers.

CHAPTER 27

LASH—Ukraine Dutch Treat

Continuing our fleet renewal and expansion over the next two years, 1995 and 1996, we invested a total of $184.8 million in new assets. These vessels were financed with new debt of $115 million and $69.7 million from internal corporate sources.

By 1995/1996 the *Acadia Forest* and the first *Atlantic Forest* were over 25 years old. The *Rhine Forest* was over 20 years old. We had re-registered the first *Atlantic Forest* to U.S. flag, renamed her *Jeb Stuart* and time-chartered her with a supply of LASH barges to the Military Sealift Command. We began thinking about replacements for the first-built LASH vessels. The indicated newbuilding prices in the mid-1990's in Japan were approximately six times what we had paid for the *Acadia Forest*. We were induced to seek another source. The only other LASH ships built to Jerome Goldman's specifications (aside from those built in Japan by Sumitomo for our company, those built in the United States by Avondale for PFEL, Prudential, Central Gulf, Waterman and Delta Line and those built in Belgium for Holland America Line and Hamburg America Line) were five ships built at the Kherson Shipyard in Odessa, Ukraine. We focused on the latter ships as possible replacements for the earlier ships in our fleet because the Ukraine-built LASH were delivered between 1984 and 1987 and built to trade in heavy ice conditions. Lloyd's classed them highest for ice trading because they had ice-breaking bows and heavy steel hulls. They have twin screws and two engines, a somewhat awkward arrangement as compared to our other LASH ships that are not ice-class and had only a single screw and a single engine. Far East Shipping Co., or FESCO, owned one of these 1984 Ukraine-built ships and made it available for sale. After considerable negotiations through a London broker, on August 15, 1996, we acquired our eleventh LASH vessel, the *Aleksey Kosygin,* for $8.5 mil-

lion and renamed her *Atlantic Forest*. After a lengthy refurbishment in a Far East shipyard, we positioned her in January 1997 to replace the *Acadia Forest* in Forest Lines' transatlantic service. We temporarily retained the *Acadia Forest* in our fleet during the following year for auxiliary service with the Waterman fleet and for a few voyages in 1999 to allow for planned maintenance on the *Atlantic Forest* and the *Rhine Forest*.

Thirty years after she was delivered as a newbuilding the world's first LASH vessel, the *Acadia Forest,* made her final voyage, after which we sold her at book value to a demolition yard in February 1998.

Our initial effort to employ the *Atlantic Forest* in a new service, pending her allocation to Forest Lines' transatlantic service, was unsuccessful. We withdrew her from an exploratory service between the U.S. and Brazil due to insufficient cargo volume, and incurred $1.3 million in termination expenses. The attractive price made it worthwhile for us to take delivery of this ship as soon as she became available, even though we did not have immediate employment for her. Retiring the *Acadia Forest* opened up a place to employ the newer *Atlantic Forest* in our Forest Lines' transatlantic operation.

A year after we bought the *Atlantic Forest* (ex *Aleksey Kosygin*) from FESCO, we discovered that her sister ships were also available from the Black Sea Shipping Company, which operated a joint LASH service with FESCO out of Odessa between the Black Sea and North Vietnam. Apparently this service had become unprofitable, forcing them to abandon it. The owners had no other use for the LASH vessels. This explains why the *Aleksey Kosygin* became available. The Black Sea Shipping Company was financially strapped and by early 1997 its entire LASH fleet of four vessels (and its other ships) were arrested at various ports around the world. We learned that three of these four LASH vessels might be available for sale either by settlement with the admiralty courts or by paying the outstanding claims. We made contact with the owner through a London broker to buy three of these vessels, *Le Duan, Gaysin* and *Indira Ghandi,* hoping to get at least two. We actually made a contract with the Black Sea Shipping Company to purchase all three ships: *Indira Ghandi* for $8 million, *Gaysin* for $5 million and the *Le Duan* for $5 million. The *Le Duan* was arrested in Rotterdam. Despite the owners' efforts, they were unable to raise the funds to pay off the claims. Therefore, after allowing the owners a lengthy period of time to raise funds, the admiralty court in Rotterdam decided that the only way the ship could be released was to auction her. In the meantime, we had made a contract with the owners to purchase the ship. On June 4, 1997, we agreed to amend the contract. The amendment stated that the owners would allow the ship to be auctioned and that the maximum price we would pay would be $5 million or, alternatively, the auction price (with the understanding that the sellers would pay off the claims against the ship, about $406,000, thereby releasing the ship). Of course, we were then obligated to pay whatever costs necessary to put the ship in first-class operating condition, and we had not yet arrived at that number—but we considered it would be acceptable if the offering price did not exceed $5 million.

Niels W. Johnsen, representing the Company, went to Rotterdam to participate in the auction. Hugo Hansen, our agent in Rotterdam, was also present, together with a lawyer licensed in the Netherlands, to act as interpreter. The entire proceedings of the Rotterdam court would be held in the Dutch language.

The auction was held on June 18, 1997. A Dutch auction in the admiralty court is a formal affair. Five or six judges arrived in the courtroom in their black robes and gray wigs. A bailiff explained in Dutch how the auction would proceed. The bids would be up or down in 50,000-guilder increments—in other words, the winning auction price ultimately would be in guilders. In the first session, whereby the bids would go up, the party who made the highest bid would get a commission of 0.05%. When the bidding stopped, the highest bid would be recorded, after which there would be a recess. The second session, in the afternoon, would begin with the bailiff starting at a high point, whatever he chose. Then, depending upon whether there were any bids, he would go down from the high point at the agreed rate to a low point. In the process of going down, the first bidder who said "mine" would get the ship.

In the morning session, Niels W. Johnsen bid up the price of the ship to the high point of 3 million guilders. The guilder at that time was valued at 1.9308 to the U.S. dollar. To Johnsen's surprise, during the intermission between the bid up and the bid down, the only other party who was bidding against our Company sent a message over to Johnsen saying that if we would like him not to make any further bids, he would cease bidding if we paid him 200,000 guilders. Johnsen, of course, told him that not only was his proposal unethical, it was absolutely ridiculous to even consider, and told him to forget it. This was an amusing episode in an otherwise complicated bidding process. In the afternoon Johnsen went back into the courtroom to proceed for the second session, where the bailiff would call for bids down. As it turned out, the bailiff started at 3 million guilders. Since we were the morning's high bidder, we made no further bid and neither did the opposition bidder. So, in essence, we got the ship by default, because the opposition bidder had understood the message that he'd better forget trying to get a payoff for not bidding. He realized that we were serious and we weren't going to take nonsense for anything more than it was worth.

Therefore after settling all legal fees, claims of the admiralty court, and miscellaneous expenses, we ended up paying about the equivalent of $3,145,000 for the vessel. After the auction we settled on an en bloc price for the *Indira Ghandi* and the *Gaysin* of $16,838,354. The result of this complicated process was that we actually got the *Le Duan* for whatever we settled with the court, plus an allowance for the so-called "right of retention claim" and other expenses to take delivery of the *Le Duan* in Rotterdam.

We renamed the *Le Duan* the *Willow*. She was a 1987-built, 41,000-DWT LASH vessel, constructed in the Ukraine. She was otherwise an exact sister ship to the *Aleksey Kosygin*. After considerable efforts to make the *Gaysin* and the *Indira Ghandi* free of claims so they could be safely delivered to us without fear of having them arrested again, we finally determined that the claims were too complicated on the *Indira Ghandi* and we had to give up the opportunity of getting delivery. We did, however, free up the *Gaysin,* then in the Black Sea area, and took delivery at a safe port in the Mediterranean in January 1998. We paid $5 million for her and renamed her the *Hickory*. She was built in the Ukraine in 1989. Both the *Willow* and the *Hickory* were intended as replacements for older LASH vessels in our fleet, but we used them temporarily to perform auxiliary service for Waterman in the Indian Ocean area. We ultimately sold the *Willow* for scrapping in India but we retained the *Hickory,* which is still operating in our fleet. We sold her to one of John Hatleskog's companies and took her back on bareboat charter for five years.

ISC Board of Directors in 1995. Left to right: Raymond V. O'Brien, Jr.; Niels M. Johnsen; Laurance Eustis; Niels W. Johnsen, Chairman; Erik F. Johnsen; Edward K. Trowbridge; Edwin Lupberger; Harold S. Grehan, Jr., and Erik L. Johnsen.

CHAPTER 28

Big Hits—Some Winners!

Late in 1998 we began a company-wide and fleet-wide program to determine what measures, if any, were necessary to assure continued safe performance of our systems and equipment at and beyond January 1, 2000 (Y2K), when there were concerns about computer failures. All systems entered the new millennium without difficulty. Also in preparation for the new millennium the Board decided to take advantage of the ability to issue "high yield" bonds again to pay off ship mortgage debt, refinance part of the Company's existing 9% notes maturing in 2003, and other corporate requirements. On January 22, 1998, the Company issued a new series of 7¾% senior notes due 2007, with aggregate principal amount of $110 million. Standard and Poor's rated these notes BB+ and Moody's Investors Service rated them Ba3. The issue was over-subscribed and the entire $110 million sold on the first day. We used the net proceeds from this issue, together with a line of credit for $25 million, to repay secured amortizing bank debt pending the date for retiring the 2003 9% notes.

We acquired another Pure Car/Truck Carrier (the 1994-built *Green Point*) in April 1998, registered her under the U.S. flag and fixed her on a long-term charter to a major Japanese shipping company. Late in 1998, we sold one of our older foreign-flag car carriers, the *Cypress Pass,* and reported a gain on the sale of $7,762,000—*a Winner!* We replaced her with a new-building, a sophisticated Car/Truck Carrier, Hull #1098, paid for with funds from a $50 million line of credit pending a permanent loan. She was named *Asian King* by her sponsor, Karen Q. Johnsen, wife of R. Christian Johnsen, the Company's Washington, D.C., attorney. The *Asian King* was delivered from its South Korean shipbuilders, Hyundai Heavy Industries, Ltd., in December 1998 for operation under foreign

flag. We paid $57,750,000 on delivery. She simultaneously was entered into a long-term time charter to a major Far Eastern company. The *Asian King* has capacity to carry heavy and large rolling stock in addition to automobiles and trucks.

We also made a $7,753,000 gain (*a Winner!*) on the sale of the *Cypress Trail,* sister ship of the *Cypress Pass,* and replaced the *Cypress Trail* with Hull #1099, named the *Asian Emperor* by her sponsor, Lisa J. Kane, daughter of Niels M. Johnsen and wife of Michael Kane. The *Asian Emperor* is an exact sister ship of the *Asian King* and also was delivered in December 1998 from the same shipyard at the same price. Permanent financing for both the *Asian King* and *Asian Emperor* was provided by a long-term loan from a syndicate of banks arranged by Citibank, New York, with equity from the Company's own resources.

Freight rates for Cape-size bulk carriers continued to be depressed. Diminished need for ocean transportation of iron ore and coal, the main ingredients for Asian and European steel mills, reflected the substantially reduced demand for steel worldwide.

On December 15, 1998, Seminole Electric Cooperative, Inc. notified our Central Gulf Lines, Inc., subsidiary that effective December 31, it was unilaterally terminating the coal transportation contract it had signed in 1981—(*a Big Hit*). The annual shipments under this contract had averaged 3 million tons of coal, including the 2.7 million tons we had transported in 1998 from the Ohio River area to Northeast Florida. The contract had six years left to run. Seminole filed a lawsuit in Florida in an effort to confirm its right to terminate the contract but admitted it was obligated to pay damages for this surprising cancellation. The suit also asked the Florida court to fix the damages we suffered as a result of Seminole's conduct. We asked the

Sponsor Lisa Johnsen Kane, daughter of Niels M. Johnsen (left), and wife of Michael Kane (right), at the launching of MV *Asian Emperor*. After the traditional smashing of the champagne bottle on the hull, Mrs. Kane applauds as her mother, Marlene M. Johnsen, looks on. Later, automobiles were driven off the vessel (below) as part of the ceremony.

MV *Asian Emperor,* launched and delivered in December 1998, by Hyundai Heavy Industries, Ulsan, South Korea, is an exact sister ship of MV *Asian King.*

Karen Q. Johnsen, wife of R. Christian Johnsen, about to cut the ribbon to release streamers and balloons and name the Pure Car/Truck Carrier MV *Asian King* as she floats out of building dock at Hyundai Heavy Industries, Ulsan, South Korea, in December 1998.

court to order Seminole to arbitrate the dispute as required under the contract. The arbitration proceeded shortly thereafter. The barges and river towboats used for this contract were leased and were the obligation of Seminole. However, Central Gulf Lines Inc. had built and owned the Material Transfer Inc. coal-handling terminal in Gulf County, Florida.

In 1999 the arbitration panel reached its decision. It was in our favor and awarded the Company a settlement of $22,975,000 after allowing for certain expenses—*a Winner!*

We had a gain of $2,408,000 on the sale of river fleeting space no longer needed for some of our LASH barges, and in the fourth quarter 1999, gained $1,412,000 on the sale of a tugboat—*a Winner!*

In February 1999, one of the Company's U.S.-flag LASH vessels, the *Green Island,* sustained severe hull damage in heavy weather on her inbound crossing of the Atlantic. Fortunately, hull insurance covered most of the repair cost of about $10 million. However, the *Green Island* lost about 200 days while under repair. Loss of earnings not covered by insurance cost the Company an extra $14 million—*a Big Hit.*

The U.S.-flag LASH *Austral Rainbow's* charter to the Military Sealift Command ended in August 1999.

MV *Asian King,* newbuilding Pure Car/Truck Carrier from Hyundai Heavy Industries, Ulsan, South Korea, December 1998. LOA 199.98 meters, (659',11"); DWT, 21,511 metric tons; draft 10 meters (33'); speed, 20 knots on 58.2 metric tons HVF; gross tonnage, 56,729; car-carrying capacity, 6,402 standard cars.

MV *Green Point,* built May 1994, at Mitsubishi Heavy Industries, Nagasaki, Japan. Acquired April 1998. LOA, 180 meters (594'); beam 32.36 meters (106'9"): DWT, 14,930 metric tons; gross tonnage, 57,819; speed, 19 knots on 46 mt HVF. Car carrying capacity 5,120 units.

After redelivery from the MSC, she made two voyages in our transatlantic service and one voyage in our U.S. Gulf/Southeast Asia service before we sold her for scrapping in India. The other three U.S.-flag LASH vessels on MSC charters continued, two into the fourth quarter of 2000 and one into the third quarter of 2001. The MSC charters on three ro/ro vessels run until 2010.

We purchased the *Altair Leader,* a newbuilding Pure Car/Truck Carrier that had been delivered from a Japanese shipyard in September 1999, renaming her *Green Dale.* Her sponsor was Marlene Johnsen, wife of Niels M. Johnsen. We registered the ship under U.S. flag, placed her in the Maritime Security Program and chartered her to a major Japanese ship operator. This brought our fleet of modern vehicle carriers under U.S. flag operating with MSP contracts to four—*another Winner!*

In April 1999 we joined Coeclerici (an Italian group) and Ceres Shipping, a Greek (Livanos) group, in forming the Coeclerici Cape-Size Pool. The *Amazon* then immediately began operating in this pool with 11 similar-size vessels. We decided to write off $7 million of the *Amazon*'s book value to reflect her lower market value—a *Big Hit.*

We offset some of the Big Hits in 2000 by making a total gain of $5,911,000 from: (1) a gain of $848,000 on the sale of surplus items including tugboats previously used on two LASH vessels that had been redelivered from MSC; (2) an after-tax gain of $446,000 on the early retirement of some of the Company's 7.75%

MV *Green Point* loading military aircraft in United States for Middle East.

SS *Green Island,* U.S.-flag LASH carrier. Photos taken at port of refuge, Bermuda, after vessel sustained severe hull damage in heavy weather in February 1999.

notes; (3) the gain on the sale of two LASH vessels no longer required for service (the *Willow* and *Austral Rainbow*); (4) the gain on the sale of the multipurpose, ice-strengthened *Green Ridge* after redelivery from MSC charter, and (5) the gain on the sale of the Pure Car Carrier *Green Bay,* coincident with the purchase of her larger replacement, the *Green Cove.*

We continued to reduce our debt by repurchasing at a discount certain of our 7¾% notes maturing 2007 and 9% notes maturing 2003. The Company, as of December 14, 2001, had repurchased: (1) 9% 2003 notes—$57,810,000 par value at an average price of 100.35 (the outstanding $42,190,000 of an original issue of $100 million) and (2) 7¾% 2007 notes—$25,570,000 par value at an average price of 90.3 (the outstanding $84,430,000 of an original issue of $110 million).

In 2000 the increased cost of bunker fuel oil impacted both the Forest Lines and Waterman services by an extra $8.1 million, even though the increase was partially offset by fuel oil hedges.

During 1998, the Company acquired a 37.5% interest in Belden Cement Carrier Companies, a cement carrier management company, and three cement carrier companies—Echelon, Shining Star Shipping, Inc. formerly known as Shining Star Malta Ltd. and Carson Shipping, Inc.—for approximately $3.4 million. During 1999, the Company sold 7.5% of its interest in each of these companies for approximately $806,000. Then the Company acquired a 30% interest in another cement carrier company, Goodtime Shipping Inc., for approxi-

mately $633,000, and another 30% interest for $600,000 in the cement carrier company, Yakuma Shipping Inc. In October 2000, the Company sold its interest in Carson for approximately $511,000, resulting in a loss of approximately $273,000. Also, Goodtime was then liquidated due to a constructive total loss of its cement carrier for which the Company received approximately $1 million as its portion of the insurance recovery on the lost vessel. The liquidation resulted in a gain of approximately $295,000.

The Company acquired a 30% interest in three additional cement carrier companies in 2001, Tilbury Shipping Inc., Emblem Shipping Inc. and Mattea Shipping Inc. for $1,400,000, $700,000, and $512,000, respectively. The Company also acquired a 30% interest in BCH, which is a holding company for each of the aforementioned cement carrier companies. Echelon, Shining Star, Yakuma, Tilbury, Emblem, and Mattea each own and operate one cement carrier under medium- to long-term contracts managed by Belden.

These investments are accounted for under the equity method of accounting in the Company's consolidated statements of income net of taxes. The Company's share of their combined earnings was $389,999 as of December 31, 2001, and $114,000 and $131,000, respectively, at the end of 2000 and 1999. No distributions were made during 1999, 2000 or 2001, except for the sale of Carson and liquidation of Goodtime in 2000. The successful ending to the Belden investment came in the fourth quarter of 2006, when we sold our inter-

MV *Green Dale* sponsor, Marlene M. Johnsen, with her husband, Niels M. Johnsen, at delivery of vessel in September 1999, and, above, presenting traditional gift to master of the vessel.

MV *Green Dale* (ex *Altair Leader*) Car/Truck Carrier built and delivered September 1999 at Kanasashi Shipyard in Japan. Registered U.S. flag, car-carrying capacity, 4,148 units. LOA, 179 meters (587.12'); beam, 32.28 meters (105.88'); draft, 9.22 meters (30.24'); 19 knots on 44 metric tons HVF.

MV *Green Cove,* Car/Truck Carrier built March 1994 at Kanasashi Shipyard, Japan. Registered U.S.-flag. LOA, 179 meters (587.12'); beam, 32.28 meters (105.88'); draft 9.22 meters (30.24'); speed 19.45 knots on 45 metric tons HVF. Car-carrying capacity 4,148 units.

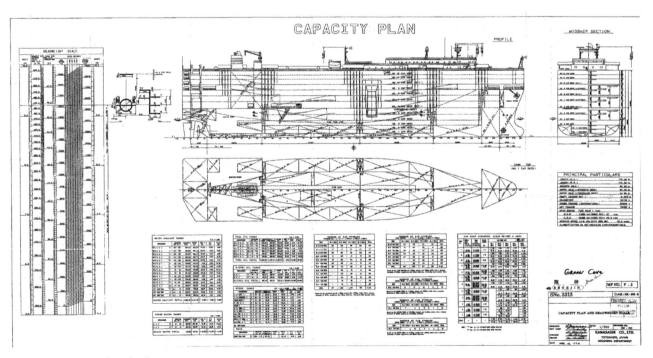

MV *Green Cove* "pocket plan."

Stern view of *Bali Sea* departing loading dock with partial load of railroad cars aboard existing single deck. (Photo from Captain James McNamara)

Bali Sea and *Banda Sea* operation showing railroad cars being rolled aboard prior to installation of second deck level. (Photo from Captain James McNamara)

Railroad cars are positioned to roll onto *Bali Sea* at dock previously used by vessel at New Orleans.

MV *Bali Sea,* built in March 1982 as float-on/float-off semi-submersible vessel, was converted in 2001 to roll-on/roll-off railroad car carrier. She is used with sister ship *Banda Sea* in regular service between U.S. Gulf and Coatzacoalcos, Mexico. LOA, 177 meters (580.56'); beam, 35.84 meters (117.56'); draft, 5.6 meters (18.37'): 12 knots on 25 tons HVF, carrying capacity 54/60 railcars of 55-foot maximum length. Each vessel's capacity will be increased to 100/116 railcars after installation of second deck. (Photos from Captain James McNamara)

est, which was then 26.1% of that company, for a gain of $27,581,000—*another Winner!*

The *Banda Sea* and *Bali Sea* were redeployed from service under the ocean transportation contract with Freeport Copper and Gold Mining Company in Irian Jaya, Indonesia. After reviewing the alternative re-employment opportunities for these two dock ships, we decided their structural configuration made it technically feasible to convert them to railroad boxcar and tank car carriers. We therefore installed railroad tracks fore and aft on the ships' decks while retaining their float-on/float-off capability. A locomotive pushes or pulls the boxcars through the ship's open stern transom. With this conversion the dock ships accommodate up to 60 standard boxcars each. Immediately we began marketing a new service to carry railcars by ship between Mobile, Alabama, and Coatzacoalcos, Mexico, making an "end-run" around the congested Rio Grande border.

CG Railway, Inc., had its first sailing in February 2001, with a sailing scheduled every four days in each direction. The ships also offered a three-day transit between the U.S. Gulf and Mexico, making 90 round-trips each year. In 2005, with the encouragement of the governor of Louisiana, we moved the U.S. terminal from Mobile to New Orleans. We constructed the new dock at the head of the Mississippi River Gulf Outlet at Elaine Street in New Orleans East. This area had excellent rail connections with the port's hinterland. It was reached from the Gulf of Mexico through a 36-foot dredged channel. Under a law passed in 1960, this channel was to be kept navigable by the Army Corps of Engineers as a national waterway. At the same time we decided to install a second deck to virtually double the capacity on each vessel to more than 100 rail cars. The ships' loaded draft would be increased to 22 feet.

On August 29, 2005, just two months after we opened the new terminal at New Orleans, the city and surrounding region were devastated by Hurricane Katrina, the most destructive storm in U.S. history. Damage to the port and inland rail connections at New Orleans forced us to suspend our service—*definitely another Big Hit.*

The hurricane and flooding also forced us to close our New Orleans office and station our staff in Baton Rouge and Mandeville, Louisiana, and Houston, Texas,

for the next three months while we awaited the reopening of New Orleans' downtown and residential areas. The Mexican railcar ferries operation resumed service in November 2005 with only one of the two ships. The second ship went back on line in February 2006. Adding second decks to the two ferries would have to wait.

One multipurpose vessel, a small tanker, and two container ships, continued to service the long-term ocean transportation contract to and from Irian Jaya, Indonesia.

By early 2001 the Company faced growing operating costs on its U.S.-flag LASH vessels sailing between the U.S. Gulf and South Asia. Loss of time due to repairs and an increase in the cost of fuel oil significantly impacted the Company's bottom line. In the first six months of 2001 the service had 228 "out of service" days for unplanned maintenance on two of its LASH vessels—costly and disruptive to the service. These and other LASH vessels of the same vintage (1973) needed extensive steelwork maintenance. Over the previous two or three years, LASH vessels had required a significant number of additional days out of service, plus heavy shipyard costs. During the first six months of 2001, the operation of these vessels accounted for approximately 50% of the Company's total revenues but caused a reduction of gross voyage profits of $9.4 million and accounted for approximately 50% of the Company's administrative and general expenses. These incidents, following the serious damage to the hull of the *Green Island* in heavy weather during an Atlantic crossing in February 1999 (which cost $10 million and over 200 idle-time days to repair), convinced the Company's management that it was time to retire the Waterman LASH fleet of four vessels. The Company had already decided in early 2001 to dispose of the three LASH vessels that had been on time charter to the MSC.

On June 30, 2001, the Company took the next *Big Hit*. It adopted a plan to charge impairment for the separation of the LASH service and other obsolete or idle vessels (the *Amazon* and special-purpose barges previously used under the contract with Freeport Copper and Gold Mining Company) from the rest of the fleet. The plan, in effect, meant that the Company wrote these assets down to scrap value at June 30, 2001, rather than over the following five to 10 years. It meant

MV *Green Lake,* Car/Truck Carrier, built June 1998, Shin-Kurushima Dockyard, Japan. Registered U.S. flag. LOA, 199.93 meters (655.77'); beam, 32.26 meters (105.81'); draft, 10 meters (33'); speed, 19.3 knots on 57 mt HVF. Car-carrying capacity 5,055 standard units.

that a non-cash charge of $81 million would be taken against the book value of these assets. The after-tax effect was to reduce the stockholders' equity from $181,532,000 to $114,905,000. Despite the severity of this move, the Company management was of the opinion it would get the lost equity back in less than 10 years. Could it?

These assets, written down to $45 million, were reclassified in the balance sheet as "assets held for disposal" at the written-down value. Debt attributed was $17.4 million.

Despite these heavy charges, the Company remained financially liquid and was able to continue its plan of reducing debt. The Company called at par $10,000,000 of its 9% 2003 notes leaving a balance outstanding of $28,085,000 of the 9% notes at the end of December 2001. As of the same date, $84,730,000 of the 7¾% 2007 notes remained outstanding. In addition, during 2001 the Company retired $24,900,000 of scheduled bank debt, resulting in total reductions in debt in 2001 of $135,000,000.

The aforementioned three LASH vessels referred to as having been sold after MSC charters ended resulted in a loss of $4,700,000 over book value. This loss was offset by a gain of $4,485,000 on the sale in the third quarter of 2001 of the *Green Lake,* one of the first Pure Car Carriers acquired in 1987. At the same time we replaced her with a newer and larger U.S.-flag Pure Car/Truck Carrier to which we gave the same name.

Subsequent to taking the charge for impairment on June 30, 2001, the Company was able to continue certain cargo contracts for its transatlantic LASH service. Therefore, the charge for two of the LASH ships (the *Rhine Forest* and *Atlantic Forest*) and barges used in this service was reversed, and operation of these two vessels continued. Of the four U.S.-flag LASH vessels used in the Waterman service, the Company then sold two for demolition together with some associated LASH barges at prices about equal to the written-down book values. The other two vessels continued in operation to fulfill cargo commitments until the following year. The third remaining Waterman LASH vessel, the *Hickory,* remained in layup until we sold it to John Hatleskog's Norwegian company and leased it back to Forest Lines for five years for use in the transatlantic service as a replacement for the *Atlantic Forest*. The latter was transferred to U.S. flag and reassigned to Waterman service between the U.S. Gulf and South Asia.

We sold the bulk carrier *Amazon* in September at about its written-down value.

In December 2002, the Company repurchased $1,052,000 of the 7¾% unsecured notes maturing 2007. This transaction brought the total of these notes repurchased to date to $26,322,000 par value, leaving outstanding $83,678,000 par value. The average market price of the 7¾% Notes repurchased was 89.89, a savings of about $2,660,867.

As of March 29, 2002, the balance of the 9% 2003 notes outstanding was $27,187,000. By December 31, 2002, the Company called all of the outstanding 9% notes due 2003 ($9,076,000 par value). We were able to completely repay the outstanding amount of the original issue of $100 million by the end of 2002 (a year earlier than required) and, at the same time, meet the scheduled principal payments on other debt from the proceeds of operating income, sale of "assets held for disposal," and some refinancing of other debt. We reduced total debt by $47,204,000—from $260,863,000 as of December 31, 2001, to $213,659,000 exactly a year later. At the end of 2003, total debt of the Company was down to $179,010,000.

After the Company transferred the *Atlantic Forest* to U.S. flag, we assigned her as a substitute under MSP contract MA/MSP-45 for the *Robert E. Lee,* which we sold for demolition. Under the MSP, the *Atlantic Forest* then became one of seven vessels in our fleet that received annual payments of $2.1 million to cover part of the extra cost of operating U.S.-flag vessels vis-à-vis foreign vessels. To preserve the viability of two of the MSP contracts held by Waterman, the Company assigned them to two gearless container vessels owned by CP Ships (Lykes Lines Limited). These were the *Lykes Motivator* (43,715 tons summer deadweight and 2,954 nominal TEU capacity) and the *Lykes Explorer* (44,966 tons summer deadweight and 3,050 nominal TEU capacity. The Company bareboat-chartered in and time-chartered out these ships on July 15, 2002,

and September 11, 2002, respectively. The Company chartered these vessels short-term (until November 22, 2004), pending the decision for the long-term substitutions. We allocated the remaining MSP contracts to our four U.S.-flag car/truck carriers, thereby completing the assignment of all seven MSP contracts allocated to Waterman and Central Gulf.

At the Company's annual shareholders' meeting in April 2003, Niels W. Johnsen retired as chairman of the Board and was immediately succeeded in that position by Erik F. Johnsen. Niels M. Johnsen then became president of the Company. The directors and officers elected at the April 2003 annual meeting were:

Erik F. Johnsen	Chairman and Chief Executive Officer
Niels M. Johnsen	President and Director
Erik L. Johnsen	Executive Vice President and Director
Gary L. Ferguson	Vice President and Chief Financial Officer
Niels W. Johnsen	Director
Harold S. Grehan, Jr.	Director
Raymond V. O'Brien, Jr.	Director
Edwin Lupberger	Director
Edward K. Trowbridge	Director
H. Merritt Lane, III	Director (appointed March 2004)

At the April 2006 annual meeting, Gary Ferguson retired as vice president and chief financial officer and was succeeded by Manuel G. Estrada, formerly vice president and comptroller.

As a substitute for the Cape-size *Amazon* the Company acquired a 12½% interest in four newly built Cape-size bulk carriers (each about 170,000-DWT carrying capacity). We entered the vessels in the Coeclerici Cape-size ship pool from which the *Amazon* was retired.

In the third and fourth quarters of 2003 the Company sold its 12½% interest in the four newly built Cape-size bulk carriers for about breakeven. We simultaneously purchased a 50% interest in two of these vessels, the *Bulk Africa,* christened by Giuliana Clerici, wife of Paolo Clerici, managing director of the Coeclerici Pool, and *Bulk Australia,* christened by Marlene M. Johnsen. Both vessels continued to operate in the Coeclerici Pool.

The charter market for Cape-size vessels firmed in second half 2003 and remained strong going into the next couple of years. China was the main driver in this firm market. For example, in 2003, world seaborne

MV *Bulk Australia*'s sponsor, Marlene M. Johnsen, wife of Niels M. Johnsen, at naming ceremony at Sasebo Heavy Industries Co., Ltd., Japan. The Cape-size, international-flag vessel was delivered January 9, 2003.

MV *Bulk Africa*—Sponsor Guiliana Clerici, wife of Paolo Clerici, with owner representatives. Left to right: Peter Livanos, Guiliana Clerici, Paolo Clerici and Niels M. Johnsen.

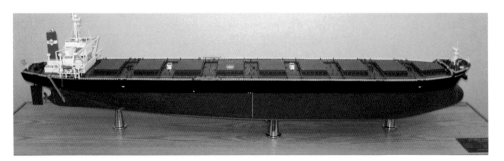

MV *Bulk Australia*—Scale model in our New York office. Total deadweight 170,578 metric tons; LOA, 289 meters (947.29'); beam, 44.98 meters (147.54'); draft loaded, 17.976 meters (58.96'); 14.7 knots. In Cape-Size pool with exact sister ship *Bulk Africa*.

MV *Green Ridge,* U.S.-flag Car/Truck Carrier built 1998 at Imabari Shipyard, Japan, acquired October 2004 as our eighth U.S.-flag vessel operating with a Maritime Security Program contract. DWT, 21,523; LOA, 199.94 meters (659.8'); beam, 32.2 meters (106.26'); draft, 10.06 meters (33.2'); gross registered tons, 57,449; car-carrying capacity, 6,000 units.

trade grew by 92 million tons, with China accounting for 80%, or 74 million tons of that growth.

Continuing our program of reducing debt, the Company repaid $34 million of secured bank loans. Taking advantage of repurchasing the Company's bonds at a discount, the Company was able by mid-2006 to acquire $59,507,000 par value of its 7¾% 2007 notes for $55,178,758, or a discount of $4,328,242. The Company had thus reduced the outstanding par value amount of the 7¾% 2007 notes to $48,583,000 (after allowing for $1,960,000 held by Bay Insurance Co.).

Early in the third quarter of 2003 USGen New England, Inc. filed a petition for bankruptcy. USGen has our U.S.-flag conveyor-equipped coal carrier *Energy Enterprise* on long-term time charter. Even though USGen continued payment of charter hire and compliance with the charter's terms, its petition for bankruptcy created an event of default under the vessel's financing and other loans. USGen's default required us to refinance immediately the balance of the *Energy Enterprise's* existing loan of $17 million, which also committed us to pay a "make whole" penalty of $2.6 million. However, the new financing

was at a reduced interest rate so that the "make whole" premium was partially offset. In addition to the $2.6 million impacting our 2003 earnings, approximately $2 million of unanticipated vessel repair costs on other vessels in our fleet, and accelerated deferred charges also occurred in this third quarter. On a positive note, the *Energy Enterprise* continued to operate at full applicable charter hire for the entire year. Her operating profit for the period about equaled that which we would have obtained from employment at full current market rates.

In October 2004 Congress passed and President George W. Bush signed the Jobs Creation Act of 2004. This act provides U.S. shipowners an option to use a modest fixed tonnage tax payment in lieu of a U.S. corporate income tax for earnings of eligible vessels in international trade. In December we exercised this option on eligible vessels to use the tonnage tax. As a result, our net income for 2004 increased by $7.7 million, because of a reversal of certain items in the deferred tax account. The standard Internal Revenue corporate tax treatment continues to apply to our vessels in U.S. coastwise (domestic) trading.

The fourth quarter 2004 was particularly active as certain promising events indicated that we were beginning to recover from the write-off we took on June 30, 2001:

(1) In October, Congress passed and the president signed a renewal of the Maritime Security Program. The act provided for another 10-year program commencing October 1, 2005, and revised the annual payment to $2.6 million. It grandfathered our existing seven MSP contracts, and awarded the Company an additional contract for an eighth vessel, which we assigned to the newly purchased Car/Truck Carrier *Green Ridge* (ex *Hercules Leader*).

(2) In November, Dominion Energy New England Inc., a subsidiary of Dominion Resources Inc., purchased substantially all of USGen New England Inc.'s power generation assets, including the contract employing the *Energy Enterprise*.

(3) The Company decided to add a second rail cargo deck to each of the *Bali Sea* and *Banda Sea,* the two vessels operating in the railcar ferry service between the U.S. Gulf and Coatzacoalcos, Mexico.

(4) The Company concluded a five-year, $50 million secured credit line with several banks, effective December 6, 2004.

(5) In December 2004 the Company purchased from P&O Nedlloyd, an established container liner company, two second-hand geared container sister ships (the *P&O Nedlloyd Vera Cruz* and *P&O Nedlloyd Buenos Aires*) to replace the two chartered-in vessels (the *Lykes Motivator* and *Lykes Explorer*) operating under the Company's MSP contracts. We simultaneously registered both vessels under the U.S. flag and time-chartered them back to Farrell Lines, a U.S. subsidiary of P&O Nedlloyd. The time charters are for an initial period ending late 2008, when two substitute newbuilding vessels may be mutually agreed upon as replacements or the charters will end. Each vessel has a total deadweight capacity of 29,930 tons, nominal TEU capacity of 1,755, two cargo cranes with 40-ton capacity each and speed of about 16 knots. After we acquired these two vessels, P&O Nedlloyd was purchased in its entirety, including Farrell Lines, by Maersk Inc. The time charters with Farrell remained unchanged. However, we renamed the ships *Santa Cruz* (to avoid

ISC Board of Directors at annual meeting, April 24, 2007; in new headquarters, Mobile, Alabama. Seated, from left: Niels W. Johnsen, retired chairman; Erik F. Johnsen, retired chairman; Niels M. Johnsen, new chairman; Erik L. Johnsen, new president. Standing: Edward K. Trowbridge, Edwin Lupberger, Raymond V. O'Brien, Jr., H. Merritt Lane III, Harold S. Grehan, Jr.

confusion with two other unrelated ships named *Vera Cruz*) and *Buenos Aires*.

(6) The Company issued $40 million of 6% Convertible Preferred Stock, which it completely sold on January 6, 2005. These funds helped finance the railcar ferry expansion work, acquire the container vessels, and other corporate purposes.

The Company's balance sheet as of December 31, 2005 (four and one half years after the June 30, 2001, writedown), shows a net worth (stockholders' equity) of $178,000,000 (including preferred stock of $37,554,000).

FLEET LIST AS OF MARCH 31, 2006

	Flag	Year Built	# of Units	Speed (Knots)	GRT	DWT	LWT	Employment
1. ROLL ON/ROLL OFF								
a. Car/Truck Carriers								
Green Lake	USA	1998	5,055 cars	19	57,623	22,799	16,108	Time charter to Japanese operator carrying about 5,000 automobiles each voyage, with return cargoes of heavy vehicles
Green Point*	USA	1994	5,120 cars	19	57,819	14,930	15,125	"
Green Cove	USA	1994	4,148 cars	19.45	50,308	16,178	13,277	"
Green Dale*	USA	1999	4,148 cars	19	50,887	16,157	13,298	"
Green Ridge	USA	1998	6,000 cars	19.3	57,449	21,523	17,351	"
Asian King*	Panama	1998	6,402 cars	20.1	55,729	21,511	16,412	Time charter to Korean operator carrying about 6,000 automobiles each voyage
Asian Emperor	Panama	1999	6,402 cars	20.1	55,729	21,479	16,438	"
Cypress Pass**	Norway	1988	4,864 cars	17	42,447	12,763		" 5,000 autos
b. Heavy Vehicles (MSC Charters)								
Sgt. Matej Kocak	USA	1981 chartered	536 TEU + vehicles	20	29,091	25,073	26,539	Long-term charter to Military Sealift Command
PFC Eugene A. Obregon	USA	1982 chartered	536 TEU + vehicles	20	29,091	25,073	26,539	"
Maj. Stephen Pless	USA	1983 chartered	536 TEU + vehicles	20	29,091	25,073	26,539	"
c. Railroad Box Cars/Tank Cars								
Bali Sea	Singapore	1982	1 DK 60 cars	12	29,594	22,220	10,571	Regular service between Coatzacoalcos, Mexico, & U.S. Gulf, carrying railroad freight cars
Banda Sea	Singapore	1982	1 DK 60 cars	12	29,594	22,239	10,571	"
2. FLOAT ON/FLOAT OFF								
Dock Ship								
Spruce	Marshall Islands	1975	15 BGS	9.5	7,258	8,172		Feeder service N. Europe Transatlantic LASH service
3. CONTAINER SHIPS								
Santa Cruz	USA	1989	1,755 TEU	16	23,790	29,930	10,830	Time charter to liner operator
Buenos Aires	USA	1989	1,755 TEU	16	23,790	29,930	10,830	"
Java Sea	Singapore	1988	256 TEU	12.5	2,854	3,169	1,702	Contract with Indonesian mining company

	Flag	Year Built	# of Units	Speed (Knots)	GRT	DWT	LWT	Employment
4. LASH								
Atlantic Forest	USA	1984	82 BGS	15.5	37,464	48,093	21,120	Liner service: U.S. Gulf/S. Asia
Rhine Forest	Marshall Islands	1972	83 BGS	17.5	35,826	44,799		Liner service: Transatlantic
Hickory**	Panama	1989	82 BGS	15.5	38,282	40,798	21,120	"
850 LASH BARGES	USA	var				340,690		
5. USA Domestic Service								
Sulphur Enterprise molten-sulphur tanker	USA	1994	N/A	15	16,771	27,241	9,298	Long-term contract coastwise molten sulphur trade
Energy Enterprise conveyer-equipped self-unloader	USA	1983	N/A	14.47	24,900	38,234	10,566	Long-term contract coastwise coal trade
6. Multi-Purpose Ships								
Lautan Arafura**	Indonesia	1979	619 TEU	16	9,751	12,487		Contract in Indonesia with Indonesian mining company
Ocean Gurnard***	Singapore	1996	Tanker	13.5	7,463	13,496		Carrying oil supply for Indonesian mining co.
7. Bulk Carriers (international registries)								
a. Ore/Coal carriers (50% owned)								
Bulk Australia	Liberia	2003	N/A	15	87,590	170,578 Cape-size		Cape-size bulk Carrier pool
Bulk Africa	Liberia	2002	N/A	15	87,590	170,578 Cape-size		"
Bulk Cedar	Liberia	1998	N/A	14.5	38,995	73,322 Panamax		Panamax-size Bulk carrier pool
Bulk Fern	Liberia	1998	N/A	14.5	38,995	73,326 Panamax		"
b. Cement Carriers (26.1% owned)								
Alcem Calaca**	Australia	1979/1998	N/A	12	29,873	12,274		Bulk cement trade
Alcem Lugait	Singapore	1984/1998	N/A	14	18,284	28,608		"
Bel Anna	Panama	1983	N/A			27,213		"
Glory Kuah (tug)	Singapore	1993	N/A	10	399			"
Langkaw (barge)	Singapore	1993			4,061	8,398		
Glory Moon	Panama	1973	N/A	12.5	16,534	25,424		"
Glory Ocean	Singapore	1996	N/A	13.5	10,337	16,264		"
Glory Pacific	Singapore	1996	N/A	13	10,508	16,000		"
Glory Sky	Singapore	1996	N/A	13.5	10,508	16,264		"
Glory Star	Panama	1984	N/A	12.5	6,774	10,678		"
Glory Sun	Philippines	1985	N/A	12	15,879	24,938		"
Mariana III	Panama	1981	N/A	13.	10,971	16,960		"
Glory Atlantic		2006						

40 ships, 850 LASH barges (= Total DWT 1,594,419 tons), 1 Tugboat

*	leased	GRT	Gross Registered Tons
**	chartered	DWT	Deadweight ton capacity
***	chartered tanker	LWT	Light Weight Tons

INTERNATIONAL SHIPHOLDING CORPORATION
Consolidated Statements of Income, 2006

(All amounts in thousands except share data)

Revenues	$274,881
Operating Expenses	
Voyage Expenses	230,510
Vessel and Barge Depreciation	23,735
Impairment Loss	8,866
Gross Voyage Profit	11,770
Administrative and General Expenses	18,765
(Gain) Loss on Sale of Assets	(5,125)
Operating (Loss) Income	(1,870)
Interest and Other:	
Interest Expense	11,147
(Gain) Loss on Sale of Investments	(23,058)
Investment Income	(1,397)
Loss on Early Extinguishment of Debt	248
	(13,060)
Income from Continuing Operations before (Benefit) Provision for Income Taxes and Equity in Net Income of Unconsolidated Entities	11,190
(Benefit) Provision for Income Taxes	
Deferred	(1,137)
State	4
	(1,133)
Equity in Net Income of Unconsolidated Entities (Net of Applicable Taxes)	4,725
Income from Continuing Operations	17,048
Net Income	$17,048
Preferred Stock Dividends	2,400
Net Income Available to Common Stockholders	$14,648
Basic and Diluted Earnings Per Common Share	
Net Income Available to Common Stockholders—Basic	
Continuing Operations	2.40
Discontinued Operations	
	2.40
Net Income Available to Common Stockholders—Diluted	
Continuing Operations	2.39
Discontinued Operations	
	2.39
Weighted Average Shares of Common Stock Outstanding	
Basic	6,116,036
Diluted	6,122,578

ASSETS (all amounts in thousands except share data)

Current Assets
Cash and Cash Equivalents	$44,273
Marketable Securities	6,545
Accounts Receivable, Net of Allowance for Doubtful Accounts of $216 in 2006	
Traffic	13,348
Agents	3,948
Claims and Other	8,889
Federal Income Taxes Receivable	322
Deferred Income Tax	67
Net Investment in Direct Financing Leases	4,400
Other Current Assets	2,798
Material and Supplies Inventory, at Lower of Cost or Market	3,508
Current Assets Held for Disposal	681
Total Current Assets	88,779

Investments in Unconsolidated Entities	12,409
Net Investment in Direct Financing Leases	70,497

Vessels, Property, and Other Equipment, at Cost
Vessels and Barges	376,802
Leasehold Improvements	20,054
Other Equipment	2,077
Furniture and Equipment	3,037
	401,970
Less – Accumulated Depreciation	(175,033)
	226,937

Other Assets
Deferred Charges, Net of Accumulated Amortization of $11,114 in 2006	14,577
Acquired Contract Costs, Net of Accumulated Amortization of $25,796 in 2006	4,729
Due from Related Parties	4,015
Other	6,099
	29,420

$428,042

LIABILITIES AND STOCKHOLDERS' INVESTMENT

Current Liabilities
Current Maturities of Long-Term Debt	$50,250
Accounts Payable and Accrued Liabilities	34,418
Total Current Liabilities	84,668

Billings in Excess of Income Earned and Expenses Incurred	700
Long-Term Debt, Less Current Maturities	98,984

Other Long-Term Liabilities
Deferred Income Taxes	11,837
Lease Incentive Obligation	17,890
Other	22,673
	52,400

Commitments and Contingent Liabilities

Convertible Exchangeable Preferred Stock	37,554

Stockholders' Investment
Common Stock, $1.00 Par Value, 10,000,000 Shares Authorized, 6,792,630 Shares Issued at December 31, 2006	6,793
Additional Paid-In Capital	54,927
Retained Earnings	101,992
Less - 673,443 Shares of Common Stock in Treasury, at Cost, at December 31, 2006	(8,704)
Accumulated Other Comprehensive (Loss) Income	(1,272)
	$153,736

$428,042

Hurricane Katrina's 20-foot storm surge overflowing levee at Entergy Corporation's Michoud electric generating plant on the Mississippi River Gulf Outlet at New Orleans. This photo was taken August 29, 2005, by Don McCrosky, plant manager, from a safe location at the plant.

EPILOGUE
MRGO NoGo – Move to Mobile

As time passed, it became clear that the aftereffects of Hurricanes Katrina and Rita were more significant on the Company than they first appeared. The evolution of the impact is best described in the following comments based upon paraphrasing memoranda written by Erik F. Johnsen, then chairman of the Company, to the Board of Directors and other interested parties after the Company was able to reopen its headquarters offices on the 17th floor of Poydras Center in New Orleans.

1. Memo dated January 3, 2006

Hurricane Katrina left its mark throughout coastal Louisiana and Mississippi. The devastation was declared as the most severe in the history of the country. The U.S. Army Corps of Engineers dredged the Mississippi River Gulf Outlet in the 1960's when the Port of New Orleans believed its future rested in moving the port to the Industrial Canal area, where it would have excellent rail facilities and interchange with the interstate highway system then being constructed by the federal government.

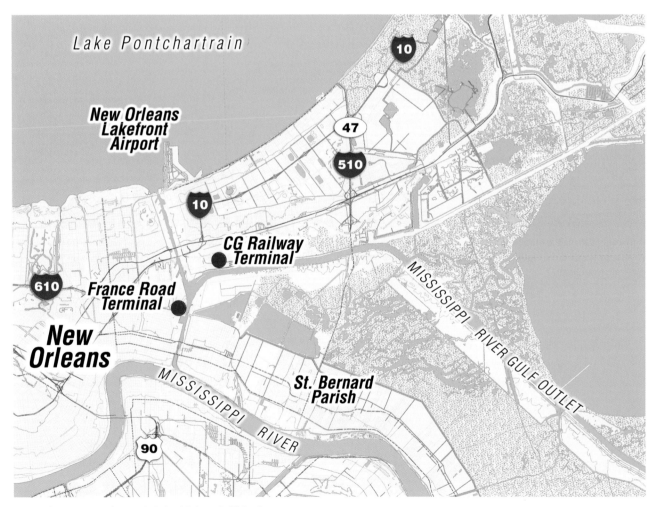

CG Railway Terminal on Mississippi River Gulf Outlet.

The belief resulted from the conclusion that container traffic would need a good highway system that was inaccessible to the Mississippi River wharves, which were adjacent to residential property for their entire 11-mile length.

When the MRGO was completed, Congress passed legislation designating it an essential federal waterway, and mandated a 36-foot channel. This waterway has been in existence now over 40 years. During that time a number of industries have developed on the Industrial Canal and the MRGO. It is the port's view that 30% of its revenue was derived from activities on the MRGO.

Prior to Hurricane Katrina, there had been some discussions with the St. Bernard Parish Council and the St. Bernard president to determine whether or not further protection should be given to the St. Bernard residents in the event of a hurricane. We understand Parish President Junior Rodriguez had contracted, on behalf of the parish, for an independent engineer to make a study of the approaches to St. Bernard, not only from MRGO, but also from Lake Borgne. All of this was carefully handled over the last several years with the governor's office and the Port of New Orleans, and it was the view of the governor and the port that MRGO must be maintained. Furthermore, they opined that the Industrial Canal locks should be materially enlarged to enable seagoing vessels (similar in size to our *Bali Sea*) to transit from the Mississippi River into the Industrial Canal, which is at the head of the MRGO. The Congress had been working on this project now for some ten years, and when we at CG Railway contracted with the state to locate our terminal at the head of the MRGO, we were assured by the governor, as well as the port, that they would continue to maintain the MRGO in the port's future plans.

No one envisaged a hurricane of such intensity as Katrina, which roared across the area and in doing so, breached the levees at the London Avenue and Seventeenth Street canals, flowed over the levees of the MRGO, and overwhelmed all barriers that the Army Corps of Engineers had put up at the Lake Borgne border into the Industrial Canal. Immediately after the hurricane, the entire area for miles around the Industrial Canal was flooded, in many areas to second floors of the homes. The destruction was overwhelming. There was a significant loss of life, although fortunately no one in our Company's families was injured, even though they all suffered from the inconvenience of being displaced and the loss of some of their homes. A large number of homes were lost or rendered uninhabitable. Huge areas of New Orleans were abandoned by residents and still not reoccupied for months after Hurricane Katrina. The former home of Niels F. Johnsen at 9 Audubon Place suffered a spontaneous electrical fire when electricity was finally restored, after over five months. The house burned to the ground. Amongst other houses lost by members of the Company was Erik L. Johnsen's in the Metairie area of New Orleans, which remained flooded to over six feet for two weeks. He decided to sell rather than repair. Nguyen Van Minh [who three decades earlier had escaped from Vietnam] ironically again lost his home, this time to the flooding in the Lakefront section of New Orleans.

The hurricane caused a breach in the Industrial Canal large enough to allow a stray barge to float into a residential neighborhood. Simultaneously oil storage tanks broke open at the Murphy Oil refinery in St. Bernard, causing significant pollution damage to the properties in and around MRGO and, for that matter, much of St. Bernard Parish. Prior to Hurricane Katrina, the population in St. Bernard Parish was estimated to be 58,000 people. After the hurricane the estimate was 800 people. There is some slow movement of additional people back to the parish. Whether or not the other residents will return is questionable. Be that as it may, it was an emotional event for all concerned, and immediately, as CNN interviewed the evacuees, all were expressing concern about the MRGO and indicating that it acted as a funnel neck that forced the waters into the parish. This idea was picked up by CNN nationwide, and emotion took over from reason. There became a fixation amongst the populace and the parish council in St. Bernard that the cause of the flooding was the MRGO. It contributed directly to the twenty-foot surge of water from Lake Borgne and Lake Pontchartrain to overflow any levees previously constructed, so ran the emotional reaction. The chance of MRGO surviving the aftereffects of Hurricane Katrina was daily less and less.

The Times-Picayune

MONEY

Industrial Canal firms hurting

*Rebound is slow,
while their futures
are uncertain*

By Jaquetta White
Business writer

For the eight **Port of New Orleans** tenants who operate on the Industrial Canal, returning to business has not been easy.

Warehouses devastated by floodwaters have reopened slowly, if at all, and growing support for the closure of the Mis-

sissippi River-Gulf Outlet, their lifeline to commerce, means that at least two of the firms will not return, port President and CEO Gary LaGrange said.

Four months after the storm, none of the businesses, which include cement and wallboard manufacturers, a cold storage warehouse and a shipyard, has fully recovered.

The port plans to begin talks with the firms to "look at all of the many opportunities and the options we may have" to support their return, LaGrange said.

Most of the port's revenue is generated by leasing property to terminal operators and other businesses, including those lo-

cated along the Industrial Canal. The state agency also collects docking fees from shippers and rental fees from companies that use its stevedoring equipment.

The rent paid by Industrial Canal tenants makes up about 30 percent of the port's revenue, and those businesses also generate millions in direct spending to the local economy.

But their operations were washed away in Hurricane Katrina, while the rest of the port's activity, concentrated on the Uptown portion of the Mississippi River, escaped major damage.

See **INDUSTRIAL**, *C-8*

STAFF FILE PHOTO BY JOHN McCUSKER

Rotten meat and other items are removed from the New Orleans Cold Storage dockside facility after Hurricane Katrina struck Aug. 29. With the possible closure of the Mississippi River-Gulf Outlet, many companies on the Industrial Canal are facing tough shipping choices.

Narrow locks restrict shipping

INDUSTRIAL, *from C-7*

The port has revised leasing agreements with several of the tenants as an inducement for them to remain in business.

But that won't be enough to keep at least two of the firms, LaGrange said.

"There's a possibility that one or two of them may move out of the state. The realistic case is that there are five we really think we have a chance at keeping and retaining," LaGrange said. He declined to name the companies that could relocate.

The major drawback in the port's efforts to retain the business is the controversy surrounding the Mississippi River-Gulf Outlet.

The manmade channel reaches across St. Bernard Parish to connect Breton Sound to the Industrial Canal. Nicknamed MR-GO, the channel is a shortcut for deep-sea ships. For years it has been the center of debate between St. Bernard Parish residents and shipping interests. While the maritime industry has argued that the channel is a necessary link in the region's shipping chain, parish residents have said it has weakened the area's storm protection and caused other environmental damage.

The debate came to a head after Katrina, when the outlet was blamed for some of the

flooding in St. Bernard. The Army Corps of Engineers, which maintains the outlet, has suspended dredging of the channel for the next year. As a result of the storm, the channel filled in enough that the clearance for ships is now only about 23 feet.

That's far from the 36-foot draft firms such as **Vulcan Materials Co.** need to operate. The company, which brings in crushed stone from the Yucatan Peninsula for construction projects, is planning a move from the port because the ships is relies on can no longer pass through the canal, spokesman David Donaldson said.

"Our desire would be to stay right where we are, but we're in a situation where, with the absence of dredging, we can't do that," Donaldson said.

Vulcan is considering several options, he said, including a move to the **Port of St. Bernard.** It would cost about $2.5 million to relocate, Donaldson said. The hefty price tag, he said, doesn't compare with what it would cost to break down the shipments so that they could be sent by shallow-draft barges through the channel.

"The economics of bringing this in by barge are not feasible," Donaldson said. "At this point, we've just got to look at other options."

New Orleans Cold Storage, where

52 million pounds of chicken famously rotted in the heat when electricity failed after the hurricane, is bumping into the same obstacle. The firm, which blast-freezes, stores and then ships chicken parts abroad, requires a deep draft to move the product.

The company will have to incur and pass along additional costs when it becomes operational again next week. With just one dry-dock warehouse open, the chicken will have to be trucked to the waterside Jourdan Road location for shipping.

Beyond that, without a deep-draft channel, vessels that call on the warehouse will have to travel on the Mississippi River and through the narrow Inner Harbor Navigational Canal lock, which could prove problematic, said Mark Blanchard, executive vice president of New Orleans Cold Storage.

"The problem with the locks is the width," he said. "The larger vessels can't fit."

The solution would be to divide shipments between several ships, Blanchard said.

"We wouldn't be locked out of the business because of the locks. It just hinders us," he said. "We're limited by what can fit through the lock. Our competition is not limited in that way."

Not all of the Industrial Canal tenants are having as tough a time. Business at **United States**

Gypsum Co., a wallboard manufacturer, is at just two-thirds of its pre-Katrina levels, but that's because of a shortage of employees, not a transportation problem, spokesman Bob Williams said.

"It's not an issue for us because we use barges," Williams said. "And they require a shallow draft."

The firm's staff, however, has fallen from 150 to 100.

Those who are affected by the MR-GO controversy, however, are planning to turn to the government for help. Blanchard, who has traveled to Washington to encourage the state's congressional delegation to support the dredging of the MR-GO, said it would only make sense to compensate the businesses that depend on it.

"We made this investment based on this waterway being accessible and navigable," he said.

LaGrange agreed. Current estimates, he said, indicate that it would cost $360 million to rebuild the firms that remain on the canal and relocate those that intend to move to the Mississippi River.

"Because of the fact that the general consensus seems to be in favor of closing the MR-GO, then the next logical option seems to be some mitigation by the federal government to pay for the relocation of those companies," LaGrange said.

The port is working on a plan

to move one of it largest tenants, container terminal operator **APM Terminals**, which is a subsidiary of shipping line **Maersk Inc.**, to the Mississippi River. The terminal is not operating now, and its business is being rerouted to Houston.

The terminal is not on the list of businesses LaGrange believes will leave New Orleans.

"We're doing everything to keep them and I feel pretty confident that we will," he said.

Meanwhile, the port is turning its attention to finding new use for the spaces that will be abandoned.

"Our game plan will be to utilize all that space with better levee protection and flood protection," he said.

Before Katrina, LaGrange had identified the areas adjacent to the Industrial Canal as targets for potential expansion projects. Although those plans are less certain now, LaGrange insists there is still room for development.

"Should the (Army) Corps (of Engineers) decide not to redredge the MR-GO, we'll use the space for medium to low-dredge vessels," LaGrange said. "We have to retool. Don't think for a minute that it will be dead space."

• • • • • •

Jaquetta White can be reached at jwhite@timespicayune.com or (504) 826-3494.

The Army Corps of Engineers firmly stated that the cause of the flooding was low levees in Lake Borgne and the breaches at the Seventeenth Street and London Avenue canals. Furthermore, the president of St. Bernard Parish, Junior Rodriguez, subsequent to the hurricane levees breach of MRGO, met with the Port of New Orleans and worked out a compromise plan set forth in a memorandum of understanding, which called for reducing the MRGO channel to 28 feet, and simultaneously having the Corps construct higher levees on the Lake Borgne side of the channel, and construct a floodgate in the MRGO that would be closed in case of another hurricane. This plan was embraced by the Port of New Orleans as well as the industries that were working in the MRGO waterway, including CG Railway. The memorandum of understanding was taken before the St. Bernard Parish Council. The council rejected it and voted to discontinue dredging of the MRGO. Having had this wide adverse publicity in the media, it became clear that the Corps of Engineers would elect to do no further dredging of MRGO until a long-term solution was decided upon. Furthermore, when the emergency funding package was concluded in the Congress just before Christmas 2005 to help restore Louisiana and Mississippi, language was put into that agreement that prohibited any of those funds to be used for dredging the MRGO. We have had discussions with the Corps of Engineers, whose officials tell us that they still are convinced that the main problem was low levees on the eastern side of the MRGO which bordered Lake Borgne. Be that as it may, five months after Hurricane Katrina, we became convinced, as did the Port of New Orleans, that the Corps would not in the immediate future change its viewpoint. MRGO would continue to be neglected, as were large areas of New Orleans that suffered devastating flood damage.

It became obvious that we had to have further discussions with the Louisiana congressional delegation in Washington, as well as with the director of the Port of New Orleans. The latter decided to have the various interests, which totaled in excess of 12, join with him to meet with the Louisiana congressional delegation. The majority of the delegation were in favor of giving all of the political participants a year to a year and a half to make plans for what would finally be decided. The

exception was Senator David Vitter, who announced that he would not enter the fray since he had been contacted by the St. Bernard people and had come to the conclusion that it was too hot a political matter to do anything else but take the stance of no immediate dredging pending further investigation. CG Railway could not accept the financial cost and risk of losing an important segment of its business for an uncertain future. We needed a new facility for our CG Railway services.

Subsequent to these meetings, Congress passed and the president signed the $29 billion aid package, primarily for Mississippi and Louisiana, and, marginally, for Texas and Alabama. In the $29 billion package, there is included $11.2 billion that has been appropriated and is to be handled through HUD. This particular fund is to be utilized by the governor of each state (Louisiana will receive 54%) for the purpose of granting reconstruction monies as decided by the governor. Additionally, the law allows for relocation expenses of businesses affected by the hurricane. It was estimated by the New Orleans port director that if the MRGO is not dredged, a number of businesses would have to be relocated at an estimated cost of $380 million.

As a result of the hurricane, the MRGO has already silted up in several places so that the current channel water depth is 23 feet. Our ships (with only one rail car deck) draw a little less than 20 feet of water and, therefore, we are maintaining our operation in the MRGO temporarily. However, we continue our program of installing the second deck on both vessels. When this is completed later in 2006 or early 2007, we will be drawing 21 to 22 feet in loaded condition and, therefore theoretically could continue to use the MRGO, but we would actually be "one hurricane away" from further silting that would prevent our long-term operation. Therefore, as a result of the current status, we had no alternative but to re-look for other locations, first within Louisiana. We were unable to locate a suitable place in Louisiana with connecting rail facilities. We again surveyed Mississippi and Alabama. After careful study we concluded that our alternative ports for relocation would be either Pascagoula, Mississippi, or Mobile, Alabama.

As far as Louisiana is concerned, you will remember the estimate for putting the terminal at New Orleans was right at $31 million. We obtained from the state $15 million toward that cost, and from the City of New Orleans, $2 million. We can confirm that we indeed received this sum and the state issued bonds in the amount of $15 million and the city, $2 million. Our matching investment was right at $14 million. We talked to the contractor who had constructed the terminal in New Orleans. He stated that he could remove the facility from the Elaine Street Terminal and relocate it at a much lower cost than the initial pricing at New Orleans. As we wrote this memorandum, we were in the process of setting up meetings with the governor of Louisiana and the governor of Mississippi. The purpose of the meeting with the governor of Louisiana was to achieve an agreement that the State of Louisiana would reimburse us the $14 million that we have invested in the terminal, and that we got clear title to all of the equipment. The meeting with the governor of Mississippi was for the purpose of getting his support for establishing our hub at Pascagoula, receiving from Mississippi a grant of funds to construct the terminal and upgrade other facilities at the Port of Pascagoula to enhance our overall operation.

2. Memo dated January 9, 2006

Further to the above memo of January 3, Erik F. Johnsen and Erik L. Johnsen met with Governor Blanco of Louisiana on Wednesday, January 4, at her office in Baton Rouge. Attending that meeting were the executive director of the Port of New Orleans, his deputy, and the economic development director for the State of Louisiana. We reviewed with the overnor the current status of MRGO. The port director pointed out that the industries on the MRGO actually contribute $2.29 billion annually of economic benefit to the State of Louisiana. Even so we advised the governor that we had come to the conclusion, with emotions extant, we must for the security of our own company, look for an alternative location for CG Railway.

We asked the governor to turn over to her economic development director the responsibility of unwinding all of our agreements, giving us clear title to all equipment that had been installed at the Elaine Street Terminal and reimbursing us the $14 million

that we had put up concurrent with the state's support over the last year and a half. She was receptive. It is too early to say what we can achieve. We do hope, however, to be able to get title to all of the equipment that was used for the construction of the Elaine Street Terminal.

On Friday, January 6, Erik F. Johnsen and Erik L. Johnsen met with the governor of Mississippi. In attendance were the governor's chief of staff and a deputy economic development project representative. We explained to the governor our interest in relocating our CG Railway service to Pascagoula. We had surveyed the port and came to the conclusion that it could serve our purposes. We told the governor that we needed the State of Mississippi to upgrade the rail yard then existing at Pascagoula, and to improve the dock facilities so as to accommodate our rail ferry ships. We also, after some discussion, advised him that we would have an open mind about the relocation of our headquarters to Mississippi. He obviously took note of all that we said, and said he would go into it together with his economic development staff. Erik L. Johnsen worked with that staff over the next three weeks. The governor was very business-like. He stated that he knew it had to be good for us, but it also had to be good for Mississippi.

3. Memo dated January 12, 2006

Hurricanes Katrina and Rita caused extensive damage throughout southeast and southwest Louisiana. Our CG Railway service was adversely impacted because of the extensive damage ashore and silting in the waterways. More important, however, was the long-term result of Katrina and Rita.

There was continued controversy within the state and at the federal level on what to do generally for protection against future flooding in the State of Louisiana, while specifically focusing on the future of MRGO. Since CGR is dependent on the use of MRGO, it became clear to us that for the protection of our investment in the CGR service our Company had to be proactive. The newspaper article reprinted on page 223 shows the economic impact of the closure of MRGO.

On April 21, 2007, International Shipholding Corporation moved into new headquarters on the 17th and 18th floors of the RSA (Retirement Systems of Alabama) Battle House Tower Office Building, Mobile's tallest building, on the western shore of the Mobile River. (Photo from Thompson Ventulett Stainback and Associates, Inc.)

Two one-of-a-kind docks for two one-of-a-kind ships: Specially designed two-tier railroad docks under construction in Mobile, Alabama, (photographed) and Coatzacoalcos, Mexico, will enable us to roll up to 116 railroad cars on and 116 railroad cars off within six to eight hours at each port. The average loaded railcar has a net weight of 70 tons. The *Banda Sea* and *Bali Sea* will make a total of 85 calls at each dock each year beginning in the third quarter of 2007, meaning a total inbound and outbound tonnage for each full year of 1,250,000/1,500,000 tons. The round voyage between Mobile and Coatzacoalcos will take about eight days. On April 24, 2007, the Mobile dock was 99% complete and the slipway was being dredged. The CG Railway operation with the second decks will be up and running by summer 2007. Up to 500 railroad cars can be held in the railroad yard at a time.

4. *Memo dated May 11, 2006*

At our last board meeting, we spent a lot of time discussing the effects of Hurricane Katrina as well as the various discussions we have had with the respective state officials in connection with the required relocation of our CG Railway terminal from New Orleans to either Mississippi or Alabama. We also discussed the various financial considerations involved in that transaction. Erik F. Johnsen, therefore, set forth to the board management's current thinking of where it believed the Company was heading with the CG Railway program.

Firstly, as we discussed, we are convinced that the Port of Mobile offered us the best alternative for long-term benefit to the CG Railway service. We had concluded on satisfactory terms, as a first step, cancellation of the cooperative endeavor agreement we had executed with the State of Louisiana for the construction of the Elaine Street Terminal. We continued negotiating with the State of Louisiana and, of course, with the states of Mississippi and Alabama on the final proposals respecting relocation of the port for the CGR service. The State of Mississippi was unresponsive, while the State of Alabama offered us an economic package that included a prerequisite that ISC relocate its headquarters office from New Orleans to Mobile.

5. *Memo dated June 9, 2006*

Since May 11, management had quietly met with officials of the State of Alabama in order to firm up their proposal for the relocation of our operations to Mobile. The State of Alabama, in offering us a grant to potentially offset the construction cost of a new railroad dock in Mobile, tied this to a commitment that we move our headquarters from New Orleans to Mobile. To enable us to accomplish the relocation of the headquarters, the State of Alabama offered us other financial incentives.

Alabama listed the advantages and incentives they offered. From their point of view they offered us attractive savings over the next ten years. We concluded the overall estimated savings and incentives came to around $15 million.

On May 24, 2006, citing force majeure, we signed an amendment to the cooperative endeavor agreement with the State of Louisiana, thereby officially canceling the mutual obligations of the state and the Company connected thereto. As soon as that agreement was executed, Erik F. Johnsen met with the commissioner of administration of the State of Louisiana on June 1. At that meeting he reviewed with the commissioner the series of events connected with the Company's CGR operations. He explained to the commissioner the incentives and grant that Alabama offered us. In our view we did everything in our power to convince the authorities in Baton Rouge of the merit of assisting us in this matter. However, the State of Louisiana offered nothing to mitigate our losses. The offer from Mobile could not be rejected.

The demise of MRGO was confirmed on June 2, 2006, when the governor of Louisiana wrote to Major General Don T. Riley, director of civil works, U.S. Army Corps of Engineers, and the Louisiana economic development secretary sent his letter of June 8, 2006, to Erik F. Johnsen.

At the July 26, 2006, directors' meeting of International Shipholding Corporation held in New York City, Erik F. Johnsen stated, "It is difficult for us to assess New Orleans and Louisiana today. Yet one must recognize that a high percentage of the city is in disrepair. Granted, there will be money pouring into the area for reconstruction, but undoubtedly some time will pass before any of this occurs. The climate in Alabama is very positive, and they have offered real incentives for us to relocate to Mobile. I don't take lightly the toughness involved in a transition of this type, and I know it won't be easy. I ask each of you herewith to join with me in confirming your acceptance of the offer from the State of Alabama and relocate ISH headquarters to Mobile."

Ship owning is a very risky business: *"not for widows and orphans."*

Appendix

State of Louisiana
OFFICE OF THE GOVERNOR
Baton Rouge
70804-9004

KATHLEEN BABINEAUX BLANCO
GOVERNOR

POST OFFICE BOX 94004
(225) 342-7015

June 2, 2006

Major General Don T. Riley
Director of Civil Works
United States Army Corps of Engineers
441 G Street, NW
Washington, DC 20314

Dear General Riley:

I am encouraged by the historic partnership formed between the U.S. Army Corps of Engineers and the State of Louisiana to develop a comprehensive master plan for the protection and restoration of our fragile coast, as mandated by the Congress and our state Legislature. I am pleased that the Corps and the State have responded quickly and are committed to making these two plans become one vision for coastal Louisiana.

Last November, our Legislature created the Coastal Protection and Restoration Authority (CPRA) of Louisiana to develop, implement and enforce a comprehensive coastal protection master plan that for the first time in our state's history will truly integrate coastal restoration and hurricane protection. By law, this single state entity will be your partner, representing the State in the long journey to establishing a safe and sustainable coast.

Our integrated team, comprised of Corps leadership and the CPRA, has been hard at work on the comprehensive coastal protection and restoration plan, with the interim report due to Congress on June 30. I understand that this report will recommend that certain projects be advanced to bring immediate solutions for our most vulnerable coastal areas and that the final report on comprehensive protection will be made in December 2007. As we work together as partners on this critical planning effort, I believe it is essential that we communicate clearly and openly on each and every aspect of this plan.

Therefore, I write to unequivocally express the policy of this State regarding the future of the Mississippi River Gulf Outlet (MRGO). Our people have spoken, our Legislature has made its will clear, and my Advisory Commission on Coastal Protection, Restoration and Conservation has recommended the immediate closure of this channel.

Over the years, MRGO has compromised the safety of countless communities and contributed to the loss of vital coastal marsh areas. The closure of the MRGO must ensure that communities are safe and our ecosystems are protected from further saltwater intrusion and coastal land loss.

Letter from Louisiana Governor Kathleen B. Blanco to Major General Don T. Riley, U.S. Army Corps of Engineers, June 2, 2006 (2 pages).

General Riley
Page 2
June 2, 2006

Specifically, our work must include a more precise plan for closure, restoration of the extensive wetlands lost as a direct result of the MRGO, and the integration of this closure into the comprehensive hurricane protection plan. We must also consider the navigation needs that will be affected by closing the MRGO to deep draft navigation, including expediting the construction of the new IHNC Lock and relocation of businesses currently depending on the MRGO.

As this report is formulated, I will be communicating this policy on MRGO through the CPRA directly to our Congressional Delegation. I urge you to join me in advocating with one voice on this issue, as well as on other critical near term aspects of our plan.

I understand, as do the people of Louisiana, that there will be many tough decisions in the coming months and years. Implementing these policy choices and determining their long term sustainability will not be easy. However, I am confident that working together, with a strong commitment to public input and thoughtful direction from our legislative leaders, we will set Louisiana on the right path for a safe and prosperous future.

Sincerely,

Kathleen Babineaux Blanco
Governor

State of Louisiana

LOUISIANA ECONOMIC DEVELOPMENT

Kathleen Babineaux Blanco
Governor

Michael J. Olivier, CED
Secretary

June 8, 2006

Mr. Erik L. Johnsen, President
CG Railway, Inc.
650 Poydras Street, Suite 1700
New Orleans, LA 70130

Via Fax & U.S. Mail
Fax: 504.593.2503

Dear Mr. Johnsen:

Louisiana Economic Development has, together with the Division of Administration, reviewed Mr. Erik F. Johnson's meeting of last week with Commissioner LeBlanc in which the parties discussed the options facing CG Railway in the Port of Orleans after Hurricane Katrina and the decision of the Corps of Engineers to cease dredging operations in and around the Mississippi River Gulf Outlet (MRGO).

The State invested $15 million in improvements at the Port to assist CG Railways in bringing about its railcar ferry transportation system to operate between Mexico and the Port of New Orleans, in large part based upon our desire to work with a longstanding New Orleans company in a new venture. Indications are that but for the hurricane and resultant decisions by the Corps and Congress, the increased cargo capacity and frequency of operations together with improvements made by the State and CG Railway to the facility, would have resulted in a resounding success for the State, the Port and CG Railway.

Since the hurricane we have worked with you and reached agreement on a number of matters necessary to resolving issues arising from the Hurricane and its aftermath. At all times we have sought to minimize the consequences to CG Railway of these unfortunate circumstances and to assist your business in the recovery of its investment while being mindful of the substantial investment made by the State.

Unfortunately, we cannot accede to the request that the State of Louisiana pay CG Railway an additional $18 million (for a total state payment of $33 million) that would allow CG Railway to finance a similar facility in the Port of Mobile. We understand your position that this may result in the movement of your parent company's headquarters from New Orleans to Mobile and acknowledge that this is an unfortunate result for both Louisiana and your employees who returned home following Hurricane Katrina. We do appreciate your expressed desire to continue to have business offices and other ongoing operations in the State and look forward to working with you in those endeavors.

Letter from Michael J. Olivier, Louisiana secretary of economic development, to Erik L. Johnsen, June 8, 2006 (2 pages).

Mr. Johnsen
Page 2
June 8, 2006

We have also worked with CG Railway and the Port of New Orleans to support the mutual efforts of each to reach agreement on an operating lease that will allow the investment in the Port to continue to be used, albeit with different operations from those originally contemplated.

As has been demonstrated in the past, we continue to wish to work with you and look forward to further discussions of future opportunities.

Sincerely,

Michael J. Olivier
Secretary

c: Commissioner Jerry Luke LeBlanc, Division of Administration
      Mr. Erik F. Johnsen, Chairman, CG Railway, Inc.
      Ms. Maris LeBlanc, Division of Administration
      Mr. Richard House, LED
      Mr. Fred Chevalier, Jones Walker

[CHAPTER 82]

AN ACT

To provide for the sale of surplus war-built vessels, and for other purposes.

March 8, 1946
[H. R. 3603]
[Public Law 321]

Be it enacted by the Senate and House of Representatives of the United States of America in Congress assembled, That this Act may be cited as the "Merchant Ship Sales Act of 1946".

Merchant Ship Sales Act of 1946.

DECLARATION OF POLICY

SEC. 2. (a) It is necessary for the national security and development and maintenance of the domestic and the export and import foreign commerce of the United States that the United States have an efficient and adequate American-owned merchant marine (1) sufficient to carry its domestic water-borne commerce and a substantial portion of its water-borne export and import foreign commerce and to provide shipping service on all routes essential for maintaining the flow of such domestic and foreign water-borne commerce at all times; (2) capable of serving as a naval and military auxiliary in time of war or national emergency; (3) owned and operated under the United States flag by citizens of the United States; (4) composed of the best-equipped, safest, and most suitable types of vessels, constructed in the United States and manned with a trained and efficient citizen personnel; and (5) supplemented by efficient American-owned facilities for shipbuilding and ship repair, marine insurance, and other auxiliary services.

(b) It is hereby declared to be the policy of this Act to foster the development and encourage the maintenance of such a merchant marine.

DEFINITIONS

SEC. 3. As used in this Act the term—

(a) "Commission" means the United States Maritime Commission.

"Commission."

(b) "War-built vessel" means an oceangoing vessel of one thousand five hundred gross tons or more, owned by the United States and suitable for commercial use—

"War-built vessel."

(1) which was constructed or contracted for by or for the account of the United States during the period, beginning January 1, 1941, and ending with September 2, 1945; or

(2) which, having been constructed during the period beginning September 3, 1939, and ending with September 2, 1945, was acquired by the United States during such period.

(c) "Prewar domestic cost", as applied to any type of vessel, means the amount determined by the Commission, and published by the Commission in the Federal Register, to be the amount for which a standard vessel of such type could have been constructed (without its national defense features) in the United States under normal conditions relating to labor, materials, and other elements of cost, obtaining on or about January 1, 1941. In no case shall the prewar domestic cost of any type of vessel be considered to be greater than 80 per centum of the domestic war cost of vessels of the same type.

"Prewar domestic cost."

Limitation.

(d) "Statutory sales price", as applied to a particular vessel, means, in the case of a dry-cargo vessel, an amount equal to 50 per centum of the prewar domestic cost of that type of vessel, and in the case of a tanker, such term means an amount equal to 87½ per centum of the prewar domestic cost of a tanker of that type, such amount in each case being adjusted as follows:

"Statutory sales price."

(1) If the Commission is of the opinion that the vessel is not in class, there shall be subtracted the amount estimated by the Commission as the cost of putting the vessel in class.

(2) If the Commission is of the opinion that the vessel lacks

desirable features which are incorporated in the standard vessel used for the purpose of determining prewar domestic cost, and that the statutory sales price (unadjusted) would be lower if the standard vessel had also lacked such features, there shall be subtracted the amount estimated by the Commission as the amount of such resulting difference in statutory sales price.

(3) If the Commission is of the opinion that the vessel contains desirable features which are not incorporated in the standard vessel used for the purpose of determining prewar domestic cost, and that the statutory sales price (unadjusted) would be higher if the standard vessel had also contained such features, there shall be added the amount estimated by the Commission as the amount of such resulting difference in statutory sales price.

Subtraction for normal depreciation.

(4) There shall be subtracted, as representing normal depreciation, an amount computed by applying to the statutory sales price (determined without regard to this paragraph) the rate of 5 per centum per annum for the period beginning with the date of the original delivery of the vessel by its builder and ending with the date of sale or charter to the applicant in question, and there shall also be subtracted an amount computed by applying to the statutory sales price (determined without regard to this paragraph) such rate not in excess of 3 per centum per annum in the case of a vessel other than a tanker, and not in excess of 4 per centum per annum in the case of a tanker, for such period or periods of war service as the Commission determines will make reasonable allowance for excessive wear and tear by reason of war service which cannot be or has not been otherwise compensated for under this subsection.

Restriction on adjustments.

No adjustment, except in respect of passenger vessels constructed before January 1, 1941, shall be made under this Act which will result in a statutory sales price which (1) in the case of dry-cargo vessels (except Liberty type vessels) will be less than 35 per centum of the domestic war cost of vessels of the same type, (2) in the case of any Liberty type vessel will be less than 31½ per centum of the domestic war cost of vessels of such type, or (3) in the case of a tanker will be less than 50 per centum of the domestic war cost of tankers of the same type.   For the purposes of this Act, except section 5, all Liberty vessels shall be considered to be vessels of one and the same type.

Liberty vessels.

"Domestic war cost."

(e) "Domestic war cost" as applied to any type of vessel means the average construction cost (without national defense features) as determined by the Commission, of vessels of such type delivered during the calendar year 1944, except in case of any type of vessel the principal deliveries of which were made after the calendar year 1944, there shall be used in lieu of such year 1944 such period of not less than six consecutive calendar months as the Commission shall find to be most representative of war production costs of such type.

"Cessation of hostilities."

(f) "Cessation of hostilities" means the date proclaimed by the President as the date of the cessation of hostilities in the present war, or the date so specified in a concurrent resolution of the two Houses of the Congress, whichever is the earlier.

"Citizen of the United States."

39 Stat. 729.
46 U. S. C. §§ 802, 803.
"Affiliated interest."
Post, pp. 46, 49.

(g) "Citizen of the United States" includes a corporation, partnership, or association only if it is a citizen of the United States within the meaning of section 2 of the Shipping Act of 1916, as amended. The term "affiliated interest" as used in sections 9 and 10 of this Act includes any person affiliated or associated with a citizen applicant for benefits under this Act who the Commission, pursuant to rules and regulations prescribed hereunder, determines should be so included in order to carry out the policy and purposes of this Act.

SALES OF WAR-BUILT VESSELS TO CITIZENS

Sec. 4. (a) Any citizen of the United States may make application to the Commission to purchase a war-built vessel, under the jurisdiction and control of the Commission, at the statutory sales price. If the Commission determines that the applicant possesses the ability, experience, financial resources, and other qualifications, necessary to enable him to operate and maintain the vessel under normal competitive conditions, and that such sale will aid in carrying out the policies of this Act, the Commission shall sell such vessel to the applicant at the statutory sales price.

(b) At the time of sale, the purchaser shall pay to the Commission at least 25 per centum of the statutory sales price. The balance of the statutory sales price shall be payable in not more than twenty equal annual installments, with interest on the portion of the statutory sales price remaining unpaid, at the rate of 3½ per centum per annum, or shall be payable under such other amortization provisions which permit the purchaser to accelerate payment of the unpaid balance as the Commission deems satisfactory. The obligation of the purchaser with respect to payment of such unpaid balance with interest shall be secured by a preferred mortgage on the vessel sold. *Payment.*

(c) The contract of sale, and the mortgage given to secure the payment of the unpaid balance of the purchase price, shall not restrict the lawful or proper use or operation of the vessel. *Use of vessel.*

CHARTER OF WAR-BUILT VESSELS TO CITIZENS

SEC. 5. (a) Any citizen of the United States and, until July 4, 1946, any citizen of the Commonwealth of the Philippines, may make application to the Commission to charter a war-built dry-cargo vessel, under the jurisdiction and control of the Commission, for bare-boat use. The Commission may, in its discretion, either reject or approve the application, but shall not so approve unless in its opinion the chartering of such vessel to the applicant would be consistent with the policies of this Act. No vessel shall be chartered under this section until sixty days after publication of the applicable prewar domestic cost in the Federal Register under subsection 3 (c) of this Act.

(b) The charter hire for any vessel chartered under the provisions of this section shall be fixed by the Commission at such rate as the Commission determines to be consistent with the policies of this Act, but, except upon the affirmative vote of not less than four members of the Commission, such rate shall not be less than 15 per centum per annum of the statutory sales price (computed as of the date of charter). Except in the case of vessels having passenger accommodations for not less than eighty passengers, rates of charter hire fixed by the Commission on any war-built vessel which differ from the rate specified in this subsection shall not be less than the prevailing world market charter rates for similar vessels for similar use as determined by the Commission. *Rates.*

(c) The provisions of sections 708, 709, 710, 712, and 713, of the Merchant Marine Act, 1936, as amended, shall be applicable to charters made under this section. *49 Stat. 2009. 46 U. S. C. §§ 1198–1200, 1202, 1203.*

SALE OF WAR-BUILT VESSELS TO PERSONS NOT CITIZENS OF THE UNITED STATES

SEC. 6. (a) Any person not a citizen of the United States may make application to the Commission to purchase a war-built vessel (other than a P-2 type or other passenger type and other than a

Liberty type collier or tanker), under the jurisdiction and control of the Commission. If the Commission determines—

(1) that the applicant has the financial resources, ability, and experience necessary to enable him to fulfill all obligations with respect to payment of any deferred portion of the purchase price, and that sale of the vessel to him would not be inconsistent with any policy of the United States in permitting foreign sales under section 9 of the Shipping Act, 1916, as amended; and

39 Stat. 730.
46 U. S. C. § 808.

(2) after consultation with the Secretary of the Navy, that such vessel is not necessary to the defense of the United States; and

(3) that such vessel is not necessary to the promotion and maintenance of an American merchant marine described in section 2; and

(4) that for a reasonable period of time, which in the case of tankers and "C" type vessels shall not end before ninety days after publication of the applicable prewar domestic cost in the Federal Register under subsection 3 (c) of this Act, such vessel has been available for sale at the statutory sales price to citizens of the United States, or for charter under section 5 to citizens of the United States, and that no responsible offer has been made by a citizen of the United States to purchase or charter such vessel;

then the Commission is authorized to approve the application and sell such vessel to the applicant at not less than the statutory sales price. In case of application submitted by a citizen of the Commonwealth of the Philippines, paragraph (4) of this subsection shall not apply. Notwithstanding paragraph (4) of this subsection, not to exceed ten "C" type vessels, except C–3's, may be sold to noncitizens at any time after such date of publication at not less than the statutory sales price.

Application by citizen of Philippines.

Restrictions.

(b) Notwithstanding any other provision of law, no war-built vessel shall be sold to any person not a citizen of the United States, except in accordance with subsection (a), or upon terms or conditions more favorable than those at which such war-built vessel is offered to a citizen of the United States, but where the vessel so sold is being transferred to foreign register and flag, the mortgage securing the unpaid balance of the purchase price and interest thereon shall contain provisions according to such mortgage the priorities over other liens and encumbrances accorded such mortgages on merchant vessels under the laws of such registry and flag.

ORDER OF PREFERENCES

Citizen and noncitizen applicants.

SEC. 7. (a) In exercising its powers under this Act and under other provisions of law with respect to the sale and charter of war-built vessels, the Commission shall give preference to citizen applicants over noncitizen applicants, and as between citizen applicants to purchase and citizen applicants to charter, shall, so far as practicable and consistent with the policies of this Act, give preference to citizen applicants to purchase. In determining the order of preference between citizen applicants to purchase or between citizen applicants to charter, the Commission shall consider, among other relevant factors, the extent to which losses and requisitions of the applicant's prewar tonnage have been overcome and shall in all cases, in the sale and charter of a war-built vessel, give preference in such sale or charter, as the case may be, to the former owner of such vessel, or to the person for whom the vessel was constructed but to whom delivery thereof was prevented by the United States. In determining the order of preference between noncitizen applicants to purchase, the Commission shall give preference to citizens of the Commonwealth of the Philippines, and in determining the order of preference between other noncitizen applicants to purchase shall consider the extent to which losses in prewar tonnage

Citizens of the Philippines.

of the various member nations of the United Nations, incurred in the interests of the war effort, have been overcome, and the relative effects of such losses upon the national economy of such member nations.

(b) After the cessation of hostilities, operation of vessels in commercial service by the United States, either for its own account or through operating agents under agency agreements, shall, except as to the Panama Railroad Company and other services specifically authorized by law, be continued only to the extent necessary to effect orderly transfer of vessels to private operation.

Operation after cessation of hostilities.

EXCHANGE OF VESSELS

SEC. 8. (a) The Commission is authorized to acquire, in exchange for an allowance of a credit on the purchase of any war-built vessel under section 4 or any vessel acquired through exchange under subsection (d) of this section—

(1) Any vessel owned by a citizen of the United States, other than a vessel purchased under this Act; or

(2) Any vessel owned by a foreign corporation, if—

(A) the vessel was constructed in the United States, and has, after December 7, 1941, been chartered to, or otherwise taken for use by, the United States; and

(B) the controlling interest in such corporation is, at the time of acquisition of such vessel hereunder, owned by a citizen or citizens of the United States, and has been so owned for a period of at least three years immediately prior to such acquisition; and

(C) such corporation agrees that the war-built vessel purchased with the use of such credit shall be owned by such citizen or citizens and shall be documented under the laws of the United States.

Such allowance shall not be applied upon the cash payment required under section 4. A war-built vessel shall be deemed a "new vessel" for the purpose of section 511 of the Merchant Marine Act, 1936, as amended, and section 510 (e) of such Act shall be applicable with respect to vessels exchanged under this section to the same extent as applicable to obsolete vessels exchanged under section 510 of such Act.

(b) (1) If, prior to December 31, 1946, the owner of a vessel eligible for exchange under subsection (a) makes a firm offer binding for at least ninety days, to transfer the vessel to the Commission in exchange for an allowance of credit provided in subsection (a), the amount of such allowance shall be the fair and reasonable value of the vessel as determined by the Commission under this section. In making such determination the Commission shall consider: (A) The value of the vessel determined in accordance with the standards of valuation established pursuant to Executive Order 9387 (8 F. R. 14105) as of the date of such offer, (B) any liability of the United States for repair and restoration of the vessel, (C) the utility value of the vessel, (D) the effect of this Act upon the market value of such vessel, and (E) the public interest in promoting exchanges of vessels as a means of rehabilitating and modernizing the American merchant marine. In no event shall the amount of such allowance, in case of dry cargo vessels and tankers, exceed (A) (1) if the vessel or vessels tendered in exchange are of equal or greater dead-weight tonnage than the war-built vessel or vessels being acquired, 33⅓ per centum of the statutory sales price (unadjusted) of the war-built vessel or vessels, or (2) if the vessel or vessels tendered in exchange are of lesser dead-weight tonnage than the war-built vessel or vessels, such proportionate part of 33⅓ per centum of the statutory sales price (unadjusted) of such war-built vessel or vessels as the dead-weight tonnage of such

Credit allowance.

54 Stat. 1106; 53 Stat. 1184.
46 U. S. C. §§ 1161, 1160 (e); Supp. V, § 1161.

Amount of allowance.

50 U. S. C., Supp. V, app. § 1295 note.

Dry cargo vessels and tankers.

vessel or vessels tendered in exchange bear to the dead-weight tonnage of such war-built vessel or vessels, or (B) the liability of the United States in connection with the repair or restoration of such vessel under any charter to which the United States is a party, whichever is higher.   In the case of passenger vessels tendered in exchange, the amount of the allowance shall not exceed the percentages of statutory sales price computed under (A) (1) and (2) above by gross tons instead of dead-weight tons, or such liability for the repair or restoration of such passenger vessel, whichever is the higher.   In any case where the vessel tendered in exchange was acquired from the United States, the exchange allowance under this section shall not exceed the price paid the United States therefor plus the depreciated cost of any improvements thereon.   In the case of any vessel tendered in exchange which has been restored to condition by the United States for the purpose of redelivering such vessel to its owner in compliance with the charter of such vessel with the United States, or where, for such restoration a cash allowance has been made to the owner, there shall be deducted from the amount of the allowance of credit for such vessel determined by the Commission under this section, an amount equal to the liability of the United States for such restoration or such cash allowance made to the owner.

(2) If, after such offer is made, and prior to its acceptance, or prior to the acquisition of the vessel, by the Commission, the vessel is lost by reason of causes for which the United States is responsible, then in lieu of paying the owner any amount on account of such loss, the offer shall, for the purposes of subsection (a) and this subsection, be considered as having been accepted and the vessel as having been acquired by the Commission under subsection (a) immediately prior to such loss.

(c) The Commission is also authorized to make available any war-built vessel for transfer in complete or partial settlement of any claim against the United States (1) for just compensation upon requisition for title of any vessel, or (2) for indemnity for the loss of any vessel which was acquired for use by the United States, but only to the extent such vessel is available for sale to the claimant.

(d) In the case of any vessel constructed in the United States after January 1, 1937, which has been taken by the United States for use in any manner, the Commission, if in its opinion the transfer would aid in carrying out the policies of this Act, is authorized to transfer to the owner of such vessel another vessel which is deemed by the Commission to be of comparable type with adjustments for depreciation and difference in design or speed, and to the extent applicable, adjustments with respect to the retained vessel as provided for in section 9, and such other adjustments and terms and conditions, including transfer of mortgage obligations in favor of the United States binding upon the old vessel, as the Commission may prescribe.

ADJUSTMENT FOR PRIOR SALES TO CITIZENS

SEC. 9. (a) A citizen of the United States who on the date of the enactment of this Act—

(1) owns a vessel which he purchased from the Commission prior to such date, and which was delivered by its builder after December 31, 1940; or

(2) is party to a contract with the Commission to purchase from the Commission a vessel, which has not yet been delivered to him; or

(3) owns a vessel on account of which a construction-differential subsidy was paid, or agreed to be paid, by the Commission

Passenger vessels.

Reconditioned vessels.

Loss prior to acquisition, etc.

Transfers in settlement of claims.

Adjustments with owners.

under section 504 of the Merchant Marine Act, 1936, as amended, and which was delivered by its builder after December 31, 1940; or

49 Stat. 1998.
46 U. S. C. § 1154.

(4) is party to a contract with a shipbuilder for the construction for him of a vessel, which has not yet been delivered to him, and on account of which a construction-differential subsidy was agreed, prior to such date, to be paid by the Commission under section 504 of the Merchant Marine Act, 1936, as amended;

Supra.
Price adjustments.

shall, except as hereinafter provided, be entitled to an adjustment in the price of such vessel under this section if he makes application therefor, in such form and manner as the Commission may prescribe, within sixty days after the date of publication of the applicable prewar domestic costs in the Federal Register under section 3 (c) of this Act. No adjustment shall be made under this section in respect of any vessel the contract for the construction of which was made after September 2, 1945, under the provisions of title V (including section 504) or title VII of the Merchant Marine Act, 1936, as amended.

Ante, p. 41.

49 Stat. 1995, 2008.
46 U. S. C. §§ 1151–
1155, 1156–1161, 1191–
1204; Supp. V, §§ 1152–
1161, 1194, 1195.
Date of sale.

(b) Such adjustment shall be made, as hereinafter provided, by treating the vessel as if it were being sold to the applicant on the date of the enactment of this Act, and not before that time. The amount of such adjustment shall be determined as follows:

Determination of
amount.

(1) The Commission shall credit the applicant with the excess of the cash payments made upon the original purchase price of the vessel over 25 per centum of the statutory sales price of the vessel as of such date of enactment. If such payment was less than 25 per centum of the statutory sales price of the vessel, the applicant shall pay the difference to the Commission.

Credit for excess payments, etc.

(2) The applicant's indebtedness under any mortgage to the United States with respect to the vessel shall be adjusted.

Mortgage indebtedness.

(3) The adjusted mortgage indebtedness shall be in an amount equal to the excess of the statutory sales price of the vessel as of the date of the enactment of this Act over the sum of the cash payment retained by the United States under paragraph (1) plus the readjusted trade-in allowance (determined under paragraph (7)) with respect to any vessel exchanged by the applicant on the original purchase. The adjusted mortgage indebtedness shall be payable in equal annual installments thereafter during the remaining life of such mortgage with interest on the portion of the statutory sales price remaining unpaid at the rate of 3½ per centum per annum.

(4) The Commission shall credit the applicant with the excess, if any, of the sum of the cash payments made by the applicant upon the original purchase price of the vessel plus the readjusted trade-in allowance (determined under paragraph (7)) over the statutory sales price of the vessel as of the date of the enactment of this Act to the extent not credited under paragraph (1).

Credit for excess payments, etc.

(5) The Commission shall also credit the applicant with an amount equal to interest at the rate of 3½ per centum per annum (for the period beginning with the date of the original delivery of the vessel to the applicant and ending with the date of the enactment of this Act) on the excess of the original purchase price of the vessel over the amount of any allowance allowed by the Commission on the exchange of any vessel on such purchase; the amount of such credit first being reduced by any interest on the original mortgage indebtedness accrued up to such date of enactment and unpaid. Interest so accrued and unpaid shall be canceled.

Interest.

(6) The applicant shall credit the Commission with all amounts paid by the United States to him as charter hire for use of the

Charter hire.

vessel (exclusive of service, if any, required under the terms of the charter) under any charter party made prior to the date of the enactment of this Act, and any charter hire for such use accrued up to such date of enactment and unpaid shall be canceled; and the Commission shall credit the applicant with the amount that would have been paid by the United States to the applicant as charter hire for bare-boat use of vessels exchanged by the applicant on the original purchase (for the period beginning with date on which the vessels so exchanged were delivered to the Commission and ending with the date of the enactment of this Act).

Exchange allowance.

(7) The allowance made to the applicant on any vessel exchanged by him on the original purchase shall be readjusted so as to limit such allowance to the amount provided for under section 8.

Ante, p. 45.

Overpayments and deficiencies in Federal taxes.

(8) There shall be subtracted from the sum of the credits in favor of the Commission under the foregoing provisions of this subsection the amount of any overpayments of Federal taxes by the applicant resulting from the application of subsection (c) (1), and there shall be subtracted from the sum of the credits in favor of the applicant under the foregoing provisions of this subsection the amount of any deficiencies in Federal taxes of the applicant resulting from the application of subsection (c) (1). If, after making such subtractions, the sum of the credits in favor of the applicant exceeds the sum of the credits in favor of the Commission, such excess shall be paid by the Commission to the applicant. If, after making such subtractions, the sum of the credits in favor of the Commission exceeds the sum of the credits in favor of the applicant, such excess shall be paid by the applicant to the Commission. Upon such payment by the Commission or the applicant, such overpayments shall be treated as having been refunded and such deficiencies as having been paid.

Purchase price.

For the purposes of this subsection, the purchase price of a vessel on account of which a construction-differential subsidy was paid or agreed to be paid under section 504 of the Merchant Marine Act, 1936, as amended, shall be the net cost of the vessel to the owner.

49 Stat. 1998.
46 U. S. C. § 1154.

Adjustment subject to binding agreement.

(c) An adjustment shall be made under this section only if the applicant enters into an agreement with the Commission binding upon the citizen applicant and any affiliated interest to the effect that—

(1) depreciation and amortization allowed or allowable with respect to the vessel up to the date of the enactment of this Act for Federal tax purposes shall be treated as not having been allowable; amounts credited to the Commission under subsection (b) (6) shall be treated for Federal tax purposes as not having been received or accrued as income; amounts credited to the applicant under subsection (b) (5) and (6) shall be treated for Federal tax purposes as having been received and accrued as income in the taxable year in which falls the date of the enactment of this Act;

(2) the liability of the United States for use (exclusive of service, if any, required under the terms of the charter) of the vessel on or after the date of the enactment of this Act under any charter party shall not exceed 15 per centum per annum of the statutory sales price of the vessel as of such date of enactment; and the liability of the United States under any such charter party for loss of the vessel shall be determined on the basis of the statutory sales price as of the date of the enactment of this Act, depreciated to the date of loss at the rate of 5 per centum per annum; and

(3) in the event the United States, prior to the termination of the existing national emergency declared by the President on

May 27, 1941, uses such vessel pursuant to a taking, or pursuant to a bare-boat charter made, on or after the date of the enactment of this Act, the compensation to be paid to the purchaser, his receivers, and trustees, shall in no event be greater than 15 per centum per annum of the statutory sales price as of such date.

55 Stat. 1647.
50 U. S. C., Supp. V,
app., note prec. § 1

(d) Section 506 of the Merchant Marine Act, 1936, as amended, shall not apply with respect to (1) any vessel which is eligible for an adjustment under this section, or (2) any vessel described in clause (1), (2), (3), or (4) of subsection (a) of this section, the contract for the construction of which is made after September 2, 1945, and prior to the date of enactment of this Act.

49 Stat. 1999.
46 U. S. C. § 1156.

LIMITATION ON ELIGIBILITY FOR BENEFITS OF ACT

SEC. 10. No person shall be eligible to purchase or charter a war-built vessel under this Act, or to receive an adjustment under section 9, unless such person makes an agreement with the Commission binding upon such person and any affiliated interest to the effect that the liability of the United States under any charter party or taking for use, made or effected prior to the date of the enactment of this Act, for the loss, on or after such date of enactment and prior to September 3, 1947, of any vessel owned by such person and under charter to the United States (excluding a vessel with respect to which an adjustment is made under section 9) shall be limited to an amount equal to just compensation as of the date of said loss, determined pursuant to existing law, or such amount as may be mutually agreed upon subsequent to the date of the enactment of this Act as just compensation under the provisions of existing law.

NATIONAL DEFENSE RESERVE FLEET

SEC. 11. (a) The Commission shall place in a national defense reserve (1) such vessels owned by it as, after consultation with the Secretary of War and the Secretary of the Navy, it deems should be retained for the national defense, and (2) all vessels owned by it on December 31, 1947, for the sale of which a contract has not been made by that time, except those determined by the Commission to be of insufficient value for commercial and national defense purposes to warrant their maintenance and preservation, and except those vessels, the contracts for the construction of which are made after September 2, 1945, under the provisions of the Merchant Marine Act, 1936, as amended. A vessel under charter on December 31, 1947, shall not be placed in the reserve until the termination of such charter. Unless otherwise provided for by law, all vessels placed in such reserve shall be preserved and maintained by the Commission for the purpose of national defense. A vessel placed in such reserve shall in no case be used for commercial operation, except that any such vessel may be used during any period in which vessels may be requisitioned under section 902 of the Merchant Marine Act, 1936, as amended.

49 Stat. 1985.
46 U. S. C. § 1101
et seq, Supp V, ch. 27.

49 Stat. 2015.
46 U. S. C. § 1242;
Supp. V, § 1242.

(b) Any war-built vessel may be made available by the Commission to any State maintaining a marine school or nautical branch in accordance with the Act of July 29, 1941 (Public Law 191, Seventy-seventh Congress; 55 Stat. 607).

34 U. S. C., Supp. V,
§§ 1122, 1123a–1123e.

GENERAL PROVISIONS

SEC. 12. (a) The Commission is authorized to reconvert or restore for normal operation in commercial services, including removal of national defense or war-service features, any vessel authorized to be sold or chartered under this Act. The Commission is authorized to make such replacements, alterations, or modifications with respect to

Reconversion, etc.,
of vessels.

80634°—47—PT. I——4

any vessel authorized to be sold or chartered under this Act, and to install therein such special features, as may be necesary or advisable to make such vessel suitable for commercial operation on trade routes or services or comparable as to commercial utility to other such vessels of the same general type.

Contracts.
58 Stat. 787.
50 U. S. C., Supp. V, app. § 1657.

(b) The provisions of section 202 of the War Mobilization and Reconversion Act of 1944 shall not apply to contracts of the Commission for or relating to construction of ships.

Eligibility to engage in coastwise trade.
41 Stat. 999.
46 U. S. C., Supp. V, § 883 note.

(c) Notwithstanding the provisions of section 27 of the Merchant Marine Act, 1920, as amended (U. S. C., title 46, sec. 883), no vessel sold or chartered by the Commission under this Act to a citizen of the United States shall be prohibited from engaging in the coastwise trade of the United States while owned by or chartered to such citizen or citizen successors in interest merely because it was under foreign registry on or after May 27, 1941, and prior to its sale or charter under this Act to such citizen, if it is otherwise entitled under the laws of the United States to engage in such trade.

Receipts and expenditures.

49 Stat. 1986, 1987, 1988, 2016.
46 U. S. C. §§ 1111 (d), 1114 (b), 1117, 1119 (a), 1244 (c).

(d) All moneys received by the Commission under this Act shall be deposited in the Treasury to the credit of miscellaneous receipts. The provisions of sections 201 (d), 204 (b), 207, 209 (a), and 905 (c) of the Merchant Marine Act, 1936, as amended, shall apply to all activities and functions which the Commission is authorized to perform under this Act.

REPORTS

SEC. 13. The Commission shall on July 1, 1946, and every three months thereafter, make a report to Congress with respect to all activities or transactions under this Act which have not been covered by any previous such report.

TERMINATION DATE

SEC. 14. No contract of sale or of charter shall be made under this Act after December 31, 1947.

Approved March 8, 1946.

TERMINATION DATE

SEC. 14.[7] No contract of sale shall be made under this Act after January 15, 1951, and no contract of charter shall be made under this Act after June 30, 1950, except as provided for charter under subsections (e) and (f) of section 5 hereof, as amended.

Approved March 8, 1946.

ESSENTIAL TRADE ROUTES, TRADE AREAS, AND SERVICES

Pursuant to Section 211 of the Merchant Marine Act, 1936, as amended, the following trade routes, trade areas, and services have been determined to be essential for the promotion, development, expansion, and maintenance of the foreign commerce of the United States:

Trade Route No.	Description
1	**U.S. Atlantic/East Coast South America.** Between U.S. Atlantic ports (Maine-Atlantic Coast Florida to but including Key West) and ports in Brazil, Paraguay, Uruguay, Argentina, and Falkland Islands.
2	**U.S. Atlantic/West Coast South America.** Between U.S. Atlantic ports (Maine-Atlantic Coast Florida to but not including Key West) and ports in Pacific Coast Colombia, Ecuador, Peru, and Chile.
4	**U.S. Atlantic/Caribbean.** Between U.S. Atlantic ports (Maine-Atlantic Coast Florida to but not including Key West) and ports in the Gulf of Mexico and Caribbean Sea (Mexico-French Guiana, inclusive), all islands of the Caribbean and West Indies (except Puerto Rico), the Bahama Islands, and Bermuda.
5-7-8-9	**U.S. North Atlantic/Western Europe.** Between U.S. North Atlantic ports (Maine-Virginia, inclusive) and ports in the United Kingdom, Republic of Ireland, and Continental Europe (Germany south of Denmark to northern border of Portugal).
6	**U.S. North Atlantic/Scandinavia and Baltic.** Between U.S. North Atlantic ports (Maine-Virginia, inclusive) and ports in Scandinavian and Baltic ports and Iceland, Greenland, and Newfoundland.
10	**U.S. North Atlantic/Mediterranean.** Between U.S. North Atlantic ports (Maine-Virginia, inclusive) and ports in Portugal, Southern Spain, Azores, Atlantic Morocco, and the Mediterranean Sea (including the Adriatic Sea, Aegean Sea, Black Sea, and other seas which are arms of the Mediterranean).

Essential Trade Routes, U.S. Atlantic and Gulf Ports, designated under Merchant Marine Act of 1936 (3 pages).

Trade Route No.	Description

11   **U.S. South Atlantic/Western Europe**. Between U.S. South Atlantic ports (North Carolina-Atlantic Coast Florida to but not including Key West) and ports in the United Kingdom, Republic of Ireland, and Continental Europe north of Portugal.

12   **U.S. Atlantic/Far East**. Between U.S. Atlantic ports (Maine-Atlantic Coast Florida to but not including Key West) and ports in Japan, Taiwan, Philippines, and the Continent of Asia from the Union of Soviet Socialist Republics to Thailand, inclusive.

13   **U.S. South Atlantic and Gulf/Mediterranean**. Between U.S. South Atlantic and Gulf ports (North Carolina-Texas, inclusive) and ports in Portugal, Spain south of Portugal, Atlantic Morocco, and the Mediterranean Sea (including the Adriatic Sea, Aegean Sea, Black Sea, and other seas which are arms of the Mediterranean).

14-1(41)   **U.S. Atlantic and West Africa**. Between U.S. Atlantic and ports on the West Coast of Africa from the southern border of Morocco to the southern border of Angola including Madeira, Canary, Cape Verde, and other islands adjacent to the West Africa Coast.

14-2(42)   **U.S. Gulf and West Africa**. Between U.S. Gulf and ports on the West Coast of Africa from the southern border of Morocco to the southern border of Angola, including Madeira, Canary, Cape Verde, and other islands adjacent to the West Africa Coast.

15-A(51)   **U.S. Atlantic/South and East Africa**. Between U.S. Atlantic ports (Maine-Atlantic Coast Florida to but not including Key West) and ports in South and East Africa from the southern border of Angola to Cape Guaradful in the Somali Republic, including the Ascension and St. Helena in the South Atlantic, the Malagasy Republic, and adjacent in the India Ocean not east of 60o east longitude.

Trade Route No.	Description

15-B(52)   U.S. Gulf/South and East Africa. Between U.S. Gulf ports (Key West-Texas, inclusive) and ports in South and East Africa from the southern border of Angola to Cape Guardaful in the Somali Republic, including the Islands of Ascension and St. Helena in the South Atlantic, the Malagasy Republic, and adjacent islands in the Indian Ocean not east of 60° east longitude.

16   U.S. Atlantic and Gulf/Australia and New Zealand. Between U.S. Atlantic and Gulf ports (Maine-Texas, inclusive) and ports in Australia, New Zealand, New Guinea, and South Sea Islands.

17   U.S. Atlantic, Gulf, and Pacific/Indonesia, Malaysia, and Singapore. Between U.S. Atlantic, Gulf, and Pacific Coast ports and ports in Indonesia, Malaysia (Malaya, Sarawak, and Sabah), Singapore, Brunei and Southern Asia.

18   U.S. Atlantic and Gulf/India, Persian Gulf, and Red Sea. Between U.S. Atlantic and Gulf ports (Maine-Texas, inclusive) and ports in Southwest Asia from Suez to Burma, inclusive, Ceylon and Africa on the Red Sea and Gulf of Aden.

19   U.S. Gulf/Caribbean. Between U.S. Gulf ports (Key West-Texas, inclusive) and ports in the Gulf of Morocco and Caribbean Sea (Mexico-French Guiana, inclusive) and all islands of the Caribbean and West India (except Puerto Rico.

20   U.S. Gulf/East Coast South America. Between U.S. Gulf ports (Key West-Texas, inclusive) and ports in Brazil, Paraguay, Uruguay, Argentina, and Falkland Island.

21   U.S. Gulf/Western Europe. Between U.S. Gulf ports (Key West-Texas, inclusive) and ports in the United Kingdom, Republic of Ireland, and Continental Europe north of Portugal.

22   U.S. Gulf/Far East. Between U.S. Gulf ports (Key West-Texas, inclusive) and ports in Japan, Taiwan, Philippines, and the Continent of Asia from the Union of Soviet Socialist Republics to Thailand, inclusive.

244

New York, New York

September 25, 1969

AMENDMENT NO. 4 TO "LASH" CONTRACT
OF AFFREIGHTMENT DATED OCTOBER 31,
1967, BETWEEN CENTRAL GULF STEAMSHIP
CORPORATION AND INTERNATIONAL PAPER
COMPANY_____

It is hereby agreed by and between the parties hereto that

the aforesaid LASH Contract of Affreightment be and hereby is amended

as follows:-

PARAGRAPH 13 - VESSEL'S NAME:

The name of the vessel is "ACADIA FOREST".

CENTRAL GULF STEAMSHIP CORPORATION

By _____
Vice Chairman

_____
Witness

INTERNATIONAL PAPER COMPANY

By _____
Vice President

_____
Witness

Excerpts from Central Gulf Steamship Corporation/International Paper Company contract and amendments (20 pages).

New York, New York

January 3, 1969

AMENDMENT NO. 3 TO "LASH" CONTRACT
OF AFFREIGHTMENT DATED OCTOBER 31,
1967, BETWEEN CENTRAL GULF STEAMSHIP
CORPORATION AND INTERNATIONAL PAPER
COMPANY.

It is hereby agreed by and between the parties
hereto that the aforesaid LASH Contract of Affreightment
be and hereby is amended as follows:

1.   Paragraph 10(b)(I) is amended to read as
follows:

"(I) to time charter the VESSEL and all
BARGES in the system from OWNER under the
terms and conditions of a time charter in
the form annexed hereto as EXHIBIT "F" at
a charter hire rate of $9,000.00, U.S.
currency, per day;"

2.   Paragraph 10(b)(II)(viii) is amended to read
as follows:

"(viii) OWNER represents that the VESSEL
fully loaded is capable of steaming about
18 knots in good weather and smooth water
on a consumption of about 82.8 metric tons
fuel oil and 3.6 metric tons diesel oil
suitable for the VESSEL per twenty-four (24)
hours, as more specifically set forth in
EXHIBIT "A" to the CONTRACT."

3.   The following is added to Paragraph 10 as sub-
paragraph (e):

"(e) Insofar as the terms, or any of
them, of this Paragraph 10 may be deemed
inconsistent with any of the terms of the
WAR RISKS CLAUSE or the GENERAL WAR CLAUSE,
the terms of this Paragraph shall prevail,
and insofar as any of the terms of the
WAR RISKS CLAUSE may be deemed inconsistent
with the terms of the GENERAL WAR CLAUSE,
the terms of the WAR RISKS CLAUSE shall
prevail. As used in the GENERAL WAR CLAUSE,
the words 'expenses of discharge', 'discharging expenses', and equivalent, shall
apply to expenses of discharging cargo from
BARGES, but shall not be deemed to apply to
any expenses in discharging BARGES from
VESSEL or any other cost or expense relating
to the items enumerated in Paragraph 5(d) of
this CONTRACT."

4.   Clause 6 of EXHIBIT "F" is amended to read as
follows:

"6.   The Charterers to pay as hire:
As per Paragraphs 10 or 21 of Contract of
Affreightment referred to in Clause 40 below,
as may be applicable."

5.   Clause 21(E) of EXHIBIT "F" is amended to read
as follows:

"(E) In the event of the nation under
whose flag the VESSEL sails becoming involved in war, hostilities, warlike operations,
revolution, or civil commotion, and such war,
hostilities, etc., preventing the VESSEL from
operating under this Charter, both the Owners

and the Charterers may cancel the Charter and, unless otherwise agreed, the VESSEL to be redelivered to the Owners at the port of destination or, if prevented through the provisions of section (A) from reaching or entering it, then at a near open and safe port at the Owners' option, after discharge of any cargo on board."

6.   (a)   EXHIBIT A - Description of heavy lift crane is changed to read as follows:

"Vessel equipped with one (1) 510 - Short Ton (455 L/T) Heavy Lift Crane for loading and discharging Barges."

(b)   EXHIBIT B - Estimated weight light Barge is changed to read as follows:

"Not more than 82.366 Long Tons"

CENTRAL GULF STEAMSHIP CORPORATION

By _____
                    Vice Chairman

_____
        Witness

INTERNATIONAL PAPER COMPANY

By _____
                    Vice President

_____
        Witness

New York, New York
February 13, 1968

AMENDMENT NO. 2 TO "LASH" CONTRACT OF
AFFREIGHTMENT DATED OCTOBER 31, 1967,
BETWEEN CENTRAL GULF STEAMSHIP CORPO-
RATION AND INTERNATIONAL PAPER COMPANY

OWNERS having signed a formal barge building contract and
specifications for the construction of the BARGES, and so notified
SHIPPER in writing on January 23, 1968, in fulfillment of the terms
of Clause 22 of the aforesaid Contract of Affreightment as amended
by Amendment No. 1, it is hereby confirmed that the said Contract
of Affreightment is in full force and effect.

CENTRAL GULF STEAMSHIP CORPORATION

By_____
          Vice Chairman

_____
          Witness

INTERNATIONAL PAPER COMPANY

By_____
          Vice President

_____
          Witness

New York, New York
December 26, 1967

AMENDMENT NO. 1 TO "LASH" CONTRACT OF AFFREIGHTMENT DATED OCTOBER 31, 1967 BETWEEN CENTRAL GULF STEAMSHIP CORPORATION AND INTERNATIONAL PAPER COMPANY

OWNERS having signed a formal shipbuilding contract and specifications for construction of the VESSEL dated December 15, 1967, it is hereby agreed by and between the parties that Clause 22 of the aforesaid Contract of Affreightment be and hereby is amended to provide that if a formal barge building contract and specifications are not signed on or before January 31, 1968, AND SHIPPER so notified in writing by that date, the said Contract of Affreightment should be null, void and of no further effect.

CENTRAL GULF STEAMSHIP CORPORATION

_____   By _____
Witness   Vice Chairman

INTERNATIONAL PAPER COMPANY

_____   By _____
Witness   Vice President

T A B L E   O F   C O N T E N T S

TABLE OF CONTENTS - Page 2

TABLE OF CONTENTS - Page 3

<u>LASH</u>

<u>CONTRACT OF AFFREIGHTMENT</u>

Dated: New York, N. Y.
October 31, 1967

IT IS THIS DAY MUTUALLY AGREED between CENTRAL GULF STEAM-
SHIP CORPORATION, New Orleans, Louisiana, Owner, Chartered
Owner, or Disponent Owner (hereinafter referred to as OWNER)
of the vessel referred to herein and INTERNATIONAL PAPER
COMPANY, New York, N. Y. (hereinafter referred to as SHIPPER)
that OWNER will provide a vessel and barges and will carry
cargoes provided by SHIPPER, and SHIPPER will pay freight
and other charges, all as more specifically provided for
herein, for the duration of this Contract of Affreightment
(hereinafter referred to as the CONTRACT) on the following
terms and conditions:

1.   <u>VESSEL AND BARGES:</u>

OWNER will provide, to perform under this CONTRACT,
and operate as herein provided, a new building First Class
LIGHTER-ABOARD-SHIP (LASH) vessel (hereinafter called the
VESSEL), to be named, more fully described in EXHIBIT "A"
hereto, together with barges (hereinafter referred to as
BARGES), more fully described in EXHIBIT "B" hereto, required to sustain the system in operation without delay
to the VESSEL.

254

(1) Cargo insurance shall be for SHIPPER's account.

4. CONTRACT PERIOD:

(a) DURATION - For a period of ten (10) consecutive contract years (a contract year is twelve (12) consecutive months, commencing with the initial tendering date of the VESSEL, as specified in Appendix #1 hereto, or any anniversary of that date) SHIPPER will provide cargo for each Eastbound voyage, for up to seventy-three (73) BARGES, of wood pulp and/or paper products and/or other general cargo, excluding liquid in bulk, and OWNER will carry said BARGES on the VESSEL, which will make consecutive voyages, all in accordance with the terms and provisions hereof.

(b) VOYAGES - OWNER agrees that the VESSEL will embark on no less than six (6) Eastbound voyages per half contract-year period to Range 1, as defined in Exhibit "C". If a port in Range 2 is nominated for more than two (2) voyages during any such period, then OWNER agrees that the VESSEL will embark on no less than five (5) Eastbound voyages during such period.

(c) It is understood that OWNER has the right to carry liquid or other dry cargo in side tanks or other spaces, within the limitation of VESSEL's carrying capacity, not occupied by the seventy-three (73) BARGES, either for SHIPPER's

-11-

account (at freight rate[s] to be agreed upon in addition to the lump sum freight shown in EXHIBIT "C", which rate[s] shall not exceed that charged other shippers for comparable cargo) or for the account of others. It is agreed that SHIPPER shall have the option at any time to contract for the use of all or any portion of said side tanks or other spaces not then under contract to another shipper.

5.   FREIGHT RATE:

(a) Full freight on each voyage as provided herein, regardless of the number of BARGES loaded, is to be prepaid by SHIPPER to OWNER in New York in U.S. currency upon telegraphic advice of bills of lading having been marked "On Board" VESSEL, pursuant to paragraph 3(h) hereof, and is to be considered earned as cargo is taken on board BARGE, ship and/or barge and/or cargo lost or not lost, regardless of the number of BARGES loaded on the VESSEL

(b) SHIPPER shall prepay to OWNER a lump sum, U.S. currency, per voyage for each Eastbound voyage pursuant to the terms hereof according to the rate schedule set forth in EXHIBIT "C", except that SHIPPER shall not be liable to pay freight for more than seven (7) voyages per half contract-year period except on a pro-rata basis per barge for individual BARGES containing SHIPPER's cargo carried on a voyage or voyages in excess of seven (7) voyages per half contract-year.

-12-

(Par. 5, cont'd)

    (c)   TOWAGE - In addition to the above, SHIPPER shall reimburse OWNER within ten (10) running days after receipt of OWNER's duly supported invoice for all towage expenditures (including fleetage and tollage, if any, and necessary insurance to cover all risks other than as otherwise provided for herein) by OWNER in transporting BARGES (i) between the VESSEL's customary discharging/loading point at or near New Orleans, and Vicksburg and Natchez, and return, including towage at and between holding areas at or near said customary discharging/loading point and the VESSEL's stern or side under her heavy lift gantry crane while she is at said customary discharging/loading point; (ii) between the VESSEL's customary discharging/loading point at Panama City and SHIPPER's facility at Panama City, and return, including towage at and between holding areas at or near said customary discharging/loading point and the VESSEL's stern or side under her heavy lift gantry crane while she is at said customary discharging/loading point; and (iii) between the VESSEL's customary discharging/loading points at U.K./European ports of discharge of the VESSEL and points to which the loaded BARGES are towed, and return, including towage at and between holding areas at or near said customary discharging/loading point and the VESSEL's stern or side under her heavy lift gantry crane while she is at said customary discharging/loading point; PROVIDED THAT in any case in which cargo of any other shipper is towed on

-13-

all or any portion of the aforesaid routes, then the towage
to be paid by SHIPPER hereunder shall be reduced by the full
amount of the cost of the towage attributable to such other
cargo on such route at the rates prevailing hereunder. For
the purpose of computing such reduction, the towage cost of
a flotilla of more than one BARGE shall be divided by the
number of BARGES to arrive at a towage charge per BARGE.
"Customary discharging points" of the VESSEL as that term is
used herein shall be as follows:

    At or near New Orleans: any point on the Mississippi
    River within 100 miles of the Port of New Orleans.

    Panama City: any point within one (1) mile of SHIPPER's
    facility.

    Rotterdam: any point within the inner harbor of
    Rotterdam.

    Liverpool: any point as close to the inner harbor as
    permitted by port authorities, and safety of VESSEL.

    London: any point SHIPPER designates within the Thames
    Estuary or River to which VESSEL can safely proceed.

Any towage costs other than as specified herein shall be for
OWNER's account.

    Towage hereunder shall be arranged by OWNER for its ac-
count, and OWNER shall give SHIPPER at least six (6) months'
written notice of the name of the towing company, and of
rates and terms to apply and of any changes therein. The
cost of such towage as is for SHIPPER's account as specified
herein shall be reimbursed to OWNER by SHIPPER as aforesaid

-14-

upon duly supported invoices, and data concerning towage of other cargo, submitted by OWNER to SHIPPER, PROVIDED that within sixty (60) days of written notice from OWNER to SHIPPER of rates and terms to apply SHIPPER may arrange the reimbursable towage for all or any portion of the BARGE movement at either end of the voyage, or require that such towage be arranged, with any other reputable towing company nominated by SHIPPER, such arrangement to commence upon the termination of the existing towage contract.

(d) Payment by SHIPPER to OWNER in accordance with subparagraphs 5(a), (b) and (c) hereof shall be deemed full payment to OWNER for all services to be rendered by OWNER hereunder, and includes, without limitation, towage, loading expenses of the BARGES onto the VESSEL, all port charges, pilotage, agency fees, bunkers and/or normal VESSEL costs at all ports of loading and discharge.

(e) It is understood that the rate of freight specified **above** covers only Eastbound transportation of cargo and only cargo carried in the seventy-three (73) BARGES.

6. DISCHARGING PORT:

Promptly upon completion of loading of BARGES at U.S. ports, VESSEL shall proceed directly to the ports nominated by SHIPPER for the particular voyage in accordance with the terms hereof.

-15-

7. **AGENTS:**

OWNER's agents are to be employed at both loading and discharging ports at OWNER's expense.

8. **PENALTIES:**

(a) SHIP DEMURRAGE - SHIPPER shall have the option of requesting, and shall receive if so requested, additional time not exceeding five (5) running days on any single round voyage in which to make delivery of BARGES to OWNER in accordance with the provisions of sub-paragraph (f) of Appendix #1 on the first voyage or 3(f) on subsequent voyages, PROVIDED, that SHIPPER shall pay OWNER demurrage at the rate of $7,500.00 U.S. currency, for every day, or pro rata for any part thereof, for the period of time which VESSEL is delayed in sailing by reason of SHIPPER's utilizing such additional time. Demurrage shall not be paid for a period of delay exceeding the amount of time requested and utilized by SHIPPER. In the event such additional time is used by SHIPPER in any given half-year period, the number of voyages provided for that period, as specified in sub-paragraph 4(b) hereof, shall be reduced to the extent that the completion of the number of voyages otherwise provided is prevented solely by the use of such additional time.

(b) BARGE DEMURRAGE (U.S.) - SHIPPER will pay OWNER the additional sum of $3,010.00* per BARGE (except for voyages on

---

* U.S. currency

-16-

(Par. 8, cont'd)

which SHIPPER has nominated Range 2, in which case the amount
paid shall be $3,870.00* per BARGE) for the excess of (i) the
total number of BARGES which OWNER delivered empty to SHIPPER
for use on the next Eastbound voyage, or the total number
which the VESSEL is capable of loading and carrying on that
voyage, whichever is less, over (ii) the number of loaded or
empty BARGES delivered or tendered by it to OWNER at U.S.
points, for a given Eastbound voyage, IF AND ONLY IF, (i)
SHIPPER's failure to deliver said total number of BARGES is
in no way contributed to by any act or omission of OWNER,
(ii) SHIPPER's failure to deliver said total number of BARGES
results in the VESSEL's necessarily sailing on the next voyage
with less than its total capacity of BARGES, and (iii) the
BARGES comprising such difference were scheduled to carry
cargo on a subsequent Westbound voyage but will be precluded
from being so used by such failure.

    (c) BARGE DEMURRAGE (U.K./Europe) - SHIPPER will pay
OWNER $140.00 per day per BARGE U.S. currency, or pro rata
for any part of a day, for each day in which said BARGE is
used by SHIPPER at a U.K./European port in excess of the allowed free time, as stipulated in sub-paragraph 3(j) hereof.
Such demurrage will cease to accrue upon redelivery of the
BARGE to OWNER, which shall be deemed to have occurred when
the empty BARGE is made available to OWNER at the place and

---

* U. S. currency

-17-

25. <u>NOTICES:</u>

All notices provided for herein shall be in writing and addressed as follows:

To: Central Gulf Steamship Corporation
     One Whitehall Street
     New York, New York 10004

To: International Paper Company
     220 East 42nd Street
     New York, New York 10017

CENTRAL GULF STEAMSHIP CORPORATION

By _____
              Vice Chairman

_____
            Witness

INTERNATIONAL PAPER COMPANY

_____   By _____
            Witness   Vice President

262

<u>E X H I B I T   A</u>

NEWBUILDING LIGHTER ABOARD SHIP   "TO BE NAMED"
OUTLINE SPECIFICATIONS OF VESSEL

Total deadweight at 28' (8.5 Meters) SSW Draft   About 25,000 Long Tons

Total deadweight at 36' 10 - 29/32" SSW Draft   About 43,000 Long Tons

Total capacity of cargo holds and on deck 73 Barges, each Barge as described in EXHIBIT "B".

Vessel equipped with one (1) 500 - Short Ton (446 L/T) Heavy Lift Crane for ✓ loading and discharging Barges.

Vessel's capacity lifting 73 Barges, including the weight of the cargo, at 446 L/T or grand total of 32,558 Long Tons

Length between Perpendiculars	About 767' 8 - 1/2" (234 Meters)
Length over - all	About 859' 6 - 7/8" (262 Meters)
Moulded Breadth	About 106' 7 - 1/2" (32.5 Meters)
Extreme Breadth	About 107'
Service Speed at 36' 10 - 29/32"	About 18 Knots
Service Speed at 28'	About 19 - 1/2 Knots
Fuel (Maximum 1500 Seconds Redwood No. 1) Consumption	About 82.8 Metric Tons per 24 hours
Diesel Oil Consumption	About 3.6 Metric Tons per 24 hours

Vessel will be powered by a 9 RND 90 Sulzer Engine.

E X H I B I T   A

EXHIBIT B

NEW BUILDING LIGHTER ABOARD SHIP
OUTLINE SPECIFICATIONS OF BARGES

The Lighter is essentially a floating container, box shape configuration, fitted with either large manually operated folding hatch covers, water - tight pontoons, or steel cross backs with wooden hatch covers covered with water - tight tarpaulins and four substantial lifting and stacking posts (as per the attached drawing):

Over-all length	About 61' 6"
Over-all beam	About 31' 2"
Depth of Hull	About 13'
Draft	8' 8"
Displa cement	500 Short Tons
Estimated weight light Barge	Not more than 76 Long Tons
Capacity - Bale	19,900 Cubic Feet
Capacity - Grain	20,600 Cubic Feet

Any extra fittings or equipment required in addition to that necessary for service as contemplated under the terms of the CONTRACT will be for Shipper's account.

This is a proforma to be substituted by actual Specifications to be mutually agreed upon prior to signing of Shipbuilding Contract.

EXHIBIT B

264

Glossary

Anchorage. A place in or near a port where vessels may drop their anchor for temporary holding.

Ballast. A heavy substance used to improve the stability and control the draft of the ship. When used as "in ballast," a voyage without cargo, carrying only said substance or only fuel and potable water.

Bareboat Charter. A "net lease" in which the charterer takes full operational control over the vessel for a specified period of time (usually medium- to long-term) for a specified daily rate that is generally paid monthly to the vessel owner. The bareboat charterer is solely responsible for the operation and management of the vessel and must provide its own crew and pay all operating and voyage expenses.

Berth. A safe dock for a ship to lie afloat while loading or unloading cargo or awaiting orders.

Breakbulk Vessel. An ocean-going vessel that transports general cargo in its hold in individual bags, bales or other units without first loading such cargo in separate containers. Loading and unloading of a breakbulk vessel requires shoreside assistance.

C-2, C-3, C-4, EC-2, AP-2, AP-3. U.S. Maritime Administration (MARAD) designations given to certain U.S. vessels built during World War II and immediately thereafter.

Bulk Cargo. Cargo stowed unpackaged in a vessel's hold, not enclosed in any container such as a box, bale, bag or cask and not subject to mark or count.

Cargo. The commodity of other revenue-producing material carried on a ship or barge in domestic or international transportation.

Car/Truck Carrier (Ro/Ro). An ocean-going vessel especially designed/constructed to carry wheeled vehicles. She has multiple decks with ramps to and from a dock and between decks to permit the loading and unloading of wheeled vehicles without any shoreside or shipboard cargo-handling equipment. The vehicles are rolled on or rolled off the vessel, either self-propelled or towed.

Charter. A contract for employment of a vessel.

Classification Society. Internationally recognized organizations that establish and issue to the shipowner technical standards for ship design, construction and operation. The principal classification societies are: American Bureau of Shipping (ABS), Bureau Veritas (BU), Det Norske Veritas (DNV), Lloyds Register (LR), Nippon Kaiji Kyokai (ClassNK) and the Russian Maritime Register of Shipping (RS).

Coasting Vessel. A ship engaged in domestic short-sea trades.

Construction Differential Subsidy (CDS). Government payments to a shipowner or ship builder under the Merchant Marine Act of 1936 to compensate for higher cost of U.S. ship construction vis-à-vis foreign competition.

Container Ship. A vessel specifically designed to carry standard-size cargo containers.

Contract of Affreightment. A contract or charter by which the vessel owner undertakes to provide space on a vessel for the carriage of specified goods or a specified quantity of goods on a single voyage or series of voyages over a given period of time between named ports (or within certain geographical areas) in return for the payment of an agreed amount per unit of cargo carried. Generally, the vessel owner is responsible for all operating and voyage expenses.

Deadweight (DWT). The weight of cargo, fuel, water and other portable items a vessel may legally load and carry on her assigned draft.

Demolition. Ships past their useful life are sent to facilities in certain seaports for breaking up (scrapping) after having reached the end of their economic usefulness.

Dock. A safe berth.

Dock Ship. A special-purpose ship configured so as to partially submerge or emerge to enable cargo to be loaded or unloaded by floating on or off the vessel.

Draft. The depth to which a ship is submerged below the surface of the water (see "Plimsoll Mark").

Drydock. A large, submersible dock in the form of a basin into which water will flow and into which a ship is floated for cleaning and repair of underwater surfaces after the water is emptied and the dock emerged.

Dunnage. Sawn lumber or similar material used in securing safe stowage of cargo in a vessel's holds or on deck.

EBITDA. Acronym for "Earnings Before Interest Taxes Depreciation and Amortization."

FEU. Acronym for "Forty-foot Equivalent Unit: a shipping container of standard size (40' length x 8' height x 8' width) used to describe the carrying capacity of a container ship.

FLASH. Acronym for "Feeder Lighter Aboard Ship": a non-self-propelled barge designed and built to carry about eight LASH barges for towage between main ports and subsidiary ports.

Fleet. The ships owned or operated by a shipowner. Also, the barges owned by a ship or barge owner assembled in a specific area within a port or on a river.

Float-On/Float-Off. Special-purpose vessel that can be partially submerged to receive barges in floating position after submerging and float barges out after emerging (see "Dock Ship").

FIO. Acronym for "Free in and out" - Loading and unloading expenses of the cargo are paid in full by owners of the cargo.

Freight. The revenue earned for the carriage of cargo. Also sometimes refers to the cargo itself.

Gantry Crane. A crane for loading or unloading cargo containers, barges or other heavy weights mounted on rails aboard ship or on shore so as to move from one position to another as part of its lifting operation while straddling the area between the rails. The LASH Mother Vessels are each equipped with a Gantry Crane capable of lifting a fully loaded LASH barge weighing about 500 long tons.

Hatch. The opening in a ship's deck through which cargo is loaded or unloaded.

Intermodal. The system of handling the movement of cargo from one transportation mode (such as ship carrying containers) to another (such as a trucking line or railroad) to on-forward the containers.

International Flags of Convenience. The national ensigns of countries that grant most favorable tax treatment to ship owners whose ships are operated under their registry.

LASH. Acronym for "Lighter Aboard Ship": the designation given to the type of ship pioneered by Central Gulf Lines, Inc. to carry about 83 standard LASH barges as more fully described in Chapter 10.

LASH Barge. "Lighter Aboard Ship" Barge of standard dimensions (61' 6" length x 31' 2" width x 13' 0" height; 80 long tons weight empty, 375 long tons cargo capacity; 19,900 cubic feet bale capacity) (see illustration, Chapter 10) for use aboard LASH vessels, as described in Chapter 8. The Company registered the LASH Barges under the U.S. flag; home port, New Orleans, Louisiana.

Liberty Ship. Designation given to WWII-built cargo vessel as described in Chapter 1 as EC-2 type.

Liner Service. A principal trade route offering regularly scheduled vessel sailings between advertised ports of call.

LOA. Length Overall of a vessel.

Long-Term Contract. A contract with a duration of more than five years.

MARAD. U.S. Maritime Administration, an agency of the U.S. Department of Transportation.

Maritime Security Act. See Operating Differential Subsidy (ODS).

Medium-Term Contract. A contract with duration of three to five years.

Military Sealift Command (MSC). A branch of the U.S. Navy that awards charters/contracts for the ocean transportation of military supplies for all military services.

Military Prepositioning Service (MPS). Ships chartered or owned by MSC loaded with strategic military equipment, fully manned and stationed in areas of the world, ready to respond to U.S. military needs.

Mother Vessel. A LASH vessel that carries LASH barges or a container ship that carries standard containers in liner service or other employment.

National-Flag Carrier. A ship owner whose vessels are registered in and fly the flag of its home country.

Newbuilding. A ship under construction or just completed by a shipbuilder.

On the Berth. A vessel loading cargo on Liner Service.

Operating Differential Subsidy (ODS). Payments made to shipowners qualified under the Merchant Marine Act of 1936 to provide regular Liner Service on Essential Trade Routes in accordance with Federal Maritime Board approval. Congress replaced ODS on October 8, 1996, with the Maritime Security Act, which provided payments of a fixed amount for 47 vessels, of which the Company had seven vessels qualify. Annual payments per vessel were $2.1 million from December 20, 1996, to September 30, 2005; $2.6 million from October 1, 2005, to September 30, 2008; $2.9 million from October 1, 2009, to September 30, 2011, and $3 million from October 11, 2012, to September 30, 2015. After 2005 the number of vessels qualifying increased to 60, of which the Company had eight.

Plimsoll Mark. The official designation inscribed (welded) on the hull of a vessel to certify its freeboard to which depth a vessel may be submerged after loading cargo or ballast. The freeboard allowed is divided into that which is applicable in summer salt water, tropical salt water, winter salt water and fresh water, depending upon where the vessel is located at applicable times of the year.

Probo. An ocean-going vessel with holds or tanks that are rapidly self-cleaning so as to permit the transportation of dry bulk and liquid products on back-to-back voyages.

Roll-On/Roll-Off (Ro/Ro). An ocean-going vessel designed to load and unload wheeled vehicles by driving them on and off the vessel. Generally a roll-on/roll-off vessel can also carry containers.

Ship's Gear. The cargo winches, booms, and/or cranes used for loading and/or unloading cargo.

Shipowner. The legally registered owner of a vessel.

Shipper. The agent or the cargo consignor of the commodity or items legally carried by a vessel.

Shoring Cargo. Securing cargo loaded aboard a ship to make it safe for carriage without movement even in heavy sea conditions.

Short-Term Contract. A contract with duration of less than three years.

SPLASH. Acronym for "Self Propelled Lighter Aboard Ship, a vessel designed to carry up to 18 LASH Barges or equivalent

amount of cargo by means of Float On/Float Off or lift/on lift/off the vessel.

Stability. The safely loaded or proper distribution of weights (solid or liquid) aboard a ship so that she may operate in any reasonable sea condition and always maintain vertical upright buoyancy position.

Tanker. A ship designed to carry only liquid cargo such as petroleum, chemicals, or their derivatives.

TDW. Total deadweight.

TEU. Acronym for "Twenty-foot Equivalent Unit": a shipping container of standard size (20' length x 8' height x 8' width) used to describe the carrying capacity of a containership.

Time Charter. A contract in which the charterer obtains the right for a specified period to direct the movements and utilization of the vessel in exchange for payment of a specified daily rate, generally paid semi-monthly, but the vessel owner retains operational control over the vessel. Typically, the owner fully equips the vessel and is responsible for normal operating expenses, repairs, wages and insurance, while the charterer is responsible for voyage expenses, such as fuel, port and stevedoring expenses.

Title XI Guaranteed Financing. Financing, the repayment of which is guaranteed by the U.S. Government, for the construction of a U.S. registered ship in a U.S. shipyard, thus enabling the shipowner to qualify for a favorable interest rate.

Ton. A unit of weight, short (2,000 pounds), long (2,240 pounds), or metric (2,204.6 pounds).

Trade Route. One of essential Trade Routes on which a U.S. flag subsidized vessel was approved to operate and for which U.S. Government approval was qualified to receive ODS. Also, any established Liner Service.

Underwriters. Insurance companies that cover the various risks of shipowners.

U.S. Coast Guard. The U.S. Government agency, part of the Department of Homeland Security, which establishes the rules and regulations for ship operation and crew performance for U.S.-flag vessels.

U.S. Maritime Administration. See *MARAD.'*

Victory Ship. Designation given to WWII-built cargo vessel as described in Chapter 1 as AP-2 or AP-3 type.